Family Therapy: A comprehensive overview

RONALD F. LEVANT
Boston University

D0068738

Prentice-Hall, Inc.   Englewood Cliffs, New Jersey 07632

Library of Congress Cataloging in Publication Data

LEVANT, RONALD F.
  Family therapy.

   Bibliography: p. 281
   Includes index.
     1. Family psychotherapy. I. Title. [DNLM:
1. Family therapy. WM 430.5.F2 L655f]
RC488.5.L465 1984 616.89'156 83-10958
ISBN 0-13-302885-2

To my families

Editorial/Production Supervision
  and Interior Design: *Barbara Kelly Kittle*
Cover Design: *Lundgren Graphics, Ltd.*
Manufacturing Buyer: *Ron Chapman*

Printed in the United States of America

10 9 8 7 6 5 4 3 2 1

ISBN 0-13-302885-2

Prentice-Hall International, Inc., *London*
Prentice-Hall of Australia Pty. Limited, *Sydney*
Editora Prentice-Hall do Brasil, Ltda., *Rio de Janeiro*
Prentice-Hall Canada Inc., *Toronto*
Prentice-Hall of India Private Limited, *New Delhi*
Prentice-Hall of Japan, Inc., *Tokyo*
Prentice-Hall of Southeast Asia Pte. Ltd., *Singapore*
Whitehall Books Limited, *Wellington, New Zealand*

Contents

Part Two: Family Therapy

Part Three: Beyond Family Therapy

Preface

This book is designed to provide for advanced graduate students and professionals in the mental health and human service fields a comprehensive overview of the field of family therapy. It is based on my experience teaching a year-long course on family systems and family therapy to such an audience for the past eight years. It assumes a working knowledge of mental health concepts and procedures.

The book's primary emphasis is on theory and conceptual models, although the empirical research, and, to a lesser extent, practical applications, are brought into the discussion. To balance the predominantly theoretical narrative, I have included resource sections at the ends of chapters two, four, five, six, and eight. These sections list the case materials which are available to illustrate in depth the various approaches. These include full-length case studies and filmed or videotaped interviews, some of which have been transcribed and published with a side-by-side running commentary which discusses particular interactions or interventions. It was my hope that these sections would be of use both to readers (accessing materials which they might pursue on their own) as well as to professors, who, in teaching a course on family therapy, might want to know where to find compatible case studies or videotapes.

This book is organized into three parts. In part one, the topic of family systems, or dynamics, is presented. It has often been observed that family therapy is not so much a matter of having the whole family in the treatment room as it is of the therapist having a family concept or map which guides his or her interventions. The objective of this part of the book is to help the reader develop this capacity to think in family terms. Chapter one addresses the problem of how to conceptualize the family unit as a social and psychological entity, bringing to bear both socio-logical/academic models as well as those developed in the clinical fields. Seminal theories, such as communication theory and general systems theory are also presented. In chapter two, the relationship between family interaction and individual patienthood is considered, a relationship which lies at the very foundation of the field of family therapy. First, I present the conceptual models developed in the early phases of the family therapy movement (such as "double-bind"; "marital schism and skew"; "pseudomutuality, pseudohostility, and the rubber fence"; "mystification," etc.), as well as the more recent and comprehensive models. Then the domain of empirical research bearing on the relationship between family inter-action and individual psychopathology is discussed.

Part two presents the field of family therapy. The scaffolding for this part is built in chapter three, which develops a conceptual scheme for classifying the various approaches (or schools of family therapy). This scheme groups 22 schools of family therapy into three more general models of family change, which are termed the historical, structure/process, and experiential models. These models are differentiated in terms of several dimensions: The time perspective taken in viewing the family's problems (whether oriented toward the past, the "functional" present—including the recent past and immediate future, or the immediate "here-and-now" present); the focus of the efforts to effect therapeutic change; the role of the therapist; the usual duration of therapy; and the fundamental theoretical orientation employed (whether psychoanalysis, systems theory, learning theory, existentialism, or phenomenology).

The three models are then discussed in chapters four, five, and six. Each chapter begins with a discussion of the general assumptions, boundaries, and at-tributes of the particular model of family change, and then describes the major schools within the more general model. The discussion of specific schools empha-sizes theory and conceptual models, and considers the conceptualizations of family dynamics, family dysfunction, and family change inherent in each school. Some examples from practice are introduced in these chapters to illustrate theory, and each chapter includes a resource section which details the available case material. Chapter four gives the historical model. This includes the psychodynamic, multi-generational, and intergenerational-contextual schools of family therapy. In general, these schools are concerned with the individual within the family, with particular attention to those aspects of their interpersonal functioning which are distorted by unresolved attachments to figures in the past, and which will likely be transmitted to future generations. Chapter five presents the structure/process model, which in-cludes the communicational, structural, and behavioral schools of family therapy. These approaches are concerned with the current patterns of interaction of the family, and the relationship of these patterns with the symptoms or presenting problem of the identified patient or client. The experiential model is described in chapter six. This includes the Gestalt, experiential, and client-centered schools of family therapy. These schools emphasize experience, in the present, of individual family members, conceived in existential terms, and understood through the phenomenological method of viewing experience through the internal subjective frame of reference of the person.

To round out the discussion of family therapy, chapter seven takes up the matters of evaluative research, training, and professional issues. First, family therapy outcome research is reviewed, considering both the substantive findings as well as some of the methodological issues. The objective is to present what is known and unknown about the efficacy of these various family therapy approaches, and also to indicate that family therapy (or any therapy, for that matter) does not always work. Second, training in family therapy is discussed, in order to provide the reader with suggestions for how to obtain training if that is desired, and to highlight some of the conceptual and empirical issues involved in training. Finally, the topic of professional issues is considered, with examinations of the regulation of the field of marital and family therapy, and of professional associations and ethics.

In part three we take up the advancing edges of the field, and examine trends which extend beyond the customary boundaries of family therapy—such as the idea of the family as the unit of treatment, and of treatment as the objective of intervention. Chapter eight presents a discussion of special forms and techniques of working therapeutically with families, considering the following topics: The crisis-oriented approaches of family crisis therapy and multiple impact therapy; the "mega-group" approaches which extend beyond the family as the unit of intervention to multiple family groups and social networks; non-verbal techniques such as family sculpture and the use of videotape and other aides; specialized techniques for dealing with certain aspects of marraige (sex therapy, divorce therapy); and the issue of specialized techniques for including children. Finally, chapter nine takes up the topic of psychological-educational, skills-training approaches toward working with the family, which extend beyond therapy toward development and prevention. These programs have emerged as a growing trend within family therapy (particularly from the client-centered and behavioral schools), as well as from the related fields of parent education, marriage enrichment, family life education, child-birth education, premarital counseling, and divorce counseling. The discussion considers the nature of the interventions as well as the evaluative research.

Acknowledgments

1. The section on conceptual models in Chapter 1 (pp. 9-24) is an expanded version of an earlier article: Levant, R. F. Clinical and sociological models of the family: An attempt to identify paradigms. *American Journal of Family Therapy,* 1980, *8*(4), 5-20. Copyright, 1980, Brunner/Mazel Publishers. Reprinted by permission.

2. Chapter 3 is a revised version of an earlier article: Levant, R. F. A classification of the field of family therapy: A review of prior attempts and a new paradigmatic model. *American Journal of Family Therapy,* 1980, *8*(1), 3-16. Copyright, 1980, Brunner/Mazel Publishers. Reprinted by permission.

3. The section on client-centered family therapy in Chapter 6 (pp. 177-186) is a revised version of an earlier article: Levant, R. F. Family therapy: A client-centered perspective. *Journal of Marriage and Family Counseling,* 1978, *4*(2), 35-42. Copyright, 1978, The American Association for Marriage and Family Therapy. Reprinted by permission.

4. The section on special techniques for children in Chapter 8 (pp. 228-230) includes some material from a previously published article: Levant, R. F., and Haffey, N. A. Toward an integration of child and family therapy. *International Journal of Family Therapy,* 1981, *3*(2), 130-143. Copyright, 1981, Human Sciences Press. Reprinted by permission.

5. Chapter 9 is a revised version of an earlier article: Levant, R. F. Toward a counseling psychology of the family: Psychological-educational and skills-training programs for treatment, prevention, and development. *The Counseling Psychologist,* 1982, *11*(3). Copyright, 1983, The Counseling Psychologist. Reprinted by permission.

6. Figure 3-1 (p. 77) is an adaptation of figure 4 (p. 132) of: Foley, V. D. *Introduction to family therapy.* New York: Grune and Stratton, Inc., 1974. Reprinted by permission.

7. Quotations in Chapter 1 and Figure 1-4 (p. 22) from Hill, R. and Hansen, D. A., The identification of conceptual frameworks utilized in family study. *Marriage and Family Living,* 1960, *22*(4), 299-311. Copyright, 1960, The National Council on Family Relations. Reprinted by permission.

8. Quotations in Chapters 1, 2, 3, 5, and figures 1-6 (p. 27), 1-17 (p. 29), 1-18 (p. 29), and 2-1 (p. 62), from Minuchin, S. *Families and family therapy.* Cambridge, MA: Harvard University Press, 1974. Reprinted by permission.

9. Quotations in Chapter 6 from Laing, R. D. *The politics of the family and other essays.* New York: Pantheon Books, 1969, 1971. Copyright, 1969, 1971, Pantheon Books, A division of Random House, Inc. Reprinted by permission.

10. Figure 1-3 (p. 20) is an adaptation of figure 3 (p. 46) of: Parsons, T. and Bales, R. F. *Family, socialization, and interaction process,* New York: The Free Press, 1955. Copyright, 1955, The Free Press, a division of Macmillan Publishing Co., Inc. Reprinted by permission.

11. Figure 1-1 (p. 13) is an adaptation of figure 1 (p. 352) of: Powers, W. T. Feedback: Beyond behaviorism. *Science,* 1973, *17*(9), 351-356. Copyright, 1973, The American Association of the Advancement of Science. Reprinted by permission.

12. Quotations in Chapter 1 and figure 1-5 (p. 23) from Rodgers, R. H. Toward a theory of family development. *Journal of Marriage and the Family,* 1964, *26*(3), 262-270. Copyright 1964, The National Council on Family Relations. Reprinted by permission.

13. Figure 1-19 (p. 32) is reprinted by permission of the author and publisher Virginia Satir, *People making,* 1972, Science and Behavior Books, Inc. Palo Alto, CA. USA.

14. Figure 7-2 (p. 192) is reprinted by permission of the publisher, and is taken from the *Handbook of Psychotherapy and Behavior Change: An empirical analysis* (2nd ed.) by A. E. Bergin and M. J. Lambert. John Wiley & Sons, Inc., New York, 1978.

15. Figure 1-21 (p. 35) is taken from Evaluation of Family system and genogram, *Family Therapy: Theory and Practice,* D. J. Guerin (ed.). Reprinted by permission of Gardner Press, Inc., New York, 1976.

16. Figure 6-1 (p. 165) is from Gestalt theory and therapy of intimate systems (unpublished paper) by Melvin A. Rabin, 1980. Reprinted with permission.

part one: family dynamics

1

The Family as
a Social System

The aim of this chapter is to provide the reader with the means for understanding the family as a social system. The plan for this chapter will follow a course parallel to that of the inductive method, building up from considerations of data to conceptual frameworks. Thus, we will first consider the nature of the data or information that one obtains when observing a family for clinical or research purposes. Second we will briefly consider several methods for systematically gathering data from a family. And, finally, we will review in some detail the conceptual models that are used to help order and interpret this data.

GATHERING DATA
FROM THE FAMILY

The initial experience of a trainee beginning to observe families is often a paradoxical one. The beginner, on the one hand, feels overwhelmed with information and impressions of various sorts yet, on the other hand, feels that there are not sufficient data to understand many of the things that are going on in the family. In the midst of a wealth of data, key information seems to be missing—information that might help resolve apparent contradictions and piece together a unifying theme. Or perhaps this important information is available, yet is not recognized as such.

The hypothetical trainee is experiencing problems intrinsic to the assessment of the highly complex social system that is the family. Enormous, often overwhelming amounts of information are available when one observes such a system. Some of the data can be readily understood. The meaning of other data is obscure and needs to be inferred.

To know which data to selectively attend to, and how to infer meaning from the more obscure data elements, requires education and training in family assessment. We will begin that process in this section of Chapter 1. First, an overview of communication theory will be presented, in order to help the reader develop an appreciation for the various types and aspects of family communication. Second, several procedures currently used to gather data from families will be briefly reviewed.

Communication Theory

The data gathered in family observation and assessment concern, at some level, the communication of family members. Some theorists consider all behavior in an interpersonal context to be communicative. This is based on the premise that "one cannot *not* communicate." (Watzlawick, Beavin, & Jackson, 1967, p. 49). Even a refusal to communicate constitutes communication. In this discussion I will follow this general premise, and describe the many different ways in which behavior may be communicative.

Communication is the subject of study by several scientific disciplines. *Semiotics* is the general field concerned with signs, symbols, and languages. Within this general field, there are three kindred disciplines: *syntactics,* concerned with the relation of symbols to other symbols, as in the study of grammar; *semantics,* which is concerned with the relationship of the symbols to the objects and events which they represent; and *pragmatics,* which is concerned with the relationship between signs and their human interpreters. It is this last field that is of most interest to professionals concerned with the family. In particular, interest is primarily on the sender-receiver relationship as mediated by communication, and less on the relations between sender and sign and between receiver and sign.

In considering the different types of communication, one of the first distinctions to be made is that between verbal and nonverbal communication.

Verbal communication. Verbal communication is what one usually thinks of when one thinks about communication; the words and sentences spoken by one person to another. Verbal communication is communication by symbolic language— that is, language that uses symbols to refer to the actualities of the real world. This is in contrast to the direct representation of objects and events by, for example, gesturing to point out an object or drawing a picture of it.

Nonverbal communication. On the other hand nonverbal communication is the more interesting aspect of communication, particularly from the point of view of emotional relationships. Several types of nonverbal communicative behavior have been described in a review of this field by Kendon (1973). *Paralinguistic* phenomena are vocal sounds that are not part of the language. This category includes qualities of the voice (loudness, "tone of the voice") as well as emotional sounds such as cries, sighs, gasps, and laughter.

Kinesic communication generally refers to body movement, and includes facial expression, head, hand, and arm movements (gesticulations and gestures), posture, and whole-body movements (embraces of one person by another, aggressive acts). Kinesic communication is particularly important in the areas of affiliation and power. Facial gestures, raised eyebrows, sidelong glances, and preening and flushing may be used to signal a desire for the development of a friendly interaction or a romantic involvement. The thrust of the jaw, locking of the arms, posture, and body movement are used to indicate power differentials or dominance-submission reciprocals (Scheflen & Scheflen, 1972). Alliances are also communicated by body movement, such as crossing of legs or pointing an elbow so as to form a barrier around two people, as well as by synchronous movements of two family members. Also included in this category of kinesic communication are movements that may seem random and noncommunicative, or whose communicative meaning may seem unclear, such as postural changes, hair-stroking, foot tapping or jiggling, and rearranging of objects. These movements generally indicate discomfort or anxiety. A final type of kinesic communication is nonvocal sounds such as finger-snapping, thigh-slapping, foot-stamping, and applause, in which the meaning is generally very clear—in fact demonstrative.

Two other categories of nonverbal communicative behavior are the *appearance* of individuals (dress, grooming) and the *spatial arrangement* of a group of individuals. This latter area includes considerations such as the positioning of individuals in relation to each other (indices of alliances and splits) and the degree to which communicating individuals are facing each other or turned to the side (a good index of the degree of engagement between the two communicants).

Modes of transmission and reception of messages. The above discussion of verbal and nonverbal communication referred to the modes by which messages are transmitted. Also important are the modes by which messages are received. Verbal communication is primarily received through the auditory channel, whereas nonverbal messages are received through the visual channel, although some types may be received through the auditory channel (for example, nonvocal sounds), the tactile channel (as in embraces and handshakes), and the olfactory channel (natural body smells, perfumes, and colognes).

Report versus command aspect of communication. The distinction of the report versus command aspects of communication was made by Bateson (Ruesch & Bateson, 1951, pp. 179–181). The report aspect refers to the conveying of information from one person to another, whereas the command aspect refers to the way in which the message is to be regarded—that is, to the behavior expected of the receiver of the message. For example, a question such as "where is my mail?" may be a request for information ("It's on your desk") or a demand that the mail be produced at once. Thus, following Watzlawick, et al. (1967), the report aspect of communication refers to the *content* of the message, whereas the command aspect refers to information indicating the nature of the message and, therefore, refers to the *relationship* between the communicants. Verbal communication most typically conveys content, though it can be used to refer to the relationship level, whereas nonverbal communication generally refers to the relationship level, although it can be used to convey information in a direct denotative way, as in, for example, pointing north in response to the question "which way did he go?"

Metacommunication.   The idea of metacommunication was also developed by Bateson and associates (Bateson, Jackson, Haley, & Weakland, 1956; Bateson, 1972a). The group used as its foundation the theory of logical types (Whitehead & Russell, 1910), in which the central premise is that a member of a class exists at a different (lower) level of abstraction (or logical type) than the class itself; thus, a member of a class can never be the class, nor can a class be a member of itself. In human communication, this theory was used to point to the existence of different levels of communication: there is the message, and then there is the message about the message. Communication about communication is metacommunication. From our previous discussion it can be seen that the command aspect of communication is a form of metacommunication: it is a message about the message, indicating how the receiver is expected to respond.

In general, a metacommunication modifies a primary-level message. It can perform a command function, by indicating the nature of the message, whether question or statement, request or demand, and the behavior expected of the recipient of the message. It can amplify and deepen an emotional message, as a soft tone of voice and a gaze does to the message, "I love you." And it can contradict and deny a primary message, as a metallic tone of voice and a stiff, closed posture does to the same message, "I love you."

In the above example the metacommunication was intertwined with the primary communication, and it was transmitted through the nonverbal mode. Metacommunication can also occur separated from the primary-level message and can be sent through the verbal mode as (for example) when one clarifies one's message ("I meant that as a joke"), or seeks clarification ("Did you mean you wanted your mail brought to you or that you wanted to know where I had put it?").

Congruent versus incongruent communication.   In the process of communication, then, we send messages through verbal and nonverbal modes of transmission, and we send simultaneous messages at different communicative levels. When all components are properly in phase—the verbal and the nonverbal messages complement and/or clarify each other, and the different levels of the message are consonant—congruent communication is the result. When receiving congruent messages, we generally have the feeling that the sender means what has been said, and a sense of trust is fostered. On the other hand, when messages at different levels conflict, incongruent communication results, which often leaves the receiver feeling confused, not sure what the other person really meant. Double-level messages of this sort are fairly common. They can often be clarified by a request for additional information, or by a statement of one's own "muddle" as a result of the double message. That is, the receiver of an incongruent message can send a metacommunicative message as a means of resolving the paradox. As will be discussed in Chapter 2, in dysfunctional relationships the possibility for clarification of incongruent messages does not exist, with the result of a continued *mystification* of the process occurring in the relationship (Laing, 1965).

Communication patterns. The material in this discussion follows Watzlawick, et al. (1967). The basic unit of communication is the *message,* with a transmitter at one end and a receiver at the other. A series of several messages is generally called an *interaction.* A still larger unit is the *communication* or *interaction pattern,* which consists of a particular sequence of interactions. A sequence of interactions forms a communication pattern as a result of *punctuation.* Punctuation is a form of metacommunication that defines the initiation or termination of a sequence of interactions, and as such, it reflects the relationship between the communicants. There are many cultural conventions of punctuation that organize interactional sequences and that reflect the relationship of the interactants. The exact nature of the relationship, of course, varies with the content of the interactional sequence. In some situations, for example, the act of initiation of a sequence reflects a power hierarchy in which the initiator is the more powerful, at least in the particular domain involved in the sequence. In other cases the initiator may be a petitioner, making a request of a more powerful person. In addition to cultural norms, families evolve their own forms of punctuation, which organize their interactions into patterns. In some cases, sequences may be punctuated differently by the two parties to an interaction, as is often the case in marital discord. For example, consider the husband who says he drinks because his wife nags him. Yet his wife complains that she nags because he drinks.

So far in this discussion of communication patterns, a dyadic relationship has been assumed. The situation gets more complex with the addition of other people. In triadic and larger-group interaction, there is the consideration of *who interacts with whom:* Which dyadic interactions tend to occur with frequency, and which do not? And what about larger group interactions involving three, four, or more people? In these group sequences, do interactants participate as individuals or are there coalitions, in which two or more people tend to communicate with one or more other persons?

In families, communication patterns tend to recur with some regularity, reflecting the stable and continuous relationships of family members. Later in this chapter I will discuss conceptual models used in observing and interpreting these regularities of family process.

Techniques for Gathering Data

The nature of communication in families has been described in some detail, and this *is* the data that one collects in family assessment. Several techniques are available for collecting data. As is true of investigations in all branches of science, the techniques used will influence the particular data that result. Moreover, the approach that is taken—the assessment techniques that are employed, the aspects of family life that are assessed—often reflect the assessor's conceptual model of the family. In this section two types of assessment techniques will be covered: family tasks and interviews. The presentation will be selective rather than exhaustive. For a more detailed discussion of the area the reader is advised to consult the following reviews of the field: Bodin, 1968; Lickorish, 1971; Cromwell, Olson, & Fournier, 1976; and Fisher, 1976. In addition Straus and Brown (1978) have published a comprehensive compendium of family-measurement techniques.

Family tasks. The first approach involves giving family members a task of some sort and observing the process of their interaction. This approach is most often used in family research, but it can be applied to clinical family assessment. The task can be familiar or novel. The former gets at usual and habitual interaction patterns, whereas the latter brings out the family's response to new situations and highlights its adaptive capacity. There are four categories of family tasks, on a continuum from highly novel to highly familiar: Problem-solving, decision-making, conflict-resolution, and naturalistic tasks (Cromwell, et al., 1976).

Problem-solving tasks attempt to assess family members' behavior in a standardized situation. These tasks often employ structured games of various sorts that are often quite removed from situations of everyday family life. They have the advantage of being highly objective, but they also have the disadvantage of being difficult to interpret in terms of, or extrapolate to, the actualities of family life. Examples are the Simulated Family Activity Measure (SIMFAM) (Straus & Tallman, 1971) and the Bodin Parchesi Test (Bodin, 1969). In these tests, the family is instructed to play a game (such as Parchesi) while their interactional behavior is observed (and sometimes videotaped). The family's behavior during this standardized task is then scored according to preestablished protocols in order to yield ratings of such variables as dominance, support, problem-solving ability, and communication clarity.

Decision-making tasks are closer to the realities of family life. These tasks require family members to make a joint decision about a hypothetical but conceivable family situation, such as where to go on a vacation, what to do on a Sunday outing, how to spend lottery winnings, or how to celebrate an anniversary or a birthday. An example is the Plan Something Together Task of the Mental Research Institute's Structured Family Interview, in which the family is simply asked to jointly plan something, while their behavior is observed and scored according to protocol (Watzlawick, 1973).

Conflict-resolution tasks present the family with an actual conflict and require them to seek resolution. Several of the Wiltwyck Family Tasks are of this type, particularly the third, fourth, and fifth tasks. (Elbert, Rosman, Minuchin, & Guerney, 1964, p. 890). The third task requires family members to assign "blame-labels" to each other, such as who is the "bossiest, fights the most, biggest cry-baby." The fourth task asks individual family members to discuss what they like and dislike about the other family members. And the fifth task requires the family to describe an argument and how it got resolved. Strodtbeck's Revealed Differences Technique (1954) is another conflict-resolution task. In this procedure, family members are first interviewed individually in regard to aspects of their family life, and then are presented as a group with their differences of opinion, which they are asked to reconcile.

Naturalistic tasks involve observing the family in its own context while they are engaged in a normal activity. Some researchers, such as Kantor and Lehr (1975) place observers in the home, or tape-record family process over extended periods of time, or both. And some clinicians, such as Bloch (1973a) and Friedman (1965) recommend the use of the home visit for both diagnostic and therapeutic purposes.

Family tasks can be given to the whole family, the marital pair, or to some other subgroup. Satir (1966) has recommended administering the Plan Something Together task to the following series of subgroups: whole family; all except father; all except mother; children only; mother and daughter(s); mother and son(s); father and son(s); father and daughter(s); husband and wife. This process allows the disentanglement of the relationships in the family, which can otherwise appear as a "can of worms."

Family interviews. The second approach involves interviewing the family members together. This approach is often used in clinical settings as a part of the intake procedure. Compared to other methods, family interviewing tends to emphasize the verbal mode of communication, although the sensitive interviewer does not neglect the nonverbal mode. Family interviews can be relatively structured or unstructured, and they can either take a historical approach or assess current fields of family life. The following discussion will be brief, since this subject is treated in greater detail in Part II.

Satir (1967) has developed a method of family interviewing that she calls "taking a family life chronology." This is a structured historical procedure that focuses on the marital pair as the "architects of the family." She also places a good deal of emphasis on how family members see themselves as similar to or different from each other, since in her estimation family members often fail to differentiate themselves sufficiently. A more comprehensive structured historical format is the Family Case History Outline developed by the Group for the Advancement of Psychiatry (1970). This format includes the following dimensions:

1. Presenting problem

2. Family composition and characteristics
3. Multigenerational history
4. Current relationships with extended family
5. Developmental history of parents: Infancy through adulthood
6. Courtship period
7. Development of family: From marriage to the present
8. Current family relationships
9. Diagnostic impression
10. Changes during treatment
11. Final evaluation and prognosis
12. Follow-up

Minuchin's assessment scheme (1974, p. 130), on the other hand, is ahistorical, focusing on current family functioning. The following aspects of family life are evaluated:

1. Family structure
2. Family's flexibility and capacity for change
3. Family "resonance"—its responsiveness to individuals, from high ("enmeshed") to low ("disengaged")
4. Family's ecological context
5. Family's developmental stage
6. Role of identified patient in maintaining family structure

Minuchin's interviewing approach is midrange on the dimension of structured versus unstructured. He follows the movements of the family part of the time, and at other points he leads the family in certain preplanned directions. Minuchin's assessment procedure is unique also in its emphasis on the process of "joining the family" as a means of making an assessment. The result is an "interactional diagnosis" that "changes as the family assimilates the therapist, accomodates to him, and restructures, or resists restructuring interventions" (Minuchin, 1974, p. 131).

Phenomenological approaches also emphasize joining the family. The objective here is to gain an "insider's" perspective to the greatest extent possible—to understand experientially what being a member of this family means to the family members. This procedure is the least structured. General assessment schemes are not used, but instead, the unique organization of family dimensions and issues that characterize *this* family are described as they unfold. The process of understanding the family, in which the interviewer is involved, is shared with the family on an ongoing basis, and the responsibility for problem formulation and goal setting is left with the family (Levant, 1978a).

This completes our brief discussion of assessment. We will now turn to a consideration of the conceptual models that shape and inform the assessment process.

CONCEPTUAL MODELS
OF THE FAMILY

For better or for worse, one of the features of the family field is that, rather than one unified conceptual framework, it is characterized by many different conceptual models arising out of different frames of reference. To make matters even more complicated, these models arise out of several disciplines, each with its own methods and language systems, so that it is exceedingly difficult to compare and reconcile the various conceptual models that exist. The approach followed here will be to present the most current and widely accepted models. But first, we need to take up some preliminary considerations concerning the nature of conceptual models, the dimensions of the family, and the disciplines involved in the study of the family.

Preliminary Considerations

Conceptual models, in general, differ in the degree of their elaboration and refinement. At the low end of the scale, Rodgers (1964, p. 262) has defined the term "conceptual approach," which is "a set of concepts which are rather loosely tied together and which are not in any definite sense interrelated and interdefined."

At a higher level of sophistication there is the "conceptual framework," which Hill and Hansen (1960, pp. 300–301) have defined as "clusters of interrelated but not necessarily interdefined concepts generally applicable" to the area of interest. Finally, there is the "theory." Rodgers (1964, p. 262) has defined a theory as "a set of interrelated propositions which are empirically verifiable, universally valid, and parsimonious in their explanation of phenomena." At this stage in the development of the field of family study, we have several well-delineated conceptual frameworks, but do not yet have a unified theory of the family.

Howells (1971) delineated five dimensions of the family. The individual dimension is concerned with the psychological attributes of family members. The relationship dimension reflects the interaction and communication of family members and is concerned with particular dyadic relationships, such as the marital relationship and the parent-child relationship. The group-properties dimension is concerned with the dynamics of the family as a small group. The material-circumstances dimension refers to the socioeconomic status of the family. And the dimension of family-community interaction deals with the family in ecological perspective. For the most part, the conceptual models of the family that will be considered here focus on the relationship and group-properties dimension, with the other dimensions in view but receding into the background.

As noted above, the family has been the subject of study by many academic and applied disciplines: anthropology, education, home economics, law, the ministry, psychiatry, psychology (social, developmental, counseling, and clinical), social history, social work, and sociology. Although there has been some collaboration, these disciplines have operated to a considerable extent independently of one another, elaborating their own conceptual models without full awareness of the work done by colleagues in other disciplines (Riskin & Faunce, 1972). It was probably necessary in the early stages of the field to sharply focus on the family through the lens of one's own discipline. But it is now time to bridge the different disciplines and interrelate their contributions in order to work toward a unified and comprehensive theory that does justice to the complexity of family life.

This process has been going on for some time now among the academic disciplines, under the leadership of sociologists. For the past 30 years there has been a movement of increasing momentum toward taking stock of the contributions of sociology and of other closely related academic fields such as anthropology, social history, and social psychology (Christensen, 1964a; Hill & Hansen, 1960).

At the same time that sociology was moving toward a consolidation of the family field, new conceptual models and research investigations proliferated in the clinical fields (psychiatry, psychology, and social work). This latter development was stimulated by certain clinical observations regarding the relationship between the interaction patterns of families of psychiatric patients and the patient's symptoms, observations that challenged the intrapsychic conceptual models holding sway in these fields (see Chapter 2). These emerging perspectives were influenced by general systems theory, an approach that was originally elaborated at the end of World War II in the field of biology and that entered psychiatry through the field of medicine in the 1950s (Gray & Rizzo, 1969; von Bertalanffy, 1969). General systems theory is part of a paradigm shift or new epistemology, in which the concern with linear, cause-and-effect relationships is replaced by a concern with wholeness, patterns, and circular feedback loops. General systems theory was introduced into the field of sociology in the late 1960s (Buckley, 1967). Leaders of the sociological movement toward consolidation and unification of the family field have recently attempted to integrate some of their previous work with general systems theory (Broderick, 1971; Hill, 1974).

Since general systems theory has influenced contemporary thinking about the family in both academic and clinical circles, it will be discussed first, before systematic treatment of, on the one hand, the major conceptual models of the family developed by sociology and the social sciences, and on the other hand, the more recent models elaborated by the mental health fields.

General Systems Theory

General systems theory, along with kindred fields such as information theory, game theory, cybernetics, operations research, and ecology, constitutes a fundamental shift in epistemological perspective. The older epistemology was concerned with linear, one-way, cause-and-effect principles of relationship, which were developed by the observation or manipulation of nonliving objects. This Galilean-Newtonian mechanistic world view, concerned as it was with undirected events, eschewed vitalistic explanations of intrinsic purpose, directedness, or teleology, and sought only the explanation of how a given cause created a given effect. In the pursuit of such understanding, this science sought to isolate variables and to reduce nature to its most fundamental units (von Bertalanffy, 1969).

The newer perspective represented by general systems theory was initially developed as a science of living systems. As such, it focused on the characteristics of whole systems, which are more than the sum of their parts. A fundamental characteristic of whole living systems is *organization,* which is a highly improbable (negentropic) state, according to the second law of thermodynamics. Characteristics of organized whole systems include differentiation of parts, and order and directedness of processes. By developing an understanding of the unique characteristics of whole systems, general systems theory was able to resolve the old mechanistic-vitalistic controversy. It developed an expanded and unified science, in which mechanistic science is seen as but one domain; and it developed explanations of living systems based on their physical properties, so that vitalism was no longer a necessary assumption. Above and beyond the resolution of this ancient issue, proponents of general systems theory see it as having much potential for the general problem of unification of all of science—the physical, biological, social, and behavioral branches—and the humanities. "It is," according to Gray and Rizzo (1969, p. 7) "a new approach to the unity-of-science problem which sees organization rather than reduction as the unifying principle, and which therefore searches for general structural isomorphisms in systems." For example, certain differential (mathematical) equations that describe the process of diffusion in chemical reactions may also describe "such apparently diverse systems as the spread of information, the spread of rumor, divorce rates, accident rates, and others" (Gray & Rizzo, 1969, p. 14).

The discussion of general systems theory will define the term "system," differentiate open from closed systems, describe feedback loops, present a typology of open systems, and consider the application of this typology to the family.

Definition of system. Von Bertalanffy, who first propounded general systems theory, defined system as "complexes of elements standing in interaction" (1968, p. 33). Buckley provides a more elaborate definition. A system is

> a complex of elements or components directly or indirectly related in a causal network, such that each component is related to at least some others in a more or less stable way within any particular period of time. . . . The particular kinds of more or less stable interrelationships of components that become established at any time constitute the particular structure of the system at that time, thus achieving a kind of "whole" with some degree of continuity and boundary. (Buckley, 1967, p. 41)

Open versus closed systems. Systems are relatively open or closed, depending on the degree to which they are organized to enter into transactions with the environment.

At the extreme end, closed systems are not organized to enter into transactions with the environment. Closed systems are nonliving, simple mechanical entities and are of two types: (1) machines, operating on principles of linear causality and Newtonian physics, which are characterized by *organized simplicity*; (2) natural mechanical systems, such as gases, operating on principles of particle mechanics and characterized by *chaotic complexity.*

Closed systems return to an end state of high probability (that is, of minimal organization, or high entropy), such as chemical or thermodynamic equilibrium. This end state, or equilibrium, is completely determined by the initial conditions of the system.

Open systems are organized to enter into transactions with the environment. They process information and can handle a great range of environmental input; some types of open systems can respond to unpredictable input by modifying or elaborating structural elements. Open systems are characterized by *organized complexity* and include complex mechanical systems (such as servomechanisms), biological systems, and sociocultural systems. Depending on the type of system, open systems either return to a preset end state or evolve to a new state. In either case, the end state is one of low probability (highly organized, negentropic). It is a steady state of balanced tension maintained by the taking in and utilization of energy. Living systems do this by taking in "complex molecules high in free energy, and so negentropic" (Gray & Rizzo, 1969, p. 12).

Feedback loops. Feedback loops are information-processing mechanisms. Information processing is characteristic of open systems. In closed systems, such as simple mechanical processes, energy exchange is the basis for the relationship of parts: Part A, bearing energy *x,* comes into contact with Part B, to which it transfers energy *y,* causing B to move to point M. In open systems, the complexly organized parts are related through information exchange. This is based on the principle of "trigger action" (von Bertalanffy, 1968), in which an insignificant amount of energy (that is, information) produces a major change in the system.

In general terms, feedback loops are information-processing mechanisms by which a system determines the nature of its present state, or the nature of an environmental disturbance, or both and responds.

Figure 1-1 is a diagram of a feedback loop. Input signals can arise from the environment (as feedback on the environmental effect of an output or as information on an environmental disturbance) or internally, from the system itself (as system readings on internal parts and processes or as feedback on the internal effect of an output). Input signals are received by the sensor function, which transmits a sensor signal into the system. In the comparator, the nature of the sensor signal is determined by comparing it to a reference signal, which is an index of the system's desired parameters. An error signal is emitted, which reflects the deviation of the sensor signal from the desired state. The error signal activates the effector function, which produces an output in order to effect the desired state. The output may be directed internally or into the environment. Information on the effect of this output is transmitted back to the system as an input signal.

The thermostat is an example of a feedback loop. The air in the room (en-

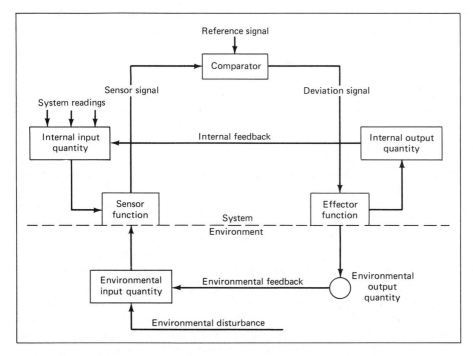

FIGURE 1-1   Diagram of feedback loop. (Adapted from Powers, 1973.)

vironmental input) comes into contact with a thermal-sensitive element (sensor) sending in a signal regarding current room temperature. This signal is then compared (in the comparator) to the temperature setting (or reference signal). If the current room temperature differs from the temperature setting, a deviation signal is sent out. Depending on whether the room is too hot or too cold, the furnace is either turned off or turned on, respectively (effector function).

There are two types of feedback loops. *Negative-feedback* loops respond to a deviation signal by a counteraction of the deviation, in order to restore the prior state. Negative feedback loops are also known as deviation-counteracting, or "constancy" feedback loops (Kantor & Lehr, 1975, p. 14). The thermostat described above is an example of a negative-feedback loop. *Positive-feedback* loops respond to a deviation signal by output that amplifies the initial deviation, in order to evolve to a new state. Positive feedback loops are also known as deviation-amplifying, or "variety" feedback loops (Kantor & Lehr, 1975, p. 14). Positive feedback is characteristic of living systems.

Open systems.   There are three types of open systems, characterized by the kind of feedback loops that are employed. (The ideas presented here were derived in part from two other three-way classification schemes, but with significant modification: Kantor & Lehr, 1975; Buckley, 1967). The three types of open systems are homeostatic, balanced-growth, and random systems.

Homeostatic systems are governed by negative feedback alone. They seek a preset end point and are *homeostatic* and *morphostatic* (structure maintaining). Examples of homeostatic systems include mechanical systems such as thermostats, servomechanisms, and robots; physiological processes such as the control of heart rate and respiration, or the response of the body to illness and injury; and family and social rituals.

Balanced-growth systems are governed by both positive and negative feedback. They operate on the principle of *equifinality* (von Bertalanffy, 1968), which means that a given end state can be reached from a variety of initial conditions. They alternate periods of evolution of new structure (or *morphogenesis,* Buckley, 1967) with rest phases (periods of *homeodynamic* equilibrium). Examples of balanced growth systems include futuristic electronic systems, such as self-evolving computers; embryological development; governmentally regulated processes, such as economic growth in a developed nation, or regulated social change; and the development of cognition through a sequence of stages.

Random systems are governed by positive feedback alone. They constantly evolve new structural features and operate on the principle of *multifinality* (or *equipotentiality*) (Buckley, 1967), in which given initial conditions may lead to a variety of dissimilar end states. Examples include Hal, the computer in the film *2001*; biological evolution; a host of social processes such as the rise of cultures, the escalation of international conflict, and vicious cycles such as formation of deviant individuals or subcultures; and compound interest and the growth of capital.

Families and systems. Some writers (for example, Satir, 1967) have tended to equate functional families with open systems and dysfunctional families with closed systems. While it is true that dysfunctional families may develop very rigid boundaries, a family could not be a closed system, as we have defined it: even the most dysfunctional families interact with the environment and exist at some level of organization (even if the organization is psychologically very primitive). Families are open sociocultural systems, of which there are three basic types. However, whereas in the preceding discussion of types of open systems, two of the types utilized only one kind of feedback and experienced *either* stability *or* change, families utilize both kinds of feedback and experience both change and stability. However, they may *tend* toward one or the other extreme. This we can describe as homeostatic, balanced-growth, and random family types. Families of any of these types can be functional or dysfunctional, depending on the quality of the family process. For example, the homeostatic-type family was the original paradigm for the dysfunctional family, particularly the family with a schizophrenic member (Jackson & Weakland, 1961). However, homeostatic-type families can be quite functional; an example is as the efficient and disciplined McKenzie family (Kantor & Lehr, 1975), a large family existing on very limited resources. Balanced-growth families seem to typify a model of positive functioning, yet it is still possible for families of this sort to experience dysfunction. An example would be a highly developed couple, capable of both change and stability, yet for whatever reasons incompatible.

Finally, random-type families would include both highly creative, artistic families, and disorganized multiproblem families. Sketches of these three family types in functional forms have been developed by Kantor and Lehr (1975), and are reproduced below.

1. Homeostatic-type family: the McKenzies (Kantor & Lehr, pp. 123–124).

"They're back," calls out Maureen, the McKenzies' eleven-year-old daughter, from the window at which she has been watching for the family DeSoto. Immediately, the other children start gathering in the kitchen, breaking off their other activities. "Hey, how about some hands on these bags?" Father calls up the stairs. John, Stephen, and Kevin, the McKenzies' three oldest children at ages fourteen, thirteen, and twelve, hop down the stairs and accompany their father to the car where they pick up the family's grocery bags from out of the trunk. Each boy makes several trips with his bags up to the kitchen, where Maureen supervises their unpacking and Patty and Tina, the McKenzie "babies" help out by putting canned goods in pantries and cabinets, wherever they can reach. Bryan McKenzie, the ten-year-old, also helps with the unpacking until he notices a pack of Hershey bars in one of the bags. He tears off one bar, smacks his lips, and tosses the bar into the air. "Hey, you can't eat that now," Maureen shouts. "I know that," he replies. "I was just thinking how good it was gonna taste." He puts the bar back in the bag with the rest and resumes helping with the unpacking. When the last bag is picked up from the car, Mr. McKenzie locks up the trunk and says, "We'll be back in ten minutes." "Where are you and Ma going?" John asks. "That's none of your business," Father replies. "I bet it's a treat," Kevin says. "You'll all find out soon enough," Mother adds. By the time the parents return with an angel food cake and some ice cream some ten minutes later, all the groceries are put away and bags folded up neatly for subsequent use as waste basket liners. Mother slices the cake and Father scoops out the ice cream in quantities appropriate to the age of each of the children, who stand in line for the goodies. "You all did a very good job with the groceries," he says.

2. Balanced-growth-type family: the Clouds (Kantor & Lehr, 1975, pp. 130–131).

"What would you like for dinner?" Mrs. Cloud asks her nine-year-old daughter. "Steak or . . . ?" "Cereal," replies Susanna who has recently decided to be a vegetarian. "Okay," replies Mrs. Cloud. "What about you, Pamela?" Mrs. Cloud asks Susanna's friend who is staying for supper. "Steak or something else?" "Steak," says Pamela. Susanna grimaces. "A little bit of steak and a big bowl of cereal," Pamela adds. Susanna smiles. During dinner, Mr. Cloud looks across the table and says, "Peter, I'm afraid I've got a bone to pick with you." "What's that?" "The mess from your mice is getting out of hand. I almost broke my neck in the hallway outside your room this afternoon. When we agreed to let you keep those mice it was on the condition that you clean their cages." "I do clean them," Peter counters, "once a week." "Well, it's not enough," Father says. "Their excrement's piling up on the floor." "That's because they're getting out of their cages," Peter replies. "Because you've got too many mice," says Father. "No, because you won't give me the money to buy new cages." "Wait a minute," interjects Mrs. Cloud. "Dad's right, Peter. Something's got to be done about the mess. But Peter's got a point too, Dad. Those cages are falling apart." "I'm glad somebody believes me," Peter remarks. "We can't afford new cages," says Father. "Well, what about the two of you getting together to repair the ones that are in there now? That might solve both your problems," says Mother. "On one condition," agrees Father. "You agree to clean them twice a week." "Agreed." says Peter.

3. Random-type family: the Canwins (Kantor & Lehr, 1975, pp. 137–138).

"That bathroom door handle is off again," shouts Maria Canwin. "Teddy, will you fix it?" she calls to her nine-year-old son. "I'll do it," her husband Herbert volunteers. "That's what you said last week," retorts Mrs. Canwin. "I'm sorry, dear, I put it on the repair list, but I can't seem to find the list," he replies. Now Teddy, who, in spite of his young age, is more skillful than his father in most mechanical matters, starts looking at the door handle. Meanwhile, a huge toolbox stands as a monument of promise, blocking the doorway to Mr. Canwin's study. Melissa, recently turned thirteen, perches statuesquely on the toolbox. Dancing in gracefully slowed movements, she sings in falsetto to an unseen audience, laughing in uncensored self-admiration. Moments later, Maria Canwin answers the telephone. She lodges the receiver loosely between her ear and shoulder so she can continue stirring her dinner pots on the stove. Ringlets of smoke from the burning haddock in the oven play around her nose, but she fails to notice it. Waving a glass of wine in her free hand, she is deep in a fiery conversation, punctuated by raucous laughter. An old college chum, phoning on a layover from the airport has just been stampeded into coming over. "We'll save dinner for you," Maria says, hanging up. "No you won't. You've burned the fish again," Herbert remarks, snorting under his breath. A shrieking Teddy, leaping from the stairs to a chair and onto his father's back in an impossible acrobatic sequence shouts, "I heard that, skunk-head." Enter Melissa, trying to peel her brother off her father's back. "Get off, jerk." She also tries simultaneously to pry her parents apart from a cluttered and obviously too energetic embrace. "Leave him alone, Mom. I want him now. You can have him later." Meanwhile Teddy shouts, "Put up your dukes, Herby!" "Stop it." roars Maria, suddenly overcome with the chaos. Sound and motion come to an instant stop. The three onlookers check in with each other: Does she mean it? "One of you three children can set the table. We're having a guest."

This concludes our brief tour through general systems theory. We will now turn to a discussion of the sociological and clinical models of family.

Sociological Conceptual Models
of the Family

Sociology has made the family a subject of study since about the mid-nineteenth century. Christensen (1964b) identified four stages in the development of the sociology of the family. The "preresearch" stage (prior to 1850) was characterized by poetic, religious, and philosophical approaches to the family, but not yet by a systematic study of family phenomena. In the stage of "social Darwinism" (approximately 1850-1900), scholars produced a literature that treated the family as an institution that was viewed over broad sweeps of time. As was characteristic of the general tone of the times, family scholars sought to explain the evolution of the family, from primitive to advanced forms. Often the works were tinged with an ethnocentric bias and a naive faith in progress. The methodology employed in this era was weak, relying heavily on anecdotal accounts of missionaries and the like. The "emerging-science" stage (approximately 1900–1950) involved several shifts in perspective. There was a shift relatively early from a somewhat moralistic posture to a more value-free position. Over the entire period there was a development of a more rigorous methodology, using empirical data and quantitative methods of data analysis. There was also a shift from a predominant concern with the sociological and historical study of the family as a social institution to an increasing concern with the social-psychological study of internal family processes. The stage of "systematic theory building" (1950 to the present) involves attempts to take stock of the existing research findings and schools of thought, with the aim of unifying the field of family study.

The initial impetus for systematic theory building came from Hill and colleagues (Hill, Katz, & Simpson, 1957; Hill & Hansen, 1960; Hill, 1966). This group initially catalogued seven conceptual frameworks (Hill et al., 1957), of which two were later dropped from consideration as full-fledged conceptual frameworks for family study. The remaining five frameworks were presented in an article that delineated in taxonomic tables their major features and underlying assumptions (Hill & Hansen, 1960). The five frameworks are the institutional-historical, the structure-functional, the symbolic-interactional, the situational, and the family developmental.

The five frameworks were treated in commissioned chapters in Christensen's landmark work, *Handbook of marriage and the family* (1964b). The demise of two of the frameworks occurred in that volume. Sirjamaki (1964), writing on the institutional framework, argued that when this approach is stripped of the remaining vestiges of the social Darwinism with which it evolved, it is not a conceptual framework at all, but rather is a comparative *methodology* (using cross-cultural and historical comparisons). And Stryker (1964) effected an integration of the symbolic-interactional and situational conceptual frameworks.

Two years later, Nye and Berardo (1966) published a similar collection of commissioned chapters. Their volume included the original five frameworks, and six others. These latter approaches are not sociological conceptual frameworks, but rather, they represent the contributions of other disciplines and professions to the study of the family: anthropology, social psychology, psychoanalysis, economics, law, and the ministry.

Of the original five frameworks, only three survived rigorous scrutiny in two later review articles: The structure-functional, the interactional-situational, and the family developmental (Klein, Calvert, Garland, & Palma, 1969; Broderick, 1971). Broderick added four new conceptual models, which have been developed in other fields and which look promising for the field of family study. These conceptual models are balance theory, game theory, exchange theory, and general systems theory.

The three major sociological frameworks will be described in the remainder of this section. This will be an abbreviated discussion. For more detail, the reader is referred to Christensen (1964a).

Structure-functional framework.   Like general systems theory, the structure-functional framework is concerned with properties of whole systems. In fact, the structure-functional framework can be seen as a specialized science of homeostatic systems. This is fairly clear from its assumptions (Hill & Hansen, 1960, p. 309):

1. Social conduct is best analyzed for its contribution to the maintenance of the social system, or for its nature under the structures of the system.
2. A social human is basically a reacting part of the social system; self-elicited (independent) action is rare and asocial.
3. The basic autonomous unit is the social system, which is composed of interdependent subsystems (e.g., institutions, family systems, etc.).
4. It is possible to profitably study any subunits of the basic system.
5. The social system tends to homeostasis.

The general approach of functional analysis involves identifying the structural elements, or subsystems, of a given social system, and specifying their functional significance in the overall maintenance of the system. Function in this sense refers to the particular part played by the subsystem. Function is also thought of in terms of the "interrelationship of the parts which compose the system" (Hill & Hansen, 1960, p. 303). In this second sense, two subsystems (or two systems) have a *functional relationship* with each other by virtue of their interdependence: Each is a function of the other (Pitts, 1964). *Functional equivalents* refers to the situation in which two structural elements have the same functional significance. This term is isomorphic with the term "structural isomorphism."

Functional prerequisites refers to the needs or requirements of a social system for its maintenance. Parsons has developed an analytic model of social systems in which he differentiated four subsystems that specialize in handling four functional problems of social systems: adaptation, goal gratification, integration, and pattern maintenance (Pitts, 1964). This model as applied to society as a whole is presented in Figure 1-2.

It can be seen that this model is differentiated along two axes: external versus internal orientation (manifest versus latent); and means versus ends (instrumental versus expressive). The first axis differentiates functions according to whether they are oriented externally, toward relationships with other systems, or internally, toward the maintenance of the system. The second axis differentiates functions that are instrumental means from those that are ends (or expressive acts). Bell and Vogel (1968) see the following institutions as the subsystems responsible for fulfilling the functional prerequisites of society as a whole: (1) The economy serves the function of adaptation, through the creation and distribution of goods and services. These are the *means* by which individual and social goals are attained. (2) The polity tends the function of goal gratification through the administration of goal-

	Means (instrumental)	Ends (Expressive)
External Orientation (Manifest)	Adaptive- instrumental	Goal-gratification (consummatory)
Internal Orientation (Latent)	Pattern maintenance (norms, values)	Integration

FIGURE 1-2   An interpretation of Parson's model of society. (Bell & Vogel, 1968.)

oriented policies (*ends*). (3) The community deals with the problem of integration. It provides affective bonds (expressive function) to integrate the individual into the larger society (ends). (4) The value system (religion, education) serves the function of pattern maintenance by providing orienting principles and normative expectations (means).

In terms of the family, the structure-functional framework has been applied both to internal processes of the family, and to the relation between the family and other social systems. Bell and Vogel (1968) have developed a set of functional relationships that obtain between the family and the four functional subsystems of society. They have also applied this model to the relations between the family and personality, and to the internal activities of the family. In this latter study, the adaptation function is represented by task performance, goal gratification by family leadership, integration by solidarity and intimacy, and pattern maintenance by the family value system (values, normative expectations).

Parsons's work (Parsons & Bales, 1955) has extended beyond the structure-functional frame of reference. In his theoretical formulation of the process of socialization, he integrated the structure-functional framework with a developmental theory (specifically, Freudian psychosexual developmental theory). And he has articulated the structure-functional framework with the interactional framework by describing internal family process in terms of the differentiation of roles. This latter model is presented in Figure 1-3. Family roles are differentiated along an axis of power (superior versus inferior) and along the instrumental-expressive axis. This particular formulation of sex-typed roles has influenced certain clinical formulations of family dysfunction (Lidz, 1973). It has also been the focus of a good deal of controversy as a result of the women's movement (Perrucci & Targ, 1974), and it has been challenged in empirical studies on sex-role typing and stereotyping (Bem, 1974; Bem, Martyna, & Watson, 1976).

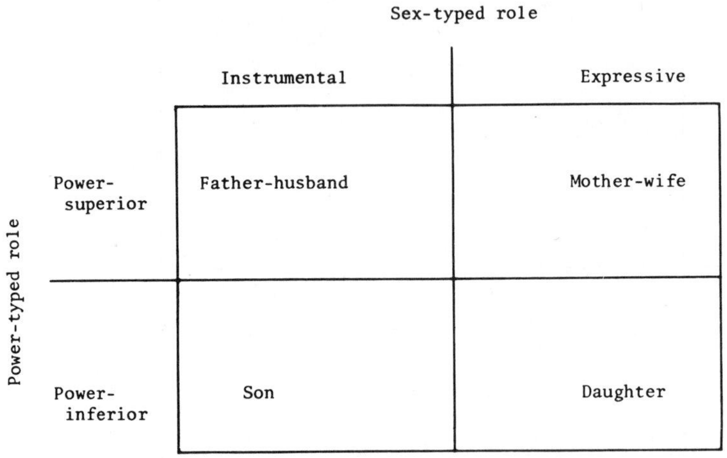

Sex-typed role

	Instrumental	Expressive
Power-superior	Father-husband	Mother-wife
Power-inferior	Son	Daughter

Power-typed role

FIGURE 1-3 Parsons's model of role differentiation in the nuclear family. (Adapted from Parsons & Bales, 1955.)

Interactional-situational framework. This conceptual model originated during the third, or "emerging science" stage that Christensen (1964b) identified in the development of the family field of study. The interactional school, also known as symbolic interactionism, was developed by G. H. Mead and associates at the University of Chicago. Of this group, Burgess (1926) was the first to apply the interactional framework to study of the family, which he defined as "a unity of interacting personalities."

Symbolic interactionism rests on two fundamental premises. The first is that human beings respond to their environment not in terms of its physical properties but rather in terms of the meaning that the environment has for them, as mediated through symbolic processes. The second is that such meanings are derived from (and modified in) the process of social interaction. Hill and Hansen (1960, p. 309) list the assumptions of this approach as follows:

1. Social conduct is most immediately a function of the social milieu.
2. A human is an independent actor as well as a reactor to his situation.
3. The basic autonomous unit is the acting individual in a social setting.

The situational model is best viewed as a natural counterpart to the interactional framework (Stryker, 1964). Like the interactional framework, it views the family as a unity of interacting personalities, but instead of focusing on the interactional processes of the family as such, it views these processes as stimuli impinging on family members. That is, family interaction is a situation, to which individual family members respond. The bridge between these two conceptual models is the emphasis that both give to the primacy of subjective factors, as seen in the concept of "the definition of the situation." This notion asserts that "if men define their situations as real, they are real in their consequences" (Thomas & Thomas, 1928, p. 572).

The interactional-situational framework, unlike the structure-functional framework, is not applied to the study of the relations between the family and external social systems, but rather is focused exclusively on the internal processes of the family. Also, unlike the structure-functional framework, the interactional school emphasizes growth and change rather than homeostasis; furthermore, it sees individuals as active creators of their symbolic-social context, rather than as passive reactors to social realities. Because of the emphasis on subjective meanings as well as social interaction, this approach is best viewed as a social-psychological model.

The mode of analysis of the interactional-situational framework starts from the premise that the family is a unity of interacting personalities. Each family member occupies certain social *positions*. Position is a term similar to status, and it refers to both ascribed positions (such as age, sex, race) and achieved positions (such as marital status and occupation). By virtue of occupying these positions, family members are assigned *roles*. Roles are defined in two ways: (1) by normative expectations and the expectations of the *reference group* (which are sensed by the individual through the process of *role-taking*, or empathy); (2) by reference to the individual's *self-concept*, which involves the process of *role-making*, or the active creation of one's own role. The study of family process, then, involves the study of the interactions of role-playing members so defined. The fundamental methodological principle of this framework is that the researcher must see the world from the frame of reference of the subject (Stryker, 1964).

As a final note, the interactional framework has yielded an approach to family therapy (Hurvitz, 1975). The symbolic-interactional approach to therapy has much in common with the experiential model of family therapy (see Chapter 7).

Family developmental framework.   This conceptual framework is the newest of those discussed here, having been elaborated in (and being very representative of) Christensen's fourth stage in the development of family sociology—systematic theory building. Unlike the other conceptual frameworks, which originated in other fields of social science and were applied later to the study of the family, the family developmental framework was formulated by family scholars with the needs of the family field of study clearly in view (Hill, 1974). As such, it has had the advantage of being able to select those aspects of other models best suited to the study of the family. The result has been a theoretical eclecticism:

> From rural sociologists it borrowed the concept of stages of the family life cycle. From child psychologists and human development specialists came the concepts of developmental needs and tasks. From the sociologists engaged in work in the professions it incorporated the concept of the family as a set of intercontingent careers. From the structure-function and interactional approaches were borrowed the concepts of age and sex roles, plurality patterns, functional prerequisites, and the many concepts associated with the family as a system of interacting actors (Hill & Hansen, 1960, p. 307).

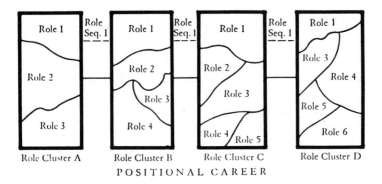

FIGURE 1-4   Role sequence, role cluster, and positional career. (From Rodgers, 1964.)

Rodgers (1964) developed a longitudinal conceptualization of roles and role relationships. In his approach, a family member occupying a given position has several roles, which in turn are made up of several norms. The collection of roles operative in a given position at a particular time is a *role cluster.* The change of a single role over time is a *role sequence.* A *positional career* is the longitudinal development of the role cluster. These concepts are diagramed in Figure 1-4. A *role complex* consists of the role clusters of two or more positions at a given point in time. A *family career* is the longitudinal development of role complexes over the family life cycle. The concepts of the role complex and family career are diagramed in Figure 1-5.

The family developmental framework starts from the interactionist concept of the family as a unity of interacting personalities, and then specifies the nature of their interrelatedness over time. Family positions are conceived not only as age positions modified by gender (and by ordinal position, in the case of children), but also as relatedness positions, in which the normative expectations of reciprocity are expressed. These relatedness positions are: husband-wife, brother-sister, mother-daughter, mother-son, father-daughter, father-son, brother-brother, and sister-sister. Over time, the role content of the positions changes (chiefly due to changes in normative expectations as a result of changes in age). Since the positions are interrelated, the change in role content of one position leads to a change in every position containing roles reciprocal to it. For example, the nature of the mother's role changes when the child's role changes from preschool toddler to elementary-school pupil.

The family developmental framework uses the concept of *developmental task.* This concept is treated at the levels of the individual family member and the family as a whole. At the level of the individual, the age-based changes in role expectations constitute *positional developmental tasks.* The concept of the *family developmental task* refers to the changes in normative expectations for the family as a whole in terms of the functions which it is expected to fulfill for its individual members and for society. Hill lists six functions that "form a series of tasks which each family fulfills in various ways, depending in part on its age and sex composi-

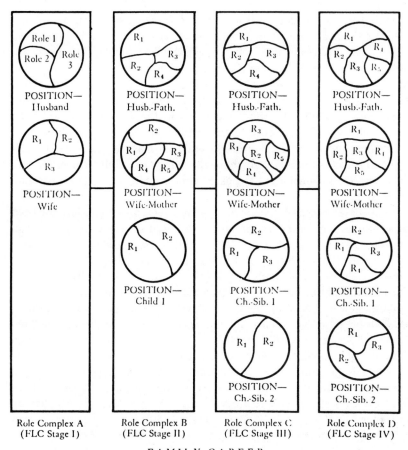

FAMILY CAREER

FIGURE 1-5 The family career. (From Rodgers, 1964.)

tion. It should be noted that these tasks have a variable urgency at different points in the family life cycle." The functions are

1. Physical maintenance for family members through providing food, shelter, and clothing.
2. Addition of family members through reproduction or adoption and releasing them when mature.
3. Socialization of children for adult roles in the family and in other social groups.
4. Maintenance of order within the family and between family members and outsiders.
5. Maintenance of family morale and motivation to carry out tasks in the family and in other groups.
6. Production and distribution of goods and services necessary for maintaining the family unit. (Hill, 1974, p. 308).

The family life cycle is described in terms of *developmental stages.* Hill and Rodgers (1964) present an eight-stage model, based on three categories of change. The first category is changes in family size, from childless couple, through an expanding period, a stable period, a contracting period, and a postparental period. The second is changes in age composition, which in the model is keyed to the developmental stages of the oldest child: infancy, preschool child, school child, adolescent, and young adult. The third is changes in the age-role content of the breadwinner(s), with specific reference to the retirement stage. Putting these three categories together, the eight stages are: (1) childless married couple; (2) childbearing stage; (3) preschool family; (4) school-age family; (5) adult trainees (adolescence); (6) young-adult launching; (7) postparental middle years; (8) postretirement-aging years.

The family developmental framework, being of recent origin, has not been worked out as fully as it might be, and it has not yet been subjected to rigorous empirical validation. Even at this early stage, however, it offers considerable promise as the starting point for the development of a unifying framework—and perhaps ultimately, a theory—not only for family sociology but also for the multidisciplinary study of the family. First of all, it represents an integration of the major sociological conceptual frameworks. Second, the family developmental framework continues to be involved in the process of theory building and consolidation through the integration of relevant perspectives. Hill (1974) has recently considered family development in the light of general systems theory. An integration of systems thinking would greatly enrich the family development framework, as well as provide a bridge to the clinical family frameworks. Third, a start on this particular bridge has been initiated from the clinical area, where a developmental approach to family therapy is emerging (Solomon, 1973; Carter & McGoldrick, 1980). Finally, there are moves within the field of developmental psychology, in which human development is being reconceptualized in an interactive and ecological frame of reference. Bronfenbrenner defines the "ecology of human development" as

> the scientific study of the progressive mutual accommodation, throughout the life span, between a growing human organism and the changing immediate environments in which it lives, as this process is affected by relations obtaining within and between these immediate settings, as well as the larger social contexts, both formal and informal, in which the settings are embedded. (1977, p. 514)

This new direction clearly provides a bridge between developmental psychology and the family developmental model.

Clinical Models of Family Functioning

Clinical models of family functioning are a relatively recent development. They have emerged in the past 30 years, as part of the rapid development of the field of family therapy. These models have been influenced to varying degrees by general systems theory. While many have been formulated without an explicit attempt to articulate with existing sociological conceptual models, there are some striking correspondences. The structural model has much in common with the structure-functional framework; the family process models share many concepts and assumptions with the symbolic-interactional framework; and the multigenerational model takes a longitudinal perspective, similar to the family developmental framework.

This section will present a brief overview of these three clinical models, with attention to their general orientations, and their approaches to describing family life. Certain aspects of these clinical models will be discussed in more depth in the next chapter and in the chapters on schools of family therapy in Part II.

Mapping family structure. Several structural models have been developed. First, there is the McMaster model of family functioning (Epstein, Bishop, & Levin, 1978), a model of clinical assessment that considers six dimensions of family functioning: problem solving, communication, roles, affective responsiveness, affective involvement, and behavior control. The influence of structural-functional sociology is evident in the subdivision of the first three dimensions into instrumental and affective categories. Second, there is the circumplex model of marital and family systems (Olson, Sprenkle, & Russell, 1979; Olson, Russell, & Sprenkle, 1980a), which is based on two orthogonal dimensions—cohesion and adaptability. Cohesion refers to emotional bonding, along a continuum from enmeshment (high cohesion) to disengagement (low cohesion), whereas adaptibility refers to the ability of the family to change its structure in response to changed circumstances, along a continuum from chaotic to rigid. The model divides each dimension into four zones and derives 16 family types on the basis of the simultaneous placement of the family on both dimensions. The third model is Minuchin's (1974) structural model. Owing to space limitations, the first two models will not be discussed further, and the remainder of this section will be devoted to Minuchin's model.

Minuchin's structural model has much in common with the structure-functional framework of family sociology, particularly in the use of concepts such as functional prerequisites, and differentiation into subsystems in order to carry out functions. In fact, Minuchin has acknowledged the influence of Parsons in his early work (Minuchin, Montalvo, Guerney, Rosman, & Schumer, 1967). However, Minuchin's model differs from the structure-functional framework in the particular systems characteristics that are ascribed to the family. Whereas the structure-functional framework sees the family as a homeostatic system, Minuchin sees the family as a balanced-growth system—or, in his terms, an "open sociocultural system in transformation" (p. 51). The family maintains itself: "It offers resistance to change beyond a certain range, and maintains preferred patterns as long as possible" (p. 52). But it is also able to adapt to changed circumstances: The family is "able to transform itself in ways that meet new circumstances without losing the continuity that provides a frame of reference for its members" (p. 52).

Minuchin defines family structure as "the invisible set of functional demands that organizes the ways in which family members interact" (p. 51). He starts with the observation that the communication or interaction of family members is patterned, a process that is described above, in the section on communication (Minuchin terms these communication or interaction patterns "transactional patterns"). He then proceeds to delineate the types of organizational structures that maintain the transactional patterns of the family. There are two categories of such organizational structures: (1) "Idiosyncratic" organizational structure, which is based on "the mutual expectations of particular family members" (p. 52). These expectations are built up over years of family life, and represent the accommodation of family members to one another. (2) "Generic" organizational structure, applicable to all families. This includes the "complementarity of functions" and the "power hierarchy." Complementarity of functions refers to the interdependence and reciprocity of the functions that family members must assume. The husband and wife may allocate functions according to the traditional "instrumental-expressive" division of labor (Parsons & Bales, 1955) or along less traditional lines. For example, many contemporary couples have developed unique patterns in which both share in the domestic and breadwinning responsibilities. The power hierarchy is usually differentiated along generational lines, such that the greater power lies with the parents. One or the other parent may have a greater degree of power and authority ("matriarchial" versus "patriarchal" forms). Power can also be shared within the nuclear family in a more-or-less democratic fashion. This is sometimes seen in families with young-adult offspring who continue their close ties to home. Less commonly, power can reside in the children. This may be a situation in which an older child helps out by assuming certain parental functions (the "parental child"—Minuchin, 1974, p. 53). Such a circumstance is to be distinguished from the situation in which children are forced prematurely into adult responsibility ("parentification" of children—Boszormenyi-Nagy & Spark, 1973). Finally, power can reside outside the nuclear family—that is, in the grandparent generation. This pattern was more common before World War II, particularly among European immigrant families.

The family carries out its functions by differentiating into *subsystems.* Subsystems can consist of an individual, a pair, or a larger group, and they can be formed on the basis of sex, age, function, or mutual interest. The enduring family subsystems include the spouse subsystem (for marital functions), the parental subsystem (for parental functions), and sibling subsystem (for peer socialization). Subsystems are differentiated from the rest of the family system by *boundaries,* which are defined as the rules governing who participates in a given subsystem, and under what circumstances.

When assessing families, Minuchin attends to the clarity of the boundaries. Boundaries between subsystems should be clear and consistent. At times, however, boundaries can become *diffuse,* as in, for example, the relationship between a mother and her infant. Boundaries can also become *rigid,* as for example, around the maternal-infant subsystem. However, when boundaries are characteristically and inappropriately diffuse or rigid, a dysfunctional situation exists. The family is thought to be *enmeshed,* in the case of inappropriately diffuse boundaries, or *disengaged,* in the case of overly rigid boundaries.

Minuchin also attends to the relationships within and among the subsystems

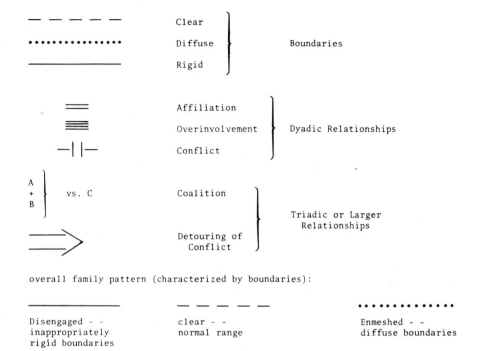

overall family pattern (characterized by boundaries):

Disengaged - - inappropriately rigid boundaries	clear - - normal range	Enmeshed - - diffuse boundaries

FIGURE 1-6   Symbols for mapping family structure. (Adapted from Minuchin, 1974.)

of the family. He determines whether the relationship between two family members is one of *affiliation, overinvolvement,* or *conflict.* In the case of three or more family members, he looks for coalitions of two (or more) family members against one (or more) other family member(s), and for the *detouring* of conflict between two family members through their mutual relationship with a third person.

Minuchin has developed a scheme for mapping family structure, with particular attention to subsystems and boundaries, and to relationships within and among subsystems. The symbols that he uses to describe these structural qualities are reproduced in Figure 1-6. Some examples of how these symbols are used to map family structure will now be presented.

First, some variations in the executive subsystem of the family will be mapped. The usual pattern, of mother and father fulfilling parental functions, with clear boundaries between the parental subsystem and the sibling subsystem, can be depicted as shown in Figure 1-7.

M F

Children

FIGURE 1-7

Another pattern, which is becoming more common, is the single-parent family (Figure 1-8).

M
— — — — —   F →
Children
FIGURE 1-8

In single-parent families an older child often helps out with executive functions and has a certain degree of authority with the other children. For example, an adolescent child may be in charge of the home from the time that the younger children come home from school to the time that mother comes home from work. Such a child is called a parental child, and is indicated by the symbol PC (Figure 1-9).

M, PC
— — — — —
Siblings
FIGURE 1-9

A situation that may arise in both single- and two-parent families is the involvement of members of the extended family (particularly grandparents) in executive functions. Two such patterns are mapped in Figure 1-10.

MGM   MGM
— — — — — —   — — — — — —
M F   M
— — — — — —   — — — — — —
Children   Children
FIGURE 1-10

In both examples we have depicted a clear boundary between the maternal grandmother (MGM) and the parental subsystem. This is not always the case. Particularly in two-parent families, the involvement of a grandparent in the executive subsystem often indicates a diffuse boundary, and overinvolvement of the parent with the grandparent (Figure 1-11).

MGM   MGM ≡ M
· · · · · · · · · ·
M   or
———   ———
F, Children   F, Children
FIGURE 1-11

Another common pattern involves a rigid boundary between the grandparent generation and the parental subsystem (Figure 1-12). In the "isolated nuclear family" this pattern of rigid boundaries is generalized to the rest of the extended family.

Grandparents
———————
M F
— — — — — — — —
Children
FIGURE 1-12

Next, some variations in the sibling subsystem will be mapped. Two-child families (the common pattern for the middle class family of the 1950s and 1960s) and single-child families are shown in Figure 1-13.

```
        M F                M F
      ------             ------
        C1 C2              C1
```

FIGURE 1-13

More complex patterns include larger families with an imbalance among siblings relative to gender (that is, all siblings one sex; one sibling of the opposite sex to the other children). These patterns are shown in Figure 1-14.

```
        M F                    M F
     ----------            ----------
     B1 B2 B3 B4, etc.     G1 G2 G3 G4 I B1
```

FIGURE 1-14

And, there is the "two-family" structure, a group of older children and a second group of younger children, with a large age-gap between the two groups (Figure 1-15).

```
        M F                      M F
      -------              -------------
      Adolescents    or    Adolescents I Toddlers
      -------
      Toddlers
```

FIGURE 1-15

Finally, we will map some examples of how conflict is handled in families. Given their greater power and influence, the conflict that is often of primary interest is that between the parents. This conflict can be expressed directly—that is, when two parents engage in an argument (Figure 1-16).

```
        M—II—F
      -------
       Children
```

FIGURE 1-16

Parental conflict can also be expressed indirectly, through their relationship with one of their children. For example, two spouses may begin to engage in argument, but stop and criticize their child. This process is called detouring of conflict, and is diagramed in Figure 1-17.

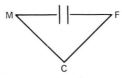

FIGURE 1-17   Detouring of conflict.

Or, two spouses may begin to argue, and one will seek the support of a child, forming a coalition with the child against the other spouse (Figure 1-18).

```
         M  )
      ....... } F
         C  )
```

FIGURE 1-18   Coalition.

Minuchin's scheme is a useful one, but it does have certain limitations. For one thing, while this scheme is quite useful for describing the structural organization of the family, it tends to depict family life as relatively static, particularly in comparison to the process models we will describe next. Also, Minuchin's model is not adequate for describing complex relationships in the extended family. For this purpose the genogram is more helpful.

Coding family process.   The family process models begin at the same point as the structural model—namely, with the observation that communication, or interaction process, is patterned. Whereas the structural school sought to define the organizational structures that undergird the interaction patterns, the process models attempt to describe the dynamic nature of the interaction patterns.

Interaction patterns could be said to be an operational definition of the interaction *rules* of the family, which determine who interacts with whom, under what circumstances, and in what manner. Put another way, what we are concerned about here is the parts or roles that family members play in the process of family interaction. Kantor and Lehr (1975) have coined the term *psychopolitics* to refer to family interaction process. The concept of psychopolitics is defined in a way that is analogous to the symbolic-interactionist use of the term *role,* with attention both to the subjective sense of self of the individual, and to the external expectations and systems constraints, as codeterminants of an individual's part or role:

> We use the term "psychopolitics" to denote that thematic area of family process in which family members try simultaneously to cope with the institutional requirements of the family's unit and interpersonal subsystems and the individual's right to be himself. The term *psychopolitics* itself—*psycho* representing the interior person and *politics* representing observable family interactions—is an expression of our concern for connecting analyses of family-system matters with personal-system goals and behaviors (Kantor & Lehr, 1975, p. 179)

A number of psychopolitical models of family process have been developed, dealing with two, three, and four player parts. Two-player models are used to describe marital interaction. Bowen (1966) described the "overadequate-inadequate reciprocity" in which one partner takes charge and dominates and the other is passive or helpless. Fogarty (1976d) delineated the "distancer-pursuer dynamic," in which one partner chases as the other flees emotional involvement. Closely related to this is the notion of "abandonment" and "engulfment" (Karpel, 1976), in which the pursuer chases as a way of compensating for feelings of abandonment; but the pursuit leaves the distancer feeling engulfed. As a result, the distancer flees more vigorously, which in turn fuels the pursuer's need to pursue.

Ackerman (1967) formulated a three-player model to describe the scapegoating process that he observed clinically. The three roles are "persecuter," "victim," and "healer." The persecuter attacks the victim, and the healer rescues the victim, thus neutralizing the attack and setting the stage for a repeat of the circular process.

Satir (1972) developed a four-player model of dysfunctional family communication, in which the parts are "blamer," "placater," "computer," and "distracter" (see Figure 1-19). These parts are enduring, generalized roles. They may appear in any combination in families. For example, there might be a fault-finding father (blamer), an ultrareasonable mother who feels that all problems can be resolved if we simply discuss them long enough (computer), a teenage daughter who is anxious to please (placater), and a silly, irreverent, and irrelevant primary-grade son (distracter). Satir views these roles as manifestations of incongruent communication. Family members using these roles do not express their real feelings (or, if they do, they contradict them at a metacommunicative level), because they do not have sufficient self-esteem and self-confidence to know that it is acceptable to express their real feelings. For example, blamers often feel unloved, alone, empty, and unhappy. Rather than express these feelings, they attack others for any number of reasons, most of which are disguised instances in which the blamer has experienced feelings of not being loved, etc. Placaters, on the other hand, often feel that they will not be loved if they disagree, or are different, or are independent of a parent or spouse. Rather than test these hypotheses, they live in a state of terror and deny themselves in order to please the other. The alternative to these dysfunctional roles, according to Satir, is "leveling," or congruent communication, in which one says what one is feeling directly.

The two- and three-player models discussed above can be described in terms of Satir's model. For example, a distancer often operates as a computer, and pursuers can either take the role of blamer or placator. In Ackerman's model, the persecuter is a blamer, the healer is a placater, and the victim (usually a schizophrenic child) is a distracter.

So far, with the exception of the leveler role, the psychopolitical models have represented dysfunctional family process. Kantor and Lehr (1975, p. 181) have developed a four-player model that is a more general model, valid for both functional and dysfunctional family situations. The four parts are "mover," "opposer," "follower," and "bystander." The mover is the initiator of the action. The opposer reacts to the mover's move by challenging or blocking it. The follower reacts to the mover's move by joining with it, and supporting it. The bystander is neutral, stays out of the action, and views it from a position of distance and perspective. The bystander is often important in resolving conflicts and in facilitating process because of this perspective and neutrality. Like Satir's roles, these roles may appear in any combination in families. Unlike Satir's roles, they are not necessarily generalized nor enduring, but are usually specific to certain situations. Thus, a family member may be a mover in one dimension and a follower in another. In fact, the degree to which roles are generalized, such that family members are "stuck" in one role, is an indicator of family dysfunction.

Kantor and Lehr's psychopolitical model of family interaction is part of their comprehensive model of family process. This is a "distance-regulation" (p. 221) model that attempts to answer two primary questions: (1) "How does a family set up and maintain its territory?"; and (2) "How does it regulate distance among its own members?" (p. 7). With respect to the first question, three subsystems are defined that describe the different types of boundaries existing between family members and the external world. These are depicted in Figure 1-20. The outermost boundary surrounds the "family-unit subsystem" (p. 23) and separates the family

FIGURE 1-19   Drawings representing the roles of blamer, placater, computer, and distracter. (From Satir, 1972, pp. 65, 67, 69, 71. Copyright, 1972. Science and Behavior Books, Inc. Reprinted by permission of the author and publisher.)

Distracter   Blamer

Computer   Placater

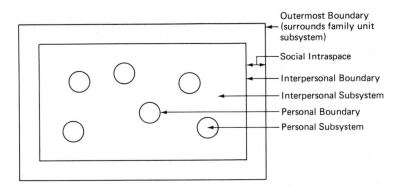

FIGURE 1-20   Boundaries and subsystems in Kantor and Lehr's model of family process. (Kantor & Lehr, 1975.)

from the community at large. It is "spatialized" as the perimeter of the household. Official visitors to the family are allowed to enter the family unit subsystem, but are usually confined to the "social intraspace" (p. 26). This is conceptualized as the space between the family-unit boundary and the interpersonal boundary, and is spatialized as the front hallway, or foyer, or perhaps the living room. Friends and relatives usually have access to the "interpersonal subsystem," but only intimate friends and close relatives are allowed into the "personal subsystems" (p. 23) of individual family members.

With respect to the second question, Kantor and Lehr's model describes the ways in which the family regulates the interrelationships of its members. Family members are conceptualized as seeking access to certain goals. Access is defined in terms of three dimensions, which are "the physical media through which each family system marks off its pathways for attaining" goals (p. 37). These "access dimensions" are time, space, and energy. The goals themselves are defined in terms of "target dimensions," of which there are three: (1) "affect," which is defined as "intimacy and nurturance—that sense of loving and being loved by someone in our world"; (2) "power," which is defined as "the freedom to decide what we want, and the ability to get it—whether it be money, goods, or skills"; and (3) "meaning," which is defined as a "framework that provides us with explanations of reality and helps us define our identity" (p. 37). "Strategies" (p. 103) are the recurring interactional patterns—through which family members, playing certain parts, gain access to targets.

Tracing family history: The multigenerational approach. Whereas the two clinical models of family functioning just considered are quite closely related to their counterparts in family sociology, the multigenerational approach is only roughly analogous to the family-development framework. The major point of similarity is the use of a longitudinal perspective. The actual time frame of interest, however, is quite different in the two models. Whereas the family-developmental framework is concerned with the life cycle of the nuclear family as it moves from formation through expansion and then contraction, the multigenerational model is concerned with the microhistory or genealogy of the family over three and sometimes more generations.

Several multigenerational models of the family have been developed. These include a psychodynamic model based on object-relations theory (Framo, 1970), the intergenerational model that admixes existentialism and psychoanalysis (Boszormenyi-Nagy & Spark, 1973), and Bowen's multigenerational model (Bowen, 1976). The similarities and differences of these three models will be described in detail in Chapter 4 and will not be covered here. Instead, Bowen's multigenerational model will be presented as representative of the group, since it presents in clearest form the fundamentals of a multigenerational conceptual framework, and since it has an associated schema for mapping generational history. The multigenerational model builds on the preceding models in the sense that it views symptoms as embedded in an interactional pattern that is maintained by an organizational structure. It then goes on to trace the evolution of that structure over several generations of a family.

In briefest outline, the model states that two people who are at approximately the same level of maturity ("differentiation of self"—which is the relative balance of "solid self" to "pseudo-self") meet, marry, and have children, forming a "nuclear family emotional system." Depending on their levels of maturity, they will have varying degrees of emotional difficulty ("fusion systems"), which they will handle through one or more of the following ways. First, one of the spouses may become dysfunctional. This occurs through the formation of an "overadequate-inadequate reciprocity," wherein the adaptive spouse becomes increasingly helpless to the point of becoming psychologically or medically symptomatic, while the dominant spouse assumes the role of caretaker. Second, the marriage may become discordant, with a high degree of conflict and turmoil. Third, the emotional difficulties may extend beyond the marital pair and their relationship to the involvement and impairment of one or more of their children. This process occurs through the formation of triangular structures involving the two parents and one of the children. Bowen refers to this as the "family projection process," by which he means the transmission of parental immaturity to the child. The multigenerational model, then, is concerned with the "pattern that emerges over the generations as the parents transmit varying levels of their immaturity to their children." (Bowen, 1966, p. 363). This is termed the "multigenerational transmission process."

The multigenerational pattern is mapped through the use of generational maps, or *genograms* (Guerin & Pendagast, 1976; Pendagast & Sherman, 1977). Figure 1-21 shows the symbols that are used in constructing a genogram. An example of a genogram is presented in Figure 1-22.

In constructing a genogram, one first gathers factual information about family members: names and nicknames, ages, dates of marriages, separations and divorces, births, deaths, and other important events such as the establishment of separate households, graduations, and promotions. Each of these events requires some reorganization of the family system, which in turn requires some change in family members. Consequently, one can note certain events coinciding with others,

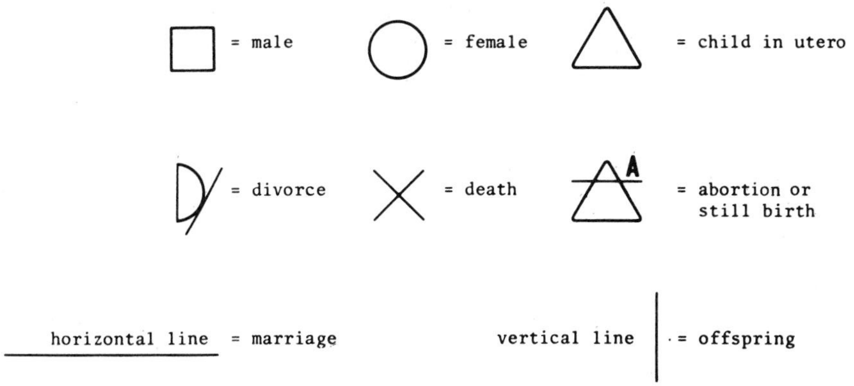

FIGURE 1-21   Symbols for genograms. (Adapted from Guerin & Pendagast, 1975.)

such as father becomes depressed around the time of the birth of the first child, or mother goes back to college when the youngest child enters adolescence.

One seeks information concerning the physical location of family members. Families can be classified as "explosive" or "cohesive," depending on their distance from the location of their family or origin. Frequency and types of contact (whether by visits, letter, phone calls) are noted, as are the patterns of closeness and distance among the manifold relationships of the family. Specific relationships can be characterized in terms of the pursuer-distancer dynamic. One should also observe the way in which family members have separated from their parental families. Both prolonged living at home and "emotional cut-offs" are indications of unresolved emotional attachment (fusion) to the parents. The "sibling positions" (Toman, 1976) and relationships should also be noted.

Finally, one seeks information concerning certain general characteristics of the family. One of these is the "toxic" issues—those emotionally laden topics about which conversation is strictly regulated. These often involve some aspect of the general topics of sex, money, death, religion or ethnicity, and parenting. There may be also some toxic issues that are specific to a particular family. The way in which the family handles these toxic issues is also an important indicator of the degree of differentiation. In addition to the toxic issues, one should also note the cultural characteristics of the family: ethnicity, religion, and socioeconomic status. These variables are obviously important for understanding many aspects of family life.

Sociological and Clinical Models: Shared Features

In examining the major conceptual models of the family developed by sociologists on the one hand and clinicians on the other, many correspondences between the two groups of models can be observed.

First, it can be noted that Parsons's structure-functional model and Minuchin's structural model have certain features in common. Both models are concerned with

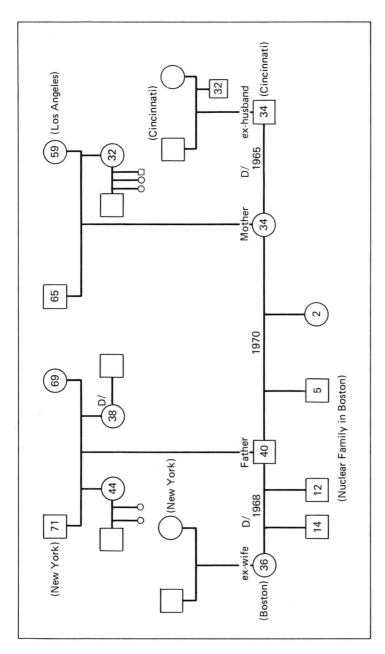

FIGURE 1-22 Example of a genogram.

the *organizational structure* of the family. They both examine the subsystems of the family in terms of their functional relationships or complementarities, and in terms of their placement in the power hierarchy. Both models, additionally, are capable of taking family phenomena into view at several levels: The level of family interactional processes; the level of the relationship of the family to external social systems; and the level of the relationship between the family system and the internal states of individual family members. Finally, both models emphasize the homeostatic or stable properties of the family. In this case, however, it should be noted that Minuchin's model does take family change into account to a greater extent than does Parson's model.

Second, it can be observed that the interactional-situational model and the family-process models have several similarities. Both models attempt to describe the *dynamic process* of family interaction. They both examine the family as a unity of interacting personalities: "Unity" is considered in terms of the complementarity or "fit" of family members' roles; "interacting personalities" is conceptualized by a definition of the term "role" that includes both externally imposed normative features and internally determined subjective features. In addition, both models tend to consider the family at two levels: The level of family interactional processes, and the level of the relationship between the family and the internal state of individual family members. Finally, both models emphasize the family's homeodynamic features and change processes.

Third, the family developmental and multigenerational models share certain features. Both models attempt to describe the *development* of the family system over time. However, they take different perspectives on time. Whereas the family developmental model is concerned with describing the family as a unity of interacting personalities as it progresses through various stages of its life cycle in one generation, the multigenerational model attempts to infer the manner in which present family interactions patterns have developed over several generations of the family's history. Additionally, both models tend to view the family at two levels: The level of family interactional processes, and the level of the relationship between the family and the internal states of individual family members. Finally, both models tend to give equal weight to the problems of stability and change.

Thus, sociology and clinical psychology both appear to have arrived—to a large extent, independently—at three basic ways of conceptualizing the family as a social entity. As Bateson (1972a) has noted, the discovery of similar patterns of thought within different intellectual disciplines, each with its own sets of data and disparate methods, points to the existence of more general paradigms or orientations toward viewing the phenomenon under study. The three paradigms of the family are, then, the structural, the process, and the historical. In general terms, the structural paradigm is concerned with describing the enduring organizational structure of the family and analyzing the underlying function and hierarchical relationship of its components. The process paradigm is concerned with depicting the dynamic flow of family interaction, with an emphasis on the interrelatedness of the players. The historical paradigm views the development or evolution of the family over a time frame of one or more generations.

Before we close this discussion let us focus for a moment on the relationships among these three paradigms. First, consider the relationship between the concepts of structure and process. "Structure" is a static concept and refers to the way in which the family is patterned and organized. "Process" is a dynamic concept, and refers to the ongoing flow of interaction in the family. Yet, as we have learned from our study of communication, and as one can verify by observing families, the flow of interaction is patterned: Certain sequences of interaction recur with regularity and can be seen to reflect stable organization features of the family. Hence, an examination of process ultimately leads to a study of structure. On the other hand, if one begins by examining the structure of the family, after a while it becomes evident that the structured elements are continually changing and evolving; a study of structure thus becomes an examination of process.

Our study of general systems theory introduced the notions of morphogenesis and morphostasis, which indicate (respectively) that ongoing social systems such as the family have periods of change and periods of stability. Though certain families may tend to emphasize one or the other of these processes, both are invariably present to some degree. The dimension of time allows one to view both change and stability in a family. Hence, the concept of history, viewed from the vantage point of general systems theory, allows the integration of the concepts of structure and process.

Finally, it should be noted that each paradigm has its own strengths and domain of application. Whereas the process paradigm offers the "best seats in the house" for observing immediate family interaction, the structural paradigm allows one to step back a bit in order to both make inferences about the organizational characteristics that undergird family interaction, and to take into view the family in its sociocultural context. The historical paradigm allows one to conceptualize both change and stability in the family: From this perspective one can observe the stable regularities of family structure as well as follow the dynamic processes of adaptation and development that change the structure of the family over time.

SUMMARY

This consideration of the family as a social system began with an examination of the nature of family communication. Communication is complex and involves both verbal communication and nonverbal communication (the elements of which include paralinguistic and kinesic factors, the individual's appearance, and the spatial arrangement of the family group). Communication has report and command functions, and occurs at different levels, including that of metacommunication. In families, a sequence of interactions becomes organized into a pattern through the metacommunicative phenomenon of punctuation. Family communication *is* the data one collects in the process of family assessment. Techniques for gathering information include (1) the assignment of tasks of one or more of these four types: problem-solving, decision-making, conflict-resolution, and naturalistic, and (2) the use of family interviews, which vary in their degree of structure and in their orientation toward the past or the present.

A number of conceptual models of the family as a social system have been proposed. Several of these models involve a shift in epistemological perspective, the focal point of which is general systems theory. Concepts central to general systems theory include the notion of a system, the distinction between open and closed systems, and the feedback loops essential to information-processing systems such as the family. On the basis of the nature of their feedback loops, open socio-cultural systems can be typed as homeostatic, balanced-growth, or random; and this typology can be applied to the family. Turning to the conceptual models themselves, parallels can be drawn between the major sociological conceptual models—structure-functional, interactional-situational, and family developmental—and the newer clinical models—structural, process, and multigenerational. The similarities between these groups suggest the existence of three more general models or paradigms of conceptualizing the family: structural, process, and historical. In the relationship of these paradigms to one another, it appears that the historical paradigm, viewed from the perspective of general systems theory, has the capacity to integrate the structure and process paradigms.

Having assimilated these ideas about how families communicate and interact, how they are organized or structured, and how they adapt or develop over time, the reader should now be in a good position to take up the issue of dysfunction in families, a topic to which I will turn in Chapter 2.

2

The Relationship
between Family Interaction
and Psychopathology

This chapter will focus on attempts to conceptualize the nature of family dysfunction. To be exact, it will review the hypotheses that have been formulated about the role of the family as a social system in the development and/or maintenance of the clinical psychopathology of one of its members. Although the problem of the family's role in the development of social pathology (for example, domestic violence, child neglect, crime, and delinquency) is also of compelling interest, only a little work has been done in this area. That work has taken a clinical perspective and, hence, can be subsumed under the discussion of the family's role in psychopathology. Another topic of importance is the problem of family dysfunction viewed in terms of the relationship and the group-properties dimensions (Howells, 1971), as contrasted with the individual dimension (problems such as marital discord, parent-child conflict, or general family dysfunction). But in this area I am not aware of any attempts to explicate the role of the family as a social system in either producing or stabilizing the dysfunction of one of its subsystems or of the whole. The work that has been done either has simply described the dysfunctional subsystem (for example, a characterization of the interaction of a marital couple) or has sought explication of the dysfunction in terms of the attributes of the individuals—their personalities, expectations, and other characteristics. Hence, this problem will not be discussed here.

GENERAL CONSIDERATIONS

Etiology versus Maintenence

The conceptual formulations that will be discussed, then, concern the family's role in the etiology and/or maintenance of psychopathology. I wish to focus for a moment on the phrase "etiology and/or maintenance." The formulations to be discussed can be arranged along a continuum according to the extent to which they are concerned with the etiological causes of psychopathology, or with the family interaction patterns that maintain the psychopathology and allow it to continue. This continuum reflects the shift in epistemological perspective from linear causal models to circular-systemic models (discussed in Chapter 1). At one end of this continuum are the psychodynamic formulations that deal explicitly with the process of development and that specify the ways in which normal development is adversely affected by particular attributes of the family (Lidz, Cornelison, Fleck, & Terry, 1957a; Wynne, Ryckoff, Day, & Hirsch, 1958). Beyond the midpoint, tending toward the opposite end, are the communicational formulations that specify the family conditions to which the particular form of psychopathology is adaptive and functional, but that either do not deal with, or have relatively undeveloped ideas regarding, the genesis of the individual's psychological disturbance (Bateson, et al., 1956a; Laing & Esterson, 1970). These investgators have questioned the illness model of schizophrenia. Consequently, they have been less interested in investigating its etiology than in studying the context within which the seeming nonsense of the schizophrenic symptoms begin to make sense. These models, however, have not completed the transition from a linear and dyadic to a circular-systemic frame of reference. At the far end of the continuum are positions that dismiss the problem of the etiology of psychopathology as irrelevant to therapeutic change. Invoking the principle of equifinality (see Chapter 1), it is asserted that "the system is . . . its own best explanation" (Watzlawick, et al., 1967, p. 129). Such positions focus on the factors that currently support and maintain the psychopathology, and they attempt to alter those factors directly. For example, Minuchin's diagnostic procedure (1974) involves mapping the structural dysfunction of the family, of which the identified patient's symptoms are an expression, in order to develop a prescriptive plan for structural intervention.

Historical Background

Historically, some of the studies to be discussed here are related to the birth of the family-therapy field. These studies departed both from the sociological tradition in family research (of studying the family through the verbal report of one member, usually the mother) and the traditional psychoanalytic approach in the clinical fields (which frowned on the notion of involving the patient's family for fear of disturbing the patient-therapist transference). These investigators of the 1950s and early 1960s were doing clinical research on schizophrenia, and they observed whole families. Their findings implicated the family as an etiological agent in schizophrenia (Lidz et al., 1957a; Wynne et al., 1958; Bateson et al., 1956).

Zuk and Rubenstein (1965) described in some detail the events that took place in the 1940s and early 1950s in the clinical fields, paving the way for a departure from the psychoanalytic orthodoxy that was dominant at the time. First, a number of important clinical studies investigated the parent-child relationship. These include Levy's research (1943), which found a relationship between "maternal over-protection" and disturbance in offspring; Fromm-Reichmann's formulation (1948) of the "schizophrenogenic mother"; and Johnson and Szurek's investigation (1954) that found a correlation between the type of antisocial behavior of children and the particular moral blind spots ("superego lacunae") of their parents. These studies were important in that they focused attention on family factors as etiological agents. The importance of their findings, however, was limited by that fact that, out of the multitude and complexity of the relationships that exist in families, only a few aspects were focused on, and these were treated as if they operated in isolation. Spiegel and Bell (1959) and Frank (1965) have reviewed this literature, noting the consequent lack of consistency in the findings. Second, newer psychodynamic theories were developed, such as those of Sullivan and Erikson, which emphasized the influence of social interaction and current life stress on personality function and dysfunction. Finally, there were innovations in clinical technique, such as group therapy, and the collaborative treatment of children and parents that was developed by the child guidance clinics. The success of these approaches diminished the fear of involving individuals other than the designated patient in therapy. These events, of course, were part of a larger process—namely, a press toward innovation in clinical methods, growing out of the impatience that resulted from the lack of efficacy of traditional psychoanalytic methods for clinical syndromes such as schizophrenia and antisocial disturbances of childhood and adolescence.

In the 1950s a number of investigators independently established research projects involving the observation and/or treatment of families with a schizophrenic member. On the West coast, Bateson developed a research project on human communication, in which schizophrenia was studied as a particular case exemplifying the more general problems of communication with which he was concerned. His project, based in the Palo Alto (California) Veterans Administration Hospital, was founded in 1952. He hired Haley, Weakland, and Fry in 1953. Jackson joined the project in 1954 as a consultant, initially to provide clinical supervision for the work with schizophrenic families, but he became a principal figure very quickly. The Bateson project continued until 1962, after which Bateson became the director of Lilly's dolphin laboratory in the Virgin Islands. Bateson, Jackson, Haley, and Weakland (1956) formulated the well-known "double bind" hypothesis to account for the disordered communicational context that characterized the families of schizophrenics.

Several centers of activity emerged on the East coast. In Bethesda, at the National Institute of Mental Health (NIMH), Bowen established a monumentally ambitious project in 1954, in which families of schizophrenics lived in hospital wards for periods of up to two and a half years (Bowen, 1960). Bowen had actually begun his work eight years earlier at the Menninger Hospital. In this earlier work Bowen had focused on the mother-child dyad, with attention to the symbiotic nature of their relationship. His later studies led to the multigenerational conceptualization of the family (presented in Chapter 1). Some of Bowen's concepts of family dysfunction include "triangulation," "emotional divorce," and the "overadequate-inadequate" reciprocity.

Bowen left NIMH in 1959 to take a position at Georgetown University Medical School. He was succeeded as Chief of the Family Studies Section of NIMH by Wynne. Wynne's early research was concerned with the influence of family role structure on the development of schizophrenia. Wynne utilized Erikson's epigenetic theory of development and viewed the role relations of the family as a learning environment for the development of a sense of identity. Wynne and his colleagues coined such terms as "pseudomutuality," "pseudohostility," and the "rubber fence" to describe the nature of the role relations in schizophrenic families (Wynne et al., 1958; Wynne, 1961). Wynne left NIMH in the early 1970s to take a position at the University of Rochester Medical School.

A similar line of inquiry took place at the Yale Psychiatric Institute in New Haven. In 1952, Lidz started an intensive investigation of the intrafamilial environment of a small sample ($N = 17$) of families of schizophrenic patients. Lidz's research was concerned with the influence of the age-sex structure of the family on the development of schizophrenia. Using a blend of psychoanalytic theory to account for individual development and the very compatible structure-functional sociology of Parsons (Parsons & Bales, 1955) to conceptualize family structure, he described two types of pathogenic families characterized by the nature of the marital relationship. The terms "marital schism" and "marital skew" were coined to label these two family types (Lidz et al., 1957a).

Laing's research in London, begun in 1958, provided limited cross-cultural validation for the studies taking place in the U.S.A. Using an existential-phenomenological theoretical orientation, Laing asked the question "Are the experience and behavior that psychiatrists take as symptoms and signs of schizophrenia more socially intelligible than has come to be supposed?" (Laing & Esterson, 1970, p. 12). In attempting to answer this question, he postulated that the schizophrenic experience results from a process of "mystification" (Laing, 1965). Mystification is a transpersonal process that has some similarities to the double-bind concept.

These research groups, headed by Bateson, Bowen, Wynne, Lidz, and Laing, produced many of the pioneering conceptual formulations regarding the family contribution to psychopathology. Their conceptualizations, of course, were based only on studies of schizophrenia. In the early 1960s, encouraged and stimulated by these early studies, investigators began to branch out and to explore the family contribution to other forms of psychopathology. Many of these studies are reviewed by Bloch (1973b); they include attention to the following clinical syndromes: phobias, psychosomatic disorders (for a review of this work, see Meissner, 1966), learning difficulties, delinquency, addictive states, homosexuality, and depression and suicide. In addition, a few studies attempted to reformulate some of Freud's original cases in terms of family systems ideas (Strean, 1962; Schatzman, 1971). For the most part, those studies did not involve new conceptualizations of family dysfunction, but rather, they applied the seminal concepts of the researchers of the 1950s to new areas. There are two exceptions. One is the group of sociological studies, such as Cleveland & Longaker (1957) and Vogel & Bell (1968). These studies started from the vantage point of viewing the family as a socializing and acculturating agent, and they sought to explain how these functions might become sufficiently disordered to produce psychopathology. Their concepts of "cultural value conflict" and the effects of the use of "disparagement" as a socialization technique contributed to our understanding of certain forms of triangulation, particularly the scapegoating of a child.

The second exception is the work of Minuchin. In the early 1960s Minuchin began his work with the families of delinquent boys at the Wiltwyck School for Boys in New York. In this work he began to develop his concepts of family structure, with particular attention to the structural problems of the "disorganized and disadvantaged family" (Minuchin et al., 1967). In the late 60s he moved to the Philadelphia Child Guidance Clinic, where he was joined by Haley (who had moved from California) and Montalvo and Rosman (who had come from Wiltwyck with Minuchin). At Philadelphia, Minuchin's attention shifted to psychosomatic families, with particular focus on the families of anorexia nervosa patients (Minuchin, Rosman, & Baker, 1978). During the late 60s and early 70s he further developed his structural theory of the family (presented in Chapter 1). Minuchin's concepts of family dysfunction focus on triangulation, and they specify the types of triangulated systems and their structural underpinnings (Minuchin, 1974).

The remainder of this chapter has two major sections. The first and larger section will present the conceptual formulations of the family's contribution to psychopathology that have been developed by Bateson, Bowen, Wynne, Lidz, Laing, and Minuchin. The second section will examine the empirical research that has attempted to test these various conceptual formulations.

CONCEPTUAL FORMULATIONS
OF THE RELATIONSHIP
BETWEEN PSYCHOPATHOLOGY
AND THE FAMILY

The conceptual formulations discussed here will be organized along the continuum from a concern with etiology to a concern with maintenance of psychopathology. At one end of the continuum, the work of the Lidz and Wynne groups represents a relatively traditional approach, in which psychodynamic theory is adapted to the study of the family as an etiological agent through the admixing of Parsons's structure-functional sociological theory (Parsons, 1955). A greater departure from tradition is represented by the work of the Bateson and Laing groups. These investigators attempted to make the schizophrenic symptoms intelligible by viewing them within the communicational context of the family. Finally, an integration of Minuchin's structural model with parts of Bowen's model—with particular attention to the patterns of dysfunction—yields a synthesis that represents the most general conceptual formulation of family dysfunction, one that allows the development of a taxonomy of dysfunctional family patterns.

Psychodynamic Conceptual Formulations

The work of Lidz and associates. Lidz's interest in the families of schizophrenic patients dates back to 1940, when, during his psychiatric residency at Johns Hopkins in Baltimore under Adolf Meyer, he and his wife began a study comparing the family backgrounds (as recorded in psychiatric case histories) of 50 young schizophrenic patients with those of 50 psychotically depressed patients. (The study was delayed for years because of World War II.) They found the two groups had very different family backgrounds. The schizophrenic group showed an overwhelming array of adverse intrafamilial factors. In fact,

> Only five of the fifty schizophrenic patients could be said to have clearly come from reasonably stable homes in which they had been raised by two stable and compatible parents according to fairly acceptable principles of child rearing. (Lidz & Lidz, 1949, p. 343)

This study led to an intensive investigation based at the Yale Psychiatric Institute, which ran from 1952 to 1965. Seventeen families of schizophrenic patients were the primary subjects, but they were studied against the backdrop of several hundred other families of patients treated at the Institute during the period, who were studied less intensively. In addition, there was a comparison group of 10 families with a delinquent child, but the data for these families were not reported, owing to a variety of methodological problems. The study was exploratory in nature, with the objective of developing hypotheses about the particular types of problems that occur in these families, and their relationship to etiology. They reported their findings in a series of articles published between 1957 and 1965 and subsequently collected into one volume (Lidz, Fleck, & Cornelison, 1965).

They found that the fathers were significantly impaired in their ability to fulfill the paternal role (Lidz, Cornelison, Fleck, & Terry, 1957b). They were, as a group, insecure in their sense of masculinity, and they needed a great deal of attention and admiration from their wives and other family members. A significant number were given to paranoid ideation and irrational behavior, which adversely affected family life. They distinguished five types of fathers: fathers who were locked in bitter dispute with their wives and tried to win over their daughters as allies; fathers who were very needy of their wife's attention and behaved as rivals to their sons; fathers whose extremely high estimations of themselves smacked of paranoid grandiosity; fathers who were obvious failures in life and pathetic figures in the home; and passive fathers who functioned as adjuncts to their very disturbed wives.

The mothers were similarly unable to carry out the maternal role (Lidz, Cornelison, Singer, Schafer, & Fleck, 1965). Two types of mothers were distinguished according to the gender of the schizophrenic child, a variable that Lidz had come to view as of paramount importance (Fleck, Lidz, & Cornelison, 1963). One group of mothers of schizophrenic sons fit the "schizophrenogenic" pattern. This is a nearly or actually psychotic woman who is profoundly egocentric, who cannot establish boundaries between herself and others, who wanted a son to bring completion to her life, who is impervious to her son's needs (except those that fit her rigid preconceptions), and who is anxiously oversolicitous and intrusive. Other mothers who did not fit this pattern were either overprotective or openly seductive with their sons. The mothers of schizophrenic daughters were involved in a great deal of marital turmoil that further undermined their already low self-esteem as women. These mothers had an amorphous quality and were unable to invest themselves in the maternal role.

The marriages of parents of schizophrenic offspring were markedly disturbed (Lidz, Cornelison, Fleck, & Terry, 1957a). The Lidz group described two patterns, which were based on the nature of the marital partners' attempts to achieve role reciprocity and which were labeled "schism" and "skew." Schismatic marriages were characterized by severe chronic disequilibrium and discord. There was a complete failure to achieve role reciprocity. Both spouses were unable to gain emotional support from each other; both sought to force each other to conform to their expectations. There were periods of intense conflict, in which threats of separation were issued, followed by periods of mutual emotional withdrawal. These marriages were also characterized by continuing strong ties to spouses' families of origin, which may have prevented a genuine investment in their family of procreation. Within the nuclear family, the generational boundaries were unclear, as parents involved the children in the marital conflict by competing for their affection and loyalty. Three types of schismatic marriages were observed: male-dominated competitive marriages, in which the husband would periodically gain an upper hand through force; female-dominated competitive marriages, in which the wife would win out through effectively excluding and isolating her husband; and dual immature dependency marriages, in which both spouses looked to each other to provide leadership and direction.

The skewed marriages were characterized by a superficial peace and seeming harmony, which was based upon a rather insidious situation. In these marriages a dominant partner with serious psychopathology was married to a dependent spouse who provided support in exchange for leadership. Conflict was denied and hidden, creating an unreal atmosphere, in which what happened differed from what was said to have happened. In some cases the disturbed thinking of one spouse was supported and shared by the other, forming a *folie à deux* or even a *folie à famille*. Two types of skewed marriages were observed, distinguished according to whether the supportive and adaptive spouse was the husband or wife.

The siblings of schizophrenic patients were found as a group to have serious psychopathology (Lidz, Fleck, Alanen, & Cornelison, 1963). Those with better adjustments had managed to sever ties with the family of origin. Yet even so, these siblings showed marked emotional constriction on projective tests. Lidz found that the factor of gender was of major importance in determining the degree of psychopathology in the siblings. The siblings who were of the same sex as the schizophrenic patient were more disturbed than the opposite-sex sibling. Encouraged by this finding, the Lidz group reexamined their data separately for male and female schizophrenic patients, focusing on the parent-child relationships (Fleck, Lidz, & Cornelison, 1963). They found that the parents of male patients consisted of a dominant mother who could not set boundaries, was engulfing or seductive, intrusive and overprotective, and impervious to her child's needs. The father was weak and ineffectual, unable to enact a paternal role, and a poor role model for the son. Their marriages were predominantly of the skewed type. The parents of female patients consisted of a mother who provided a very poor model of the female role, who was low in self-esteem, uninvested in the maternal role, and unempathic. Typically, she was undercut and derogated by a dominating husband who had very great needs for attention and admiration, and who was seductive toward the daughter. Their marriages were typically of the schismatic type.

The Lidz group also found that the families in general were characterized by an atmosphere of irrationality and faulty communication. This distorted ideational climate provided "training in irrationality," both implicitly and explicitly (Lidz, Cornelison, Terry, & Fleck, 1958). The corrosive influence of the home was further reinforced by the limitations that were placed on extrafamilial socialization (Lidz, Cornelison, & Fleck, 1965).

As Lidz pointed out, the examination of the characteristics of the 17 families did not consume the 12 years that were spent on this study (Lidz, Fleck, & Cornelison, 1965). Much of this time was spent in reconceptualizing psychoanalytic theory. The initial task was to broaden the psychoanalytic perspective in order to take into account the influence of family structure on the development of personality, using Parsons's theory as a guide (Parsons, 1955). Second, there was an attempt to incorporate theories of language and cognitive development, in order to be able to account for the schizophrenic thought disorder. The revised theory was published in small volume (Lidz, 1963) and, most recently, in Lidz (1973).

The family was described in terms of the functions it fulfills for the parents, for their children, and for society. For the children there are three interrelated functions, each of which has important implications for personality development. First, there is the provision of *nurturance,* broadly defined to extend from the total care required by the newborn to the fostering of the adolescent's separation from the family. The quality of the nurturance will influence the child's sense of trust, sense of autonomy, and self-esteem as a male or female. Second, there is the provision of a sound family *structure.* This includes the ability of the spouses to form a parental coalition, to maintain the boundaries between the generations, and to adhere to their respective gender-linked roles. Lidz uses the traditional definition of these roles proposed by Parsons: instrumental leader for the husband-father and expressive-affectional leader for the wife-mother. These structural features are posited to be necessary for the resolution of the Oedipal phase, and for the development of a secure gender identity. These structural features are also necessary for the socialization of the children. For one thing, basic social roles (parents, children; boy, girl; man, woman; husband, wife; mother, father) are learned by a process of identification with role models. In addition, values and morality are inculcated by identification and superego formation, which occurs with the resolution of the Oedipal phase. Third, the family is required to transmit the *instrumental techniques* of the culture, particularly its language, with its systems of logic and meaning.

All the families of schizophrenics were deficient in all three functions, leading Lidz to conceive of schizophrenia as a "deficiency disease" (Lidz & Fleck, 1965). However, a more specific etiology can be formulated when one views the different characteristics of the families of male and female schizophrenic patients in the light of the differing developmental requirements for boys and girls as posited by psychoanalytic theory. In general, in these families, the patient has a poor relationship with the same-sex parent and is engulfed or seduced by the opposite-sex parent. The patient gets caught in either completing the opposite-sex parent's life or in saving the marriage. For the male patients, development is disturbed by a skewed pattern with a dominant mother who cannot establish boundaries (which is thought to be less critical for females, who need not break away from the early mother-child closeness as completely as males) and by a weak, ineffectual father who cannot enact the paternal (instrumental) role. The boy is unable to separate from the mother and identify with the father. Thus he is unable to resolve the Oedipal phase, with the result that incestuous wishes and castration fears are not repressed, a superego is not formed, and an identification with the male role is not made.

The female patient, with her aloof, uninvested, and amorphous mother, and her seductive father who undermines and derogates her mother, is damaged in her ability to identify with the female role. She is further damaged by her triangulation between the schismatic parents, whose marriage she tries to salvage. She is often torn between the two parents, for loyalty to one means betrayal to the other. The irreconcilable parents become irreconcilable introjects, seriously distorting her personality development.

For both males and females, then, the developmental process is disabled at an early age. For such children, the profound developmental tasks of adolescence are then insurmountable, with the result of a schizophrenic break. Lidz (1973) views the schizophrenic thought disorder in relationship to Piaget's theory (1963) of cognitive development and Vygotsky's theory (1962) of language acquisition. Within each stage of cognitive development there is a progression from a relatively egocentric position to one that is more "decentered." Lidz argues that the schizophrenic patient has in fact traversed the sensorimotor, preoperational, and concrete operational stages of cognitive development, as is evidenced by having developed language and the ability to think both concretely and abstractly. The schizophrenic gets stuck in an egocentric position during the adolescent cognitive stage of formal operations, as a result of being overwhelmed by the developmental challenges of this period of life. The resulting "cognitive egocentricity" is characterized by "egocentric overinclusiveness," in which one believes that extraneous events refer to oneself. Unable to decenter cognitively, the patient regresses to earlier forms of cognition characterized by omnipotence of thought (in which one's wishes are believed to become reality), or even by a failure to differentiate self from nonself. At this more profound regression, category formation breaks down, and the patient finds "a fantasied living space in the intercategorical realm with confusions of sexual identity, fusions with the mother, infantile dependency, (and) polymorphous perverse fantasies" (Lidz, 1973, p. 91).

Thus Lidz developed a conceptual formulation of the etiology of schizophrenia, based on an expanded version of psychosexual developmental theory designed both to take into account the influence of family structure and to give consideration to cognitive factors. The earlier work of Wynne resembles that of Lidz to some degree.

The earlier work of Wynne and associates.   Wynne's research began in 1954, when he was a member of the Family Studies Section of NIMH, and accelerated in 1957, when he took over as Head of the Section. This work rests upon a psychodynamic theoretical foundation. However, in contrast to Lidz, whose work has a more traditional psychosexual theoretical core, Wynne aligned himself with Erikson's epigenetic theory and with ego psychology, with its distinction of form from content and its emphasis on form. Although Wynne utilized structure-functional sociological theory (Parsons, 1955), he did so to a lesser extent than did Lidz. On the other hand, Wynne tended to focus more on the communication and interaction of family members. This emphasis is reflected in his conceptualization of the etiology of schizophrenia, which lies midway between the developmentally based formulation of Lidz and the impact and learning models utilized by the communicational group. In Wynne's model, schizophrenia is the result both of processes of internalization (or identification) and induction (that is, a complementary response to the impact of parental behavior).

Wynne's early formulations were concerned with the form of relatedness or role structure of the families of schizophrenics. Positing that people have twin needs for relatedness and for a sense of separateness or identity, he described three forms of role complementarity. *Nonmutual complementarity* is a role-limited form of relatedness, which is typified by commercial or official transactions. It is "functionally specific for a particular role rather than functionally diffuse for the relation" (Wynne et al., 1958, pp. 207-208). *Mutual complementarity* is, on the other hand, based on a broader context of relatedness than a particular role. As a consequence, specific divergences in complementarity not only do not threaten the existence of the relationship, but also, in fact serve as stimuli to the deepening of the relationship. Or, in Wynne's description:

> Each person brings to relations of genuine mutuality a sense of his own meaningful, positively-valued identity, and, out of experience or participation together, mutual recognition of identity develops, including a growing recognition of each other's potentialities and capacities." (Wynne et al., 1958, p. 207)

Finally, *pseudomutuality* involves a miscarriage of complementarity. In this situation, potential divergences in role complementarity are perceived as threatening to the entire relationship and hence are avoided. There is "a predominant absorption in fitting together, at the expense of the differentiation of the identities of the persons in the relation" (Wynne et al., 1958, p. 207).

Pseudomutuality occurs in many families. In families with a schizophrenic offspring, pseudomutuality takes a particularly intense form. The social organization of such families consists of a fixed constellation of engulfing roles. The roles may be either well defined and stereotyped, or vague and amorphous. The former type of role constellation was clinically observed to be associated with acute or reactive schizophrenia, and the latter with process schizophrenia (Ryckoff, Day, & Wynne, 1959). The role constellation will remain unchanged, although there may be considerable variation in the occupants of particular roles. For example, Wynne described a family in which one daughter was rebellious and the other daughter was conforming, "a model of 'goodness'," who " 'never needed correction'."

> In late adolescence the "wild" daughter became passive, quiet, and dutiful, and, in a sense, exchanged roles with her "good" sister who erupted with violently hostile rebellion in an acute schizophrenic episode. The family role structure as a whole remained essentially unchanged. (Wynne et al., 1958, p. 209)

In schizophrenic families it is fairly typical for the role constellation to become very rigid, to the point that it will not be changed even when role definitions clash with age or sex characteristics or obvious behavioral traits. Thus the pseudomutual role constellation becomes a myth that often conflicts with observed reality.

Pseudomutuality is very close to the concept of *sham* used by Henry to describe some of the processes he observed in families with a schizophrenic member.

> Alienation, in its most painful form, occurs in a social system such as the family, for example, when satisfaction is demanded but cannot be obtained; when, as in the family, unity is necessary but division is the reality, and when frankness is impossible. Alienation is a complex emotion, made up of feelings of estrangement, powerlessness and vulnerability: A person feels cheated that he is cheating; he feels contemptuous and belittled, and covers up his vast hostility with—sham. Sham is the outer face of alienation. (Henry, 1973, p. 105)

Pseudomutuality is a type of superficial "alignment" of family members that conceals the underlying divergences and "splits," on the one hand, and that on the other hand prevents the formation of deeper relationships and closer alignments based on recognition and appreciation of individual family members' actual identities.

Pseudohostility is a similar superficial phenomenon that serves to obscure the deeper actualities. In this case there is a split or alienation that can be quite intense, but that is confined to a relatively less important issue. It serves to conceal not only moves toward closeness, but also more serious splits that could sever the relationship (Wynne, 1961).

Both pseudomutuality and pseudohostility, then, are forms of relatedness in which what appears to exist differs from what actually exists. This distortion is necessitated by an experience that is perceived as threatening to the existence of the relationship. Thus pseudomutuality and pseudohostility serve functions on a family level analogous to those served by the intrapsychic ego-defense mechanisms (Singer & Wynne, 1965a). Like the ego-defense mechanisms, these forms of relatedness have mechanisms that prevent the exposure of the family myth.

Wynne coined the term *rubber fence* to describe certain shared family mechanisms used to maintain pseudomutuality. When family members get caught up in the desperate attempt to maintain the facade of togetherness, as happens in the schizophrenic family, the family's boundaries become obscured.

> The unstable but continuous boundary, with no recognizable opening, surrounding the schizophrenic family system, stretches to include that which can be interpreted as complementary and contracts to extrude that which is interpreted as non-complementary (Wynne et al., 1958, p. 211)

This elastic boundary or rubber fence serves to prevent the recognition and acknowledgement of any "splits" or conflicts within the family that might threaten the family's sense of mutuality.

Wynne was concerned with the way in which these features of the family role constellation influenced development, and he described several ways in which psychosocial development might be affected. First, the role constellation as a whole may be internalized as an organized pattern of the meanings that relationships and events have acquired. This internalization includes the identification with parents posited by psychoanalytic theory, but goes beyond it to include the family's ways of thinking and deriving meaning.

> The fragmentation of experience, the identity diffusion, the disturbed modes of perception and communication, and certain other characteristics of the acute reactive schizophrenic's personality structure are to a significant extent derived, by processes of internalization, from characteristics of the family social organization. (Wynne et al., 1958, p. 215)

Second, Wynne suggested that certain symptoms that differ from dominant family patterns may be the result not of internalization and identification with parental models but, rather, of the elicitation or induction of role behavior complementary to that of the parents (Singer & Wynne, 1965b). A third factor that may interfere with the developmental process involves the inhibition of role learning. In pseudo-mutual families the particular role assigned to the child, whether it is vaguely or stereotypically defined, is all-encompassing. This prevents the experimentation and learning of multiple roles, which is a prerequisite to the adolescent transition from identification (with a single role) to identity (which transcends roles) (Ryckoff, et al., 1959).

Relationship between Lidz's and Wynne's formulations. On first examination, Wynne's concepts of pseudomutuality and pseudohostility appear to have some similarity to Lidz's concept of marital skew and schism. While pseudomutuality and pseudohostility refer to the overall role constellation of the family, and skew and schism refer to the marital role complementarity in particular, there does appear to be some similarity between the pseudomutual family and the skewed marriage on the one hand, and the pseudohostile family and the schismatic marriage on the other. Although one might go further and perhaps integrate these conceptual formulations, it is important to note that there were important differences in the original conceptualizations of these concepts. Whereas Lidz thought of the schismatic and skewed marriages as representative of two different types of family systems, each having different developmental implications with respect to the gender of the offspring, Wynne thought of both pseudomutuality and pseudohostility as opposite sides of the same coin, both occuring within the same family. Both are familial defensive maneuvers that occur in response to potential splits or alignments which take place within the family (Wynne, 1961).

More broadly, although both groups described similar features of the schizophrenic family's social organization and discussed the relationship between these features and development, their conceptualizations had subtle but important differences: Lidz was concerned with the manner in which the particular features of the age-sex structure interfered with normal psychosexual development, whereas Wynne was concerned with the ways in which formal features of the family role constellation influenced psychosocial development.

Despite these differences, however, Wynne's early work was moving along a path parallel to that of Lidz. His later work, communication deviance research (which will be discussed momentarily), departed more fundamentally in two respects: Substantively, it represented a shift from a psychodynamic to a communicational frame of reference; and methodologically, it represented a shift from clinical research and theory construction to empirical research.

Communication deviance research. After several years of developing these concepts of relatedness, Wynne and Singer launched a program of empirical research that began with the examination of the relationship between family interaction and communication and the schizophrenic thought disorder. Their move in this direction was parallel to Lidz's interest at the time in integrating cognitive and language development into his theory in order to better account for the schizophrenic thought disorder. In fact, some collaboration between these two groups took place during this period (Wild, Singer, Rosman, Ricci, & Lidz, 1965). As time progressed, however, the divergence between the two groups increased; Wynne's research grew closer to that of the communicational group.

In an ingenious series of studies, Wynne and colleagues compared the communication styles and other aspects of the interaction among family members of schizophrenic, borderline, and neurotic hospitalized young adults. They used a predictive research strategy, in which samples of the communication behavior of family members were evaluated without any knowledge of the hospitalized offspring in order, first of all, to deduce or "predict" certain attributes of the hospitalized offspring (diagnosis, severity of disorder, form of thinking), and secondly, to match the protocols of the family members with those of the hospitalized offspring.

The form of thinking of the hospitalized offspring was conceptualized in terms of Werner's developmental principles (1957), in which differentiation of substructures from an amorphous whole is followed by the hierarchic integration of these parts. The form of thinking of the offspring was then classified along a continuum. At the low end, "amorphous" schizophrenics evidenced an undifferentiated global form of thinking. This group includes patients who had a poor adjustment prior to the onset of symptoms ("process" schizophrenics), as well as childhood schizophrenics. At the middle of the continuum, "fragmented" schizophrenics showed failures in hierarchic integration, particularly the overinclusiveness described by Lidz. This group includes the acute or "reactive" schizophrenics. At the high end are patients whose thinking is "constricted," that is, overfocused, overorganized, and underinclusive. This form of thinking is characteristic of paranoid and obsessional patients.

The communication behavior of family members that was sampled included transcripts of family interviews (Morris & Wynne, 1965), as well as psychological tests used as samples of interactional behavior of the individual family members. The psychological tests used included the Object Sorting Test (Wild et al., 1965), the Proverbs Test (Singer, Wynne, Levi, & Sojit, 1968), and the Rorschach (Wynne & Singer, 1963a, 1963b).

The protocols were evaluated along four dimensions that were considered particularly relevant to schizophrenia: (1) styles of communication, particularly the patterns of handling attention and meaning; (2) styles of relating, particularly patterns of erratic and inappropriate distance and closeness; (3) affective disorder, particularly feelings of pervasive meaninglessness; and (4) forms of relatedness, particularly the presence of pseudomutuality and pseudohostility. Of these dimensions, the styles of communication were found to be of the greatest predictive value, particularly the manner in which family members indicated that they were focusing their attention on the task at hand. A coding system was developed to evaluate the testing protocols for the quality of their attentional focus, rated along a continuum closely related to the classification of forms of thinking as amorphous, fragmented, or constricted (Singer & Wynne, 1965a; Morris & Wynne, 1965). The coding system was refined (Singer & Wynne, 1966), and the interrater reliability was established (Singer, 1967; Wynne, 1967). A review of the reliability and validity data on this coding system concluded that "although the manual will continue to be revised and refined, one is highly encouraged by the findings thus far reported" (Lerner, 1975).

In these studies, the psychological tests were administered to family members individually. In order to assess the way in which family members "fit" together, the communication style of the less disturbed parent was evaluated as to whether the effect of this parent would aggravate or counteract the pathogenic influence of the more disturbed parent (Singer & Wynne, 1965b). The next step in this research was to study the collective impact of family members directly, using a consensus Rorschach procedure (Wynne, 1968; Singer, 1968; Loveland, 1967). Later, other conjoint family procedures were utilized (Wynne, 1970), including a variety of problem-solving tasks in which information sharing is important (Reiss & Sheriff, 1970). Some of this latter research demonstrated the transactional or systemic attributes of the schizophrenic family. For example, Reiss (1971a) found that schizophrenic families are "consensus sensitive," a phenomenon similar to pseudomutuality. One of the more striking demonstrations of the debilitating effects of consensus sensitivity was the finding that the schizophrenic family does poorly on a collective problem-solving task despite that fact that each individual member does far better when working alone (Reiss, 1971b, 1971c).

At the psychodynamic end of the continuum, then, the work of Lidz and his associates led to formulation of the etiology of schizophrenia. Specifically, Lidz's theory articulated the ways in which problems in the age-sex structure of the family might interfere with psychosexual development so as to result in schizophrenia. Lidz identified two family patterns, one of which (skew) was particularly pathogenic for boys, and the other (schism) for girls. The early work of Wynne, on the other hand, at first attempted to describe the formal features of the family role constellation, using such concepts as "pseudomutuality," "pseudohostility," and the "rubber fence," and then sought to relate these role features to the disruption of normal psychosocial development. Finally, in his later empirical work, communication-deviance research, Wynne moved from a psychodynamic to a communicational frame of reference.

Communicational Conceptual Formulations

The work of Bateson and associates.   The Bateson group took a unique perspective in their use of communication theory. They considered all social behavior to be communicative. This is based on the idea that "one cannot *not* communicate" (Watzlawick et al., 1967, p. 49). Thus, their communication theory is a theory of human behavior.

The Bateson group used as their point of departure Russell's theory of logical types (Whitehead & Russell, 1910). The central premise of this theory is that a member of a class exists at a lower level of abstraction (logical type) than the class itself; thus a member of a class can never be the class, nor can a class be a member of itself. Applied to communication, the theory of logical types points to the existence of different levels of communication, such as the report (content, message) versus command (context, relationship) levels of communication, as well as the phenomenon of metacommunication (described in Chapter 1). The interest of the Bateson group was with the way in which messages at different levels of abstraction may conflict with one another to produce incongruent communication, or Russellian paradoxes.

Haley (1976a) noted that Russellian paradox is often confused with simple contradiction. In contrast to paradox, contradictory messages conflict at the *same level* of abstraction. In contradiction, one can choose one of the two conflicting messages (even though it may be a situation of the lesser of two evils), whereas in paradox one cannot choose one of the messages without also choosing the other. For example:

> If I say to someone, "I will be angry if you obey me and I will be angry if you disobey me," he can choose one or the other. However, if I say to someone, "I want you to disobey me," he has no alternative choices nor is he faced with a contradiction. He cannot choose the least bad of the two possibilities. His bind is this: If he obeys, he is disobeying, and if he disobeys, he is obeying. (Haley, 1976a, p. 71)

Bateson was primarily concerned with fundamental and general problems of communication (human and animal), and with the theory of logical types as the basis for a general theory of communication. His interest in schizophrenia was as a special case that illustrated fundamental issues in communication. The attention the double bind hypothesis received as a theory of schizophrenia was regarded by Bateson and his associates as a distraction from the more general problems with which they were concerned, and they attempted to address this issue in subsequent publications. Watzlawick, in a review of the impact of the double bind hypothesis on the psychiatric literature, pointed out that "very few of the references to the double bind theory deal with what its originators consider to be the essential concept, i.e., the *theory of logical types*" (1963, p. 134). In a closing note to the Bateson project, Bateson, Jackson, Haley, and Weakland (1963) pointed out that they had investigated a wide range of communicational phenomena in addition to schizophrenia ("the nature of metaphor, humor, popular films, ventriloquism, training of guide dogs for the blind, the nature of play, animal behavior, the formal nature of psychotherapy"–p. 154). Their work, therefore, constituted a general approach to communication, "including schizophrenia as one major case. The present and future status of the more specific double bind concept can appropriately be considered only within this, its more general and inclusive framework" (p. 155).

Consistent with these descriptions of the project, the double bind hypothesis was developed by a process of deduction. Haley was the first to recognize that the symptoms of schizophrenia indicated an inability to discriminate logical types or levels of communication. Bateson then deduced the double bind hypothesis to explain the symptoms and etiology of schizophrenia, as "a conjecture about what must have happened, granted the premises of the theoretical approach and the observations of the schizophrenic individual's way of communicating" (Bateson et al., 1963, p. 154).

The double bind hypothesis specifies six ingredients (Bateson et al., 1956). First there must be two or more persons, one of whom is designated as victim.

These individuals must be involved in an *intense relationship,* in which it is crucial that communication be clear. Second, the double bind experience must be *repeated* over a long time period, to form a learning context for the victim. Third, there must be a primary negative injunction, such as "Do not do that or I will punish you" or "If you do not do that I will punish you." Fourth, there must be a secondary negative injunction, also reinforced by threats of punishment or signals that threaten survival. The secondary injunction conflicts with the first at a different level, thus forming a Russellian *paradox.* Fifth, there must be a tertiary negative injunction that forbids the victim from leaving the field. This *no-escape* condition includes prohibitions against gaining the support of another person or commenting on the paradox (metacommunicating). Sixth, after a time the victim learns to expect the double bind experience from important relationships. At this point, the complete sequence is unnecessary to make the victim feel double bound. Almost any part of the double bind experience will be taken for the whole.

The work of Laing and associates. Similar to the Bateson group, Laing and his associates were not primarily concerned with conceptualizing the family contribution to the etiology of schizophrenia. Their concern, however, was not with general principles of communication, but rather with providing a challenge to the illness model of psychiatry. Laing and some of his associates, of course, were to become prominent in the antipsychiatry movement.

Laing studied 11 families of female schizophrenics over a three-year period, utilizing in-home observations as well as office interviews. The objective was to illustrate the social "intelligibility" of the schizophrenic's symptoms in the context of the family. The method was social phenomenology, in which he sought to illuminate each person's perspective within the family "nexus." The family nexus consists of the members of the family and other close associates in which the relationships "are characterized by enduring and intensive face-to-face reciprocal influence on each other's experience and behavior" (Laing & Esterson, 1970, p. 21). Laing made use of Sartre's concepts of "praxis" and "process." Praxis is the result of action taken by a person, whereas process is an impersonal series of events of which, presumably, no one is the initiator. "Intelligibility," another Sartrean concept, results when one can "retrace the steps from what is going on (process) to who is doing what (praxis)" (Laing & Esterson, 1970, p. 22).

Laing formulated the concept of mystification to make intelligible the behavior and experience of the person labeled schizophrenic (Laing, 1965). Mystification is a "transpersonal defense." If someone wishes to not be reminded of something disturbing, it is not enough, Laing postulates, to utilize the intrapsychic defenses such as repression and denial. One must also insure that close associates do not bring up the painful subject. This latter action is the transpersonal defense. In Laing's presentation, "the one person (p) seeks to induce in *the other* some change necessary for his (p's) security. Mystification is one form of action on the other that serves the defenses, the security, of the own person" (Laing, 1965, p. 349).

Mystification as an action induces confusion or doubt, often unrecognized as such, about what is being done or what is going on. Often what is at issue involves conflict. Mystification, then, can either conceal the existence of conflict, or substitute false issues for authentic ones.

Laing (1965) describes several ways in which mystification may occur. First, one may confirm the content of the other's experience, but disconfirm the modality (that is, actual perception versus imagination or dreams) by which the other had the experience. For example, if two persons disagree about a shared experience, one may say to the other "you must have dreamt it." Second, one may disconfirm the content of the other's experience, substituting attributions of experience consistent with one's view of the other. Laing gives the example of a mother who is tired, and instead of saying, "I'm tired and I'd like you to go to bed now," says, "I'm sure you're tired by now and would like to go to bed." The third method is to convert praxis into process. For example, an adolescent expresses anger at his mother. Mother's reply: "You don't really mean that. You're just saying those things because of the medication they are giving you."

Searles developed a similar formulation, with, however, an emphasis on the intrapsychic impact of such maneuvers. He described six modes of "driving the other person crazy," which in general involve "the initiating of any kind of interpersonal interaction which tends to foster emotional conflict in the other person—which tends to activate various areas of his personality in opposition to one another" (Searles, 1959, p. 2). Some of these modes, or interpersonal maneuvers are: calling attention to areas in the other's personality that the other is dimly aware of and that are at variance with the other's self-concept; stimulating the other sexually in a situation where it would be disastrous to seek sexual gratification; relating to the other at two or more unrelated levels simultaneously. Laing (1961) has argued that the pathogenic potential of these maneuvers lies not in their stimulation of intrapsychic conflict, but rather in their mystifying effect—the induction of confusion or "muddle" in the other, which is not even recognized.

Relationship between the double bind and mystification. At this point, it makes sense to examine the relationship between the double bind and mystification concepts. Before doing so, it is important to point out that these concepts arise from very different theoretical matrices—communication theory and the theory of logical types on the one hand, and existentialism and phenomenology on the other. In the discussion here, these concepts will be dealt with as "intermediary descriptive concepts" (Sluzki & Ransom, 1976), and will be viewed somewhat apart from the theoretical matrices in which they are embedded.

Mystification constitutes part of the double bind. Laing has noted that "the double bind would appear to be necessarily mystifying, but mystification need not be a complete double bind" (1965, p. 353). Specifically, mystification constitutes the third and fourth ingredients of the double bind, namely the Russellian paradox. The two conflicting messages in mystification are, at one level, the message from within (that is, the victim's actual experience, such as the memory of an event), and at the other level, the message from the other (that is, what the victim is told that he or she experiences, as in the comment "you dreamt it"). Sluzki and colleagues have coined the term "transactional disqualification" to label this process (Sluzki, Beavin, Tarnopolsky, & Verón, 1967).

Laing (1965) also described the existence of an extreme form of mystification, which, though not a complete double bind, places the victim in an "untenable position" from which it is impossible to extricate oneself. This situation constitutes the third, fourth, and fifth components of the double bind—that is, the Russellian paradox plus the no-escape condition. Together, these components constitute a "paradoxical injunction"—that is, a paradox (in which, for example, in order to obey the message one must disobey it) from which one cannot extricate oneself (for example by stepping outside of the frame of reference and clearing up the paradox by commenting on it) (Watzlawick et al., 1967).

The complete double bind, then, consists of repeated paradoxical injunctions taking place over a *long time period* in an intense relationship (usually of survival value), to the point that the victim has learned to perceive the world in terms of the double bind. The double bind is thus not an isolable event, traumatic in its effect, but rather a long-term, perhaps lifelong, learning context. This point is particularly important to note, because it was misunderstood by some of the earlier researchers who attempted to count the frequency of double binds (Haley, 1976a).

Wynne's model is also similar to the double bind. Although Wynne was concerned with role relationships and Bateson with communication, Bateson's "communication" (as emphasized in the preceeding paragraph) was not the isolated communicative act, but rather the long-term pattern of communication, a notion closely related to the pattern of role relationships. Wynne (1976) pointed out that his formulations were analogous to the double bind concept. The discrepancies between the level of observable family relationships (that is, lack of fit with a particular role, the lack of genuine closeness, or the existence of genuine conflict) and the mythic family relations (pseudomutuality and pseudohostility) are analogous to differences between primary injunctions and the more abstract secondary injunctions. The rubber fence constitutes the tertiary, no-escape injunction.

Etiology.   At this juncture it would be appropriate to examine how the issue of etiology is addressed in the conceptual formulations of Laing and Bateson. Laing, in his challenge to the illness model, specifically eschews any concern with etiology (Laing & Esterson, 1970, p. 12). The Bateson group postulate that schizophrenia results from being brought up in a learning context in which the victim is forced to respond to repeated exposures to paradoxical injunction. This leads to the breakdown of the ability to discriminate logical types. As a result, one would not be able to determine whether a question such as "where were you this morning? I was looking for you" was an accusation or an opportunity. Given an inability to determine the nature of messages, one might adapt one of several defensive positions: to assume that behind every message there are hidden meanings that are detrimental to one's own welfare (paranoia); to treat all messages as inconsequential and laugh them off (hebephrenia); or to try to ignore all messages, which would necessitate withdrawing from social interaction (catatonia) (Bateson et al., 1956).

It would appear that the Bateson group favors an etiological model based somewhat loosely on learning theory. The schizophrenic symptoms are learned while participating repeatedly in experiences of a certain type. This participation shapes the individual's responses, which become automatic habits over time. The individual is thus socialized into a schizophrenic mode of existence. However, as Sluzki and Ransom (1976) point out, the Bateson group did not provide a well-developed statement of etiology, leaving a certain amount of ambiguity with regard to this issue. For example, the above formulation would account for developmental psychoses and process schizophrenia, but not acute schizophrenia in which a person functions "normally" before the psychotic break.

A related issue is the dyadic and linear causal model inherent in both the mystification and double bind concepts. Both concepts include the notion of one person (usually the mother) acting upon the victim (the schizophrenic child). This is reminiscent of Fromm-Reichmann's (1948) concept of schizophrenogenic mother, although the communicational concepts deal with interpersonal interaction rather than the personality traits of the mother. Weakland (1960) sought to address this problem. Building upon the cybernetic notion of "family homeostasis" formulated by Jackson (1957), Weakland transformed the one-way "binder-victim" causal model to a circular one, in which the response of the "victim" (who might also give incongruent messages or might respond to all messages as if they were paradoxical) contributes to the maintenance of the overall pattern of family interaction. He also attempted to expand the dyadic frame of reference to a triadic one, in which two parents each give parts of the paradoxical message to the child. However, this is not a completely adequate reformulation, in that the roles of both parents are essentially interchangeable and thus collapsible within one role, reducing the model to a dyadic one. As Sluzki and Ransom (1976) point out, it may not be possible to extend the double bind concept beyond a dyadic framework without losing some of its formal precision. This is because the double bind concept is concerned with the form of messages transmitted within communication theory's essentially dyadic (sender-receiver) frame of reference. To get into a triadic, systemic frame of reference, one must leave behind the concern with the form of message inherent in the double bind concept and deal, instead, with the broader communicational (or interactional) sequences and patterns, such as Jackson and Weakland (1961) accomplished in their later modification and blending of the double bind and family homeostasis concepts.

Wider application of the double bind concept. In more recent years the double bind hypothesis has been applied to a wider range of phenomena. On the one hand, the double bind hypothesis has been studied in relation to forms of pathology other than schizophrenia. Ferreira (1960) applied the concept to the family etiology of delinquent behavior. More recently, Sluzki and Verón (1971) applied the model to neurosis (hysteria, phobia, and obsessive-compulsive neurosis). They put forward the thesis that the double bind is a "universal pathogenic situation."

On the other hand, some researchers have asked the question of whether the double bind is necessarily pathogenic. Bateson, Wynne, and Kafka raised this question in their respective contributions to the Symposium on the Double Bind, held as part of the 1969 annual meeting of the American Psychological Association. Kafka (1971), in a revised version of his presentation, suggested that there is need for ambiguity and paradox as a stimulus for development. He proposed a reformulation of the double bind hypothesis, in which rather than an overabundance of paradox as the source of disordered development, there is an underexposure, due to parental fears of ambiguity. Wynne (1976), in a later, published version of his comments, pointed out that double binds are an inevitable aspect of existence. If the anxiety and stress can be withstood, creativity and profound growth is often the result. Bateson (1972b), in his contribution to the symposium, described some of his research findings with dolphins and came up with similar conclusions:

> First, that severe pain and maladjustment can be induced by putting a mammal in the wrong regarding its rules for making sense of an important relationship with another mammal.
> And second, that if this pathology can be warded off or resisted, the total experience may promote creativity (Bateson, 1972b, p. 278).

Thus by the late 1960s and early 1970s, there was a subsiding of some of the concerns of the Bateson group regarding the overspecificity with which the double bind concept was apprehended by the mental health community. The double bind concept—ironically, by a process of induction—was (re)gaining the stature of a more general formulation of the rules governing communication.

The work of Bateson and his associates, including their specific formulation of the double bind concept, took place within a general communicational theoretical context. For Laing and his associates, and for their construct of mystification, the frame of reference was existential and phenomenological. When the relationship between the two constructs is considered, it can be observed that mystification constitutes a part of the double bind—the Russellian paradox. Similarly, when etiology is considered, it can be noted that a dyadic and linear causal model is inherent in both formulations. Later efforts to extricate the double bind hypothesis from these underpinnings were more successful in making the transition from a linear, causal model to a circular model than they were in breaking out of a dyadic frame of reference—a task that, it has been proposed, may be impossible to accomplish fully. Over the years, however, the concept of the double bind has been applied to a wider range of phenomena, and its significance has been reexamined.

An Integration
of Structural and Multigenerational
Conceptual Formulations

As do the models just discussed, the conceptual formulations of Bowen and Minuchin emphasize the form rather than the content of experience. But these models expand the focus from a concern with communication to a concern with the organizational features of the family. As was discussed above, communication, no matter how broadly conceived, is fundamentally confined to a dyadic frame of reference. The combined structural-multigenerational perspective allows the expansion to triadic (and larger) frames of reference.

The structural and multigenerational models were influenced not only by the expansion of family research from a focus on schizophrenia to the consideration of other forms of pathology, but also by the resultant findings that similar processes occurred in a wide range of family types. As a consequence, these two models are more general expressions of the relationship between the family and individual psychopathology.

The two models to be discussed have already been presented at some length in Chapter 1, particularly in regard to their conceptualizations of the family as a functional social entity. In this section, the presentation of these models will be somewhat abbreviated, focusing on their conceptualizations of family dysfunction, with an eye to integrating the two models. Furthermore, in view of their status as the later and more general formulations, the aim will be to develop an integration of these two models that can also incorporate the earlier models.

Before attempting this integration, it is important to deal with one characteristic about which the two schools differ diametrically—their position in regard to the issue of development versus maintenance of psychopathology. Bowen's theory is historical—indeed, multigenerational. It is fundamentally important in his approach to take a history of the extended family over several generations in order to elicit the transmission of family patterns and to illuminate the basis for present family structure. Minuchin, in contrast, eschews historical data for the most part, using family interaction in the present as the data from which he derives his map of family structure. Both arrive at a picture or map of present family organization. The different routes taken to reach this point reflect the different views of family change held by the two theoretician-clinicians. This is a topic which will be discussed more fully in Part II. But it is relevant to say at this point that Minuchin is concerned with modifying present family structure through direct interventions that have the principal aim of eliminating those dysfunctional structural elements that sustain or maintain the psychopathology of one or more members of the family. Bowen, in contrast, is concerned with "coaching" individual family members to free themselves from the entanglements of present family organization through their own personal maturation and their efforts to establish mature person-to-person relationships with other family members. Minuchin attempts to change the structure in order that individual family members might experience growth. Bowen attempts to help individual family members grow in order that they might free themselves from (and realign the dysfunctional elements of) their families.

In developing an integrated summary of the conceptual formulations of family dysfunction, Bowen's theory can be taken as a starting point.

Bowen (1976) described individual psychopathology in general terms, using the concept "differentiation of self." He described how relatively undifferentiated spouses tended to "fuse" with each other and how, thereby, a "we-ness" is formed from the "pseudo-selfs" of the spouses. This has two implications. First, since the spouses have formed a partnership based on pseudo-self rather than solid self, their communication is likely to be incongruent. They will not take clear "I" positions but, rather, will send confusing, contradictory, mystifying, and even paradoxical messages. Satir's player parts of blamer, placater, computer, and distracter come to mind as ready examples of the communicational stances that such marital partners might adapt. Second, since the partnership is based on pseudo-self, the marital pair will not have formed a genuine mutual complementarity. Their marital complementarity will be one of pseudomutuality.

Bowen went on to point out that marital partners with a high degree of fusion (with its attendant distorted communication and pseudomutual complementary) experience a great deal of anxiety. They are particularly concerned about togetherness, yet the signals that are sent are never quite reassuring. Bowen describes three general ways in which the anxiety is dispelled or bound. The first of these is marital discord, with repetitive cycles of closeness—conflict—distance—closeness. In this pattern, the fusion is handled within the marital relationship. In the second pattern, the fusion is also contained within the marital relationship, but it results in the dysfunction of one spouse. In these marriages, the dominant-adaptive complementarity becomes rigidified and chronic to the point that one partner becomes overresponsible and the other becomes helpless (the overadequate-inadequate reciprocity). In the third pattern, there is a failure to form a parental coalition. The fusion symptoms extend beyond the generational boundaries of the marital relationship, resulting in the triangulation and impairment of one or more of the children.

Minuchin (1974) specified several forms of triangulation. In his theory, he describes triangulation in terms of chronic boundary problems. In chronic boundary problems, the tensions of the parental subsystem are habitually deflected to another subsystem, usually one of the children. As a result of this long-term process, the boundaries around the parental subsystem become diffuse, and the boundary around the parent-child triad (which ordinarily should be diffuse) becomes rigid. This general picture of triangulation, which Minuchin terms the "rigid triad," is mapped below, in Figure 2-1.

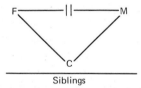

FIGURE 2-1   The rigid triad. (From Minuchin, 1974.)

Minuchin describes three types of "rigid triads." The first pattern is termed "detouring." In this pattern, tension between the marital partners is reduced to a manageable level through focusing their attention on the child. Detouring includes (1) scapegoating, as defined by Ackerman (1967) and Vogel and Bell (1968), in which the child-victim is attacked as the source of family problems because of bad behavior; and (2) overprotection, in which the parents define the child as sick or weak, and then unite to protect him or her. In both cases the child's deviance will be covertly reinforced in order to diffuse the parents' anxiety, which originates in their relationship to each other. Detouring is mapped in Figure 2-2.

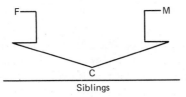

FIGURE 2-2

Minuchin employs the term "triangulation" (used by Bowen and others to describe the general class of these patterns) for the second of these patterns. In this situation the child is caught in a bind in which loyalty to one parent means rejection by the other. Because of the parents' opposing needs and injunctions, such a child cannot satisfy and feel accepted by one parent without arousing dissatisfaction or hostility in the other. The result is a tug-of-war, in which the parents compete to form coalitions with the child in the struggle against each other. This pattern, which will be termed "unstable coalitions" for the sake of clarity, is mapped in Fig. 2-3.

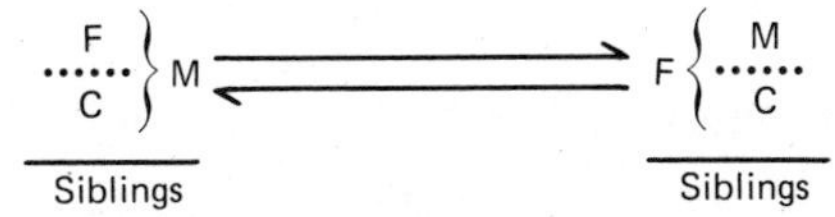

FIGURE 2-3

Note that this pattern of unstable coalitions does not necessarily involve overt conflict and discord between the parents. Their disagreements and tensions can be handled entirely through their relationships to the child. In some circumstances, however, (such as when there is a marked degree of fusion), more than one mechanism is needed to handle the tension. When the unstable coalition form of triangulation is coupled with overt marital discord, the family pattern is that of Lidz's schismatic families. Lidz's theory specified that the gender of the child is an important determinant of whether particular family structural configurations would be schizogenic. In the case of the schismatic family, the female child is thought to be more vulnerable for the development of schizophrenia. Thus, the schismatic pattern as mapped in Figure 2-4 specifies the involvement of a female child, and the greater salience of the coalition of father with daughter versus mother.

FIGURE 2-4

The third pattern is the "stable coalition," in which one of the parents joins with a child in a cross-generational coalition against the other parent. The stable coalition is mapped in Figure 2-5.

FIGURE 2-5

When a stable coalition is combined with a marital relationship marked by overadequate-inadequate reciprocity (with dysfunction in one spouse), the family pattern is that of Lidz's skewed families. In the skewed families, the male offspring is more vulnerable for the development of schizophrenia, and mother is usually the dominant figure. The skewed pattern is mapped in Figure 2-6, to portray a dysfunctional father and an enmeshed mother-son dyad.

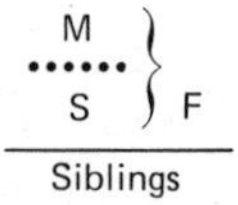

M
...... }
S   } F
———————
Siblings

FIGURE 2-6

By focusing on the organizational features of the family, then, it is possible to produce a taxonomy of the patterns of family dysfunction. These patterns can occur singly or in conjunction with others, as displayed in Table 2-1. The patterns displayed are those that have appeared in the literature so far. Other configurations, however, are also possible (such as the combination of dysfunction in one spouse with detouring).

TABLE 2-1 Patterns of Family Dysfunction

DYSFUNCTIONAL PATTERNS	COMBINATIONS OF DYSFUNCTIONAL PATTERNS
Marital discord	Schism (marital discord and unstable coalition)
Dysfunction in one spouse	Skew (dysfunction in one spouse and stable coalition)
Triangulation of child:	
Detouring	
Unstable coalition	
Stable coalition	

EMPIRICAL INVESTIGATIONS
OF THE FAMILY CONTRIBUTION
TO PSYCHOPATHOLOGY

The clinical formulations that have just been discussed gave rise to an intense period of investigation of family interaction. This research activity began in the late 1950s and reached a peak during the years 1965–71 (Jacob, 1975). By 1975, however, interest in this area had fallen off considerably in favor of what is termed "high-risk" research (Goldstein & Rodnick, 1975). In high-risk research, families of individuals thought to be at risk for certain disorders are studied longitudinally. (For a review of high-risk research see Garmezy, 1974a, 1974b).

Research into family interaction in general took the form of measuring several dimensions of family interactional behavior and comparing certain types of families along these dimensions. Stimulated by the clinical hypotheses of Bateson, Lidz, Wynne, and others, the aim was to determine whether the interaction patterns differed in families with and without a disturbed member, or if differences existed among families who had members with different types of disturbance (for example, schizophrenia versus delinquency; or process schizophrenia versus reactive schizophrenia).

Family interaction research has been reviewed on numerous occasions (Meissner, 1964; Frank, 1965; Framo, 1965a; Haley, 1972; Riskin & Faunce, 1972; Jacob, 1975; Goldstein & Rodnick, 1975; Doane, 1978a). Riskin and Faunce's review (1972) provides an excellent coverage of the methodological issues. They discuss some 21 issues regarding both the weaknesses of many of the studies (within-study issues) as well as the difficulties in comparing the results of different studies (between-study issues). They also provide an extensive bibiliography and a glossary of family interaction research terms.

Regarding substantive findings, Jacob's (1975) review is the most thorough, recent criticisms notwithstanding (Doane, 1978a; see also Jacob & Grounds, 1978; Doane, 1978b). Jacob reviewed 57 direct-observation studies that appeared between 1960 and June 1973. He first evaluated the studies in relation to six criteria of methodological adequacy. These include: (1) The experimental and control families should be comparable on certain background variables that might be related to family interaction (such as age of child, sex of child, birth order of child, family size and parents' ages, social class, religion, and ethnic group). (2) When family-interaction data are rated by judges, the judges should not be aware of whether the family is in the experimental group or the control group. (3) The judges should agree to a high degree on the presence and frequency of the behavior to be rated. (4) Separate analyses should be performed on data including male children and data including female children, since sex of child is known to influence a family's interaction patterns (Fleck, Lidz, & Cornelison, 1963; Mishler & Waxler, 1968). (5) Experimental and control families should be observed in the same setting and with the same set or expectancy. (6) Experimental and control families should be matched on hospital and treatment status to whatever extent possible.

Jacob found that in those studies comparing nonschizophrenic disturbed families with normal families, five of these six criteria were met. The criterion that few (21 percent) of these studies met was the separate analysis of data as a function of sex of child. The studies comparing schizophrenic disturbed families to normal families, however, met only one of the six criteria—the assessment of experimental and control families in the same setting. This finding is mitigated somewhat by the fact that the more recent studies were more adequate in their design.

Jacob grouped the substantive findings into four major dimensions of family interaction: conflict, dominance, affect, and communication clarity. These dimensions are thought to be related to the etiological hypotheses of the clinical investigators of the 1950s. Jacob analyzed the studies separately for the nonschizophrenic disturbed family group and the schizophrenic family groups. Two of these dimensions tended to differentiate nonschizophrenic disturbed families from normal families: dominance and affect. With regard to dominance, two tentative conclusions were drawn: (1) The power structures of normal families were more often differentiated along hierarchial lines in comparison to disturbed families; and (2) fathers are more influential in normal than disturbed families. With regard to affect, the normal families had more positive affect and less negative affect than did the disturbed families. Jacob emphasized the need to hold these conclusions tentatively, because several important contradictory findings emerged in regard to dominance. Moreover, in regard to affect, 15 of the 29 total comparisons did *not* differentiate the family groups. Even if Jacob's conclusions had emerged more unequivocally, their etiological meaning would be unclear (except in a very general sense), because they are founded on heterogenous samples of "nonschizophrenic disturbed" families, which includes a range of disturbed conditions.

With regard to schizophrenic families, only one dimension tended to differentiate them from normal families—the dimension of communication clarity. Jacob concluded that the data suggest that schizophrenic families communicate with less accuracy and clarity than do normal families. However, Jacob based his conclusion on only one study (Mishler & Waxler, 1968). He did not include the communication deviance research of Wynne and associates in his review because it did not meet his criteria of a family observational study. (In communication deviance research, data are generated in the interaction between a single family member and an examiner. The resultant communicational styles of family members are then compared and matched.) Goldstein and Rodnick (1975) did take this work into account, however, in their review of the family's contribution to the etiology of schizophrenia. They drew a somewhat stronger conclusion—namely, that (with reference to the communicational hypotheses of Bateson and others) the empirical data support the general position that schizophrenic families are characterized by disturbed communication, but that the data do not prove the specific hypotheses (for example, the double bind). This position is consonant with that of reviewers who have examined research—including studies reviewed neither by Jacob (1975) nor by Goldstein and Rodnick (1975)—specifically designed to test the double bind hypothesis (Olson, 1972; Abeles, 1976). As an aside, it should be noted that Bateson himself (1972b) did not think that the double bind hypothesis was testable with experimental methods.

Family interaction research at this point, then, has yielded only a few reliable differences between disturbed and normal families. To summarize the reliable differences: (1) Nonschizophrenic disturbed families differ from normal families in having a power structure that is less hierarchically differentiated, and in having less influential fathers, less positive affect, and more negative affect. (2) Schizophrenic disturbed families differ from normal families in having less accuracy and clarity in their communication styles.

Jacob (1975) concluded his review with a consideration of four factors that make it impossible at this time to reconcile the conflicting findings in order to make more sense out of the substantial body of family interaction research. First, there is the problem of the diagnostic status of the family groups. Many of the studies used heterogenous groups for both their schizophrenic and nonschizophrenic disturbed samples. Since these samples varied from study to study in unknown ways, the comparison and reconciliation of their findings is extremely hazardous, if not impossible. In addition to the difficulties in reconciling conflicting findings based on heterogenous samples, problems also arise in interpreting the consistent findings that do emerge. This issue has already been mentioned in regard to the findings on the nonschizophrenic disturbed family groups. In regard to the schizophrenic family groups, the lumping together of different types of schizophrenia (paranoid versus nonparanoid; process versus reactive) may result in obscuring differences between the subgroups. Goldstein and Rodnick (1975) suggested that when the data are analyzed separately for good versus poor premorbid schizophrenics, differences do emerge on several dimensions of family structure.

The second factor has to do with the unit of analysis (whether the findings are described at the individual, dyadic, or family-group level). This is a factor that, again, varied from study to study, thus limiting the meaningfulness both of cross-study comparisons and of attempts to reconcile conflicting findings.

The third factor is the background or demographic variables, which not only varied from sample to sample, limiting cross-study comparisons, but which also were not well controlled within many of the studies, limiting the validity of their findings.

The fourth factor is that of measurement. Jacob pointed out that the techniques for measuring variables differed from study to study, rendering the comparison of results across studies and the reconciliation of conflicting findings exceedingly difficult. Related to this is the more fundamental issue of the operationalization of the constructs, pointed out by Doane (1978a), Abeles (1976), and Goldstein and Rodnick (1975). Family-interaction research has not provided an adequate test of the complex clinical hypotheses generated in the 1950s, primarily because the constructs are not adequately operationalized by the measurement strategies used in this research. For example, Abeles (1976) described quite painstakingly the failure of study after study to replicate the conditions of the double bind in the experimental setting. Although her review indicated a process of successive approximation, in which later studies came closer to achieving an adequate operationalization of the construct, there does seem to be a limit to the usefulness of the experimental method in testing a hpothesis that is as abstract, complex, and "slippery" as the double bind. But even more palpable constructs of family structure, such as cross-generational coalitions or gender-reversed parental authority patterns, have not fared well in this research. These constructs are usually included under the rubric of dominance, a variable measured either by judges' ratings of family interaction—which have been criticized for lack of objectivity (Haley, 1972) —or by frequency counts of behavior such as talking time and interruptions—which have been criticized on the grounds that they may in fact not measure dominance but rather some other variable such as spontaneity (Doane, 1978a). And these two measurement strategies, both in their own way flawed, have the bewildering tendency to yield opposite results! Perhaps the answer to this problem of operationalization lies in what Riskin and Faunce (1972) have referred to as the need to formulate "intermediate-level constructs" that can provide a better link between hypotheses and measures.

Finally, at the risk of appearing nihilistic, it is pertinent to raise the question of whether the task set by the family-interaction research field is in fact "do-able." The task involves comparing families who are differentiated according to the diagnostic status of one of their members, in order to determine whether different interaction patterns obtain. One might first question whether our current psychiatric nosology can be an adequate basis for setting up comparison groups, in that the diagnostic system is replete with a wide band of error variance. Clinicians simply do not agree on diagnosis with a sufficiently high degree of reliability to insure consistent groups. The question can also be raised as to whether a valid comparison of disturbed versus normal families can be obtained, since it is impossible to equate the two groups on treatment status, expectancy, and motivation. Finally, it can be questioned whether the dysfunctional processes that are thought to differentiate diagnostic groups are not in fact present in most families to some degree; and whether the discriminable element may be the *degree of severity* of these dysfunctional processes. On this point Bowen (1976, p. 61) noted that "the results of the early studies on normal families might be summarized by saying that the patterns originally thought to be typical of schizophrenia are present in all families some of the time and in some families most of the time." Perhaps it is because of issues such as these that the field of family interaction research, once a booming business, is now largely quiescent.

SUMMARY

The family is thought to contribute to the psychopathology of one of its members either through providing an environment in which disordered development occurs in one of the offspring, or through providing a context or structure that maintains the dysfunction of one of its members. The various conceptual formulations about the family's contribution to the etiology or maintenance of the psychopathology of one of its members can be grouped into three categories: (1) Psychodynamic conceptual formulations use psychoanalytic or ego-psychological frames of reference. This category includes not only the concepts of "marital schism," "marital skew," and the gender-based theory of the etiology of schizophrenia developed by Lidz and associates, but also the concepts of "pseudomutuality," "pseudohostility," and "rubber fence" developed by Wynne and associates. (2) Communicational conceptual formulations focus on the disordered communicational context that exists in the family and to which the identified patient's dysfunction is thought to be adaptive. This category includes the double bind hypothesis of Bateson, Jackson, Haley, and Weakland, as well as Laing's notion of "mystification." (3) The later and more general formulations of Bowen and Minuchin deal primarily with family organization. The discussion of these formulations in this chapter represents an attempt to integrate Bowen's and Minuchin's ideas in such a way that the earlier models can be incorporated in the broadened frame of reference.

The research that has attempted to test all the above hypotheses has been a lively area of investigation that has yielded disappointingly few consistent findings. Several factors have contributed to the failure of this field of research investigation to provide an adequate test of clinical hypotheses of the family's contribution to the psychopathology of one of its members. These factors include not only variations in demographic and other variables across studies, unreliable diagnostic categories, and difficulties in establishing accurate measurement techniques, but also the different foci of analysis (intrapsychic, dyadic, family group) used from study to study, the difficulty in matching experimental and control families, and the presence of dysfunctional processes to some degree in all families.

RESOURCES:
CLINICAL EXAMPLES
OF FAMILY DYNAMICS

1. Science and Behavior Books (P.O. Box 11457, Palo Alto, CA 94306) has several items available on communication. *An anthology of human communication* by Paul Watzlawick is a two-hour audiotape and companion text that uses transcripts from conjoint therapy sessions to illustrate communication theory. *Communication I: Lectures and demonstrations* and *Communication II: Mini-lecture and experiential examples* feature Virginia Satir discussing and demonstrating communicational principles.
2. Psychological Films, Inc. (110 N. Wheeler St., Orange, CA 92669) has available a two-part film, *Target five,* in which Satir illustrates her player-part psychopolitical model through discussions and role plays.
3. South Beach Psychiatric Center (777 Seaview Avenue, Staten Island, NY 10305) has a number of items on communication theory and the pathology of communication. These include two Gregory Bateson tapes (*Double bind and epistemology* and *A workshop with Gregory Bateson*), one tape with Albert Scheflen (*On communication*), and one with John Weakland (*Pursuing the evident into schizophrenia and beyond*). Also available are two tapes by Lyman Wynne (*Knotted relationships and communication deviance* and *Interview with a family of double binders*).

part two: family therapy

The Field of Family Therapy: An Orientation

GENERAL CONSIDERATIONS

In Part II of the book, attention is directed to the various approaches to working therapeutically with families. The focus will be on family therapy per se, reserving for Part III the discussion of other specialized techniques and forms of treatment. The purview of the present part of the book includes the full spectrum of family therapy approaches, with attention primarily to theory.

Definitional Issues

Alexander (1963), in an early commentary on the emerging field of family therapy, called attention to three practices of mental health agencies regarding the involvement of the families of their clients. The first of these is *collaborative* treatment, used by the child guidance clinics, in which one or more members of the primary client's family are also in therapy, usually with a different therapist. The typical practice in the child guidance clinics was for the child (primary client) to be seen by a psychiatrist and for the mother to be seen by a social worker. The second practice is *concomitant* (or *concurrent*) treatment, used in marriage counseling, wherein the same therapist sees both the husband and the wife individually, with joint sessions held rarely, if at all. The third is *conjoint* treatment, in which the entire family, or a relevant subunit, is seen regularly in therapy. It is this third practice, which has evolved into the field of family therapy as we know it today, that will be the focus of Part II of the book.

As discussed in the preface, family therapy is defined more fundamentally in terms of the therapist's orientation toward viewing the presenting problems of the client—that is, in a family contextual or systemic frame of reference—than in terms of which family members are physically present in the treatment room. Thus, as the field has developed, there has been increasing variation in the choices of which family members participate in therapy. Current practice includes seeing an individual family member, a dyad (either the marital partners or a parent and child), a triad (the parents and the child), a set of siblings, the nuclear family, or three generations of an extended family.

In this context, it is pertinent to comment on the differences between marriage counseling, marital therapy, and family therapy. As Broderick and Schrader (1981) have noted in their history of the marriage and family therapy field, marriage counseling, marital therapy, and family therapy have had separate and distinct origins. Marriage counseling originated in the 1930s, as a part-time occupation of professionals such as physicians, lawyers, and ministers whose primary work sometimes involved them in people's marital difficulties. Marital therapy emerged later as a separate movement within psychiatry and involved the application of psychoanalytic theory and technique to the treatment of marital couples. Family therapy emerged in the 1950s, springing primarily from the investigations described in Chapter 2. Currently, however, these three initially separate movements are undergoing a process of amalgamation and coalescence. In the furtherance of this process, no distinction is made in this part of the book between marital as opposed to family therapy. Unless otherwise stated, the approaches to be discussed are applicable whether the presenting problem involves a child, an adult, the marital relationship, or any other family relationship. Further, it should be noted that in many approaches, the marital partners are considered to be the "architects of the family" (Satir, 1967), and—regardless of the presenting problem—the ultimate resolution is seen as residing in marital work of some sort.

Developing One's Own Approach

The objective of Part II of this book is to provide the reader with a conceptual foundation for family work. This foundation consists of two components. First, a conceptual orientation (or map) to the field as a whole is provided, so that the reader will understand the relationships between and among the at times bewildering array of schools of family therapy. Second, the theoretical foundations and methods of practice of the major schools are presented. The format used in this discussion is moderately structured. The major approaches are grouped according to their placement in the general classification scheme, and each school is discussed according to the following general outline: family dynamics, family dysfunction, and family therapy. Within this general structure, a range of subjects is treated, including: theoretical background; history of the development of the approach, as well as populations to whom it has been applied; method and techniques of assessment; process, techniques, format, and duration of therapy; the role of the therapist; and criticisms of the approach, as well as its similarities to and differences from other models. The treatment of the topics is flexible, however, and gives emphasis to those areas that are in fact emphasized in, or appropriate to, the particular school, rather than giving equal emphasis to every topic.

In and of itself, the material presented here is not sufficient to enable the reader to *do* family therapy; however, it will supply a basis for one to make an intelligent selection of which family therapies to study in greater detail or pursue training in. The plural form *therapies* is used here for several reasons. Many professionals choose to develop an eclectic integration of two or more theories, finding that single theories – in and of themselves – are insufficient to the task of understanding the families they must work with. Further, the field as a whole is increasingly moving toward synthesis and integration. Moreover, the outcome research suggests that there is wisdom in becoming fluent in more than one approach.

My recommendation to the reader interested in developing competence as a family therapist is to first get a general overview of the field and an in-depth understanding of the fundamentals of a wide range of approaches by reading Part II of this book. Then select that theory, or those theories, which best fit your personal style or "theory-in-use" and are most relevant for the clinical populations with whom you are, or plan to be, working. Additional depth in your chosen approaches can then be obtained by further reading (following up on the references and additional resources provided in each chapter), course work, and (most important) supervised experience. Supervised experience working with families is essential for two reasons: first, to learn to apply or translate the theories to real-life situations; and, second, to begin that long-term process of evolving your own approach through an artful weaving of theoretical concepts and practical experience within your own personal-professional frame of reference.

The Problem of Classification

In the early days of family therapy, its relative merits were often compared with individual psychotherapy (typically, with psychodynamically oriented therapy), as if family therapy were a unitary, homogeneous form of therapy (Haley, 1971a). In the past 30 years we have seen a proliferation of theories and techniques in the family therapy field. Today it is clear that there are numerous types of family therapy, so it is important to attempt to bring some order to the field—to characterize and classify the approaches to family therapy in order to have a better idea of what it is we are offering our clients.

In this regard we can learn from the individual psychotherapy research literature. Bergin (1967, 1971; Bergin & Lambert, 1978), in three analyses of the outcome studies, concluded that, on the average, individual psychotherapy has had a modestly positive effect. But, he went on to observe, the averages on which this conclusion was based obscure the fact that some clients gain a great deal, some gain a modest amount, some show no change, and some deteriorate after a course of psychotherapy. He pointed out that psychotherapy is not a unitary phenomenon— there is a wide range of theories and practices and a great diversity in the practitioners. What is vitally important to know, then, is "*what* treatment, by *whom,* is most effective for *this* individual with *that* specific problem, and under *which* set of circumstances?" (G. L. Paul, 1967, p. 111).

It is reasonable to expect that this question, and the principle of specificity on which it rests, will be equally important to the field of family therapy.

The preparation of a classification of the various approaches to family therapy is a necessary first step in the process of a fine-grained examination of their outcomes. A classification will not be easy, however. Because of the openness and flexibility with which the field has evolved, a great deal of cross-fertilization and exchanging of concepts and techniques has taken place among theoretically distinct groups. As a result, a lot of eclecticism has emerged, and it is somewhat difficult to discern the "pure strains" within the array of family-therapy approaches. At a more serious level, it has been questioned whether the schools of family therapy derive from comprehensive and consistent theoretical bases or are, rather, a "hodge podge of techniques and part-theories" (Zuk, 1976, p. 299). One of the aims of this chapter is to examine the issue of whether a set of distinct, theoretically based approaches to family therapy exists.

The next section will review prior attempts to classify the field of family therapy. In so doing, it will provide some additional historical perspective on the field as it has developed, and it will lay the foundation for the development of a new classification system. The final section of the chapter will present this new classification schema, which groups family therapy theories according to several of their more general characteristics.

PRIOR ATTEMPTS TO CLASSIFY THE FIELD

These prior classifications of approaches to family therapy will be discussed in chronological order and will include Haley's caricatures (1962) of leading family therapists, the GAP report on family therapy in 1965–66 (Group for the Advancement of Psychiatry, 1970), Beels and Ferber's antitheoretical view (1969), Foley's synthesis (1974), Guerin's elaboration (1976) of the GAP model, and Ritterman's world-view model (1977).

Haley's Caricatures

One of the earliest taxonomies of family therapy consisted of a set of caricatures provided by the inimitable satirist of the field, Jay Haley (1962). This appeared in the lead article of the first issue of *Family Process,* of which Haley was then editor. Haley first described three schools concerned with the families of moderately disturbed child patients: The *Dignified School of Family Therapy* (John Elderkin Bell), in which the therapist does not take sides in family conflict; the *Dynamic Psychodynamic School of Family Diagnosis* (Nathan W. Ackerman), in which the therapist takes sides with different family members at different times, gets pulled in many different directions, and often wishes it were possible to flee the room; and the *Chuck It and Run School* (Charles Fulweiler), in which the therapist does just that, leaving the family members to confront each other in an observation room equipped with recording devices. Haley then described two schools concerned with more disturbed families in which there is a schizophrenic member. Whereas in the *Great Mother School* (Virginia Satir) the therapist emanates a benevolent concern for family members and attempts to create a more friendly family atmosphere, in the *Stonewall School* (Don D. Jackson), the therapist bedevils the family into health.

> Just as a fat man is often called Skinny, the *Stonewall School of Family Therapy* derives its name from the activities of a slippery therapist who takes charge of the family in such a way that no one can come to grips with him. A characteristic of this school is the way it sprains the brains of family members. Often they leave a session batting themselves alongside the head to clear it. The therapist insists that all family members are absolutely right and absolutely wrong and that love is hate, criticism is complimentary, disloyalty is undying affection, and leaving home is really staying. Whatever direction the family members are going, in their aimless way, is accepted by the therapist but re-labeled as actually some other direction, so that the family must become less aimless to find out what the devil is really going on. (Haley, 1962, p. 76)

Finally, Haley enumerated four *Multiplication Schools* that utilize multiple therapists to ease the anxiety about family work: "Just as many swimmers who are uneasy about drowning will associate with a life preserver, so do many family therapists prefer company when they dive into a family" (Haley, 1962, p. 81). First, there is the *Eyebrows School* (R. D. Laing in England), which used two therapists in its "assault on the family." Then there is the *Brotherly Love School* (Friedman and associates at the Philadelphia Psychiatric Center), in which dual therapists met the family in the family's home, allowing family members to go about their business while the therapists tried to blend in with the family's style. There is also the *Total Push in the Tall Country School* (MacGregor and associates of the Multiple Impact Therapy Program in Galveston, Texas), in which every family member gets a therapist for a brief intensive process that combines whole-family encounters, subgroup discussions, and individual therapy sessions. Finally, there is the *Hospitalize the Whole Damn Maelstrom School* (Murray Bowen at NIMH), in which entire families of schizophrenic patients were hospitalized for months at a time on an inpatient psychiatric ward.

The Report of the Group
for the Advancement of Psychiatry

The Committee on the Family of the Group for the Advancement of Psychiatry (GAP, 1970) conducted a survey of the field of family therapy in 1965–66. Their report represents a "snapshot" of the field as it had developed by that time. The report identified three theoretical positions. "Position A" therapists are psychodynamically oriented individual therapists who view family therapy as one method within their therapeutic repertoire. They will occasionally see families but retain a focus on their individual patient. The family is seen as a stress factor with which the individual client must cope. As would be expected, Position-A therapists tend to emphasize history taking, psychiatric diagnosis, expression of affect, and the development of insight.

"Position Z" therapists use a family system orientation exclusively. They see family therapy not as a method, but as a fundamentally new orientation to mental health. All therapeutic interventions are seen as family interventions; the issue is whether or not therapists are aware of the family implications and consequences of their work. Instead of viewing the individual-in-distress as the patient, the Position Z therapist sees him or her as the "identified patient" or "symptom bearer" who is expressing the dysfunction within the family system. The family system thus becomes the focus of assessment and therapeutic intervention. Position Z therapists are ahistorical, focusing instead on the present interaction of family members. Psychiatric diagnosis is seen as inappropriate, because it presumes an intrapsychic—rather than family systemic—locus of dysfunction. The expression of affect is seen as "needless torture." Instead of forcing family members to disclose their unpleasant feelings about one another, the Position Z therapist will work toward resolving the underlying relationship problems that are producing the unpleasant feelings.

"Position M" therapists are in the middle ground—they tend to blend psychodynamic and family systems concepts.

The authors of the GAP report seemed to favor the middle-ground position. The report noted that "family theory combines two bodies of knowledge: personality dynamics and multipersonal system dynamics. The thorough integration of these two systems levels into a comprehensive theory is a long-range task" (GAP, 1970, p. 31). The report went on to observe that some proponents of family theory advocate it as a replacement for, rather than an addition to, personality theory. It predicted that the future may see the emergence of ideological struggles between therapists espousing either-or positions rather than bringing synthesis. This polarization was already being reflected in the data they had collected on the preference of the three mental health disciplines for specific theoretical orientations. Psychiatrists and social workers were fairly well polarized, preferring either psychodynamic or family theory. In contrast, psychologists' preferences were more evenly distributed among six theoretical orientations: psychodynamic, family theory, behavioral, learning, small-group, and existential.

Zuk (1971a) observed an intensification of this ideological struggle during the period 1964-1970. He listed Lyman Wynne, Ivan Boszormenyi-Nagy, and James Framo as representative of the psychodynamic camp, and Jay Haley, Don Jackson, and himself as representative of the systems orientation.

Beels and Ferber's Antitheoretical View

Beels and Ferber (1969) took a somewhat different tack in their attempt to classify family therapists. They focused on the personality style of the therapist, with particular attention to the dominance dimension. They made a distinction between "conductors" and "reactors." Conductors are dominant and participate in a group by leading it. They tend to maintain themselves on the senior side of the generational hierarchy. They are movers, in Kantor and Lehr's terminology (1975). Reactors respond to events within the family group. In Kantor and Lehr's terms, they may *follow* the flow of family interaction, *oppose* particular family members on a symmetrical, same-generational basis, or *bystand* family process by moving to the periphery of the family group when they consult with their co-therapists.

The distinction between conductors and reactors is based to a large extent on the charisma of the therapist: "Many of the conductors are vigorous personalities who can hold audiences spellbound. . . . The reactors have, on the whole, less compelling public personalities" (Beels & Ferber, 1969, p. 286).

Beels and Ferber placed the conductor-reactor dimension in a superordinate relationship to the distinction between psychoanalytic and systems theorists. This is reflected in their placing in the reactor group proponents of both theoretical orientations. As conductors they include: Nathan Ackerman and Virginia Satir as the "East and West Coast charismatic leaders," respectively; Murray Bowen and Salvador Minuchin, who are "artful stage directors"; Robert MacGregor of the Multiple Impact Therapy Group; and Norman Paul and John Elderkin Bell. As reactors-analysts they include people who explicitly subscribe to psychoanalytic theory, as well as people who work with co-therapists. This includes Lyman Wynne's group; Ivan Boszormenyi-Nagy, James Framo and associates in Philadelphia; and Carl Whitaker. The reactors–systems-purists include Don Jackson, Jay Haley, and Gerald Zuk, who, though active, have covert agendas in their therapeutic work.

Foley's Synthesis

Foley (1974) compared five leading family therapists (Ackerman, Bowen, Jackson, Haley, and Satir) in terms of three issues: "What is a family?" "What should the outcome of family therapy be?" and "How does a family change?" He also examined the therapists in terms of the emphasis given to eight specific aspects of therapy: history, diagnosis, affect, learning, values, conscious versus unconscious, transference, and therapist as teacher. Finally, he attempted to inte-

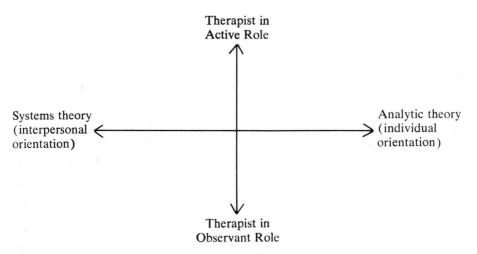

FIGURE 3-1   Foley's two-dimensional model for classifying family therapists. (Adapted from Foley, 1974.)

grate the Group for the Advancement of Psychiatry's classification system (1970), which is based on theoretical orientation, with Beels and Ferber's classification (1969) of family therapists according to the role played in therapy. He came up with the two-dimensional model displayed in Figure 3-1, although he did not attempt to place current approaches within the frame of reference of his model. In this model a therapist could take any position along the theoretical dimension, from pure analytic to pure systems theory, and could adopt a therapeutic role at any point along the continuum from observant to active.

Guerin's Elaboration of the GAP Model

Guerin (1976) pointed out that the emphasis on the style of the therapist (conductor-reactor or active-observant) reflected an antitheory trend of the late 1960s and early 1970s. The antitheory stance emerged partly in response to the excesses of the ideological struggle taking place between the analysts and the systems people. Although the antitheorists swung too far to the opposite extreme in asserting that theory was merely an after-the-fact rationalization for the practices of a given therapist, they did make a significant contribution in calling our attention to the need for a careful consideration of the relationship between theory and practice.

For his part, Guerin (1976) was more interested in developing a comprehensive theoretical classification of the schools of family therapy. Using the GAP schema as a starting point, he divided therapists into two basic groups—psychodynamic and systems—and then sketched in more fully the variety of approaches within each group.

He subdivided the psychodynamic group into four categories: individual, group, experiential, and Ackerman-type approaches. The *individual psychodynamic family therapist* is very similar to the Position A therapist in the older GAP schema. Basically, these practitioners are psychoanalytically oriented therapists who occasionally see the family for assessment or consultation. This subgroup also includes a growing number of therapists trained psychoanalytically who are becoming interested in family therapy and are starting to experiment with it. Practitioners of *family group therapy,* such as John E. Bell, Lyman Wynne, and Chris Beels use a psychodynamic group-therapy orientation, in which the family is defined as a particular type of group—a natural group as contrasted with an artificial group of strangers brought together for the purpose of therapy. Family group therapy was probably the most widespread mode of routine family therapy practice in the 1960s. The *experiential* subgroup developed during the late 1960s and reflects the spontaneous and expressive ethos of that period. Its practitioners attempt to engage the family in an "experiential happening" (Andy Ferber) or stage a growth experience for themselves (Carl Whitaker). The final subgroup—*Ackerman-type approaches*—include Nathan Ackerman and those influenced by his clinical craftiness (Norman Ackerman and Israel Zwerling).

The systems group includes four subgroups: communication-systems family therapy (Haley, Watzlawick and Weakland), structural family therapy (Minuchin), Bowenian family systems theory and therapy, and general systems thinking. Guerin considers the communications approach to be relatively narrowly focused, Minuchin's structural approach to be broader, and Bowen's theory to be the most comprehensive. General systems thinking is represented by the work of the late Al Scheflen. It operates on a fairly abstract level and as yet has found no direct clinical application.

I agree with Guerin that the style of the therapist is less important as a classificatory criterion than is theoretical orientation. The question of the relationship between theory and practice should be examined, but it should be done on a school-by-school basis, after the schools have been classified according to their theoretical orientations. However, the classification of theoretical orientations in family therapy along a single dimension, with individually based psychodynamic theory at one end and multipersonal systems theory at the other, does not do justice to the full range of theoretical positions. For example, Guerin's inclusion of the experiential therapists within the psychodynamic group ignores the fact that many experiential therapists draw their theoretical orientation from existentialism or phenomenology rather than from psychoanalysis. Moreover, the grouping of Bowen's multigenerational theory with the communications and structural approaches—although valid in the sense that all three are systems-based theories—ignores the strong parallels of Bowen's and other multigenerational approaches with psychodynamic family therapy, particularly in terms of the emphasis on family history. Bowen's theory is actually a synthesis of individual and multipersonal-systems perspectives, one that parallels very closely a psychodynamic frame of reference with regard to individuals but that operates out of a holistic perspective. Bowen reflects on this in discussing his concept of detachment:

When it was possible to attain a workable level of interested detachment, it was then possible to begin to defocus the individual and to focus on the entire family at once. . . . . Once it was possible to focus on the family as a unit, it was like shifting a microscope from the oil immersion to the low power lens, or like moving from the playing field to the top of the stadium to watch a football game. Broad patterns of form and movement that had been obscured in the close-up view became clear. The close-up view could then become more meaningful once the distant view was also possible. (Bowen, 1960, p. 351)

Although classifying family approaches along a single dimension will not do, classifications such as Steidl and Wexler's (1977), which simply describes several schools of therapy (communications, psychodynamic, structural, and the Bowen theory) without attempting a systematic articulation of the differences and similarities among them, are also not satisfactory.

Ritterman's World View Model

Ritterman (1977) attempted the more ambitious task of developing a paradigmatic classification of family therapy theories—that is, one that differentiates theories according to their "tacit knowledge" or "world view" (Kuhn, 1970). She examined two theories, the communications systems and the structural, in terms of their "pre-theoretical assumptions" or commitments to philosophical world views. She found that the communications school demonstrated assumptions consistent with the older "reductionistic" and "mechanistic" Newtonian-Galilean world view, whereas the structural school demonstrated assumptions consistent with the more recent "holistic" and "organismic" world view. Levant (1980a) attempted to expand this model to include a broader range of family therapy theories. Upon examination, however, it was found that this model had several major flaws. For example, it exaggerated the differences between the structural and communications schools, and it did not easily accomodate the multigenerational theories of Bowen and Boszormenyi-Nagy.

A NEW CLASSIFICATION SYSTEM

At this point, a fresh approach is needed. Over 15 years have passed since the GAP report predicted the blending of psychodynamic and systems concepts. This has, in fact, occurred to a significant extent. Moreover, in the 30 years since the beginning of the family therapy movement, concepts have been borrowed from all sorts of places and integrated with disparate models and theories. The important thing to notice is that the process of theory construction took place in response to the tremendous wealth of new data and experience that have emerged from the unprecedented phenomenon of working clinically with whole families.

Given this state of affairs, it seems more appropriate to examine the new conceptualizations inductively, rather than to attempt to fit them to preexisting schemata such as the GAP report or world views. By regarding the schools of family therapy as attempts to conceptualize the clinical data afresh, one could notice similarities and differences in the perspectives from which they viewed the data, and it would be possible to begin to cluster them into conceptually and pragmatically meaningful groups. This qualitative and inductive method of analysis allowed the clustering of the schools of family therapy into three groups that could be distinguished by several basic characteristics: (1) the time perspective that is taken in viewing the family, whether oriented towards the generational history of the family, the broadly conceived present (that is, including the recent past in terms of the development of the presenting problem, and the immediate future in terms of therapeutic efforts to solve the problem), or the present moment (that is, the present in its most immediate, here-and-now sense); (2) the focus of therapeutic change, whether it is to free individuals from their unresolved attachments to their family of origin, or to change the structure or process of family as a social organization, or to create an intense affective experience for the members of the family; (3) the role of the therapist—the degree and nature of the therapist's activity and the kinds of interventions used; (4) the expected duration of therapy, from short to long term; and (5) the principal theoretical background from which the various schools have developed.

The three clusters of family-therapy schools are the historical, the structure/process, and the experiential. These clusters constitute models or general orientations to therapeutic change. They do not exist at the very abstract level of world view in Kuhn's (1970) sense, but they are more general than the specific theoretical schools that they subsume. However, some overlap does exist when one considers specific schools (for example, Boszormenyi-Nagy's intergenerational school, fundamentally historical in approach, admixes some existential thinking; on the other hand, Whitaker, who has a psychoanalytic background and uses that jargon in his writings, is fundamentally committed to an experiential approach). The therapeutic models, their characteristics, and representative schools are displayed in Table 3-1. Before a more detailed discussion of each of the therapeutic models, it should be noted that confidence in this tripartite classification system has been enhanced by the appearance, shortly after the publication of this schema (Levant, 1980a), of two recent publications in which very similar classification systems are derived using different methods (Chasin & Grunebaum, 1980; L'Abate & Frey, 1981), and on the development of a family therapist rating scale based in part on this classification system (Piercy, Laird, & Mohammed, 1983).

The Historical Model

The historical model includes the psychodynamic (Wynne, Lidz, Ackerman, Framo), multigenerational (Bowen), and intergenerational-contextual (Boszormenyi-Nagy) schools of family therapy. These approaches are concerned with the individuals within the system, with particular attention to those elements of their interpersonal functioning that represent attachments to figures in the past and that will be transmitted to future generations. Basic to these approaches is a fundamental commitment to psychodynamic theory. Yet, through the integration of systemic concepts, the perspective has been broadened so that it can include the larger picture of the interactional patterns—and transmission of interactional patterns over generations—of a family of individuals (each of whom is viewed in psychodynamic or psychodynamic-compatible terms).

In general, the approach to therapy in these schools involves freeing individuals from their excessive attachments to the previous generation. This occurs through a process of uncovering these attachments, gaining insight into their inappropriateness, and gradually giving them up. The therapist's role involves facilitation of this process, either through the interpretation of the relationship between past attachments and present behavior, or through "coaching" (Bowen) clients as they attempt to form more appropriate, present-oriented, adult relationships with members of their families of origin.

For example, psychodynamic family therapy is concerned with the unconscious aspects of family members' relationships to one another. Particular reference is made to object-relations theory, which holds that we internalize (introject) images (objects) of the nurturing but frustrating parents of our infancy in order to control them. We hold on to these images or objects long after they cease to be appropriate, in order to avoid the pain of losing them. These introjected objects of the past have enormous importance in the present; we seek representatives of them in our present lives, to whom we relate, in part, as if they were these internal objects. This is known as a "narcissistic relationship," similar to the phenomenon of transference in psychotherapy. Narcissistic relationships are usually "two-way streets;" that is, each person in a dyadic relationship relates to the other as if that other actually were the internal object. Thus, narcissistic relationships are often bilateral. Family systems are seen as interlocking networks of bilateral narcissistic relationships. Therapy involves a working-through process analogous to that which occurs in psychoanalytically oriented individual therapy. In this process, the narcissistic relationships of family members and their transferences to the therapists are interpreted with the aim of helping individual family members give up their attachments to introjected objects, thus clearing the way for less distortion in their relationships with family members and others.

A number of workers have contributed to the development of psychodynamic family therapy. These include Wynne and associates; Lidz and associates; Ackerman, Beatman, Sherman, and associates at the Family Institute in New York; Framo and associates at the Eastern Pennsylvania Psychiatric Institute (EPPI); Friedman and associates at the Philadelphia Psychiatric Center; Zinner and Shapiro at NIMH; Searles at Chesnut Lodge; N. Paul in Boston; Beels in the Bronx; Skynner in London; Sager at Mt. Sinai School of Medicine; and the earlier work of Epstein and associates in Montreal.

TABLE 3-1 A New System for Classifying Schools of Family Therapy

CHARACTERISTICS	THERAPEUTIC MODELS		
	Historical	Structure/Process	Experiential
Time Perspective	Past—microhistory of the family over several generations	Present—including recent past (i.e., history of presenting problem) and near future (i.e., problem-solving efforts)	Present—in its most immediate, here-and-now sense
Focus of Therapeutic Change	Freeing individuals from attachments to past generation	Changing structure or process of family as a social organization	Intensifying affective experience for family members
Role of Therapist	Least active—interprets attachments or coaches individuals differentiating from family	Active-directive—changes patterns in session, gives prescriptions for behavior out of session	Active-encountering—participates genuinely, reflects family experience
Duration of Therapy	Long term	Short term	Intermediate term
Principal Theoretical Background	Psychoanalysis	Systems theory Learning theory	Existentialism Phenomenology
Representative Schools of Family Therapy	Psychodynamic (Ackerman, Framo, many others); multi-generational (Bowen); inter-generational-contextual (Boszormenyi-Nagy)	Communication systems (Jackson et al.); problem-solving (Haley); brief (Watzlawick et al.); structural (Minuchin); paradoxical (Palazzoli); triadic (Zuk); problem-centered systems (Epstein et al.); integrative (the Duhls); strategic (Rabkin et al.); structural-strategic (Stanton, Andolfi); behavioral (Patterson et al.); functional (Alexander)	Gestalt (Kempler et al.); experiential (Whitaker et al.); client-centered (van der Veen, Levant); humanistic communications (Satir); symbolic-interactional (Hurvitz); rational-emotive (Ellis); transactional analysis (O'Connor)

(Levant, 1980a)

The Structure/Process Model

The structure/process model originated with the communication systems school, which developed on the West Coast. It grew out of Bateson's research project on communication in families with a schizophrenic member and was based at the Mental Research Institute (MRI), founded in Palo Alto, California, in 1959 under the leadership of Jackson. The original participants included Satir, Haley, Weakland, and Watzlawick.

In addition to the original communication systems family therapy, the structure/process model includes brief problem-focused therapy (the current MRI approach of Watzlawick, Weakland, Bodin, and Fisch), problem-solving therapy (Haley's recent work), and structural family therapy (Minuchin and colleagues at the Philadelphia Child Guidance Clinic). In addition there is the paradoxical therapy of the Milan, Italy, group (Mara Selvini Palazzoli and colleagues), the triadic therapy of Zuk, the problem-centered systems therapy of Epstein and associates at McMaster University in Montreal, the integrative therapy of the Duhls in Boston, the more recently evolved behavioral family therapy (Patterson, Stuart, and others), and the eclectic syntheses of structural-strategic therapy (Stanton, Andolfi) and of structural-strategic-behavioral approaches (Rabkin, Alexander).

In general, these approaches are concerned with the current patterns of interaction of the family, and with the relationship of these patterns to the symptoms or presenting problem of the identified patient. Some variation exists among these schools in whether the interactional patterns are viewed from a structural or process perspective, whether the primary aim is broad (that is, to change the structure) or more narrow (that is, to remove the symptom), and whether the orientation is drawn from systems theory or learning theory. But as a group, they differ sharply from the historical approaches in dismissing history taking, uncovering, interpretation, and insight as irrelevant to the treatment process, and in focusing at the system level, giving little or no consideration to the psychology of the individual. They also contrast sharply with the experiential therapists in playing down the importance of feelings or affect in the treatment process.

The approach to therapy involves reordering the family system in order to remove the dysfunctional elements that produced or maintain the symptom. The therapist's role is that of expert; his or her job is to diagnose the dysfunctional elements of the system and plan a series of interventions that will alleviate them. Directives, often paradoxical ones, are used as means toward this end.

It is interesting to compare the first two therapeutic models (the historical and the structure/process) in terms of the time required for therapy. The historical model is notoriously long-term, so that only exceptionally well-motivated families and individuals are able to undergo the entire process. On the other hand, the structure/process model has been able to achieve dramatic results with symptom relief in a very short period of time. Compare, for example, the two statements below. The first is from a psychodynamic family therapist; the second is from a structural family therapist.

There are centers in the country who see a family for only several months, offering a family therapy program which does not go beyond what we consider the preliminary phases of treatment (Framo, 1965b, p. 166).

Family transformation does not follow a single intervention, but requires a continuous involvement in the direction of the therapeutic goal. But many therapists spend years meandering in the middle phases of therapy because they have lost the sense of direction that a family map makes explicit. (Minuchin, 1974, p. 14)

The Experiential Model

The experiential model includes the Gestalt, experiential, and client-centered schools of family therapy, as well as the humanistic-communicational approach of Satir. Emergent approaches include a symbolic-interactional approach (Hurvitz), a rational-emotive approach (Ellis), and an application of transactional analysis (O'Connor). The best known practitioner and conceptualizer of Gestalt family therapy is probably Kempler, who was an associate of Fritz Perls at Esalen and now has his own institute in southern California. However, in recent years a number of other workers have contributed to this approach, including Hatcher, the Kaplans, and Rabin.

Experiential family therapy was developed by Whitaker and associates at Emory University in Atlanta and, from 1965 on, at the University of Wisconsin Medical School. This approach to family therapy is probably the most atheoretical of all. In fact, the only real theoretical foundation this group has is psychodynamic theory, which they are trying to give up. This school represents, for the most part, a highly developed intuitive form of therapy, relying on the "right-hemisphere craziness" of its practitioners (who also include Warkentin, Malone, Napier, Felder, and Keith).

Client-centered family therapy is the newest entrant into the field. In this approach, which draws chiefly from the theories of Rogers, an attempt has been made to extend client-centered thinking into the area of the family. The family system is conceptualized as an internal subjective phenomenon inherent in each family member. The chief workers in this area are van der Veen at the Institute for Juvenile Research in Chicago and Levant at Boston University.

Satir, as mentioned above, was part of the original MRI group. At an early point, she diverged from that group in her emphasis on feelings and in her viewing communication from a humanistic frame of reference. She left MRI in the mid-1960s to work at Esalen Institute, in Big Sur, California, a center of the humanistic movement.

In general, the experiential approaches are concerned more with enhancing the quality of life of the individuals in the family than with alleviating symptoms or changing the family system. These schools are based principally on existential-phenomenological theoretical orientations. The approach to therapy in these schools involves providing an intensified affective experience for family members, in order that their own restorative and self-actualizing processes will take hold. The therapist's role is facilitative, following and reflecting the process of family interaction and joining the family process as a genuine and nondefensive person. Some (for example, Whitaker) go into the therapy intent on having a growth experience for themselves, knowing that this will stimulate the family to do the same.

SUMMARY

The field of family therapy developed into many different approaches, making it necessary to classify and bring order to the field. Early attempts to classify the various approaches to family therapy included Haley's caricatures of the leading family therapists in the early 1960s and the Group for the Advancement of Psychiatry's "snapshot" depicting the ideological polarization that took place in the mid-1960s. The antitheorists of the late 1960s, in reaction to the excesses of the ideological battles, suggested that the personality style of the therapist was more significant than theoretical orientation. In the mid-1970s, Foley attempted a synthesis of the theorists' and antitheorists' models; and Guerin brought us back to a consideration of theory, presenting a classification of the, by then, well-developed schools of family therapy, using the older GAP schema as a starting point. Some problems, however, were inherent in that classification's reliance on a unitary dimension (psychodynamic theory versus systems theory). In the late 1970s Ritterman examined family therapy theories in terms of their implicit underlying world views.

By 1980, a rethinking of classification seemed warranted, and a new classification system was proposed. In this schema, some 22 schools of family therapy could be grouped under three more general models of therapeutic family change: historical, structure/process, and experiential. The schools grouped under the label of each model share certain formal characteristics, particularly in regard to their operational premises concerning the nature of family dysfunction and the process of therapeutic change.

The Historical Model: Psychodynamic, Multigenerational, and Intergenerational-Contextual Schools of Family Therapy

4

The historical therapeutic model is concerned with the individual within the family system, with particular attention to those elements of interpersonal functioning that represent attachments to figures in the past, and that will be transmitted to future generations. This model blends psychodynamic and systems concepts in such a way that it can take into view the transmission of interaction patterns and personality traits over generations of a family of individuals, each of whom is viewed intrapsychically, from a psychodynamic or psychodynamic-compatible framework.

The approach to therapy in this model involves freeing individuals from their excessive attachments to the previous generation. These attachments are described variously—as "introjects" by the psychodynamic theory, as "fusion" by the multigenerational theory, and as "loyalty ties" by the intergenerational-contextual theory. Gaining freedom from these attachments occurs through a process of uncovering or discovering them, recognizing their inappropriateness, and gradually giving them up. The therapist's role involves facilitating this process, either through the interpretation of the relationship between past attachments and present functioning, or through "coaching" individuals as they attempt to develop more appropriate, present-oriented adult relationships with members of their family of origin.

In this chapter we will describe in some detail the three historical theories of family therapy—psychodynamic, multigenerational, and intergenerational-contextual.

PSYCHODYNAMIC FAMILY THERAPY

Psychodynamic family therapy is unique among the schools of family therapy in that many workers have independently contributed to its development. As a consequence, there is quite a range of positions within the rubric of psychodynamic family therapy. The psychodynamic family therapists can be clustered into four groups: (1) psychodynamically oriented clinicians and researchers who use family therapy as one modality of treatment, but who retain a primary focus on the individual patient (these are the "position A" therapists of the GAP report); (2) psychodynamically oriented clinicians who have contributed particular techniques or conceptual formulations for doing family therapy; (3) Nathan Ackerman; (4) psychodynamically oriented theoretician-clinicians who have contributed to the development of a psychodynamic theory of family therapy based on object relations theory.

Position A Therapists

The position A therapists are primarily focused on treating the individual patient and use family therapy as one procedure in their therapeutic repertoire. This group includes both neophytes (that is, psychoanalytically oriented clinicians who are beginning to experiment with family therapy) and pioneers—psychodynamically oriented clinical researchers interested in the origin and treatment of schizophrenia, some of whom (Lidz, Wynne) formulated early hypotheses regarding the role of the family in the etiology of schizophrenia (see Chapter 2).

Lidz (1973) defined the task of therapy with the schizophrenic patient as freeing the patient from the ties and obligations to parents in order to be able to devote full energies to personal development. The primary modality of therapy is individual, with a de-emphasis on free association, and with more emphasis on support than on interpretation. The aim is to foster the development of the patient's selfhood. Therapy ideally takes place in the context of a therapeutic community or hospital setting, which can provide education and resocialization as well as a psychosocial moratorium. Although awareness of the family dynamics of the schizophrenic patient are critical for proper care and treatment, family therapy is not viewed as the primary method of treatment. Family therapy is seen as having some usefulness, but it is limited: "It can prepare the way for the re-evaluation and intrapsychic reorganization of parental introjects, but it cannot by itself undo the intrapsychic distortions and disturbances that have resulted from many years of faulty intrafamilial transactions" (Lidz, 1973, p. 120).

Searles (1965), who gained his initial experience in family therapy in Wynne's project at NIMH, is in agreement with Lidz regarding the primacy of individual therapy for schizophrenic patients. Moreover, he extended some of the concepts of psychoanalytically oriented individual therapy to incorporate certain family ideas. He observed that some of his patients reacted to him as being more than one transference figure, reprojecting several introjects simultaneously. He coined the term "family transference" to describe this phenomenon. He went on to note that individual psychotherapy should be geared toward the reprojection of all of one's introjects in the transference relationship, and their ultimate reintegration via identification with the therapist:

> The patient who can find mother and father and siblings in the therapist, simultaneously, and who can, through identification with this therapist, make these projected internal images into truly integrated parts of himself becomes thereby, I believe, a more deeply integrated single individual than does the patient whose transference relationship is diverted and dispersed upon the various real members of the parental family in an exclusively family therapy approach. (Searles, 1965, p. 491)

Beels (1976), at the Family Studies Section of the Bronx Psychiatric Center, has developed a Family Service which attempts to provide care on a flexible basis, distinguishing the situations for which family therapy is advisable or not. For example, in the case of a first psychotic episode, family therapy is contraindicated if the patient is an adolescent, but is indicated if the patient is an adult. Patients with periodic and chronic patterns of schizophrenia require creative handling, depending on the particular characteristics of the social and familial situation.

Wynne (1965, 1971) has also written of the indications and contraindications for family therapy. With regard to schizophrenia, Wynne (1974) feels that family-crisis therapy is particularly efficacious in reducing the length of hospitalization when applied at intake. However, with floridly psychotic patients who have chaotic families that contribute to a stimulus overload, family therapy should be discontinued after intake, or at least deintensified and limited to manageable issues. Family therapy is particularly indicated after the patient passes through the florid stage; at this point group therapy may also be useful, if it doesn't overload the patient. For chronic schizophrenia and schizophrenia in remission, family therapy may be a useful adjunct to individual therapy, as might group therapy and vocational counseling.

Therapists Who Have Contributed
Specific Techniques
or Conceptual Formulations

Friedman and associates at the Philadelphia Psychiatric Center have developed a psychodynamic approach to seeing families on their own territories, in their homes. They began this work by seeing families of schizophrenics (Friedman, Boszormenyi-Nagy, Jungreis, Lincoln, Mitchell, Sonne, Speck, & Spivack, 1965). More recently, they have been working with lower-socioeconomic-status families of sexually acting-out girls (Friedman, Sonne, Barr, Boszormenyi-Nagy, Cohen, Speck, Jungreis, Lincoln, Spark, & Weiner, 1971). Their approach is characterized by an emphasis on working with the family from the inside, on the family's terms. For example, in their work with families of delinquent girls, they may bring a six-pack of beer over to the house, in an effort to engage the father in a discussion of family problems.

Norman Paul (1967) at Boston University developed a form of conjoint individual therapy for marital couples. In this process, each spouse gains a perspective on how the past influences the present, with particular reference to old losses that have not been adequately mourned. These old pains and losses are then grieved in the conjoint sessions, which enables the individual to live more fully in the present. The spouse gains empathy for the partner through observing this process. Paul has coined the term "operational mourning" to describe this technique.

Epstein and associates (Rakoff, Sigal, & Epstein, 1967) at the Institute of Family and Community Psychiatry of the Jewish General Hospital in Montreal, in their early work, showed how the concept of "working through," developed in the context of individual therapy, can be applied to family therapy. In individual therapy, the therapist must repeatedly point out to the patient the consistency and repetitiveness with which characterological patterns manifest themselves in a wide range of circumstances, in order to eventually overcome the patient's resistance. So too, in family therapy, the process of working through requires that the therapists repeatedly interpret the consistent interactional patterns that emerge in a plethora of contexts, in order to eventually overcome the resistance of the family to changing these patterns. (It should be noted that this group have moved to a structure/process frame of reference in their current work—see Epstein & Bishop, 1981).

Skynner (1976), at the Institute of Family Therapy in London, has developed an "open-system, group-analytic approach to family therapy," in which a very sharp focus is put on the transference-countertransference dynamic. In this method the concern is on the "projective systems" of the family (the equivalent of transference in individual therapy), and on their recognition by the countertransference stimulation of irrational emotional responses in the therapist. But he goes further, to indicate that the process of recognition is no mere intellectual exercise, but something that tests the very fiber of the therapist:

> The key requirement in the therapist is a deep awareness of his own identity which he is able to sustain in the face of overwhelming, if transient, emotional arousal engendered by encounter with profoundly disturbed family systems seeking to externalize their pathology. (Skynner, 1981, p. 71)

Skynner has fashioned a brief version of psychodynamic family therapy that relies heavily on his sharing of his irrational countertransference responses with the family. This is usually done verbally, but in some cases, it is done more dramatically, wherein "the therapist acts upon his understanding of the family dynamic in such a way that he virtually enacts the scapegoat role; that is, he voluntarily and consciously personifies the very emotion(s) the family disowns" (Skynner, 1981, p. 61). This latter process must be done delicately, and in a context of a good therapeutic relationship; under such circumstances, it can have profound reorganizing and healing effects.

Finally, Sager (1976), at the Mt. Sinai School of Medicine in New York, has contributed a psychodynamic approach to marital therapy, based on the notion of the "marriage contract." Defining contracts as occuring at three levels (verbalized, conscious-unverbalized, and unconscious), he has described how spouses each have their own individual marriage contracts (reflecting their expectations of the marriage and intrapsychic needs), and how the pair develops an interactional contract. The latter is an unconscious system that the two partners evolve to deal with each other in their attempts to fulfill their individual contracts. Sager has developed a typology of couples based in these notions. He first described seven behavioral profiles, or dominant modes by which individuals function in committed relationships: equal, romantic, parental, childlike, natural, compassionate, and parallel-partner. He then described the most common of the partner combinations, with attention to their particular vulnerability for dysfunction and to recommendations for treatment.

Nathan Ackerman

The late Nathan Ackerman was one of the dominant figures in the field of family therapy. Beels and Ferber (1969) have characterized him as the "East Coast charismatic leader."

Ackerman's interest in families developed during the Great Depression, when he studied the mental health effects of economic hardship on families. He evolved his own approach to family therapy during the late 1940s and early 1950s in his private practice. In 1965 he left the Jewish Family Service and founded the Family Institute, which provided family therapy on a sliding-scale basis. After Ackerman's death in 1971, the institute was renamed the Ackerman Family Institute, and it is now headed by Bloch.

Ackerman was a conductor. His manner was that of a kindly grandfather. His use of warmth and humor allowed him to make exceedingly direct interpretations and blunt confrontations of family members' behavior. Beels and Ferber's contention (1969) that theory is an after-the-fact justification for what family therapists do is probably more true of Ackerman than any of the other family therapists under consideration. His theory will be discussed in more detail below, but at this point the additional and related observation can be made that Ackerman's theory of family therapy is less well developed than other available theories. For example, in comparison with Framo's theory—which gives a central place to object-relations theory, takes a multigenerational perspective, and is geared not just toward symptom abatement but toward the more in-depth goal of restructuring the personalities of the family members—Ackerman's theory seems relatively short-range. His efforts are geared toward detriangling the symptomatic child through a massive interpretive assault on the family's scapegoating and defensive mechanisms. His goals are thus less ambitious than Framo's. In accordance with this, his time perspective is shorter (his therapy takes between six months and two years), and he focuses on present interaction to a much greater extent than other workers in this paradigm. In these respects, he is similar to the present-oriented structure/process therapists. Yet, in comparison with the concepts held by these workers, his theory is less well developed with respect to having a systemic frame of reference.

Ackerman's importance, however, does not rest on the degree of development of his theory. My judgement is that his importance is first of all as an early pioneer in the concept of studying and treating families, one who laid the conceptual foundation for a psychodynamic approach to the family; and secondly, as a leading family therapist, whose distinctive style and bold approach stimulated and encouraged others to work in this field.

Ackerman's view of pathology in the family is that it begins with interpersonal conflict and leads to intrapsychic conflict: "Psychopathic distortion and symptom-formation are late products of the processes of internalization of persistent and pathogenic forms of family conflict" (Ackerman, 1966, p. 75). The two levels of conflict then stand in reciprocal relationship to each other as a circular feedback system. The goal of therapy is to interrupt this cycle and reproject the intrapsychic conflict into the arena of family interaction.

Disturbed families are characterized by a failure to form an effective complementarity of roles and overall identity. This renders them susceptible to considerable anxiety in response to the perception of differences among family members. Differences are seen as threatening to the continuity and stability of the family. The particular traits that assume this ominous meaning are idiosyncratic for each family and are often related to unresolved conflicts within the family. The example of the "black sheep of the family" comes to mind.

The phenomenon of "prejudicial scapegoating" is a fairly common pattern of alignment that emerges in response to these circumstances. The family member who is different—whose difference betokens family disunity—becomes the "victim" and is punished for that difference. One member of the family may be designated to play the role of "persecutor," whereas another member of the family may elect to play the role of "healer," who ameliorates the persecution to some extent (Ackerman, 1966, p. 80). The role of healer may also be assumed by an extrafamilial person, such as the victim's psychotherapist. The degree of persecution is, of course, directly proportional to the degree of subsequent emotional impairment. Neurotic individuals were persecuted under the sacrificial theme of "the child must not be different"; whereas psychotic individuals were given the injunction "the child must not be" (Ackerman, 1966, p. 165).

The core problem in families engaging in prejudicial scapegoating is usually failure of complementarity in the marital relationship, which antedates and underlies the failure of the family as a whole to become integrated and to form an overall identity. The task of therapy then involves a "stage-by-stage shift from preoccupation with the child's problems to a confrontation of the basic disorder of the marital relationship" (Ackerman, 1966, p. 5). The therapist undercuts

the tendency of the marital partners to console themselves by engaging in mutual blame and punishment. Ultimately, he stirs hope of something new and better in the relationship. He pierces the misunderstandings, confusions, and distortions, so as to reach a consensus with the partners as to what is really wrong. In working through the conflicts over differences, the frustrations and defeats, and the failure of complementarity, he shakes up the old, deviant patterns of alignment and makes way for new avenues of interaction. (Ackerman, 1966, p. 39)

Ackerman's conceptualization of the role of the therapist is thus highly active and directive, paralleling his therapeutic style as a conductor. There is a high degree of emphasis on the use of interpretation and confrontation to break through the defensive barriers and get at what is really going on. Ackerman sees himself as forthright and at times blunt. He interprets the unconscious meaning of family interactional patterns and individual defensive maneuvers. In a sense he takes on the whole family as if it were an individual, in an analytic-confrontational mode of therapy. He is able to deliver piercing interpretations without arousing unmanageable defensiveness through his warmth and humor. He also utilizes the element of surprise, in a tactic that he calls "tickling the defenses" (Ackerman, 1966, p. 97).

Once he is able to strip away "the denials, displacements, rationalizations, and other disguises, the essential conflicts between and within family members come into clearer perspective" (Ackerman, 1966, p. 96). At this point the detriangulation of the scapegoat can be effected by bringing the underlying interpersonal conflicts to the surface, tracing the connections between these and the disablements of the scapegoated individual, and thus reprojecting the intrapsychic conflict into the arena of family dynamics.

The final task of therapy is the resolution of these interpersonal conflicts and the evolvement of "new designs for family living that offer more mutual satisfaction and a greater potential for growth to the family as a whole" (Ackerman, 1966, p. 99).

Throughout the process of therapy, Ackerman takes on a role of "true parent figure." He provides support on a selective basis, and insures the safety of family members through his "calm, firm presence." He also plays the role of participant-observer, emphasizing the use of self. He uses his own personal reactions as instruments of reality-testing for the family, his own value system as the basis for his goals for the family, and his own person as a model of mental health (Ackerman, 1966, p. 98).

Psychodynamic Family Therapy
Based on Object-Relations Theory

Individual psychoanalytic theory. It will be necessary to provide a brief discussion of individual psychoanalytic theory as a backdrop for understanding psychodynamic family therapy based on object-relations theory. This section will take up, in turn, Freudian theory, ego psychology, and interpersonal and object-relations theories.

Freud's theory of psychoanalysis is rooted in psychobiology. He viewed personality development as occurring as a function of the struggle between the biologically based instincts of the id (sex and aggression) and societal restraints against their expression (as represented by the child's parents). The sexual instinct (libido) attaches to different body zones during the course of development. Psychosexual development thus progresses from the oral stage, to the anal stage, and then to the phallic stage by age five. As the result of the conflict between the sexual instinct and parental restraint during the first five years of life, the infant acquires two personality structures: the superego, which represents an internalization of societal and parental imperatives; and the ego, whose function it is to manage the acceptable expression of id impulses.

The *ego psychologists* (A. Freud, H. Hartmann, and others) evolved the notion of a "conflict-free ego sphere," an area where the ego was not born out of conflict, and where it could function autonomously. This formulation was made to account for cerain day-to-day "neutral" functions of the ego, such as memory, perception, cognition, learning. As a result of this shift to a focus on the ego, more emphasis was placed on healthy behavior (E. Erikson), such as competence motivation (R. White).

Interpersonal and object relations theories (H. Sullivan, M. Klein, W. Fairbairn, H. Guntrip) helped separate psychoanalysis from biology, placing the person in an interpersonal context. Object-relations theory portrayed the infant as starting out not with an id teeming with animal instincts, but rather with a global ego. Libido is seen as an appetitive, nurturance-seeking reaction of the ego, and aggression as a defensive reaction of the ego to frustration. Instead of the notion of three psychosexual zones (mouth, anus, genitals), the concept is that the ego is able to libidinize any part of the body it desires in the service of making a relationship. Libido is thus a term descriptive of the object-seeking nature of the human personality.

Object-seeking is central to human existence. The process of personality development rests on the ego's relations with objects, initially and primarily in infancy, and thereafter in the unconscious, which consists of the split-off and repressed parts of the infantile ego.

Psychic wholeness is fundamental to mental health. In infancy, however, relations with nurturing objects can be sufficiently difficult so as to create ego splits; that is, poor nurturing can cause ego splits.

As the infant experiences frustration of needs, the frustrating-nurturing object is internalized in an effort to obtain better control over the provision of gratification. The frustrating-nurturing object, having bad and good parts, is then split into a good object and a bad object. The good object is reprojected onto the real external mother, who is thus idealized in order to make the relationship more comfortable. The bad object is split into an exciting object (the tempting mother who stimulates needs without satisfying them) and a rejecting object (the mother who actively denies need satisfaction).

The splitting of the object in the effort to cope with painfully frustrating experiences leads to a splitting of the ego into three parts. The central ego is the ego of daily living. It is modeled after the idealized parents, with the disturbing (exciting and rejecting) elements split off and repressed. The infantile libidinal ego, which continues to crave the nurturance from the exciting object, is the basis of compulsive overdependency in adulthood. Finally, the infantile antilibidinal ego, which is identified with the rejecting object, is analogous to Freud's archaic punitive superego.

To the extent that early life experiences are harrowing, there are greater and greater degrees of investment in the internal objects in adult life, and the unconscious preempts correspondingly greater portions of the ego. As a result, not only are external relationships interpreted at an unconscious level in accordance with the internal objects (whether in terms of one's libidinal desires or one's rejected split-off traits), but also *"active, unconscious attempts are made to force and change close relationships into fitting the internal role models"* (Framo, 1970, p. 130).

Extension of object-relations theory into the family area. This process of projecting the intrapsychic contents onto the interpersonal realm will be discussed first with respect to marital interaction, and then with regard to family interaction.

H. Dicks developed a conceptual formulation of marital interaction based on object-relations theory. He described how marital partners relate to each other in terms of their unconscious object-relational needs.

> This stressed the need for unconscious *complementariness,* a kind of division of function by which each partner supplied part of a set of qualities, the sum of which created a complete dyadic unit. This joint personality or integrate enabled each half to rediscover lost aspects of their primary object relations, which they had split off or repressed, and which they were, in their involvement with the spouse, re-experiencing by projective identification. The sense of belonging can be understood on the hypothesis that at deeper levels there are perceptions of the partner and consequent attitudes toward him or her *as if* the other was part of oneself. The partner is then treated according to how this aspect of oneself was valued: spoilt and cherished, or denigrated and persecuted. (Dicks, 1967, p. 69)

S. Lecker (1976) developed the beginnings of a typology of marriage. He started by simplifying object-relations theory, describing intrapsychic life as consisting of two "aggregates of identity," the good and the bad internal objects. Following Fairbairn, he described four basic modes by which people deal with their internal objects. In the *paranoid mode,* the person identifies with the good object, and projects the bad object onto the external world. One idealizes self and sees only bad in others. In the *hysterical mode,* the person retains the bad object as an introject, and projects the good object onto someone in his world; one idealizes others and is constantly burdened by somatic or psychic pain. The person using the *obsessional mode* retains both the good and the bad objects as introjects, siding with the good object in a constant struggle to overcome the bad object. In the *phobic mode,* the person projects both the good and the bad objects and then seeks sanctuary with those on whom the good object was projected, from those on whom the bad object was projected.

Lecker then described some possible marital combinations of persons tending to use one or another of these modes as a predominant interpersonal style. He described the *paranoid-hysteric* marriage as possibly quite stable: "The hysteric wants to find strength—the paranoid can recognize only his good internal object. The paranoid seeks weakness in others—the hysteric is eager to confess to weakness" (Lecker, 1976, p. 197). However, with the birth of the first child the situation will change dramatically. There will be considerable conflict as one parent tends to derogate and the other to idealize the child. This problem may be resolved when, with the arrival of a second child, one child is given the scapegoat role and the other the role of "angel." In contrast, the *paranoid-paranoid* marriage is explosive at the beginning: "Each partner seeks to rid himself of the bad object and find it in the other one who will become infuriated at such fault finding" (p. 197). These marriages, however, may be stabilized by the birth of a child who becomes the "repository for the bad objects of both members" (p. 197). This child is likely to be severely scapegoated.

Framo widened the application of object relations theory beyond marital interaction to include multiple generations of a family. He described the process of *irrational role assignment* or *projective transference distortion* in which

> the various children in the family come to represent valued or feared expectations of the parents, based on the parental introjects; sometimes the roles of the children are chosen for them even before they are born (e.g., the child who is conceived to "save the marriage"). . . . In every family of multiple siblings there is "the spoiled one," "the conscious of the family," and "the wild one;" the assigned roles are infinite. (Framo, 1965b, p. 192)

The process of projective transference distortion is similar to the mechanism of *externalization* described by Brodey (1959, p. 385), in which "the inner world is transposed to the outside with little modification, and the part of the outer world attended to is selected *only* as it validates the projections, *other impinging realities being omitted.*" The use of this mechanism leads to the formation of *narcissistic relationships.*

The same phenomenon has also been described by Zinner and Shapiro (1972) in terms of the defense mechanism of *projective identification* (Klein, 1946). The concept of projective identification underscores the notion that an individual is not able to lose contact with the internal objects, even the split-off, repressed ones, because the existence of splits means the internalization of conflict, and to resolve that conflict, one must continue to live it out. Thus, a projection of one's introjects requires that one stay in contact with what is projected. Contact occurs through a process of identification with the person onto whom one has projected aspects of one's self. Zinner and Shapiro (1972, p. 525) conceptualize this process of identification in terms of "the relationship between a subject and his projected part as he experiences it within the object." A person's behavior in this situation is governed by two principles. The first is that one will relate to the projected aspect of oneself in the object as if it were an internal part of oneself. The second is that one will induce or coerce the object to act in conformity with the way one perceives that object. Zinner and Shapiro quote Laing to illustrate this latter process:

We are denoting something other than the psychoanalytic term "projection." The one person does not wish merely to have the other as a hook on which to lay his projections. He strives to find in the other, or to induce the other to become, the very *embodiment* of that other whose cooperation is required as "complement" of the particular identity he feels impelled to sustain. (Laing, 1961, p. 101)

To summarize what has been presented, we have the following theoretical model with which to understand the dysfunction of individuals within a family. The parents within the nuclear family have varying degrees of attachment to their introjected parental objects, depending on the severity of experiences of loss or deprivation during their childhoods. The parents have particular modes (such as paranoid or hysterical) of handling their introjects, and they have specific object-relational needs. Their relationship represents as close a fitting as possible of their "object-relational need templates" (Boszormenyi-Nagy, 1965). This occurs through a process of bilateral projective identification. Those aspects of their object-relational needs that do not get resolved within the context of their marital relationship may get expressed in the assignment or induction, via projective identification, of irrational roles in their children.

Framo (1970) has shown how symptoms in children can be viewed as responses to the irrational role assignment—either as a form of compliance or as a method of resistance. For example, children who comply with the parental projection, and who take on the assigned role as the sole basis for their identity, are candidates for a psychotic break. Other children may exaggerate the negative role attributes with a vengeance, developing behavioral problems and patterns of delinquency. Still others may struggle intrapsychically with their partial identifications and ambivalent feelings about their assigned role. These children often develop neurotic symptoms such as obsessions, compulsions, phobias, and depression. A particularly troublesome but increasingly commonplace role assignment is one in which the child is expected to be parent to his parents (parentification). This robs the child of the opportunity to be a child, forcing a premature responsibility, and burdening the child with guilt feelings attendant upon the crossing of generational lines. Such children often do not internalize a sense of respect for authority, and they may become belligerently rebellious.

Symptoms in a spouse are a little more complicated. The formation of symptoms involves the interaction of the personality weaknesses of both spouses, developed in response to the projections of their parents, with the projective processes occurring in their marriage. Framo (1970, pp. 145–149) has described how symptoms in one spouse may represent particular internal conflicts in the other, since the spouses "collusively carry psychic functions for each other." In the "dynamic economy of their relationship system," one partner will often be overadequate to balance the underfunctioning of the symptomatic spouse. Often, if the symptomatic spouse improves, as the result of personal growth or psychotherapy, the other spouse may become symptomatic.

Process and techniques of psychodynamic family therapy. According to this model, family therapy involves two processes. First, there is a need to uncover the object-relational basis for, and meaning of, the symptom, in order to defocus or detriangle the symptomatic person and achieve symptom relief. Second, each member of the family must go through a process of uncovering, working through, and ultimately resolving his or her attachments to parental introjects. There are three phases in psychodynamic family therapy: the early phase, the intensive middle phase, and the terminal phase.

In the *early phase,* the therapist's task is to establish a foundation for the intensive work that will follow. This involves, first of all, orienting the family toward family therapy. Many families come into therapy because they are required or requested to do so as part of the treatment of one of its members, the identified patient. The family members are usually apprehensive about what will transpire in family therapy, and are likely to be on guard against the disclosure of family problems. Thus, opening questions such as "What are the problems in this family?" are likely to produce little more than a statement such as: "The major problems have to do with Mary's (identified patient's) sickness." Instead, Framo recommends taking a history of the family from the points of view of each member. This will provide opportunities for family members to make their needs known, either through their individual stories, or through their group interaction in the process of history taking. The therapist during this process accomplishes a second objective, that of making an initial assessment of the family's problems and the areas for therapeutic intervention. Through the parents' histories, it is possible to get a sense of their introjects and thus the "projective load" for the nuclear family. Through the interaction of family members, it is possible to form an impression of the unconscious processes occurring in the nuclear family. Armed with this information, the therapist is ready to tackle the third objective of this phase: obtaining the engagement of family members in the demanding process of family change. The therapist combines exploration with gentle interpretation, setting the stage for future work by indicating that "these are the things that we have to work on." This helps the family understand and assent to working on certain familial problems. Their engagement in this work comes from the sense of trust and rapport that is established as the therapist and family accommodate to each other. If the therapist is able to accomplish this, and gain entrance into the family, the therapy progresses to the next phase.

Framo sees the *intensive middle phase* as "the heart of the process" and describes the objective of this phase as follows:

> The one overriding goal of these intensive middle phases, once the therapists are part of the family, consists in understanding and working through, often through transference to each other and to the therapists, the introjects of the parents so that the parents can see and experience how these difficulties manifested in the present family system have emerged from their unconscious attempts to perpetuate or master old conflicts arising from their families of origin. (Framo, 1965b, p. 167)

The middle phase of therapy is extremely arduous. Whereas interpretations in the early phase were discussed largely at an intellectual level, in the middle phase the emotional connections are made. This is a highly demanding process that requires considerable maturity at a time when intense emotions are aroused, and/or heated family interaction is occurring. Moreover, because of the interlocking nature of family member's pathologies, there is usually opposition to the personality growth of any given member.

The middle phase will be discussed by presenting several aspects in turn: transference and related phenomena; the therapist's techniques (interpretation and working through); resistance; countertransference and co-therapy; and work with the marital partners (including family-of-origin conferences).

Transference is a common phenomenon, whereby people "transfer" fantasies, feelings, and thoughts about significant figures in their past onto others in the present. In psychoanalysis and psychoanalytically oriented individual therapy, the patient's transference is to the therapist. In family therapy, there are, first of all, the multiple transferences of individual family members to the therapist. Each of these may be composed of several introjects, as described by Searles (1965). Framo also described the transference of the family as a whole, which he has observed in less-differentiated families. Secondly, there are the transferences and related phenomena of family members to one another. The younger generations have both reality-based and transference relationships (in varying mixtures) with their parents. Moreover, transference may be a part of any intrafamilial relationship. In addition, there is the related phenomenon of projective identification, which either occurs between members of the same generation (that is, marital partners) or works in the opposite direction of transference, going from the older to the younger generation. Third, in the midst of all this is an ongoing process of conscious and unconscious perception of these distorted elements of current interaction. Thus, as Framo (1965b, p. 195) laments: "It is, therefore, an understatement to call the subject of transference in family therapy complex."

The major techniques used by the family therapist in this phase are *interpretation* and *working through.* Interpretation is a process whereby the therapist calls attention to the unconscious factors involved in a given piece of behavior. In family therapy, the therapist interprets the transference elements underlying current interaction by pointing out its irrationality or inappropriateness. As therapy progresses, the therapist may also point out how such inappropriateness reflects the fact that the person involved is relating to the other as if the other were a figure from the person's past.

A high degree of skill is required to deliver interpretations in such a way that family members accept them and begin to utilize them for their own growth. Framo recommends focusing on immediate interaction as opposed to recollections of past events, and phrasing the interpretative comment as an observation of family members' behavior rather than as an abstract formulation of motivation (for example, "Have you noticed, Mrs. Jones, that you often ask your husband to speak, and then you stop him after he's spoken only a few words?" or "Mrs. Diaz, you complain about not being able to control your son Johnny, yet just now you did not let him interrupt you while you were speaking."). Interpretations such as these point up the elements of family members' behavior of which they are unaware, and they prepare for family members' eventual receptivity to an examination of the past determinants of their behavior.

Working through is really a process of repeated reinterpretation of the unconscious elements of repetitive behavior patterns. The aim is the gradual accretion of readiness to develop insight and relinquish attachments to the past, through the wearing down of resistance.

Resistance in individual therapy is the opposition of the patient to attempts to expose unconscious motivation. In group therapy there is, additionally, the resistance of individual members to disclosing deeper aspects of themselves to others, as well as the group resistance against exploration. In families there is a family resistance that operates in addition to the individual and group resistances. Family resistance is much more formidable than other forms of resistance, in that it is based on both the interlocking nature of individual family member's personalities, and on mutual defensive patterns developed over the course of years of accommodation of family members to one another.

Framo (1965b) described a "massive resistance phase" that is a central element of the middle phase of therapy. It begins after the immediate crisis subsides—that is, when the identified patient is defocused or when the symptoms have abated. Many therapies end at just this point. Intensive family therapy, however, requires that this resistance be surmounted. Resistance, at base, arises because people fear the loss of what little they have at present—even though their current relationships are not completely satisfying and may even be destructive. Surmounting the massive resistance phases requires dealing with these pervasive fears of loss.

Framo has observed that "resistances are always a function of an intricate interplay between variables in the family and variables in the therapists" (1965b, p. 182), and, further, that "the subjective, often unconscious attitudes of the therapy team probably have more to do with the outcome of the therapy than the nature of the family problems" (1965b, p. 196). In order to deal with these subjective problems of the therapists' transference and *countertransference* to the family, *co-therapy* teams are utilized. Co-therapists can provide each other with sufficient structure and support in order that they can effectively cope with their emotional reactions to the family. In addition to strengthening the therapists, co-therapy also serves a therapeutic function for the family, by providing a model of healthy interpersonal relations, and by providing two surrogate parents for the parents of the family.

Dealing with the problems of the *marital partners* is at the very crux of the middle phases of therapy. Very often the identified patient serves the purpose of deflecting parents from dealing with their marital difficulties. Once the identified patient is defocused, the very next step involves tackling the marital problems. This will not only insure the effective detriangulation of the identified patient (and thus the separation of the generations), but will also move the therapy significantly along an intensive pathway.

In the early days, Framo would do the couples work in the context of family therapy, that is, with the children present. He "found the presence of children (to be) helpful because when the therapists assume responsibility for bringing the parents together, the children can be children again" (1965b, p. 190). More recently, Framo (1975, 1976) has described a method whereby the whole family is seen only to the point that the identified patient is defocused. Then the parents are seen in couples therapy. Initially, couples were seen in an individual-couples format, but Framo (1973) soon moved to the procedure of seeing couples in groups. He did this to both avoid the triangulating processes that occur in individual couples work, and to utilize the resources of more differentiated couples as allies or "assistant therapists."

Many marital partners are not truly married. Their commitment to each other, and thus to the family that they have created, is tenuous at best, owing to their continuing attachments to their families of origin. The objective of couples therapy is to "remarry" the partners on a firmer foundation, through the resolution of their attachments to their families of origin.

Framo (1976) has developed the technique of holding family-of-origin conferences during the course of couples therapy. This is an extremely potent procedure, which is carefully prepared. It occurs late in therapy, at a point when the spouses have exhausted conventional methods, have benefited to some extent, but are stuck with certain irreconcilable differences. These basic issues, on which neither can compromise without feeling as though he or she is giving up important parts of self, are the object-relational needs that each spouse has in relation to the other. Family-of-origin conferences can help resolve these impasses by accelerating the process of resolving attachments of the partners to their introjected families.

There is little information available about the dynamics of the *terminal phase* of family therapy, because of the infrequency with which genuine, mutually acknowledged termination occurs in long-term intensive family therapy. Framo described the process as follows:

> The family then enters a frozen state of suspended animation where the old ways are no longer effective and the new ways are not yet available. This state may last a considerable time, and families may be fixated there and never move ahead. It is a painful period for everyone. Ever so slowly, with the families who do make progress, the family members begin really to listen to each other and to the therapists. Gradually they find that the old gratifications no longer seem to work. There just doesn't seem to be much point, somehow, in continuing the relentless alienation or ruthless accusations. They are the same people, and yet there is something different in the family atmosphere; perhaps that nameless dread no longer seems to be hovering over the family. The parents may be able to be less fearful that their daughter will be raped if she goes out on a date, and the children may be less concerned with what goes on in this bedroom which has come to be occupied by both parents. The hus-

band may see the essential unhappiness behind his wife's shrewish ways and may use her less as a censuring mother. The wife may be able to feel more like a woman since she doesn't feel so compelled to see the husband as a tormentor or serf. Unlike other forms of therapy, there is not much verbalized insight; the family members seem to get along better, but have great difficulty understanding why they do. (Framo, 1965b, p. 202).

Moving from this discussion of the four general categories of the psychodynamic approach to family therapy, we will now turn to a discussion of Bowen's multigenerational family therapy. Bowen takes a somewhat broader and systems perspective on the family, but his approach remains compatible with the object-relational theory. The latter is simply viewed from a more distant perspective.

MULTIGENERATIONAL FAMILY THERAPY

Bowen is the principal developer of multigenerational family therapy. He is one of the pioneers of the family therapy movement. His work over the past 30-plus years has been primarily clinical research, with an emphasis on the development of theory. Starting from a psychoanalytic frame of reference (he was a candidate at various psychoanalytic institutes from 1948 to 1960, but resigned as a result of moving in a different theoretical direction—Berenson, 1976), he began his family studies at the Menninger Memorial Hospital in Topeka, Kansas (1946–54), with an investigation of the mother-child symbiosis in schizophrenia. From 1954 to 1959, he staged his monumental research project at NIMH, in which he hospitalized whole families with a schizophrenic member—the project that Haley (1962) referred to as the "Hospitalize the Whole Damn Maelstrom School of Family Therapy." This project afforded theretofore-unheard-of opportunities to observe families in action. It led, in the short run, to the development of a method of family therapy (Bowen, 1961) and the beginnings of a theory of schizophrenia (Bowen, 1960). In the long run, of course, it led to the development of Bowen's multigenerational theory and therapy. Bowen left NIMH in 1959 to move to Georgetown University Medical School, and he shifted his focus from schizophrenia to families with less severely disturbed members.

Bowen's theory of the family was elaborated principally in the years 1951–63, and its main elements were published in 1966. From the beginning, he was critical of the unscientific nature of psychoanalysis and psychiatry, which he traced to Freud's use of disparate conceptual models, some from the natural sciences and some from philosophy and the arts. He had a hunch that emotional illness would be traceable to that part of human functioning which is shared with lower forms of life. He made an early decision, therefore, that the theory which he would elaborate would be based on concepts that are compatible with biology and the natural sciences (such as "differentiation"—as in differentiation of cells in embryological and evolutionary processes—and "fusion") in order to prepare for the eventual development of psychiatry as a recognized science, based on the integration of psychology and biology. Thus, in this fundamental respect he has taken a path opposite to that of the modern schools of psychoanalytic thought (that is, interpersonal and object relations theories), which have attempted to remove all connections with biology and to establish the field on a foundation of psychological science instead (Guntrip, 1971). What emerged from Bowen's efforts, however, is a theory that has close parallels with the psychodynamic family therapy based on object relations theory. The chief differences are that Bowen's theory has a holistic quality; it takes the larger interactional field and historical context into view, which allows a deeper appreciation of the psychodynamics of individuals.

Bowen also developed a method of family therapy that is consistent with his theory of the family. The method of therapy went through several dramatic changes over the years, which will be discussed after Bowen's theory of the family has been presented.

Bowen's Theory of the Family

Bowen's theory of the family as an emotional relationship system consists of seven interlocking concepts. Six of these were included in his 1966 theoretical article, and one (the emotional cutoff) was added in his 1976 restatement of theory. (The 1976 paper also contained an eighth concept—societal regression—that pertained not to the family, but to society at large.) The seven concepts are differentiation of self, triangles, nuclear family emotional system, family projection process, emotional cutoff, multigenerational transmission process, and sibling position.

Differentiation of self. This is a global concept that subsumes the details of individual psychodynamics. Bowen developed this concept from his family research, through which he came to view all individuals along a single continuum. He found certain patterns of interaction in families with a schizophrenic member and then found the same patterns in families with a neurotic member and in families without symptomatic members. He further found that the intensity of these patterns was more related to the anxiety of the moment than to the diagnosis of the identified patient. In explaining these findings, he was led to challenge the traditional psychiatric view that neurosis and psychosis were qualitatively different forms of pathology. He concluded, instead, that these diagnostic entities actually represented points along a continuum of human functioning from severely dysfunctional to highly accomplished. This continuum concerns the degree of differentiation of self.

Differentiation of self is defined as the differentiation of intellectual from emotional functioning. The *emotional system* is that aspect of our existence which we share with lower life forms. The emotional system includes emotions and their associated behavior patterns (such as agitation in fight and flight, or contentment after sex or feeding), and all the automatic functions governed by the autonomic nervous system. It is synonomous with instinct in the biological usage of the term.

The *intellectual system* is governed by the cerebral cortex and is concerned with the planful cognitive direction of life processes. The *feeling system* is seen as a link between the emotional and intellectual systems which represents emotional states in awareness.

Bowen developed a "Differentiation of Self Scale" that illustrates the range of human functioning. Although termed a "scale," it is really an heuristic device for illustrating theory, and not a psychometric instrument. At the low end of the scale, undifferentiated individuals experience marked "fusion" of the emotional and intellectual systems, to the point that they are at the mercy of their automatic emotional functioning. Such individuals lack adaptability, and they become dysfunctional with low levels of stress and anxiety. They are highly dependent on those around them and inherit a disproportionate share of life's miseries, such as physical, emotional, and social illness. Bowen, in his earlier writings (1961), used the term "undifferentiated family ego mass" to refer to the emotional stuck-togetherness of the families of such individuals. More differentiated individuals are characterized by a greater autonomy of intellectual functioning. They are more adaptable and can tolerate higher degrees of stress. They are relatively independent of, and more immune from, the emotionality of those around them.

The degree of differentiation of a person can be estimated only from longitudinal observations. This is because a person's ability to function autonomously is affected heavily by stress and anxiety. Thus a highly differentiated individual, if subjected to sufficient stress, may become dysfunctional. However, such an individual will recover more quickly than a more poorly differentiated person. By the same token, a less differentiated person may be able to function well when stress is low, or in circumstances that are not anxiety-provoking, but becomes dysfunctional when stress becomes moderately high.

Like other theorists (Angyal, 1941; Bakan, 1966), Bowen (1975) postulates that there is a duality to human existence, consisting of drives for "togetherness" and for "individuality." These are represented in his theory with the concepts of *solid self* and *pseudo-self.* The solid self is a result of the drive for individuality, and the more solid self there is, the greater the differentiation of self. The solid self operates on the basis of principles extracted from life experience and thoughtfully integrated into a consistent frame of reference. This frame of reference allows the making of choices and decisions and the taking of clear stands ("I statements") in a wide range of situations. Solid self is analogous to the ego-psychological concept of autonomous ego. The pseudo-self operates from an inconsistent collection of beliefs and clichés that are adopted as a result of group pressure to belong. It results from the drive for togetherness. The pseudo-self is thus a "pretend self" designed to conform to the expectations of the immediate social group (or the object-relational needs of the significant other).

The concepts of solid self and pseudo-self form a bridge from individual to relational dynamics. In states of intimacy, two pseudo-selves fuse into each other, forming a "we-ness" in which one gives up self to other. The one who gives up self is referred to as the "adaptive" spouse; the other is the "dominant" spouse. Healthier couples manage to alternate these roles. In less differentiated individuals, the exchange of self involves most of the self and operates over a long time period. As a result the adaptive spouse may become "de-selfed" to the point of physical or psychological collapse. In an intimate relationship, this exchange of self, or fusion, is not a stable process. One person can demand more self from the other; the other can take back self. These moves generate anxiety and lead to further fluctuations in the process.

Triangles. Thus, intimate dyadic relationships are inherently unstable. They are all right as long as the anxiety level is low, but when tension runs high, dyads tend to involve a third party in their relationship, to form a triangle. Bowen describes the triangle as the "molecule"—or smallest stable unit—of any emotional relationship system. In calm moments, triangles consist of a comfortably close dyad and a less comfortable outsider, or third party. In periods of moderate tension, a triangle is characterized by conflict between two persons, and an outside person who enjoys reasonably comfortable relationships with the other two. In periods of great stress, the outside position is the most desirable but the most difficult to maintain. In these times, fourth parties, and others, are brought into the conflict to form a series of interlocking triangles. When available family triangles are exhausted, outside agencies, such as the police or social service agencies, may be triangled-in. The family has successfully externalized its tension when the outside agencies engage in active conflict regarding the family. Triangular dynamics are displayed in Figure 4-1:

FIGURE 4-1 Triangular dynamics in Bowen's Theory (1976).

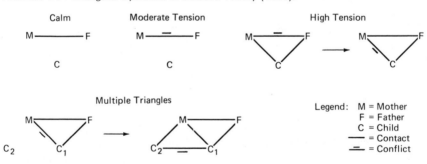

Nuclear family emotional system. In the nuclear family emotional system, the fusion of the marital partners, in which one gives up self to the other, is a major source of tension. Marital couples handle fusion symptoms in three ways. In the first pattern, the symptoms are concentrated in the marriage, which can be characterized either by distance ("emotional divorce") or by a high degree of conflict or turmoil. These latter marriages are emotionally very intense. There are repetitive cycles in which a period of emotional closeness (and fusion) is disrupted by conflict (brought about by the fusion anxiety), followed by a period of emotional distance, which leads to a makeup ceremony, which restarts the cycle. In the second pattern, one of the marital partners becomes dysfunctional. In these marriages, the dominant-adaptive complementarity becomes rigidified and chronic (that is, the fusion becomes solidified). An "overadequate-inadequate reciprocity" is established. The adaptive partner becomes increasingly helpless to point of dysfunction or even collapse, while the dominant partner assumes the role of caretaker. In the third pattern, the fusion symptoms extend beyond the marital partners and their relationship, leading to the involvement (triangulation) and impairment of one or more children.

Family projection process.   The family projection process concerns the transmission of undifferentiation from the parents to the children through the triangulation of children into the parent's relationship. "Projection" here does not refer to the intrapsychic defense mechanism, but rather to the process of transmitting parental undifferentiation. However, it does have clear parallels to the process of projective identification described in the psychodynamic theory of family therapy.

The intensity of the family projection process is related both to the degree of immaturity or undifferentiation of the parents and to the level of stress or anxiety in the family. The projection process is transmitted through the anxiety the mother feels in her relationship with her infant.

Emotional cutoff.   This term refers to the degree of emotional distancing between oneself and one's parents, either through geographic separation or psychological defensive barriers. The degree of such emotional distancing that occurs is related to the degree of unresolved attachment, or fusion, one has to one's parents. The degree of cutoff thus reflects the degree of undifferentiation that must be handled in the person's own life and that is passed on to future generations. This concept has obvious parallels to the psychodynamic concept of unresolved attachments to parental introjects.

Multigenerational transmission process.   This concept refers to the fact that undifferentiation or immaturity is transmitted over many generations. In any given generation of a family, there will be an average level of differentiation. One member of this generation of the family will experience a lower level of differentiation, reflected in a higher degree of unresolved attachment to the parental generation. This individual will marry someone at about the same level of differentiation. Together they will have a certain amount of fusion to disperse within their family of procreation. One of their children will be more triangled than the others and thus emerge with an even lower level of differentiation than the parents. Thus, in schizophrenia, "if we follow the most impaired child through successive generations, we will see one line of descent producing individuals with lower and lower levels of differentiation" (Bowen, 1976, p. 86).

Sibling positions.   This concept is an extension of the work of Toman (1976). Toman has developed a set of personality profiles based on sibling position.

For example, the oldest sibling usually develops natural managerial skills, while the youngest learns how to adapt gracefully to authority. The degree to which family members' actual personality profiles correspond to Toman's profiles can be an indication of their level of differentiation and, consequently, of their triangulation in the nuclear family emotional system. For example, when a youngest child turns out like an oldest, there is presumptive evidence of triangulation in the form of parentification.

Bowen's Method of Therapy

Bowen's method of therapy evolved over the period 1954–74. It is a unique method of therapy that is closely related to his theory of the family. The overall objective is to promote differentiation of self among family members.

His first approach, developed during the NIMH project (1954–59), consisted of seeing all of the hospitalized families together with all available staff, an approach he characterized as "multiple family-therapeutic milieu-network therapy" (Bowen, 1971). Not finding much success with this approach, he moved toward an approach of restricting the focus of such meetings to a single family while other families functioned as nonparticipant observers, an approach which he subsequently refined into a method of multiple family therapy. In the most recent version of Bowen's multiple family therapy, four families are seen in a two-hour period, with the focus on each family for one-half hour. He found that this increases the speed of therapy by about 50 percent, which he attributes to the relative ease by which clients can hear and learn from other families without reacting emotionally.

Bowen's basic model of family therapy developed after he arrived at Georgetown. He started out seeing nuclear families: father, mother, and adolescent child with behavior or school problems. He found that after about 25 to 40 sessions the family would terminate, feeling much improved. However, he could detect only superficial changes. This led to rethinking the method in the light of his concept of the triangle. He observed that therapy involving mother, father, and child simply replicated the basic triangular process occurring in the family. He hypothesized that were he to substitute a therapeutic figure for the child's position in the triangle, more substantial change might occur. Thus he began seeing couples, leaving the moderately disturbed patient-child out of the therapy and, in fact, obtained more satisfactory results.

This model of family therapy with two people is based on the premise that if you can help the two most important people in the family to increase their level of differentiation, the other will change in relation to them. Bowen has used this as the basic method in short- and long-term therapy. It works best in situations where people are capable of calm thought—that is, where anxiety is relatively low or where differentiation is relatively high.

The method consists of staying in viable emotional contact with the spouses without becoming emotionally entangled. If this can be done, the marital fusion will slowly resolve, and the two spouses will gradually increase in their levels of differentiation. Thus, the therapist must work to keep the field calm, to maintain emotional neutrality (that is, "stay out of the transference"), and to keep the focus on the process of the relationship rather than the content.

The primary technique used by Bowen is to structure the session so that each spouse talks to the therapist, in a calm, factual manner, about the emotional process of their relationship. For example, he may open the session asking the husband what progress he was able to make since the last session. During this interchange he may ask the husband to elaborate on points that may not be clear. He will then turn to the wife and ask her what she was thinking while her husband was talking. During this interchange he may ask her to elaborate her thoughts more fully. He thus elicits the fullest elaboration of the private thinking of each spouse in the presence of the other, a process he finds enormously helpful to their relationship.

Gradually, one of the spouses—usually the more differentiated of the two— will begin to make moves toward individuality in these sessions. The other spouse will respond to this with anxiety and demands for togetherness. This will lead to a period of struggles and false starts, which after about one year will be resolved by the first spouse taking definite steps to differentiate himself or herself. This will be followed by a period of relative calm and a higher level of differentiation for both. Later, the second spouse will initiate a second cycle, as he or she begins to differentiate.

In long-term therapy, Bowen will include some didactic teaching of his theory of the family. This is more effectively done later in the course of therapy, after the family has calmed considerably. Also, in the later stages of long-term therapy, Bowen will send the spouses home, to visit with their families of origin, in order to help them "differentiate a self" in their extended family.

Certain events in the late 1960s proved to be significant in shifting the focus of Bowen's method of therapy more in the direction of work with the families of origin. The first was a breakthrough in his efforts with his own extended family, which he reported at a national conference on the family in 1967 (Anonymous, 1972). The second was a serendipitous finding that psychiatric residents in a training conference that was focused on the differentiation of self in one's family of origin did better, both in their clinical work and in resolving their personal problems and difficulties with their spouses and children, than did residents who were in regular family therapy with their spouses. Bowen subsequently checked and rechecked this finding and reported in 1974 that *"families in which the focus is on the differentiation of self in the families of origin automatically make as much or more progress in working out the relationship system with spouses and children as families seen in formal family therapy in which there is a principal focus on the interdependence in the marriage"* (Bowen, 1978, p. 545).

Bowen now works with individuals, on a very sporadic basis if need be, functioning as "coach" or "trainer" to a person actively seeking to differentiate a self in the family of origin. This new posture is quite consistent with his basic premises: he has always preferred to work with the healthiest persons in the family on the basis that they are the most able to change; and he has characteristically seen himself as an educator or coach rather than as a healer or therapist.

It should be noted that while Bowen's methods of therapy are unique in certain respects, they have some close parallels in psychodynamic family therapy based on object relations theory. First of all, Bowen is similar to Framo in his emphasis on defocusing the child as soon as possible and working directly with the marital couple (although Bowen would tend to remove the child at the very beginning, whereas Framo would do so as early as possible). Second, like Framo, he has developed a form of multiple family therapy that he finds beneficial in shortening the process of therapy. (It should be noted however, that Framo tends to rely on these multiple couple groups to a greater extent than does Bowen, and that he does so to avoid the triangulation of the therapist—which, to Bowen, is at the heart of treatment.) Third, like Framo, he puts emphasis on resolving old attachments to the family of origin. (But it should be noted that the two have somewhat different procedures for handling this: Framo interprets the attachments as they emerge in the transference and the family interaction, whereas Bowen "stays out of the transference" and does not interpret; Framo holds singular family-of-origin conferences, whereas Bowen encourages the individual to make frequent visits home.)

In review, Bowen's theory of the family is based on seven interlocking concepts: differentiation of self, triangles, the nuclear family emotional system, the family projection process, emotional cutoffs, multigenerational transmission process, and sibling positions. His method of therapy evolved from seeing families in large groups ("multiple family-therapeutic milieu-network therapy"), to a more refined form of multiple family therapy, to a conjoint-nuclear-triad approach, to a dyadic approach, and ultimately, to an individual approach in which the person attempts to differentiate a self in his or her own family of origin.

Bowen is an original thinker and his theory represents an integration of psychodynamic and systems concepts within a multigenerational/historical framework. His papers have recently been brought together in an edited volume (Bowen, 1978).

INTERGENERATIONAL-CONTEXTUAL FAMILY THERAPY[1]

Ivan Boszormenyi-Nagy and Geraldine Spark are the principal developers of intergenerational family therapy. More recently Barbara Krasner and David Ulrich have helped Boszormenyi-Nagy refine and broaden the theoretical approach, which is now referred to as contextual therapy (Boszormenyi-Nagy & Krasner, 1980; Boszormenyi-Nagy & Ulrich, 1981). The contextual approach is not limited to family therapy, and is seen as a more general approach to therapy of various modalities. The following discussion will be based on the intergenerational family therapy approach, updated (as indicated) by some of the more recent writings.

[1]I would like to gratefully acknowledge the assistance of Nancy Haffey in the preparation of the first draft of this section, and of Judy Grunebaum, whose suggestions for revision were very helpful.

Ivan Boszormenyi-Nagy, or Nagy, as he is commonly referred to, moved to the United States from Hungary in 1948, acknowledging that as he made a commitment to his new country, he retained many loyalties to his family and nation of origin. His professional beginnings were as an individually oriented psychiatrist. He began to do family therapy in 1956 and was joined by Geraldine Spark as one of his co-therapists in 1963. Spark, a psychiatric social worker with extensive experience in child-guidance clinics, worked to integrate her experiences as a family therapist with her earlier training at the Philadelphia Psychoanalytic Association. Together, they worked with families having a variety of problems (ranging from minor behavioral disturbances to psychosis), from a variety of economic backgrounds (prominent community leaders to ghetto-dwellers), and in a range of settings (private practice, community mental health centers, and research projects with schizophrenic and delinquent adolescents).

Over the years they evolved a theory of family dynamics and therapy that integrates psychodynamic and systems theories within the frame of reference of existential philosophy (Boszormenyi-Nagy & Spark, 1973). They view themselves as differing from theorists (such as Lidz, Wynne, Ackerman, or Framo) who have explained relational systems in individual psychodynamic terms, and also from the structure/process theorists, in that they have created a new language to more adequately reflect the dynamic multipersonal nature of the family system. Their new language is based on the ideas of fairness and trustworthiness in family relationships.

The Intergenerational-Contextual
Theory of Family Dynamics

Nagy views the family in terms of four dimensions: (1) *Facts* concerns the factual configuration of one's roots with reference to race, nationality, ethnic group, and religion; as well as to factual events within one's family, such as illnesses, divorces, and adoptions. (2) *Psychology* concerns the intrapsychic structure of individual family members, which is understood in terms of modern psychodynamic theory. (3) *Transactions and power alignments* is the level at which the structure/process models of family therapy focus—behavior, communication patterns, and organizational structure. (4) *Merit or relational ethics* is the dimension unique to this school. It is based on Buber's (1958) existential philosophy, with particular reference to the I-Thou relationship, and its emphasis on the interdependence of human affairs. Or, as Nagy and Spark expressed it: "Naturally, the self is the experiential center of the individual's world, but the self is always a subjective I, unthinkable without some you" (Boszormenyi-Nagy & Spark, 1973, p. 9). As a result of this interdependence, a sense of justice is inherent in human relationships.

Loyalty, justice, and balance.   The dimension of relational ethics is based on the concepts of loyalty, justice, and balance. *Loyalty* refers to a set of structured expectations to which all family members are committed. Loyalty is expressed through action and is perhaps best understood in terms of who does what for whom, and how it is repaid. In order to understand families, one must know who is bound to whom in loyalty, and what that loyalty means to each member. Every family member maintains an account of the balance of give and take in his or her life. One makes investments into the account by being supportive to the needs of other family members, and one withdraws from the account by receiving support (or by exploiting others). The most fundamental loyalty, though, is not to oneself, but to the maintenance of the family.

The concept of *justice* refers to a systematic way of describing the balance of loyalty obligations, using such terms as "merit," "reciprocity," "exploitation," and "revolving slate." Merit refers to a credit, or moral surplus in one's account that is earned by contributing to the welfare of others. This contributes to one's own "entitlement," which is to be distinguished from an arrogant attitude of entitlement and from the intrapsychic sense of entitlement. The main effect of having entitlement is the liberation of the person for a productive and fulfilled life. Reciprocity refers to the balance of obligations as it exists between any two people in the family system. Any disparity between what is given and what is received is invisibly recorded and forms the basis for demands that the account be made equivalent. Exploitation refers to unequal merit accounting. One person may be exploited, either overtly or covertly, by another through nongiving or nonreciprocity, or two people may be exploited at the same time by the family system. The concept of revolving slate refers to an unsettled ledger sheet that exists between two people and that can move about so as to come between one of the original pair and a third person, who is thus scapegoated. For example, a person who has been exploited by a parent may feel angry and uncared for, but cannot express this anger directly out of loyalty to the parent. Thus, this person has earned credit or entitlement in his relationship with his parent which cannot be claimed. He may then seek to balance his account by unrealistic expectations of receiving from his spouse. Entitlement is valid only in the context of the relationship within which it is earned; hence his claim is unfair, and, if insisted upon, constitutes a form of "destructive entitlement."

Each person is embedded in a dynamically *balanced,* fluctuating, multigenerational context in which an invisible "ledger" keeps account of one's loyalty obligations. By the time a person is old enough to express loyalty through action, though, the ledger is already unbalanced. An infant who is raised in a nurturing, trustworthy environment is indebted to his or her parents. The more the environment is worthy of trust, the more one is indebted, and the less one is able to repay the benefits directly, resulting in "existential indebtedness." Thus, there is an inherent assymetry in parent-child relationships, in which the future ("posterity") is the creditor. On the other hand, an infant may be raised in a nonnurturing, exploitative environment and will have an existential credit in his or her account. Such a person may seek to balance that account by revolving the slate, attempting to make others accountable for this debt. The multigenerational nature of the ledger becomes apparent when it is realized that the infant's account is based on the environment provided by the parents, which in turn is based on the balance in the parents' own accounts.

A person frequently attempts to balance his or her account through the choice of a marital partner. A person may want to balance his account by finding a partner that will be giving, or one who is receptive to being given to. A person may be seeking the idealized parent in the spouse, or the idealized family in the spouse's family. Such expectations are unfair (since relationships are nonsubstitutable), and thus cannot be met by the marital partner; hence, the account will not be balanced in this manner. These existential debts may be settled equitably through contributing to the welfare of one's children, and/or through direct repayment to one's parents. A person's task in life is to continuously seek to restore the balance in one's relationship with one's parents, within the context of one's primary commitments to one's spouse and children.

Dialectical aspects of family relationships.   Nagy and Spark's theory of relationships is approached from a dialectical model of thinking. The term "dialectical model of thinking" refers to the process of examining the multidimensional aspects of a given phenomenon, and of exploring and synthesizing the apparent differences. Three aspects of family relationships are viewed from a dialectical model. One aspect is the *relative balance and imbalance* in family relationships. It is assumed that life is unpredictable and that changes will inevitably occur that challenge the family equilibrium and create an imbalance. An imbalance creates a sense of unfairness in the "injured" or exploited person, which demands restitution. "As injury and unfairness become balanced through restitution, the spontaneity of autonomous motions of individual members is bound to create new imbalance and new injustice which if recognized and faced, leads to a richer, safer definition of freedom and concern among members" (Boszormenyi-Nagy & Spark, 1973, p. 19). For example, a woman who feels too many demands were made upon her by her parents (an imbalance) may seek restitution (balance) by making numerous demands on her daughter. As the daughter reaches adolescence, she struggles to become autonomous, thus creating a new imbalance that, if recognized and faced, can lead to change and growth.

Knowledge of the balance or imbalance of family members' ledgers is more important than knowledge of manifest behavior patterns in determining psychological health. Overt behavioral patterns in and of themselves are not an indication of, and are not as important as, a knowledge of who is indebted to whom, and who maintains loyalty to whom. Once it is known where the loyalty imbalance exists, one can begin to seek a balancing of the accounts. The balancing of accounts must be viewed dialectically, in order to see that giving may be the means through which one receives in a relationship. When one gives up something in order to fulfill an obligation, one also reduces the debt in one's own account, and earns entitlement.

A second dialectical aspect of family relationships concerns the problem of *separation-individuation versus family loyalty.* Just as there is a strong desire to become autonomous and separate from one's family, there is an equally strong desire for closeness and attachment, and for fulfillment of loyalty obligations. Along with these desires are the fears of alienation and aloneness on one hand, and symbiotic enmeshment on the other hand. The period of adolescence is characterized by an exploration of this problem, and by a negotiation of compromises leading to both individuation and a rebalancing of loyalty obligations. The capacity to do this consitutes individuation. But it should be emphasized that Nagy has a unique understanding of individuation, which he terms "relational autonomy," reflecting both its separational ("centripetal") and relational ("centrifugal") aspects.

The third dialectical aspect of relationships is the *surface-depth dialectic.* What appears on the surface to be disloyal behavior may, on a deeper level, be loyal to the maintenance of the family system. Loyalty accounting is based on the ethics of caring and obligation, not on power. Thus paradoxically a loser, or a scapegoated family member, is a winner through being able to induce debt or guilt in other family members. The scapegoat may help to define and maintain the family system through "negative loyalty," or loyalty that on the surface appears to be disloyal because it is based on negative behavior.

Family Dysfunction:
Fixed Loyalty Imbalance

The psychological health of family relationships is not determined solely by whether or not the ledger is balanced. As mentioned previously, an imbalance can lead to growth. When an imbalance becomes fixed and unchangeable, however, a loss of trust and hope follows, resulting in a "pathogenic relational configuration," the relational counterpart to psychopathology.

Loyalty imbalances can become fixed through defensive maneuvers that are initially intended to rebalance the accounts. There are three classes of these abortive solutions: relational stagnation; substitute forms of indirect mastery; and parentification.

Relational stagnation. Relational stagnation, or the lack of movement and growth in relationships, can take several forms. One is overt failure, in which an offspring fails in all social relationships, thus maintaining total loyalty to the family. Equally stagnating is the situation in which material success or personal achievement is substituted for growth in family relationships. Another form of stagnation is sexual failure. In all marriages there is an implicit loyalty conflict between the spouse and the family of origin, which is often acted out in the couple's sexual relationship. A healthy sexual relationship may imply disloyalty in the relationship with one's family of origin; conversely, sexual dysfunction implies a stronger degree of loyalty to the family of origin than to the spouse. The conflict in loyalties between spouse and parents can also be resolved in a stagnating way by pledging total loyalty to the marital partner at the price of disloyalty or repudiation of one's family of origin. This can result in unreasonably high expectations of the marital partner and parentification of the children. A final form of stagnation is "freezing of the inner self." This can occur in response to a martyrlike parent who refuses to receive anything from his or her children. The balance of accounts is such that the child is always in debt to the parent and becomes burdened by the guilt of undischarged obligations. The child then becomes helpless and loses the capacity to relate with other people.

Substitute forms of indirect mastery. These attempts to rebalance one's loyalty accounts do not result in total stagnation, but they are ineffective in balancing the account. One such attempt is *negative loyalty,* which is seen in the process of scapegoating. The scapegoat mitigates his own guilt and controls the guilt feelings of others by suffering. For example, the adolescent boy who is perpetually given to, with no opportunity to repay his obligations to his parents, acts out and gets caught. This leads to punishment, which both relieves his guilt and induces guilt in his parents, temporarily balancing the account. The parents respond by consolidating their loyalty to each other, blaming and condemning their son, and thus decreasing their frustration over having been exploited by him. This enables them to forgive him and start giving to him again, which continues the cycle. A negative loyalty commitment often takes the form of delinquency. The delinquent shows a characteristic lack of remorse, because of the overall benefit to the family, and because the negative identity is preferable to the nonidentity of being ignored.

The mechanism of *guilt against guilt* is similar to scapegoating. In scapegoating, guilt accumulates in the persecutor. In the guilt against guilt mechanism, guilt breeds more guilt so as to create a tighter, more hostile relationship. For example, an adolescent girl becomes caught in the loyalty bind involved in the process of individuation and feels guilty for her desire for autonomy. She begins to act crazy, causing her parents to feel guilty for the demands they have made on her. The adolescent responds to her parents' guilt by feeling even more guilty, perpetuating the cycle.

Another form of indirect mastery of unbalanced invisible loyalties is *sacrificed social development as an act of latent devotion.* Nagy and Spark refer to Bowen's concept of differentiation of self, and they state that in an unbalanced family, individuals will remain undifferentiated. The family will not allow its members to become separate individuals in their own right; they will instead remain products or dependents of the family. The "undifferentiated family ego mass" requires loyalty in the form of absolute devotion, unhindered by other social involvements and commitments.

Indirect mastery of conflicting loyalties may also take the form of a *splitting of loyalties.* In this situation, one person is rejected while another becomes an object of devotion. For example, a doctor's husband may feel that his wife gives her best devotion to her patients. Such a splitting of loyalties may occur in individual psychotherapy, when a positive transference relationship with the therapist becomes an act of disloyalty to one's family. Splitting of loyalties, a more general term, is to be distinguished from the specific problem of "split filial loyalty," which occurs when the parents set up conflicting claims so that the child can offer loyalty to one parent only at the cost of his or her loyalty to the other.

Incestuous family relationships are another form of indirect mastery. Incest reinforces the symbiotic enmeshment of family members. There is a lack of both ego and generational boundaries as the child is seen as an object of gratification rather than a person in her own right. Loyalty obligations will bind the child into the incestuous relationship as she fears the loss of the parent. Thus the family structure is maintained at the expense of its members.

One of the most common mechanisms of indirect mastery of loyalty commitments is *manipulation of displaced retribution* or, simply: That which is owed to the parents is inappropriately displaced onto the children. This is a miscarriage of a normal process wherein we repay our existential indebtedness to our parents by providing good parenting for our children. For example, a martyrlike mother feels a sense of indebtedness to her parents, which she hasn't acknowledged or repaid. She feels guilty over her indebtedness; she also feels exploited as a result of the protracted indebtedness. The resultant anger makes her feel additionally guilty. The totality of these feelings creates ambiguity, which sets up an injunction against settling her account with her parents, so she tries to repay her debt by being overly devoted to her child. The mother's guilt then diminishes. The giving nature of her devotion overshadows and balances, at least in her mind, the unreasonable demands and exploitation that usually accompany the devotion. Her giving is often a material giving or a smothering with no real sharing of herself on an emotional level. Because her giving is necessary in order to relieve her guilt, she refuses to receive anything from anyone. The excessive giving, accompanied by no demands, reinforces the child's existential guilt and sense of obligation until a hopeless amount of indebtedness accrues in the child's account. Actually no one is satisfied: The grandparents feel left out, jealous, and alone; the parents feel unsupported and unappreciated; and child feels burdened, guilty, and angry.

Parentification. Parentification is a subjective distortion of relationships in which one acts as if one's spouse or child were one's parent. It occurs through wishful fantasy as well as by dependent behavior. Some parentification is healthy and normal; it becomes pathogenic, however, when it hampers the child's development or when the child is trapped in an obligational bind and must comply with parental demands. The "good child" often becomes parentified when trying to comfort the parents by being a substitute, loving parent. The emotional gain for the parent is both in the sense of security of having a parent and in not having to face the loss of one's parent. Psychologically, parentification results from the parents' own lack of individuation. They will use the child as an object so as to retain their own parents through symbiotic possessiveness. In terms of relational ethics parentification is an attempt at balancing the accounts through destructive entitlement.

Parentified children are not able to repay obligations to their parents by giving to their own children. Feelings of guilt and obligation combine with feelings of love and devotion, leading to ambivalence and hostility, until such children are unable to transfer their loyalty. A parentified child's loyalty is thus not always characterized by outward manifestations of what would appear to be loyalty; instead, it may be characterized by self-destructive and violent behavior.

Intergenerational Therapy

Nagy and Spark's theory of intergenerational family therapy derives from their theory of family dynamics and dysfunction. Families in which chronic unbalanced accounts result in pathogenic relational configurations will experience symptoms in one or more members. The therapist's task is to translate symptoms into loyalty balance equivalents, and to help the family work toward a balancing of the accounts, or "rejunction."

Nagy and Spark view intergenerational family therapy as best conducted by a co-therapy team whose members can convey complementarity, flexibility, and creativity, as well as empathy, compassion, and trust. A co-therapy team can present a balanced model to the family system as they complement one another. They can act more effectively by being able to take turns entering the family system. Most importantly, though, they must be able to remain available to each other in a trusting, respectful relationship with a capacity for openness and a toleration for differences.

In order to establish a working alliance with the family, the co-therapy team will contract to work with all family members with the goal of benefiting the family as a whole. The co-therapy team expects each family member to participate in the initial discussion of expected gains and desired goals for the family, and to contribute to the ongoing therapeutic process. The co-therapists will ally with the healthy aspects of the family by helping family members to see themselves as resources, and will work to restore a sense of trustworthiness in relationships.

The goals of intergenerational family therapy are (1) to face invisible loyalties within the family; (2) to recognize unsettled accounts; and (3) to rebalance in actuality one's obligations and relationships with one's parents, spouse, and children. Some families will find this process too difficult and painful and will opt for symptomatic relief. This will be accepted by the therapists. In other families, the regressive forces may remain hidden or invisible while the family remains fixated in symbiotic or overdistanced relationships. In these cases, therapy is seen as intolerable and will be rejected.

Initially, the family establishes a transference relationship with the co-therapists, or adopts the co-therapy team as their parents. This adoption or attempted parentification relieves some of the pressure on parentified and scapegoated children, resulting in some immediate symptom relief. In order for lasting change to occur, however, it is necessary to engage in the rejunction process, in which the family reworks stagnant imbalances in their relationships.

The initial task of the co-therapists is to create an atmosphere of trust and establish an order to communication so that all family members can express and define their entitlements and indebtedness. This is done through the co-therapists' empathic involvement with the family, and their crediting of earned merit. The co-therapists maintain an attitude of "multidirected partiality," which is based on an appreciation of the "multilateral" quality of relationships, and on the therapists' deep regard for the importance of all family members' investment in the trustworthiness of their relationships.

The co-therapists respond to the initial transference or parentification in one of two ways. On the one hand, they do not allow themselves to become parentified; rather, they insist that each family member play the appropriate family role; that is, they insist that the parents take responsibility for parenting their own children. On the other hand, the co-therapists do parent the family by using their quasi-parental authority to engage family members in the process of addressing the imbalances in their accounts in order to restore a sense of fairness in their relationships.

It is this balancing of accounts that is at the heart of the rejunction process. This process consists of exploring the many dimensions of the various relationships within the family, including the marital pair, the parents and each child, and the parents and grandparents. The co-therapists try to set up a process of dialogue between family members, in which there is mutual acknowledgment and position taking. Parents earn entitlement by speaking of their own childhood, and their relationships with their parents, to their children.

Throughout the therapeutic process, Nagy and Spark see the co-therapists as taking an active role, a role that they define as the "active programming of an ordered set of expectations for the members of the family" (p. 367). The co-therapists expect the family's commitment to responsible relating, and they respond with concerned interest, support, and empathy, and the ability to ally with different family members at different times, each of whom is asked to be accountable. They will make demands on the family, confront various aspects of family relationships, suggest alternative ways of relating, and push for the balancing of accounts and the inclusion of the grandparents in therapy.

In intergenerational therapy, in order to rebalance in reality one's accounts and obligations, it is necessary at some point to include the grandparents in the therapeutic process. It is important for the co-therapy team not to allow mutual blaming and recrimination to continue endlessly but, instead, to focus on the development of the constructive and growthful aspects of the relationships. Feelings need to be expressed, and a confrontation may be necessary in order for meaningful and mutual dialogue to ensue; the goal, however, is to facilitate a new way of relating. There may be a clarification of feelings and a modification of attitudes, but most important is a change of behavior so as to break the chain of destructive relationships. By facing one's distortions about one's parents and learning the circumstances of their lives as they see them, one learns to understand, have compassion for, and "exonerate" one's parents. The grandchildren, who have been carrying the brunt of the unsettled accounts, will then be relieved of their burden. Also, by witnessing their parents' struggles and sharing in the more meaningful aspects of their parents' lives, they learn a valuable model for the future.

Transference manifestations in family therapy may occur between family members or between a family member and the therapist. According to Nagy and Spark, the most important transference distortions operate between family members; however, it is essential also to be alert to the transference distortions of the therapist's role. The family therapist may be seen as omnipotent; the family will attempt to bring their problems to the therapist and expect the therapist to effect the magical easy cure. The family may see the therapist as a judge; they will present their differing views of justice and demand to know who is right and who is wrong. Other families will see the therapist as a blamer. If their experience with life has been to either be blamed or to be blaming others, they will expect criticism and reproachment from the family therapists. Transference feelings may originate from the ambivalence between desires for and fears of enmeshment, in which case feelings of rage or dependency may be projected onto the therapist. Finally the therapist may be seen as the parent and will be expected to see the martyrlike mother as dependent, helpless, and unchangeable, thus replacing the parentified child. However transference distortions may be manifested, the therapist must help family members understand as well as modify their relationships, thus facilitating the self-reinvesting process of mutual trust building.

According to Nagy, an understanding of behavior that will contribute to personal growth requires a consideration of the ethical dimension in human relationships. Modern psychoanalytic concepts of object relations and defense mechanisms and systems determinants are accepted, and are amplified by concepts involving existential indebtedness, merit imbalances, and loyalty obligations. While object relations theory seeks to explain the configuration of internalized objects and defense mechanisms, and systems approaches deal with patterns and hierarchy, a theory of relational ethics seeks to explain the motivating factors behind the use of defense mechanisms or cross-generational coalitions in terms of imbalances in the ledger. A new theory of motivation is thus created, in which behavior is not based solely on needs or internal drives, but on merit accounting and justice, or on what is owed both to the individual and by the individual. In seeking to integrate psychodynamic theory, systems theory, and existential philosophy, Nagy and Spark have succeeded in creating not only a new language to describe family dynamics, but a new theory with which to explain human behavior.

SUMMARY

The three major historical schools of family therapy are the psychodynamic, the multigenerational, and the intergenerational-contextual. The various workers who have independently contributed to the psychodynamic school can be grouped into four categories: position A therapists (those who retain a primary focus on the individual patient); therapists who have contributed specific techniques or conceptual formulations (the Philadelphia Psychiatric Center group, Epstein and his associates in his early work in Montreal, Norman Paul, Robin Skynner, and Clifford Sager); the approach of the pioneer family therapist Nathan Ackerman; the psychodynamic family therapists such as Dicks, Lecker, and Framo, who have extended object relations theory from the individual to relationships between individuals, first in terms of the marital relationship, and then in terms of the family. The multigenerational and intergenerational-contextual schools developed, respectively, through the work of Bowen and that of Boszormenyi-Nagy and associates.

All three schools conceptualize family dynamics and dysfunction in historical terms. The problems in any given nuclear family are seen as residing fundamentally in the lack of maturity of the individual marital partners, which in turn is a function of their relationships with their parents. This general proposition is described variously by the three schools as a lack of ego development because of the continued attachment to parental introjects, a lack of differentiation of self because of unresolved fusion with one's parents, or a fixed imbalance in one's ledger because of unsettled loyalty accounts with one's parents.

The pathology or symptoms in the family are seen as the result of an unsuccessful attempt of the marital partners to deal with their life problems. This abortive solution can result in symptoms in one of the partners, in their relationships to their parents, in their marital relationship, or in one or more of their children. In psychodynamic family therapy, dysfunction has been described in the marital relationship and in the involvement of one or more of the children through the concept of projective identification. In multigenerational theory, dysfunction has been described in one of the spouses, in the marital relationship, in one or more of the children ("family projection process"), or in relation to the grandparent generation ("emotional cutoffs"). In intergenerational-contextual theory, dysfunction has been described as a fixed loyalty imbalance that can affect *all* members of several generations of a family. It can take the form of a complete relational stagnation, or of a less crippling attempt at indirect mastery of the loyalty imbalance.

To a substantial degree, the three schools are in basic agreement with respect to their conceptualizations of family dynamics and dysfunction. With respect to therapy, they also generally agree that the approach should be directed to the more fundamental problem of lack of maturity in the parents, which is a function of their relationship with the grandparents; and that, consequently, therapy should ideally be long-term. Stylistic differences, however, can be seen in the manner in which these three schools approach the therapy situation. For example, Framo, working from a psychodynamic viewpoint, will attempt to defocus the identified child patient early in therapy. He will then work with the marital couple, preferably in a couples group, and hopefully including a family-of-origin conference late in treatment. Bowen, on the other hand, will exclude the child altogether from therapy and work exclusively with the couple. Though he will occasionally see couples in his highly structured form of multiple family therapy, he prefers to work with the individual couple. His work will be directed at coaching the individual marital partners as they attempt to differentiate themselves from their families of origin. Instead of family-of-origin conferences, he encourages visits to the parental home. Nagy and Spark, on the other hand, will tend to work with the entire nuclear family from the beginning. They will gradually push to include the grandparents in the therapy on an ongoing basis. This is consistent with their view that fixed imbalances in loyalty obligations affect all members of several generations of a family.

RESOURCES: CLINICAL EXAMPLES
OF THE HISTORICAL APPROACHES

I. *Psychodynamic Approaches*
  A. Ackerman
  1. Ackerman is one of four therapists participating in the Hillcrest Family Series (the others are Bowen, Jackson, & Whitaker). There are eight films in the series, in which one family's therapist consults with these four practitioners. Each one first conducts a half-hour consultation-assessment interview with the family and then discusses the family with the therapist who sought the consultation. The family is a "reconstituted" family. Father has custody of his two children from a previous marriage (a son, age 11, and a daughter, age 8). His son is the identified patient, with moderate behavior problems. Mother has a daughter from previous marriage. Together they have a son, 18 months of age. The films are available for rental or purchase from Psychological Cinema Register (Family Assessment Series), Audio-Visual Services, The Pennsylvania State University, University Park, PA 16802.
  2. Ackerman's book *Treating the troubled family* (1966), interweaves discussions of his conceptual approach with several case studies, which include verbatim records of interviews, with interpretive comments. The cases include: An exploratory interview with a family in crisis following the attempt of their previously well-adjusted 11-year-old daughter to stab her parents and older brother (Chapter 1); a consultation interview with a marital couple who, after six years, had not consummated their marriage (Chapter 6); a treatment interview with a family consisting of two parents and two 9-year-old fraternal twin sons, one of whom had attempted suicide (Chapter 7); an initial interview with two parents and their scapegoated, delinquent 14-year-old son (Chapter 8); and a case study and treatment interview with a family with a psychotic adolescent daughter (Chapter 9).
  3. The Ackerman Institute for Family Therapy (149 East 78th Street, New York, NY 10021—brochure available) has available for rental two case studies with Ackerman as therapist. *The enemy in myself* is a 50-minute composite of four interviews with the family with the suicidal son discussed in Chapter 7 of Ackerman's book (1966). *In and out of psychosis* is a 90-minute (two-reel) composite of interviews with the family with the psychotic daughter discussed in Chapter 9 of his book, and in Chapter 6 of Boszormenyi-Nagy and Framo (1965). Both case studies have been reviewed by Gladfelter (1972).
  4. Family Video Productions (Family Institute of Westchester, 147 Archer Avenue, Mt. Vernon, NY 10550) has available for rental a 60-minute tape, *Down on Jack Night,* consisting of excerpts with commentary from one interview of an eight-month treatment with the family of a troubled adolescent. The therapist is Norman Ackerman, Nathan's cousin, and their styles are similar. This tape was recently reviewed by Mendelsohn (1981).
  B. Framo
  1. Boston Family Institute (251 Harvard Street, Brookline, MA 02146

—brochure available) has available for rental or purchase two 60-minute tapes: *A couples group demonstration*; and *James Framo*, a tape in which Framo is interviewed about his life and work by Fred Duhl.

2. A report by Framo in Papp's collection (1977a) of case studies covers a full-length case study of the treatment of a marital couple whose problems were resolved in relation to their extended family.

C. Miscellaneous

1. The Ackerman Institute (see above address) also has available for rental *The initial interview*, a 30-minute tape in which Don Bloch and Ann Korelitz conduct a first session with a family of five, with commentary by Phoebe Prosky. This tape was recently reviewed by Greenberg (1979b). I have found that his tape goes particularly well with Franklin and Prosky's (1973) chapter on the initial interview.

2. A full-length case study of the work of C. Christian Beels with a family in which the father was the identified patient (borderline personality disorder) is in Papp (1977a).

3. The work of Norman Paul is available in two places. The Boston Family Institute (see above for address) has a 60-minute tape (for rental or purchase) in which Paul is interviewed about his life and work. And the Audio Visual Center of Indiana University (Bloomington, IN 47401) has available for rental *Trouble in the family*, a 90-minute film with excerpts from several sessions of the treatment of a middle-class family, with commentary by Ackerman.

4. Robin Skynner (1976) presents an outline of a 16-session course of treatment with a family with four children, in which the 14-year-old son was underachieving in school.

5. The work of Clifford Sager is available in two places. His book (Sager, 1976) includes a case study of his work with a marital couple in transition. Available for rental or purchase from the South Beach Psychiatric Center (777 Seaview Avenue, Staten Island, NY 10305—brochure available) is one tape, *Marital or sex therapy*, in which Sager demonstrates the clinical use of the marriage-contract concept.

II. *The Multigenerational Approach*

A. Bowen is one of the participants in the Hillcrest Family Series (see above).

B. The Georgetown University Family Center (4380 MacArthur Boulevard, NW, Washington, DC 20007—brochure available) has available for rental or purchase an extensive collection of tapes illustrating the theory and practice of Bowen's multigenerational approach. First, there are six tapes of hour-length didactic lectures by Bowen covering such aspects of his theory as triangles, differentiation of self, nuclear-family emotional system, family projection process, multigenerational transmission process, and symptom development in the family. Second, in a series of more advanced didactic tapes, Bowen is interviewed by Michael Kerr on the more subtle aspects of his theory. Titles include: *Family systems theory and therapy: An overview; The theoretical base of family systems theory; Systems therapy; Anxiety and emotional reactivity in therapy; Defining a self in one's family of origin, Part I and Part II; Issues in aging; The lawyer and the mental health expert in the courtroom; Obstacles to systems thinking; Family therapy with schizophrenia* (reviewed by Menn, 1981); *Background to systems thinking and disci-*

pleship; and *Emotional process in society.* And, finally, the following 11 clinical tapes are available (for rental only): *One year of family therapy with the same family; Focus on the extended family in family therapy; Differentiation in the three generational triangle; Psychotic reaction: A family system phenomenon; Towards resolution of the emotional attachment to the past generation; Toward differentiating a self in caring for aging parents; Divorcing family systems; The process of defining an "I position"; The family evaluation interview; Physical symptoms and aging from a family theory and therapy perspective;* and *The emotional cutoff: A clinical example.*

C. The Center for Family Learning (10 Hanford Avenue, New Rochelle, NY 10805—brochure available) has available for rental a collection of 12 tapes, both didactic and clinical, on the work of Bowen and (for the most part) two of his former students, Phillip Guerin and Thomas Fogarty. Introductory-level training tapes include *The genogram* (lecture), *A family evaluation interview* (interview), *On triangles* (lecture), *The child centered family* (lecture and interview), *Welcome back, Ted* (interview). Intermediate-level tapes include: *Therapeutic strategies and family typology* (lecture), *The clinical relevance of the multigenerational model* (excerpts of interviews), and *Marital conflict and the relevance of the extended family* (consultation interview). Advanced tapes include: *On closeness and emptiness* (lecture), *Lucille* (consultation interview), *Single parent family interview* (consultation interview), and *Family principles* (lecture). In addition, the Center publishes a journal, *The Family,* which is a good source of case studies using the multigenerational approach.

D. The South Beach Psychiatric Center (see above for address) has two Bowen tapes sets available for rental or purchase: *Schizophrenia as a multigenerational phenomenon* (lecture), and *Interview with a schizophrenic family* (interview plus discussion).

E. Elizabeth Carter has a full-length case study in Papp (1977a), concerning the long-term treatment of an Irish family with multiple instances of alcoholism over several generations. Additional case material can be found in Carter's and McGoldrick's (1980) book.

III. *The Intergenerational-Contextual Approach*

A. The Institute of Contextual Growth (126 S. Bethlehem Pike, Ambler, PA 19002) has available for rental or purchase a series of seven didactic and clinical videotapes illustrating the intergenerational-contextual approach of Nagy.

B. The South Beach Psychiatric Center (see above for address) has available for rental or purchase one set of tapes, *Consultation with a family,* in which Nagy conducts a consultation interview and discusses the family in the light of his theory.

C. Boszormenyi—Nagy and Spark present several case studies in their book *Invisible loyalties* (1973), including an extensive "reconstructive dialogue" of the treatment over three and one-half years of a family with two teenage daughters, one of whom was hospitalized following threats to kill herself or her father.

D. The Eastern Pennsylvania Psychiatric Institute (Henry Avenue and Abbottsford Road, Philadelphia, PA 19129) has a number of tapes of Nagy's earlier work. At press time, because of a reorganization that was under way, the institute was unable to supply a current list of its materials; a list is expected in due time.

The Structure/Process Model: Communicational, Structural, and Behavioral Schools of Family Therapy

The structure/process approaches to family therapy are concerned with the current patterns of interaction of the family, and with the relationship of these patterns to the symptoms or presenting problem of the identified patient. There is some variation among these schools in whether the interactional patterns are viewed from a structural or process perspective; whether the primary aim is to remove the symptom or change the structure; and whether the primary orientation is drawn from systems theory or from learning theory. But as a group, they differ sharply from the historical and experiential models. They differ from the historical approaches in several respects. The structure/process approaches are not concerned with the past, so there is no emphasis on history taking, although some approaches do take a history of the presenting problem. They are not concerned with traditional diagnostic procedures or categories, which are based on the assumption that the problems reside within the individual. They are not concerned with the intrapsychic life of the individual, or even with the shared unconscious life of the members of the family group. They are thus not concerned with uncovering unconscious dynamics through interpretation in order to achieve understanding or insight as a prerequisite for behavior change. Haley wrote:

> It is beginning to be argued by many family therapists that talking to family members about understanding each other is necessary because something

must be talked about and families expect this form of discussion, but that change really comes about through interactional processes set off when a therapist intervenes actively and directly in particular ways in a family system, and quite independently of the awareness of the participants about how they have been behaving. (Haley, 1971b, p. 7)

These approaches also differ from the experiential model in playing down the importance of affect in the treatment process.

The approach to therapy in the structure/process schools involves reordering the family system in order to remove the dysfunctional elements that produced or maintain the symptom. The therapist's role is that of expert whose job is to diagnose the dysfunctional elements of the system and plan a strategy, or series of interventions which will alleviate them. As a means toward this end, the therapist often uses directives, particularly paradoxical ones.

In their attributes, then, the structure/process approaches are *ahistorical,* with a focus on present interaction; *behavioral,* rather than insight-oriented or affective; and *interactional* (concerned with influencing interactional patterns), rather than intrapsychic or experiential; and they require of the therapist a *directive-mover style,* rather than reflective-follower, interpretive, or "coach" style.

The structure/process model includes a growing number of schools, among them:

Communication systems (Jackson, Haley, Satir, Watzlawick, Weakland)
Problem-solving therapy (Haley)
Brief therapy (Watzlawick, Weakland, Bodin, and Fisch)
Structural family therapy (Minuchin)
Paradoxical therapy (Palazzoli)
Triadic therapy (Zuk, 1971b)
Problem-centered systems therapy (the McMaster model—Epstein & Bishop, 1981)
Integrative family therapy (Duhl & Duhl, 1981)
Strategic therapy (Rabkin and others)
Structural/strategic therapy (Stanton, 1981; Andolfi, 1980)
Behavioral family therapy (Stuart, Patterson, Liberman, and others)
Functional family therapy (Barton & Alexander, 1981).

In addition, although not identified with a specific school, the following individuals have made significant contributions to the model: Gregory Bateson, Milton Erickson, Peggy Papp, and Lynn Hoffman.

Because of space limitations it is impossible to discuss all these approaches; some reference citations, however, are given above. The focus of this chapter will be (1) the communication systems school and its derivatives (emphasizing problem-solving and brief therapies, but with brief comments on several others); (2) the structural school; and (3) the behavioral school. In regard to the behavioral school, the concern here will be the application of behavioral theory and techniques to conjoint family and marital therapy. (The application of behavioral methods to the training of family members, either to be caregivers to a disturbed child or to improve marital relationships, will be discussed in Chapter 9.)

THE COMMUNICATIONAL SCHOOL
AND ITS DERIVATIVES

The communicational school originated on the West Coast. It grew out of Bateson's research project on communication and was based at the Mental Research Institute (MRI), founded in Palo Alto, California, in 1959, under the leadership of Jackson. Satir joined during the first year. She was followed three years later by Haley, Weakland, and Watzlawick. In the same year, MRI and Ackerman's New York–based Family Institute cofounded *Family Process,* the first professional journal of the field.

Communication remained the central concern of the MRI group. The original formulation of the double bind, derived by applying Russell's theory of logical types (Whitehead & Russell, 1910) to the behavior of schizophrenic patients, was extended to a more general concern with Russellian paradox, both as a pathogenic factor in family communication and as a therapeutic maneuver (the "therapeutic double bind" or "counterparadox").

In the early and middle 1960s, MRI enjoyed a reputation as a leading center in the development of family therapy, housing three of the principal pioneers in the field: Jackson, Haley, and Satir. Foley (1974), for example, includes these three individuals along with Ackerman and Bowen as the "seminal theorists of family therapy." He characterized all three as being concerned with communication, but differentiated their particular emphases. He described Jackson as concerned with communication and cognition, Haley with communication and power, and Satir with communication and feelings. Actually, Jackson's and Haley's approaches are fairly similar to each other. Both can be seen as rather clear-cut representatives of the structure/process model, whereas Satir's approach diverged from theirs at a fundamental point—namely, the frame of reference that they applied to the findings that family members send messages that are discrepant at different levels. Whereas Jackson and Haley viewed this discrepant communication within the Batesonian-Russellian frame of reference as paradoxical communication, Satir interpreted these double-level messages from the humanistic perspective. This perspective, which was blossoming at the time on the West Coast in the form of the "growth" or "human potential" movement, was influenced by Rogerian thinking, with its concepts of congruence and self-concept. Thus, Satir (1967, 1972) thought of the double-level message as incongruent communication and described the origin of incongruent styles of communication in the low self-esteem of the person who adopts them.

In the second half of the 1960s MRI lost these three leaders of the field of family therapy. Haley left to work with Minuchin at the Philadelphia Child Guidance Clinic. Satir left to become the first director of training at the Esalen Institute in Big Sur, California. And, in 1968, Jackson died at the age of 48. With the loss of these major figures, the importance of MRI receded until the mid-1970s, when its Brief Therapy Center became known for a refined form of the early communication approach to family therapy. This brief, problem-focused therapy was developed by Weakland, Fisch, Watzlawick, and Bodin (1974). It shares many elements with Haley's problem-solving therapy (1976), developed while he was at Philadelphia Child Guidance Center and, later, at his Family Therapy Institute in Washington, D.C.

These are the main elements of the multiple contributions of this very creative center, but not all of them. (For a thorough discussion of the contributions of MRI, consult Bodin, 1981). The rest of this section will discuss, in turn, the approaches of Jackson, Haley, and the Brief Therapy Center at MRI.

The Family Interactional Perspective of Don D. Jackson

Jackson laid the foundation for the communicational approach to the family by developing a cybernetic model of family function, dysfunction, and therapeutic change. The central concepts in his work are family homeostasis, redundancies and rules, the marital *quid pro quo,* punctuation, and the therapeutic double bind.

Family homeostasis. Jackson was one of the first to make the observation that when the identified patient improved (in individual therapy), another member of the family began to express symptoms. For example, he reported that the improvement in the depression of a married woman was accompanied by the deterioration of her husband, eventuating in his suicide; that the successful treatment of another married woman's sexual unresponsiveness was associated with the development of impotence by her husband; and the initial responsiveness to therapy of a young woman with anorexia nervosa was accompanied by her husband's development of a duodenal ulcer (Jackson, 1957).

These observations and others of a similar nature led Jackson to develop the notion of family homeostasis. Utilizing general systems theory, he conceived of the family as a homeostatic system, capable of a limited range of behavioral possibilities, and governed by negative (deviation-counteracting) feedback. This latter, cybernetic property of family systems occurs because "people function as 'governors' in relation to each other by reacting in 'error-activated' ways to each other's behavior" (Haley, 1963, p. 189). The behavior of the husbands described in the preceeding paragraph, in becoming symptomatic as their wives improved, are examples of negative feedback carried to the extreme (and failing). Haley (1963) gives a less extreme example: The wife, who is usually calm and rarely raises her voice, begins to scream and cry at the dinner table. The husband starts to weep, complaining that he cannot deal with her needs at this time because of the pressures he is under at work. The wife stops shouting and becomes calm, and moves to support her husband. The "status quo" has been homeostatically reestablished.

Redundancies and rules.   Given the homeostatic nature of the family systems, and the consequently limited range of allowable behavior, it follows that certain communicational sequences will recur with regularity. These recurring interactional patterns, or "redundancies," are the result of the continuing process of interaction, in which family members act as governors in relation to each other's behavior. These redundancies reflect the "rules" of the family system (Jackson, 1965b). The term *rules* is meant in a "case-law" sense: Rules are the product of the ongoing development of family relationships (rather than an *a priori* set of laws established in advance to govern family interaction). The concept of rules is also understood metaphorically: That is, family members are thought to behave *as if* such and such were the rule or expectation for their behavior. Rules are thus low-order inferences obtained from observing the repetitions in the family's interaction.

The marital quid pro quo.   The marital *quid pro quo* (literally, something for something) is a general rule that describes the foundation of the marital relationship. The marital *quid pro quo* consists of a set of implicit and explicit expectations that the spouses have of each other, built up over years of communicational exchanges. *Quid pro quo* arrangements may be either *symmetrical,* with spouses tending to mirror each other's behavior (for example, "I'll support you, then you support me" or "It's your turn to wash the dishes, I did it last night"), or *complementary,* with spouses taking differentiated roles ("I'll wash the dishes and cook if you discipline the children and bring home the bacon").

Punctuation.   This concept was discussed in Chapter 1. Spouses (or other family members) will often describe their interactional patterns in very different ways. For example, the husband might say, "My wife nags me, and therefore I find something else to do—watch TV or read the paper." The wife might say, "My husband never spends any time with me; he's always reading the paper or watching TV. Therefore I get irritated with him, and let him know about it." What is happening is that each spouse punctuates the sequence in a different manner. They are each caught in the trap of thinking that there is a linear causal relationship between one's behavior and that of the other, and cannot see the overall circular causality built into their interaction pattern: . . . wife nags, husband withdraws, wife nags, husband withdraws, wife nags . . . .

The therapeutic double bind.   Jackson's approach to intervention involved a set of methods designed to unbalance the circular and repetitive patterns of the homeostatic family system, particularly those patterns that either produced, maintained, or were—in and of themselves—the presenting problem. This was conceptualized as the introduction of positive (deviation-amplifying) feedback into the family system (Hoffman, 1971), which would produce a "runaway." Basically this involved introducing some incongruity into the therapeutic situation in such a way that people have to change their previous patterns of interaction in order to deal with it. That is, the family is placed in a "therapeutic double bind." The general class of paradoxical interventions was developed considerably after Jackson's death, and will be discussed in more detail below. It is sufficient to note here that the types of paradoxical interventions described by Jackson include prescribing the symptom, *reductio ad absurdum* (exaggerating the symptom), and relabeling. The main point to be made is that Jackson laid the theoretical foundation—using general systems theory—for this general class of interventions. A more detailed review of the contributions of Jackson can be found in Greenberg (1977).

Problem-Solving Therapy (Jay Haley)

Haley's problem-solving therapy (1976b) emphasizes obtaining a clear statement of the problem and an accurate picture of the interactional sequences that maintain it. From this, goals are set with the family, and the therapist designs a strategic series of interventions (directives) that meet the goals by both eliminating the problem and changing the sequences of interaction.

Establishing the family diagnosis.   The first interview is designed to both establish the therapeutic contract and to provide the therapist with sufficient information to formulate the family diagnosis and general strategy for change. There are four stages in the first interview: (1) the social stage, in which the family is welcomed and made comfortable; (2) the statement-of-problem stage, in which each family member is asked for his or her view on the problem; (3) the interaction stage, in which the therapist moves to the periphery and asks the family to talk with one another; (4) the goal-setting stage, in which the family is asked to specify the changes sought from therapy.

The diagnosis is developed from studying the relationship between the symptom or presenting problem and the repetitive interactional sequences or redundancies observed in the family. Symptoms are, first of all, seen as metaphors of the family situation. Haley provides an example of a man who enters therapy because of his fear of a heart attack. He has been checked out by numerous physicians, and no organic basis for his complaint has been found. The therapist should thus examine how the "heart analogy is built into the person's ecology" (1976b, p. 91). He may observe that there are numerous rules organized with reference to the father's "heart condition": The father's job and his performance are regulated by his symptoms; the children must be quiet in order to avoid upsetting father; sexual intimacies can only occur under certain conditions lest he overtax his heart; arguments must be avoided . . . and so on.

Haley also observed that the redundant interactional sequences reflect the family's hierarchical structure. (Parenthetically, this observation is reflective both of Haley's concern with both communication and power, noted by Foley (1974), and of the years he spent collaborating with Minuchin at the Philadelphia Child Guidance Center.) One observes the sequences in order to map the hierarchy. Symptoms reflect a confusion of the hierarchical structure, and they can be seen as an effort to solve the family's organizational problems. The particular types of organizational problems that are of concern are cross-generational coalitions, which may involve either two or three generations.

The typical two-generation coalition consists of the intense involvement of one parent (usually the mother) with a child, and it regularly includes *and* excludes the second parent (usually the father). This situation can be mapped, using structural notations, as shown in Figure 5-1.

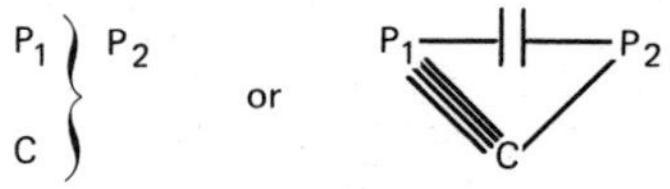

FIGURE 5-1

The interactional sequence that expresses this organizational problem often consists of the following moves:

1. P_1 is in an intense relationship with C, with both positive and negative elements, which are expressed by P_1 as affection and exasperation toward C.
2. C acts up, expressing the symptomatic behavior.
3. P_1 calls in P_2 to assist.
4. P_2 moves in to deal with the situation.
5. P_1 criticizes P_2 for not dealing with the situation competently. P_1 may attack P_2 directly or threaten separation.
6. P_2 withdraws.
7. P_1 and C resume their intense relationship, expressing a mixture of affection and exasperation, until they again reach an impasse.

The typical three-generational coalition occurs in a one-parent family situation consisting of grandmother, mother, and child, where grandmother is defined as dominating, mother as irresponsible, and the child as a behavior problem. This situation can be mapped as shown in Figure 5-2.

FIGURE 5-2

The interactional sequence that expresses this organizational problem often consists of the following moves:

1. Gm cares for C while complaining of M's irresponsibility.
2. M withdraws, letting Gm take care of C.
3. C acts up.
4. Gm protests. She should not have to discipline C; M should do this.
5. M steps in to take care of C.
6. Gm criticizes M for not dealing with the situation competently, and steps in to rescue C from M.
7. M withdraws, letting Gm take care of C.
8. C acts up.

Haley observed that this interactional sequence is also descriptive of a variety of organizational problems, both in and outside of the family context. These include: the relationships between mother, parental child, and problem child in a single-parent family; the relationships between therapist, mother, and problem child in long-term individual (child-focused) psychotherapy; the relationships between supervisor, student-clinician, and client in the clinical training situation; and the relationships between the professional staff member, the paraprofessional staff member (or ward attendant), and the client in the mental health outpatient (or inpatient) setting. These situations are mapped in Figure 5-3.

M $\}$	Th $\}$	Supervisor $\}$	Professional $\}$
$\}$ PC	$\}$ M	$\}$ Student	$\}$ Paraprofessional (Attendant)
C $\}$	C $\}$	Client $\}$	Client $\}$

FIGURE 5-3

Formulating the treatment strategy.   Once the problem is clearly defined and the interactional sequence maintaining the problem is identified, the therapist formulates a treatment strategy, consisting of an overall plan for a series of tactical interventions, called directives. (It should be noted in passing that like Haley's concern with hierarchical structure, his emphasis on this mode of intervention is reflective of his concern with communication and power. It also reflects his long association with the late Milton Erickson, the directive therapist and hypnotist. The topic of Erickson's approach and contributions to the field of therapy is, unfortunately, one that will not be covered here, because of space limitations. The interested reader, however, is referred to Haley, 1973, and Zeig, 1980.)

Directives serve several functions. First, they are tactical maneuvers designed to change both the presenting problem and the underlying interactional sequences. Second, they intensify the therapeutic relationship. Directives may be initiated in the therapy session, but are usually tasks which must be accomplished between sessions, which keeps the therapy alive. Third, they provide additional information about the family, particularly in regard to the degree and nature of their resistance (for example, whether they carry out the directive, to what degree they accomplish it, what excuses are offered if they fail to carry it out).

Directives are of two types: straight and paradoxical. Straight directives are given when the therapist wants the family to do what the directive says. This is useful in crisis situations, where the family homeostasis is destabilized. In these situations, the directive functions as negative (deviation-counteracting) feedback. Haley points out that it is easier to get someone to do something differently than it is to get someone else to stop doing something, and also that specific directives for new behavior are much more effective than "good advice" (such as "being considerate of each other"). Haley also points out the importance of properly motivating the family to follow the directive (that is, by reviewing previous efforts they have made to solve the problem on their own, emphasizing each as a failure with the punctuation "and that failed too"), of carefully designing the directive to fit the unique characteristics of each family, of involving everyone (even if a given individual's role is merely to observe and report back), and of setting up an accountability structure (the "task report," which takes place at the succeeding meeting, during which the family reports on the outcome of the task). For example, a directive for a two-generational problem, in which father sides with eneuretic daughter against his wife, would require that father wash the sheets when daughter wets the bed. This would tend to disengage father and daughter. A directive for a three-generational problem, in which grandmother sides with grandchild against mother, would require the grandchild to engage in minor misbehavior in order to irritate grandmother, and require the mother to defend her daughter against the grandmother. This would foster an alliance between mother and daughter, weakening the attachment of grandmother to grandchild.

Paradoxical directives are given when the goal is for the family to oppose the therapist. These directives are useful in stuck situations or with more resistant families, and they function as positive (deviation-amplifying) feedback. Another way of viewing paradoxical directives is as a therapeutic analogue of the Japanese martial art *aikido,* which teaches one to not directly confront one's opponent with counterforce, but rather to utilize the opponent's own momentum or force to bring about the defeat.

Haley (1976b) discusses several types of paradoxical directives. For the family as a whole, Haley suggests directives that advise against changing, a tactic known as "restraining." For example, a family with a school-phobic son might be cautioned against attempting to remedy the situation. It might be pointed out that it would upset the family if the boy suddenly started going to school. When this tactic works, the family changes in order to prove the therapist wrong. Under these circumstances, Haley recommends that the therapist both give the family credit by expressing surprise that the change happened, and "predict a relapse," saying that the change is only temporary and will not continue. The family will then stabilize the change, again in order to prove the therapist wrong.

With a dyad or individual family member, Haley suggests "prescribing the symptom." A provocative child may be asked to provoke his parents for the next week. If he does so, the parents will react differently because he has been told to do so by the therapist. More likely, he will not do so, which changes both symptom and sequence. In prescribing the symptom, it's often best to ask for more extreme behavior than the client is already doing, a tactic known as *reductio ad absurdum* or "exaggerating the symptom." An overprotective mother may be asked to watch over her child carefully all week and, in addition, to spend an hour with him discussing the perils of life. Sometimes it is effective to ask that the symptom occur in a particular manner and at a particular time, a technique known as "symptom scheduling" (Newton, 1968). A couple who presents with marital discord characterized by repetitive fighting may be asked to have a fight at a set time for a specific amount of time, say two hours.

In general, the types of paradoxical directives discussed by Haley involve asking the family members to stay the same, in a context that is defined as helping them to change, in order to counter their resistance. This is one general class of paradoxical directives, which will be placed in a broader context in the discussion below. At this point, however, it is necessary to issue a caution. Paradoxical maneuvers are advanced therapeutic techniques. It takes considerable skill, developed through supervised practice, both to sensitively design and to competently implement paradoxical procedures. When not handled well, paradoxical directives can have serious consequences, including congealing the resistance of the family to entertaining further notions of change.

Directives, whether paradoxical or straight, are basically tactical maneuvers within an overall therapeutic strategy. Haley reminds us that therapeutic change does not occur in a uniform progression, and that it cannot be made in a single leap. Rather, therapy occurs through a series of stages. Often the process involves the creation of a new malfunctioning structure as a halfway step.

Haley illustrates the process of therapy in stages by discussing the approaches to resolving the two-generational coalition depicted above in Figure 5-3. One approach is through the peripheral parent, which in this case is the father. This approach has three stages. In the first stage, the therapist works with the father and the son, and the mother is shifted to the periphery, creating the new malfunctioning structure. In the second stage, the therapist works with the mother and father, while the child is defocused and is enabled to participate in age-appropriate activities. In the third stage, the therapist disengages, leaving the couple involved with each other, and the child involved with peers. The videotaped case study *A modern Little Hans* (available from the Philadelphia Child Guidance Center) illustrates this approach. In this case, the presenting problem was the dog phobia of the eight-year-old son. The mother was the expert on the son's problem, and the father was peripheral, working two jobs and staying uninvolved in family life. In the first stage, the father, a mail carrier and a presumed expert on dogs, was asked to teach his son how to deal with dogs. In the second stage, the therapist directed the mother and father to go away for a weekend together as a reward for their son's recovery. This prompted the couple to work on their marital difficulties. In the final stage, the therapist disengaged.

Ethical considerations. Haley (1976b) gives considerable attention to the ethical issues raised by his approach, particularly the question of "manipulation." In his view, all therapeutic approaches involve interpersonal influence and manipulation, whether acknowledged or denied. Hence he considers the charges of manipulation that have been directed at his approach to therapy to be baseless. To him, a more cogent ethical issue is the degree to which a therapeutic approach addresses and resolves the presenting problems of the client or family. Therapists have set themselves up as experts and accept money for their services; they are thus obligated to use their expertise in a cost-efficient manner to help solve the presenting problem. Disregarding the family's presenting problem or attempting to sell them another goal, such as achieving insight, is in Haley's view unethical. He argues that often people have excellent insight into what their problems are, but are helpless to solve them. The therapist's expertise must be directed toward helping them do so.

Brief Therapy
(Watzlawick, Weakland, Fisch, Bodin)

Brief therapy, as developed at the Mental Research Institute is, if anything, more problem-focused than Haley's approach. Brief therapy is limited to a maximum of 10 sessions, with the goal being the resolution of the presenting problem. As with Haley, problems are conceptualized in an interactive and communicational frame of reference, but MRI brief therapy also has a particular orientation toward problems—namely, problems are seen as the result of prior unsuccessful attempts to solve a given difficulty. Also, like Haley's tactics, the interventions used are directive and emphasize the paradoxical method. Brief therapy, however, emphasizes a particular class of paradoxical interventions known as "reframing," which consist of redefining the frame of reference within which the family has conceptualized its problem and attempted its solution. Underlying these differences from Haley's approach is the fact that whereas Haley emphasized the power or control dimension, Watzlawick and his associates tend to emphasize the cognitive or meaning dimension.

Theoretical foundation.   The theoretical foundation for brief therapy derives from a consideration of the problem of persistence and change in human affairs, as captured in the French proverb

Plus ça change, plus c'est la même chose

or, "the more things change, the more they remain the same." A theoretical formulation of the problem of persistence and change is derived by extrapolation from two mathematical-philosophical theories: the theory of groups and the theory of logical types (Watzlawick, Weakland, & Fisch, 1974).

Group theory, originated by the French mathematician Galois in 1832, in its fundamentals concerns the relationships between members of a group or class. Four rules, or group properties, describe these relationships:

1. Any *combination* of members of a group will be a member of the group (for example, if the members of the group are the hours of the day, any combination of two or more members is again a member of the group). "Combination" can refer to addition, subtraction, or whatever combination rule applies to the group. Thus, no member or combination of members of a group can place itself outside of the group.
2. One can change the *sequence* of operations performed on members of the group without changing the result (for instance, using the clock example, 9:00 a.m. plus 3 hours plus 5 hours is the same as 9:00 a.m. plus 5 hours plus 3 hours, namely 5:00 p.m.). Thus, the manner in which a sequence of interactions in a family system is punctuated is arbitrary; the end result will be a restoration of the family homeostasis.
3. All groups contain an *identity number,* which, when combined with another member of the group yields that member (for example in groups that have an additive combination rule, the identity member is *zero*: $3 + 0 = 3$. In

groups that have a multiplicative combination rule, the identity member is *one*: 3 X 1 = 3.) Thus, in such cases a member of a group may act without making any change whatsoever.

4. Every member of the group has an *opposite or reciprocal member,* such that the combination of the member with its opposite yields the identity member (for example, in groups with an additive combination rule, 3 + (−3) = 0; and, in groups with a multiplicative combination rule, 3 X $\frac{1}{3}$ = 1). Thus, although a change from one member of a group to another may appear to be extreme (that is, from day to night, black to white, Nazism to Communism), nothing may have changed at all.

Group theory thus provides a framework for understanding the situation where "the more things change the more they remain the same"; that is, changes that in effect yield no substantive change can be seen as operations that take place *within* the frame of reference of a group, or class, or system. The theory of logical types, on the other hand, provides a framework for understanding changes that *transcend* the frame of reference of the group, or class, or system.

The *theory of logical types,* developed by Whitehead and Russell (1910), was mentioned above, in Part I. This theory highlights the difference in logical type, or level of abstraction, between a member of a group, or class, and the class itself. The class exists at a higher level of abstraction than the members of the class. The class of all trees is not, itself, a tree, but rather a conceptual model used for categorizing the individual objects as either "tree" or "not-tree." Not only does the class exist at a higher level of abstraction, but it also functions differently from its members. That is, the whole is greater than, and qualitatively different from, the sum of its parts. For example, the behavior of a species in adapting to the survival challenges of overpopulation is of a very different order than, and may in this instance be contradictory to, the survival behavior of individual members of the species.

Watzlawick and his colleagues use the analogy of an automobile with a standard shift to describe the transition from one logical type to the next. Within any given gear, the car has a specified range of performance capability. Any specific performance output within this range can be achieved by the appropriate use of the gas pedal. Shifting gears provides the driver with a new range of performance capability, and thus is an intervention of a higher logical type than using the gas pedal.

Watzlawick and his group emphasize that, in order to avoid confusion or paradox, it is necessary to be clear which logical type—the class, or a member of the class—is being referred to; and, also, that the transition from one level to the next higher level involves a transformation of considerable theoretical importance, since it provides a way *out* of a system or frame of reference.

Thus, group theory and the theory of logical types are complementary theories. Whereas group theory illuminates the types of changes that can occur in a system that itself remains constant, the theory of logical types gives us a frame of reference for understanding the kind of change that changes the system. Watzlawick and his associates (1974, p. 10) refer to the first type of change as "first-order change," and the second type as "second-order change." In applying this conceptual model to family therapy, it can be seen that many of the changes a dysfunctional family may go through in their own attempts to solve their problems are first-order changes, whereas successful therapy would aim for second-order change.

Problem formation. Watzlawick and his co-workers make a distinction between difficulties and problems. Difficulties are either things that can be resolved by using common sense (for example, the application of the opposite member according to group property *4,* as when the heat is turned up in order to warm a cold room, or when children are punished in order to make them behave); or they are things that cannot be resolved and simply must be lived with (such as the "generation gap," or a certain incidence of alcoholism in the population). Problems, on the other hand, are impasses, deadlocks, and knots that are created by the mishandling of difficulties. There are three general categories of problems.

The first category is called the *terrible simplifications.* In this situation, action is necessary but is not taken. The difficulty is treated as if it did not exist. In terms of group theory, this is the introduction of the identity member, which, according to group property *3,* produces zero first-order change. This type of problem is often seen in families with a schizophrenic member, such as the skewed families described by Lidz and associates (1957a), or the pseudomutual families described by Wynne and associates (1958), (see above, Chapter 2). In these families the initial difficulty (for example, conflict between family members) is compounded and transformed into a problem by the act of collusively denying that the difficulty exists. Any attempt to acknowledge the initial difficulty is attacked and is treated as an instance of "madness" or "badness" (Laing, 1965).

The second category is called the *utopian syndrome.* In this situation, action is taken when it should not be. The intervenors try to change a difficulty that is either unchangeable or nonexistent. In terms of group theory, if terrible simplification is the introduction of zero, utopia is the introduction of infinity, which Watzlawick and his colleagues consider to be a special case of group property *4.* The problem consists of accepting a premise that the ideal state of reality is more real than how things actually are. Within this frame of reference, first-order change is attempted, typically by applying the opposite member according to group property *4,* when second-order change is required (that is, leaving the frame of reference within which the ideal premise is accepted). The attempt at change then becomes a problem in its own right. For example, the prohibition era was based on a large-scale acceptance of the utopian premise that alcoholism could be eradicated by making it illegal to consume alcoholic beverages. Of course prohibition did not succeed in its goal, but rather, it made things much worse: the incidence of alcoholism increased, a whole industry was handed over to the criminal sector of our society, the quality of alcohol was decontrolled, leading to the distribution of inferior or harmful products, which in turn created public health problems.

The utopian syndrome has several variations. The "introjective" form results when the unattainability of utopian goals is taken as a sign of personal failure and inadequacy. The result is painful personal distress leading to severe depression with suicidal potential. The "procrastination" form is less serious. In this situation, the goal is recognized as large and thus the journey to reach it is expected to take a long time. Examples of this include the perpetual student, the perfectionist, and the "ne'er-do-well." In the "projective" form, the utopian blames significant others for personal failure to achieve perfection of some sort. In the extreme case this takes the form of a paranoid psychosis.

Watzlawick and his associates argue that many approaches to therapy have utopian goals, such as differentiation of self, genital organization, and self-actualization. They further assert that the more limited, problem-focused approach is more humane:

> From the foregoing, one arrives at the disturbing possibility that the limits of a responsible and humane psychotherapy may be much narrower than is generally thought. Lest therapy become its own pathology, it must limit itself to the relief of suffering; the quest for happiness cannot be its task. (Watzlawick et al., 1974, p. 57)

The third category of problems is *paradox*. In this situation, action is taken at the wrong level. An error in discriminating logical types occurs, and a "game without end" is established. This can occur in two ways. In the first way, first-order change is attempted when only second-order change will do. Watzlawick and his colleagues provide an example of a marital couple, in which the wife feels the husband is not being sufficiently open for her to know where she stands with him. She may attempt to get the information she seeks by asking questions and observing his behavior. He may then feel intruded on and respond by attempting to show her that she doesn't need to know all this information. He might choose to withhold even innocuous statements from her as a result. She may then escalate even more, feeling that there must be something wrong if he is not telling her certain things. This couple is on the way to a serious problem that is the result of their attempted solutions. Each feels he or she can modify the behavior of the other by applying the opposite member (group property *4*), which produces zero second-order change. What is needed is second-order change, in which the couple changes the rules of their relationship through metacommunication.

In the second way of establishing a game without end, second-order change is demanded when first-order change would have been sufficient. For example, a mother may demand that her son *want* to go to bed on time. It is not enough that he simply go to bed on time; he might be doing so because "he was forced" (a change in behavior induced by the appropriate application of the opposite member, thus first-order change) rather than because "he really wants to be good" (a second-order change in attitude). The endless quality of the game thus established is seen when one reflects on the "undecidability" of the son's behavior in this situation. If the son *wants* to go to bed on time, is he doing so because his mother demanded that he want to do so?

The above example is a specific case of a more general type of problem, namely, the "be spontaneous! paradox." This paradox is not only at the root of innumerable interactional problems between parents and children or spouses (which follow the paradigm of the above example), but it also is the cause of certain types of personal problems, wherein one attempts to bring about a change in oneself through the action of "willpower," and the desired change is one that can only occur spontaneously. The very attempt to control the natural process is the essence of the pathology. Examples of this include the insomniac, whose attempts to force himself to go to sleep produce only more wakefulness; and persons suffering from sexual problems such as impotence or inorgasmia, whose attempts to have a good sexual experience only insure that it will not happen.

Problem resolution.   In therapy, problem resolution occurs through a process of second-order change. Second-order change is directed at what appeared to the client or family to be the solution to their difficulties—which, as discussed above, is the chief source of the problem. The major technique for achieving second-order change is "reframing," whereby the family is taken out of the frame of reference within which they have misconstrued their difficulties and have launched abortive attempts to solve them.

To illustrate the application of second-order change, suppose an event *(x)* is imminent and undesirable. Common sense would suggest avoiding *(x)* by its opposite *(not-x)*, which would result in a first-order-change "solution." As long as the solution is sought within the dichotomy of *(x)* and *(not-x)*, one is caught in an "illusion of alternatives." Second-order change is not *(x)* but also not *(not-x)*. It rejects the idea that one must choose, and it jumps to the next higher logical level, to deal with the class (all alternatives) rather than with just one member (one or the other alternative).

Reframing is a maneuver that, operating at the "meta" or next-higher logical level in relationship to an item, changes the membership of the item from one class to another. Because class membership is a conceptual category (often with associated affects), to reframe "means to change the conceptual and/or emotional setting or viewpoint in relation to which a situation is experienced and to place it in another frame which fits the 'facts' of the same concrete situation equally well or even better, and thereby changes its entire meaning" (Watzlawick et al., 1974, p. 95). Tom Sawyer demonstrated the successful application of this technique when he reframed the whitewashing of the fence from an experience of drudgery to one of pleasure. Watzlawick and his colleagues describe the case of a man with a very bad stammer who was required by circumstances to take up a career as a salesperson. His situation was reframed from one of certain failure by virtue of his handicap to one in which his handicap was viewed as a special advantage, by pointing out to him that whereas salespersons are often disliked for the slick, glib quality of their sales pitch, people will listen patiently and with sympathy to someone with a speech handicap.

Watzlawick and his associates (1974) describe in detail 12 specific maneuvers for resolving the problems that clients and families bring in to therapy, particularly those engendered by their prior "solutions." The emphasis is on reframing procedures, although tactics such as restraining, prescribing the symptom, and exaggerating the symptom are also used. Just a few of their techniques will be discussed here. For more detail, the reader is referred to their excellent book.

For the utopian situation, Watzlawick and his colleagues point out that it is useless to counter the unrealistic goals with common sense, since common sense is the reciprocal member, which, according to group property *4,* leads to the identity member, and to a first-order-change impasse. Instead, they recommend the tactic of encouraging and even exaggerating the utopian's inflated goals and expectations.

For problems involving the counterproductive application of willpower (variants of the be spontaneous! paradox, self-imposed), they recommend paradoxical procedures that redirect the client's effort to control the problem. For example, a client who is attempting to conceal a socially embarrassing handicap, such as fear of public speaking, nervous tremors, or blushing, is advised to advertise rather than hide the handicap. Insomniacs are instructed to keep their eyes open until sleep befalls them. The treatment of sexual dysfunctions, such as impotence and inorgasmia involves, in part, instructing the client and his or her mate to be in an amorous situation and avoid having sexual relations (see Chapter 8).

Watzlawick and his associates describe a technique they call "making overt the covert," in which, for example, a spouse is made aware of her contribution to marital fights that result in her husband getting out of control. Although this technique differs from psychoanalytic interpretation in several important respects (that is, it promotes awareness about an interactional sequence rather than an intrapsychic event, it focuses on the present rather than on the past, it does not utilize concepts such as unconscious and repression), it stands as an interesting contrast to Haley's frame of reference, in which the promotion of awareness of any kind is specifically avoided. This contrast derives from certain basic differences between the two approaches, which have been mentioned above—namely, that Haley emphasizes the power dimension and uses techniques that unbalance the stuck system, whereas Watzlawick and his group emphasize the meaning dimension, utilizing methods that change the meaning of the situation, an orientation that allows the facilitation of awareness under certain circumstances. These differences also represent two general approaches to the use of paradoxical interventions—on the one hand, as a therapeutic form of *aikido* designed to overcome the family's resistance (accentuating the power dimension); and on the other hand, as a method for reordering a family's conceptual categories (accentuating the meaning dimension). While similar tactics may be used in either approach, they are used within a somewhat different theoretical matrix, and with differing intended objectives. Paradox, a technique in use by many therapists in addition to Haley and the MRI group, has been the subject of several recent review articles and compilations. For further detail, see Weeks and L'Abate (1978, 1979) and Soper and L'Abate (1977).

Recent Applications of the Communicational Approach

The communicational approach has been successfully exported to practitioners and centers that did not participate in its origination, a fact testifying to the robustness of the approach. A brief overview of these applications and elaborations of the method will be provided in this section.

The Milan group.   In Italy, Mara Selvini Palazzoli and her colleagues—Gianfranco Cecchin, Giuiana Prata and Luigi Boscolo—at the Milan Centre of Family Studies have developed a version of the communicational approach. Palazzoli, originally trained as a psychoanalyst, became discouraged with the poor efficacy of conventional psychotherapy for her anorectic patients. She began to utilize the communicational approach with families of anorectic patients in 1967, and was greatly encouraged by the rapid and long-lasting remissions that she was able to achieve (Palazzoli, 1978). In 1971, she turned her attention to the application of this method with families of schizophrenic patients. The approach she and her colleagues have developed has been described in a recent book (Palazzoli, Cecchin, Prata, & Boscolo, 1978). The goals of the approach are broader than those of the other communicational approaches. Whereas MRI's brief therapy is focused on resolving the presenting problem, and Haley's problem-solving therapy attempts to resolve both the presenting problem and the interactional sequences that maintain it, Selvini Palazzoli conceptualizes schizophrenia in a holistic/systemic fashion as an overall pattern of interaction of the family (the "schizophrenic transaction") and aims the therapy at the resolution of this overall pattern. Her goals are thus closer to those of the structural school.

The approach of the Milan group is described as "long brief" therapy, which consists of 10 sessions held at monthly intervals. A male-female co-therapy team meets with the family, while the other two members of the group provide live supervision through one-way mirrors. For most of the session the goals are diagnostic: to gather information about the transactional patterns of the family. During this period the co-therapists refrain from commenting to the family about their observations. Toward the end of the session the co-therapists leave the treatment room to confer with their colleagues and design a prescription, which is then presented to the family at the close of the session. The prescriptions are usually paradoxical and emphasize "positive connotation," a form of reframing in which the affective valence of a situation is changed from negative to positive.

Brief therapy for couples.   Peggy Papp, at the Ackerman Family Institute, has developed a form of brief therapy for use with couples groups, which blends the MRI communicational approach with "family choreography," a form of family sculpture (Papp, 1976a, 1976b. See Chapter 8 for further discussion of sculpture and of couples groups). The couples meet in groups of four couples for 12 sessions.

In the first session, they choreograph their relationships. Choreography is an analogic and kinetic mode of communication, and it can portray much more readily than words the central dilemma of the couple's relationship. This dilemma becomes the focus of change.

During the subsequent sessions the couples are divided into separate husbands' and wives' groups, in order that tasks may be assigned without the knowledge of the other spouse. The purpose of this is to introduce an element of unpredictability, and set the stage for flexibility and change. For example, during the week, spouse A is kept guessing about whether the change in spouse B's behavior is spontaneous, prescribed, or created by spouse A. The group context also helps keep up the momentum of change through both support and confrontation. The entire approach is designed to initiate and sustain rapid change:

> The first step is considered the most important in this change process; it unsticks the couples from their repetitious and predictable pattern of interaction, and sets them moving in a new direction. The rapidity of change creates hope and produces a momentum which is self-reinforcing (Papp, 1976a, p. 362).

Strategic psychotherapy.   Finally, Richard Rabkin (1977) has developed an approach which he calls strategic psychotherapy, which blends the communicational approach with hypnosis and behavior therapy techniques. Rabkin spent some time at the Wiltwyck School for Boys with Minuchin and Auerswald, and he also acknowledges the influence of Haley, the brief therapy group at MRI, and Milton Erickson. His unique contribution is the introduction of behavioral methods in what is basically a communicational frame of reference.

Overview of the Communicational School and Its Derivatives

The theoretical foundation for the communicational school and its derivatives was laid by Jackson, who used cybernetics to develop an interactional approach to family diagnosis and family treatment, and formulated the concepts of family homeostasis, redundancies and rules, marital *quid pro quo,* punctuation, and the therapeutic double bind.

In Haley's problem-solving therapy, the emphasis is on resolving the presenting problem through changing the interactional sequences which maintain it. Dysfunctional interactional sequences are seen as reflective of organizational problems of the family, particularly in regard to its hierarchical structure, where cross-generational coalitions have formed. These coalitions and their interactional sequences are altered through a strategic process of therapy in which tactical maneuvers called directives (either straight or paradoxical) are used. Therapy occurs in stages, which may include the creation of a new malfunctioning structure as a half-way step.

In the brief therapy developed by Watzlawick, Weakland, Fisch, and Bodin at

MRI, the approach is even more problem-focused than Haley's and the perspective on problems—namely, that they are the result of attempted prior solutions—is unique. This approach first developed a conceptual model of first-order change (change within the existing frame of reference) and second-order change (change of the frame of reference), utilizing two mathematical-philosophical theories as the foundation (the theory of groups and the theory of logical types). Problems result from the mishandling of difficulties, whether by simplification (action is necessary but is not taken), or by utopianism (action is taken when it should not be), or by paradox (action is taken at wrong level—either first-order change is attempted when second-order change is required, or the reverse occurs). Problem resolution occurs chiefly through changing the frame of reference within which the problem has been misconstrued, using the paradoxical technique of reframing.

Other recent applications of the communicational approach include the work of the Milan group (Palazzoli and associates), brief therapy for couples (Papp), and strategic psychotherapy (Rabkin), which admixes the communicational approach with hypnosis and behavior-modification techniques.

STRUCTURAL FAMILY THERAPY

Structural family therapy was developed by Salvador Minuchin and his colleagues, in two principal settings. The work began in New York, at the Wiltwyck School for Boys, where Minuchin served as Director of the Family Research Unit from 1962 to 1965. The school is a private residential treatment center for delinquent boys, 8 to 12 years of age, who come from the most disadvantaged sections of New York City. The research group, which included Edgar Auerswald, Braulio Montalvo, Bernard G. Guerney, Jr., Bernice L. Rosman, and Florence Schumer, was interested in studying "the structure and process of disorganized, low socioeconomic families that had each produced more than one acting-out (delinquent) child; and . . . hoped to experiment with and develop further therapeutic approaches designed for such families" (Minuchin et al., 1967, p. ix). In the late 1960s, Minuchin turned his attention to psychosomatic families, with particular interest in families with a child suffering from anorexia nervosa (Minuchin, Rosman, & Baker, 1978). This work took place at the Philadelphia Child Guidance Clinic, where Minuchin was Director of the Family Therapy Training Center. His colleagues during this period included Montalvo and Rosman from the Wiltwyck School, Jay Haley, Lynn Hoffman, Harry Aponte, Lester Baker, and Ronald Liebman.

The structural school, like the communicational approaches, focuses on the present family context and views the therapeutic task as one of directed behavior change. But the structural school has, in many respects, a broader frame of reference than the communicational approaches. In fact, it could be said that the structural school incorporates or subsumes the main elements of the communicational approaches (specifically, Jackson's and Haley's), both in regard to its perspective on the family and family assessment, and in regard to its goals and methods of producing therapeutic change. And the structural school then goes beyond this to achieve a holistic perspective on the family and on family therapy. Ritterman (1977—see above, Chapter 3) described this difference in terms of the pretheoretical assumptions of the two schools. In terms of the operational theory, the holistic quality of structural family therapy in comparison to the communicational approaches can be observed in several places.

First, with regard to the theory of the family, the structural school views the communicational sequences ("transactional patterns") not simply in terms of their cybernetic properties (that is, as elements of a negative feedback loop, serving to restore family homeostasis), but also as reflective of the overall organizational structure of the family. Minuchin makes reference to Parsons' structural-functional sociology of the family (Parsons, 1955) as an important influence in his conceptualization of family structure and organization (Minuchin et al., 1967). And not only does he conceptualize the family itself as a complex organizational system (with the cybernetic control functions as one component), but also he views the family in its ecological context (that is, socioeconomic, ethnic and cultural factors), and with reference to its developmental stage (from young marrieds to the post-retirement elderly couple) (Minuchin, 1974).

Second, with regard to family assessment, Minuchin recognizes that the data that one gathers about families is enormously influenced by the process of data-gathering:

> The therapist's impact on the family is part of family diagnosis. The therapist's entrance is in itself a massive intervention. The family therapist must recognize his influence on the picture being presented by the family. He cannot observe the family and make a diagnosis from "outside." (Minuchin, 1974, p. 131)

Thus the family diagnosis, which is derived experientially through the process of joining the family, is a holistic diagnosis that takes the therapist's influence into account. It is also an evolving diagnosis, which changes to take into account the family's response to the therapist's moves.

Third, with regard to family therapy, Minuchin has both broader goals and a richer armamentarium of treatment methods. The latter will be discussed in more detail below. With regard to the goals of therapy, although he considers it essential to provide a remission of the presenting problem, the goals of structural family therapy are the "transformation of the family system":

> In family therapy, the transformation of structure is defined as change in the position of family members vis-à-vis each other, with a consequent modification of their complementary demands. (Minuchin, 1974, p. 111)

This discussion of structural family therapy will first present the general approach to family assessment and therapy. Second, specific applications will be considered: to the low-socioeconomic-status family on the one hand, and to the "anorectic family" on the other.

Structural Family Therapy:
The General Approach

Minuchin's approach involves three general processes: *joining* the family in a position of leadership; *assessing* the family experientially, through participating in its processes in order to derive a family map or diagnosis; and *restructuring* the family according to the goals implied in the diagnosis.

Joining the family. The therapist's first task is to form a therapeutic system, through joining the family in a position of leadership. This process is akin to the participant-observer anthropologist, who both joins a culture and then disengages to examine his experience. The therapist participates in the culture of the family, immersing himself in its processes. To do this requires accepting the family's structure and style, and blending with them, "going with the flow." This provides the family with a sense of affirmation and acceptance, and helps build the therapeutic system. It also provides the therapist with a subjective sense of the family's transactional patterns. But the therapist must also periodically disengage and examine the experience with some objectivity in order to form the family diagnosis.

Minuchin (pp. 125-128) describes three operational procedures by which a therapist can *accomodate* to the family in order to facilitate the process of joining: maintenance, tracking, and mimesis.

Maintenance refers to supporting the existing structure of the family. This can be done for the entire family or for a subsystem or individual. Maintenance involves accepting, respecting, and valuing a given aspect of the family. For example, in an interview with the "Smith" family, Minuchin (1974) supports the father's role as switchboard of the family by asking permission to speak to his wife and son.

Tracking means to follow the content of the family's communication through minimal encouragers such as "umhum," or restating what has been said. Tracking is an operation that confirms the family by valuing what they have to say, and it also elicits information. In this procedure, the therapist "leads by following."

Mimesis refers to a process through which the therapist adopts the style and accomodates to the affective range of the family. In fast-moving families, he may increase his own tempo. In intellectual families, he may adopt a cognitive style. In general he might disclose aspects of himself that he shares with the family in order to enhance the sense of kinship. Mimesis is often a spontaneous occurrence. For example, in the interview with the "Smith" family, Mr. Smith removes his coat and lights a cigarette. Minuchin asks him for a cigarette (as a planned mimetic operation), and then takes off his coat (as an unplanned, spontaneous mimetic operation).

Assessing the family. Minuchin views the family as "the matrix of identity" —that is, the learning environment which, by providing its young with experiences of both belonging and autonomy or separateness, enables each of them to develop a sense of self that has both continuity with others and with the past, and a differentiation from others or a distinctness of one's own. There are many varieties of families that can satisfactorily provide this function for their children, but in general there are certain prerequisite qualities for doing so. These qualities are evaluated in the family assessment procedure (p. 130).

The first element assessed is the *structure* of the family. (In this section an abbreviated discussion of family structure is provided. For more detail, see Chapter 1.) Toward this end, it is necessary to observe the preferred transactional patterns of the family in order to determine the underlying organizational structure. The therapist attempts to ascertain the power hierarchy (does power reside chiefly in mother, or in father, or in both parents equally, or elsewhere?), the complementarity of functions (for example, does mother provide the nurturance to the younger children while dad relates chiefly to the older children?), and any idiosyncratic features of the family that organizes the ways in which members transact (such as communication rules regarding what can and cannot be discussed, range of affective expression, or style and tempo of communication). The therapist also observes the functional subsystems: Is there a spouse subsystem, or do Mr. and Mrs. Jones transact all of their business as parents? Is there a sibling subsystem? Do individuals have sufficient differentiation to constitute themselves alone as a functional subsystem? Are there other subsystems, organized around more specific functions, such as the older siblings, or the females of the household? Finally, the therapist assesses the boundaries of the subsystems. The boundaries are the rules determining who participates and under what circumstances. They are necessary in order to protect the differentiation of the subsystem, and hence its capacity to carry out its function. Thus, clear boundaries are optimal. However, boundaries may exist anywhere along a continuum from rigid to diffuse.

The second aspect of the family that is assessed is the family's *flexibility* and capacity for change. To what extent does the family have available alternative transactional patterns? How much deviance from the preferred patterns is allowed? How does the family tolerate alterations of its power hierarchy or of its subsystems? This element is most clearly seen in the family's response to the therapist's moves or probes.

The third facet of the family that is evaluated is its *resonance,* or sensitivity to the actions of individual members. The resonance of families falls along a range from disengagement to enmeshment. In disengaged families, there is a very low sensitivity or resonance to family members' actions, and thus only extreme acts are capable of mobilizing the family's deviation-counteracting mechanisms. Families such as these have generalized rigid boundaries. They may promote an overblown sense of autonomy at the expense of the individual's sense of belonging. In enmeshed families, the resonance is so high that it takes only a minor action to mobilize the families' deviation-counteracting mechanisms. Families at this pole have generalized, diffuse boundaries. They tend to promote an exaggerated sense of belonging at the expense of a sense of autonomy.

The fourth aspect of family life that is examined is the role the *identified patient* plays in the maintenance of the family's transactional patterns—particularly, the role played by the symptomatic behavior. (For example, does it defuse conflict, or does it protect another family member?)

The fifth and sixth aspects of family life that are assessed are the family's *ecological context* and *developmental stage.*

There are numerous occasions in which symptomatic or problematic behavior develops in a family member in response to the stress of a normative or transitory family crisis—for example, the birth of the first child, the marriage of eldest daughter who had functioned as a substitute mother (parental child), the death of a grandfather resulting in the taking in of grandmother, or the call to active military duty of the husband/father. In these situations, the task is to determine the structural strains resulting from the transitional event and impinging on the identified patient, in order to help the family evolve to a more functional structure.

On the other hand, severely dysfunctional families are frequently characterized by certain stable features. First, there are often cross-generational triangular structures, in which the boundaries between generations become diffuse and the boundaries around the triangular structure become rigid. These triangular structures can take the form of coalitions (either stable or unstable) or of conflict-detouring patterns (either overprotective or scapegoating). (These patterns are discussed in more detail above, in Chapter 2. See also Figure 5-4.)

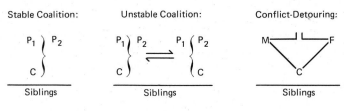

FIGURE 5-4

Second, these patterns become extremely fixed and rigid. Third, the family may either be enmeshed, disengaged, or oscillate between the two poles. Fourth, the identified patient is intimately bound up in the dysfunctional pattern, is invariably part of the dysfunctional triangular structure.

Restructuring the family. From the assessment process, a family map or diagnosis is evolved, which pinpoints the structural problems. The map implies certain goals. For example, with enmeshed families, in which the members are too involved in one another's lives, the goal is to increase the distance and strengthen the boundaries between subsystems (including individuals). Or with families that detour conflict, the goal would be to get the spouses to negotiate their conflict directly within the spouse subsystem.

The process of therapy involves a steady movement in the direction of the therapeutic goal. Disequilibrium is often introduced, as the family's preferred transactional patterns are challenged. The therapist must balance these restructuring interventions with support provided through the three accomodation procedures described above (maintenance, tracking, and mimesis). Over time, the family changes for three basic reasons: (1) They are challenged in their perception of reality; (2) they are provided with alternatives that make sense to them; and (3) once they have tried these, new relationships appear that are self-reinforcing.

Minuchin (1974) describes seven different categories of restructuring operations: "Actualizing family transactional patterns" (p. 140); "marking boundaries" (p. 143); "escalating stress" (p. 147); "assigning tasks" (p. 150); "utilizing symptoms" (p. 152); "manipulating mood" (p. 155) and "support, education and guidance" (p. 156). It will be noticed in the description of these operations to follow that some of them are paradoxical and others are direct. Minuchin does not distinguish these operations according to this dimension, because his broader frame of reference focuses instead on the overall structure and organization of the family.

In the early phases of therapy, two pitfalls are inherent in an active/directive approach to family therapy. One is that the family may make the therapist too central to the therapy and direct all of their conversation to the therapist. A second is that the family may elect to talk to the therapist about their problems, a course of action that produces a different order of data than if they were to enact their problems. To avoid these pitfalls, Minuchin recommends three procedures for *actualizing family transactional patterns.* The first is to direct family members to interact with each other with regard to a given specified topic, a procedure Minuchin terms "enacting family transactional patterns" (p. 141). The second, "recreating communicational channels" (p. 141) consists of a set of techniques for facilitating intrafamilial communication. These include such things as insisting that people talk to each other, refusing to respond when directly addressed and instead indicating by gesture that the communication should be addressed to another family member, and leaving the room to observe the family from behind a one-way mirror. Third, communication can be encouraged by "manipulating space" (p. 142). If Minuchin wants two people to conduct a dialogue, he may move their chairs so that they can be in direct contact with each other.

Two key procedures for *marking boundaries* involve working with communication and with space and positioning. Individual boundaries can best be delineated by imposing a set of communicational rules, such as: Family members should talk directly to each other rather than about each other; no one should speak for anyone else; and the family should listen to what a family member is saying and acknowledge it. Individual boundaries can also be strengthened among the children by underlining their differences, or by setting up differentiated age-appropriate expectations for both freedom and responsibility. Subsystem boundaries are effectively strengthened by manipulating space. For example, the intrusion of the children into the parental subsystem can be blocked by gathering the children off to another side of the room to play with toys while the parents discuss their relationship.

Families with a symptomatic member have typically developed dysfunctional patterns for handling stress, which usually involve its detour or denial. It is thus necessary at times to *escalate stress* in order to evolve more workable alternative patterns. There are four ways of accomplishing this. The most direct procedure involves "blocking transactional patterns" (p. 147), particularly those that are involved in the dysfunctional mechanisms. For example, if the parental child starts to answer for one of her younger siblings, the therapist might say to her "Just a minute, Mary" and "Go ahead" to the younger sibling. The second procedure is that of "emphasizing differences" (p. 148) that the family has been minimizing or glossing over. Third, the therapist can move to "develop implicit conflict" (p. 148), particularly in those situations where a family has developed rapid and efficient patterns for defusing or derailing conflicts. Finally, the therapist may "join in an alliance or coalition" (p. 148) with a family member or subsystem. This tactic may involve joining individual family members serially, providing support to each in order to facilitate their articulation of their perspectives or positions on an issue. It may also take the form of joining one family member for a longer period of time in order to bring a conflict out into the open and develop it fully, in order that it can be resolved. Joining to form an alliance or coalition requires special care on the part of the therapist. First of all, it is necessary to avoid getting drawn into the family battles. Second, it is necessary to be very attuned to the level of stress that the family members can tolerate, in order to avoid overburdening or overwhelming them.

Minuchin, like Haley, will *assign tasks,* both within and outside of the session. These tasks may be straight, paradoxical, or a combination of the two. In regard to the latter, Minuchin gives an example of a couple in which the wife controls many details of her husband's behavior. The task involved a straight directive to the husband, who was asked to purchase clothing for himself for the first time in his life, making selections solely on the basis of his own tastes. The wife was paradoxically instructed to intensify (exaggerate) her continuous monitoring and criticism of her husband. As with Haley, Minuchin views tasks as diagnostic probes, providing valuable information about the family's flexibility, resistance, and willingness to follow through with treatment.

Minuchin, again like Haley, recommends *utilizing the symptom* in therapy. Symptoms "represent a concentrated nodule of family stress . . . working with them can be, to paraphrase Freud, the royal road to family structure" (p. 152). The symptom can be "focused-on," "exaggerated," or "de-emphasized." One can "move to a new symptom," "relabel the symptom," or "change the symptom's affect" (pp. 152-155). Minuchin's special technique of holding a lunch session early in the treatment of anorectic patients illustrates several of these methods of using the symptom. The very act of having a lunch session with an anorectic patient brings the focus squarely on the symptom. The therapist may assign the parents the task of making their daughter eat her lunch, which will lead to the development of an interpersonal conflict. This conflict then becomes figural, deemphasizing the anorectic symptom. The anorectic symptom may also be relabeled as a case of disobedience on the part of the daughter; or, the therapist can move to a new symptom, putting the focus on the parents' failure to form a workable complementarity.

Minuchin, in this instance unlike Haley, will also take into consideration the feeling-tone of the family. Minuchin writes of focusing on and *manipulating mood.* The therapist, as an act of joining, may take on the family's mood, and as an act of restructuring, can elect to exaggerate the family's mood, in order to call forth counterdeviation mechanisms. Minuchin gives an example of his becoming highly punitive toward a child in the family with a very controlling, punitive mother. This maneuver forced the mother to express support and concern toward her daughter. The therapist can also manuever to heighten the intensity of, or dampen, family affect depending on the need. Affect can also be utilized to increase or decrease distance, depending on whether the therapist is dealing with a disengaged or enmeshed family, respectively.

Finally, Minuchin discusses the function of *support, education, and guidance* as restructuring interventions. Families or individuals can sometimes benefit from simple instruction—for example, in regard to communication or conflict resolution. Moreover, sometimes providing support to a subsystem, such as the parental subsystem, can enable the parents to get their bearings and handle parenting on their own.

Structural family therapy, then, calls for a careful and evolving holistic family diagnosis and a steady movement toward the therapeutic goals, with restructuring carefully balanced with accomodation and support. Although the particulars of Minuchin's approach, especially the separate functions of joining, assessment, and restructuring and their constituent operations, have been discussed here in a somewhat atomistic style, these maneuvers and functions, in actual practice, are highly intertwined. The analogy comes to mind of the contrast between a detailed description of the several classes of orchestral instruments and their constituent items, and an actual concert. When a gifted practitioner such as Minuchin works, these maneuvers are blended in an artful way to create therapeutic movement.

Another general issue is the high degree of directiveness of Minuchin's approach, and whether this is likely to promote dependence in the family. Another analogy from the arts may be useful here. Minuchin's work with a family is like that of a director (or choreographer) with actors (or dancers). After he helps the family develop their moves, they are capable of conducting their own performances.

Specific Applications
of Structural Family
Therapy

This section consists of a brief review of the application of structural family therapy, first, to lower-socioeconomic-status disorganized families with delinquent offspring and, second, to anorectic families. This will provide an opportunity to observe the relationship between theory and practice. In particular, the focus will be on the way in which the diagnosis specifies certain goals, and on how techniques are selected in order to facilitate movement toward the goals.

It must be pointed out at the beginning that Minuchin worked with these two client populations at very different time periods and points in his career. His earlier work with families of delinquents is reflective of the beginning phase of the development of his theory, when he was making the transition from a psychoanalytic to a systemic frame of reference. Consequently, the approach developed then might not represent what he would, at this time, consider to be the optimal approach for working with families of this sort. With this *caveat* in mind, we can proceed to the discussion of applications.

Disorganized, multiproblem families. Minuchin et al. (1967) described disorganized, multiproblem families as units wherein the parents have relinquished their executive function and provide little or no leadership, where boundaries shift rapidly and according to parental whim, where mood changes are abrupt and extreme, and where randomness prevails.

The families were studied in terms of four dimensions of family life: self-observation and communication, socialization of affect, modalities of contact, and family structure.

With regard to self-observation and communication, the unpredictability of the environment stunts the children's growth in several important ways. The children develop neither an objective grasp of reality, nor a sense of their competence in effecting change in reality. Consequently, they develop neither a strong sense of self, nor a capacity to self-reflect and self-observe.

The parents' abdication leaves a power vacuum that results in a preoccupation with power operations among the siblings. The child is thus trained to attend to the command level of communication (the relationship one bears to the person sending the message in terms of the power dimension) rather than to the content (or report level). This limits their ability to attend to content, to observe reality, and to communicate their observations.

Children in these homes do not expect to be heard, and thus they resort to intensity of sound to make their needs known. Conflicts in the ever-changing environment are not brought to closure. A subject is rarely carried to a conclusion, as content is virtually ignored while pitch and intensity of voice and body movements are accorded higher status.

With regard to the socialization of affect, a restricted affective range is observed. Affective expression occurs primarily in one of two forms: aggression and nurturance. Children are observed to shift rapidly from one mood to the other.

With regard to modalities of contact, disorganized families are observed at either extreme of the enmeshment-disengagement axis, or alternating between the two. At the enmeshment pole, family members are observed to relate with a kind of "fast engagement," an intense but superficial and defensive form of relating. Minuchin described the "elastic band" syndrome, which occurs during the shift from disengagement to involvement. A child acts up in the presence of a disengaged parent (perhaps intoxicated) and gets no response. The child acts up even more, and continues to get no response. Finally the child acts up enough, and gets a response— usually violent—from the irritated parent. The analogy is to stretching an elastic band to the point where it breaks; the child gets hit by the snapping back of the band.

Finally, with regard to structure, Minuchin described six basic characteristics of these families:

1. They are largely a one-parent family; the mother provides continuity through a succession of unstable father-figures.
2. In an "intact" family, the spouse subsystem functions mostly as a *parent* subsystem.
3. The nature of the parents' power is confusing. The parents are at times in absolute, autocratic power and control; at other times, they feel completely helpless.
4. The parent(s) relinquishes executive functions by: (a) delegation of instrumental roles to a "parental child" (or children); or (b) total abandonment of the family (psychologically and/or physically).
5. The sibling subsystem acquires significance as a socializing agent far beyond that which has been recognized heretofore.
6. There is a breakdown in communication between parent and children, and the sibling subsystem tends to encourage expression of opposition to parental control. (Minuchin et al., 1967, p. 219)

Minuchin and his colleagues developed a number of techniques for working with these families (Minuchin et al., 1967; Minuchin & Montalvo, 1967; Minuchin, 1965). These techniques were designed to directly change the communication patterns, the structure, and the affective system of multiproblem families. In this section, a technique for directly enhancing family members' capacity for self-observation and reflection will be presented.

In the early phases of his work, Minuchin regarded the lack of skill in introspection as the most serious problem with multiproblem families. This position reflects the fact that, being in the process of making the transition from psychodynamic to systems theory, he tended to emphasize the development of awareness as a necessary step in therapeutic change. Introspection and a capacity for observing self and others are prerequisites for the development of awareness.

Minuchin thought that to facilitate the capacity for observing self and others, he must block these families' characteristic defensive maneuver of "fast engagement," which occurs at the enmeshed pole of interaction, and in which impulse is rapidly translated into action. This was accomplished through a structured process of taking selected family members out of the fray of action and training them as observers.

This technique, which is called "conflict-resolution family therapy" (Minuchin, 1965), involves the following steps. The therapist first meets with the whole family in order to pinpoint salient conflicts and the recurring transactional patterns that impede the observing and problem-solving abilities of the family members. He then selects out the central participants and directs them to continue dealing with the conflict, giving them specific instructions on how they might do it more successfully. He then takes the other members of the family behind the one-way mirror, and teaches them to observe the interaction. Usually, the participant family members will have difficulty with their task, and revert to previous patterns. At these points, an observing family member will be instructed to return to the treatment room in order to help the participants get back on course.

This format is repeated with different subgroups acting as participants, so that the full spectrum of conflict issues is addressed, sequentially and systematically. Thus the family is trained to observe family interaction, to slow down action in order to focus on an issue, and to stay with an issue long enough to successfully resolve it. The capacity for introspection is enhanced indirectly through this overall process, and directly through enacting the participant role with the awareness that one is being observed. As Minuchin (1965, p. 284) put it: "A consciousness of being observed is an intermediary step in the process of introspection."

Anorectic families. Minuchin's work on psychosomatic and anorectic families occurred later in his career, after he had developed his structural theory of family therapy (Minuchin et al., 1978). Hence, both the descriptions of these families' characteristics and the "blueprints for therapy" are presented much more in structural terms than the earlier work. No reference is made to introspection, and there is no attempt to increase family members' awareness.

Anorexia nervosa, or self-starvation, is a psychosomatic syndrome with both physical and psychological symptoms. The physical symptoms include a loss of 25 percent or more of body weight and one or more of the following: hyperactivity, hypothermia, and amenorrhea. The psychological symptoms include a fanatical pursuit of thinness, fear of gaining weight, distorted body image, denial of hunger, struggle for control, and sense of incompetence. The syndrome is potentially fatal, with deaths occurring in 10 percent to 15 percent of the cases. It usually appears in middle-class females, typically during adolescence.

The anorectic family diagnosis consists of the following elements: enmeshment; overprotection; rigidity; transactional patterns that either avoid or defuse conflict so that conflict is neither fully acknowledged, developed, nor resolved; and the involvement of one child and the parents in a rigid triad of one of three types—stable coalition, unstable coalition, or overprotective detouring.

The approach to treatment involves short-range and long-range goals. The short-range goal is symptom remission. Treatment may involve a brief period of hospitalization for either medical or strategic reasons. Symptom remission is accomplished through a combination of behavior modification and family therapy. The behavioral program is an inpatient program, using an operant approach in which activity is the reinforcer. The program is tailored to each child; and, with each incremental gain (or loss) of weight there is an increase (decrease) in permissible activities. This program is successful in helping anorectic patients begin to gain weight after about one week of the program.

The short-range family therapy approach is built around the lunch session, which is held for both inpatients and outpatients. The session lasts two hours, and has two parts. In part I, the therapist joins the family and forms the therapeutic system. Part II begins after lunch arrives, and involves the enactment of the family's core transactional patterns. The goal of this session is the transformation of the definition of the problem from that of a sick individual to that of a dysfunctional family, in order to set the stage for long-term family therapy. A surprising finding of these sessions was that the anorectic patient began to eat immediately afterward, a vivid documentation of the effectiveness of these sessions in defocusing the symptomatic individual.

The goal of long-term therapy is to effectively change the dysfunctional family patterns. It should be pointed out that in the structural model, long-term therapy is really not that long. In the program for anorectics and their families, the median length of treatment was 6 months, with the range being 2 to 16 months.

The therapy proceeds according to the structural model and involves both joining the system and restructuring. The specific areas that are restructured correspond very closely to the family diagnosis: enmeshment, overprotection, conflict avoidance, rigidity, and the rigid triad. Specific techniques to accomplish these goals are selected according to the particular qualities of the individual family.

Finally, it should be pointed out that a particular pitfall in working with these families is their ability to appear to agree with and adopt the therapist's directives, whereas in fact they are only enacting their conflict-avoidance patterns. Minuchin states that moves of "high intensity" are required to overcome this particular form of resistance.

BEHAVIORAL FAMILY THERAPY

Introduction

The behavioral approach to family therapy, like the communicational and structural schools, is oriented toward the present interaction of family members, and emphasizes the use of directive interventions to change behavior. Although some behavioral family therapists take systems theory into account to some extent (Mealiea, 1976; Tsoi-Hoshmand, 1976), the primary emphasis is on learning theory.

The theoretical foundation of the behavioral family therapy school, has, in fact, been fairly circumscribed. For the most part, the approach has been based on what is known as social-learning theory (Bandura, 1969), which combines the methods of operant conditioning with social-psychological influencing processes such as modeling (Greer & D'Zurilla, 1975). Classical conditioning approaches (such as reciprocal inhibition and systematic desensitization) have been largely ignored, or confined to the treatment of sexual dysfunction (Masters & Johnson, 1970). So, too, the newer self-control approaches (Kanfer & Karoly, 1972) have not seen much use in behavioral family therapy. Finally, even within the social-learning/operant paradigm, the emphasis has been primarily on changing the contingencies of reinforcement—that is, on response control (or "consequation"). Only recently have programs been developed that also utilize stimulus-control procedures—that is, methods designed to alter one family member's "cues" to which another member responds (Wiltz, 1973; Jacobson, 1978).

The behavioral approach is a fairly recent entrant into the field of family therapy, with most of the work having been done from 1965 to the present. From an exploratory stage of utilizing behavioral techniques in a conjoint format of family and couple therapy (Liberman, 1970), the field moved fairly rapidly in three distinct directions: (1) the training of parents in behavior modification in order to help them change the dysfunctional behavior of their children (behavioral parent training—O'Dell, 1974; Johnson & Katz, 1973; Berkowitz & Graziano, 1972); (2) the training of marital couples in behavioral techniques and other skills in order to help them change the discordant aspects of their relationship (behavioral marital therapy—Patterson, Weiss, & Hops, 1976; Jacobson, 1977a, 1977b); and (3) the integration of behavioral techniques with other approaches in the structure/process model, whether communicational or structural (Rabkin, 1977; Liebman, Minuchin & Baker, 1974; Perlman & Bender, 1975; Rosenberg, 1978; Birchler & Spinks, 1980; Barton & Alexander, 1981).

The problem of *generalization* of treatment effects was an important factor in the move from the conjoint therapy format into either the training or the eclectic models. Forehand and Atkeson (1977) defined four ways in which treatment effects may be generalized: (1) *setting generality* refers to the maintenance of treatment effects outside of the treatment setting—that is, in the home or the school; (2) *temporal generality* refers to the maintenance of gains after the termination of treatment; (3) *behavioral generality* refers to change in behaviors other than those targeted for treatment; and (4) *sibling generality* refers to change in the behaviors of children other than the identified patient.

Early in the development of the behavioral approach to family therapy, it was reasoned that generalization would be enhanced if the therapist functioned as a trainer of change-agents rather than personally as a change-agent. An approach of this sort, in which parents or spouses were trained in the use of behavior-modification procedures would (it was argued) more thoroughly alter the family environment in which the deviant behavior occurs than would the direct treatment of the deviant behavior and its reinforcers (Patterson, Ray, & Shaw, 1968). This would guard against the reappearance of the symptom through its inadvertent reinforcement and also provide parents with the option of reinstituting behavioral procedures to prevent relapses. More optimistically, it would enable parents or spouses to utilize behavior-modification procedures to deal with any additional present or future family problems.

Eclectic combinations of behavioral and systems approaches developed in an analogous manner. It was found that behavioral methods often had profound effects in remediating a symptom (such as the use of the token economy to facilitate weight gain in anorectic patients—Minuchin et al., 1978). Unless changes were also made in the family context, however, there would be a very high rate of relapse (Pertshuk, 1974). To insure the durability of the gains, behavioral methods were wedded to communicational or structural techniques in a multipronged effort to both remediate the symptom and alter the family environment.

In this section we will present the original model of conjoint behavioral marital and family therapy. The training-oriented methods (both parent-child and marital) will be discussed in Chapter 9 as part of the general discussion of approaches that seek to empower families through educational methods to either solve or prevent individual and relationship problems. Some of the eclectic models have been discussed earlier in this chapter.

Liberman (1970) defined behavioral family therapy in terms of three processes that are analogous to the three components of structural family therapy: (1) establishing a therapeutic alliance with the family; (2) making a behavioral assessment of the family's difficulties; (3) implementing a strategy for change, utilizing behavioral principles of reinforcement and modeling.

Establishing a Therapeutic Alliance

Liberman (1970) discussed the first process, establishing a therapeutic alliance, in terms of developing trust, mutual respect, warmth, and affection between the therapist and members of the family. In behavioral terms, it is necessary for the family members to positively value the therapist in order for the therapist to serve as an effective source of reinforcement and as a model.

Assessment of the Family

Assessment in conjoint behavioral family therapy is a prerequisite for designing an effective strategy for change. Two major questions are asked during the assessment process: (1) What are the problematic behaviors that family members would like to change? (2) What current reinforcement contingencies support or maintain the problematic behaviors? Behavioral assessment involves both interviewing and observation, the latter occurring preferably in a setting natural to the family. The objective is to obtain a statement of the specific behaviors to be changed, and to determine precisely the frequency of the targeted behaviors and specify their antecedents and consequent events. Several precise recording systems have been developed to gather baseline information and monitor treatment. These include paper-and-pencil inventories (Weiss & Margolin, 1977) and electromechanical systems such as SAM (Signal System for the Assessment and Modification of Behavior —Thomas, Carter, Gambrill, & Butterfield, 1970).

The behavioral school recognizes the interlocking nature of the family, describing it as a system consisting of "mutually interdependent dyads" (Patterson & Reid, 1970). Dyadic interaction, whether husband-wife or parent-child, has been described in terms of two reinforcement processes: reciprocity and coercion. *Reciprocity* describes a relatively well-functioning dyad, in which both parents reinforce each other equitably over time, and in which positive reinforcement maintains the behavior of both persons. *Coercion* describes an inequitable exchange, in which one person's behavior is controlled by positive reinforcement, while the other's behavior is controlled by negative reinforcement (removal of an aversive stimulus). For example, in a dysfunctional family, husband may demand sex from his wife in an aversive manner. The more wife demurs, the more demanding the husband becomes. Eventually her resistance wears down, and wife gives in, positively reinforcing husband's aversive behavior. Husband ceases his aversive behavior, negatively reinforcing wife's compliance. Coercion may be one-sided, as in the above example, or two-sided, in which case, discord, impasse, and mutual withdrawal may result.

Behavioral Intervention

Once an assessment is made, intervention involves the systematic application of techniques to either increase (accelerate) or decrease (decelerate) a set of specific behaviors. Behaviors are accelerated by the contingent application of either positive or negative reinforcement. Behaviors are decelerated through the contingent application of punishment (either the presentation of an aversive stimulus or the withdrawal of a positive stimulus) or the use of extinction (discontinuation of reinforcement).

Positive reinforcement is the most common method of increasing behavior. Reinforcers may be material (money, tokens, food) or social (praise, affection). A common goal in family therapy is to increase the reinforcement value of social stimuli emitted by family members, which might be accomplished by pairing the social stimulus with a material reinforcer. In general, it is often difficult to find effective reinforcers. In this situation, detailed behavioral observation may be used to identify high-frequency behaviors. The opportunity to emit one of these high frequency behaviors can be used as reinforcement for emitting a low-frequency behavior. This principle (called the Premack principle) was utilized in the behavioral treatment of anorexia nervosa, in a strategy wherein activity (a high-frequency behavior) served as the reinforcer for eating (Minuchin et al., 1978).

When one wishes to facilitate the emission of a behavior that has a zero rate of occurence, there are several options. With more mature individuals, one can simply *instruct* the person how to enact the behavior, perhaps using *modeling* to exemplify it. In other cases, shaping may be necessary; that is, successive approximations to the target behavior are reinforced. Liberman (1970) described a case in which husband wished wife to be a better homemaker and wife wanted husband to purchase a better home. The steps along the way to these goals involved reinforcement of wife for utilizing a tablecloth at dinner and reinforcement of husband for looking at the real estate listings in the Sunday papers.

In general, when increasing behaviors through positive reinforcement, it is desirable to gradually reduce the reliance on discriminating cues and on continual reinforcement. *Fading* is a procedure whereby the controlling influence of discriminative cues (or "prompts") for the emission of the behavior is gradually reduced. For example, a retarded girl was taught to walk using an overhead rope as a prompt. The prompt was faded first by slackening it and then by cutting it. In family therapy, the therapy situation (including the therapist) serves as a prompt for the desired new behavior. This prompt is often faded by gradually reducing the contacts, substituting telephone calls for visits, and then reducing the calls. *Chaining* is a technique in which two or more desirable behaviors are brought together and maintained by the last element (reinforcer) in the chain. For example, one might initially reinforce eye contact and smiling separately, and then make reinforcement contingent on the emission of both behaviors. *Thinning out material reinforcers* is often used to bring desirable behavior more directly under the control of social reinforcers. The schedule of reinforcement is also made progressively more *intermittent,* in order to increase the durability of the desired behavior. This process works by increasing this behavior's resistance to extinction.

Negative reinforcement is not often used in family therapy, although dysfunctional families often use this method of behavior control, particularly in coercive dyadic interaction. Negative reinforcement involves the absence of aversive stimulation, either through its removal or its postponement. An example is the stopping, by one spouse, of certain aversive behavior such as nagging, demanding, or yelling.

Aversive stimulation is a form of punishment. It is also not often used in family therapy. Dysfunctional families, however, often utilize this method of behavior control, particularly in coercive interaction. The effect of the presentation of aversive stimulation is to reduce the behavior with which it is contingent. What is aversive to one person may not be so to another, but family members usually are well aware of one another's sensitivities.

Withdrawal of positive reinforcement is another form of punishment that, however, does have therapeutic utility. In this procedure, positive reinforcement is removed or denied contingent on the emission of undesirable behavior, and this tactic has the effect of reducing the frequency of that behavior. Two variants of the technique are *time out* and *response costs.* Time out refers either to the withdrawal of the person from a situation in which reinforcement occurs, as in isolation (in which the person is removed from a reinforcing environment for a specified period of time) or to leaving the person in the environment (in which they then encounter a complete absence of reinforcement—for example, the therapist looks away and does not interact for a specified period of time). Response cost is less frequently used in family therapy. It involves the subtraction or loss of reinforcers (such as tokens or coins) contingent on the emission of undesirable behavior.

Extinction involves the cessation of reinforcement that maintains a behavior, resulting in the reduction of frequency of emission of that behavior. When a behavior is maintained by positive reinforcement, extinction involves the noncontingent withdrawal of the reinforcement. Behavior maintained by intermittent reinforcement is more resistant to extinction than is behavior that is continually reinforced. Behavior maintained by negative reinforcement is extremely resistant to extinction.

The use of a combination of several of the above techniques is common in behavioral family therapy. For example, undesirable behavior may be reduced by extinction, while other behaviors (incompatible with the undesirable behavior) are strengthened through the use of positive reinforcement. In addition, there are other approaches, such as *contingency management,* in which parents are helped to rearrange their reinforcement schedules. For example, it is not uncommonly found that a child's undesirable behavior is inadvertently reinforced by parental attention. Parents are thus taught to ignore the undesirable behavior and to provide attention at other times. Finally, establishing *behavioral contracts* (which specify the contingencies of reinforcements) have been found to be effective in family therapy (Firestone & Moschetta, 1975).

Conjoint Behavioral Therapy
vis-à-vis Other Structure/Process Approaches

The behavioral school of family therapy has undergone relatively recent development from a conjoint marital and family format into training formats (behavioral parent training and behavioral marital therapy) and into eclectic forms (in which behavioral techniques are integrated with communicational or structural methods). The approach of conjoint marital and family therapy involves the three processes of forming the therapeutic alliance, making a behavioral assessment, and implementing behavioral change. The analogy of these processes to those of the structural school (joining, assessing, and restructuring) has been noted.

There are differences, however, between the early conjoint behavioral approach and the other schools in the structure process model. The most obvious, of course, is the reliance on learning theory rather than on systems and related theories. Somewhat related to this is the reductionistic position that behavioral family therapy takes in relationship to the family. This is perhaps most evident in its approach to assessment, which involves an exceedingly fine-grained examination of behavior, with the establishment of frequency counts and antecedent-consequent relationships. But it is also seen in its approach to treatment, where the focus is on the acceleration or deceleration of specific behaviors. Hence in Ritterman's terms (1977), the behavioral school is much more committed to a mechanistic world view than are the other structure/process schools, even the communicational.

Another difference between the behavioral school and others in the structure/process paradigm is that, although it uses directives, it uses straight directives exclusively. Paradoxical methods are not found in the strict behavioral-therapy repertoire. This rational-directive problem-solving orientation is basic to the behavioral school and is related to its views on resistance. Lebow (1972) is representative of this position when he argues that failure to bring about therapeutic change is the result of the failure of the therapist to adequately define, assess, and implement a sound treatment plan, and not of any resistance on the part of the client or family.

Gurman (1980) finds that, given this difference regarding resistance between the early representatives of the behavioral school and the other structure/process schools, the eclectic syntheses that have developed are noteworthy indeed. In his view,

> it is not surprising, then, that as behavior therapists have begun to recant their earlier stance on this issue (of resistance), they have chosen to align themselves with models of intervention which offer the most explicit techniques for increasing the therapists' influence and leverage against the family's efforts to maintain the status quo. (Gurman, 1980, p. 87)

SUMMARY

The three major structure/process schools of family therapy are the communicational, the structural, and behavioral. In the communicational school and its derivatives, the pioneering family interactional perspective came from the work of Don

D. Jackson. The later representatives of the communicational school are Haley's problem-solving therapy and the MRI brief therapy. Both approaches are brief and problem-focused, and both utilize paradoxical interventions. Haley's approach examines the relationship between interactional sequences and organizational hierarchy. Accenting the power dimension, his interventions resemble a therapeutic form of *aikido,* designed to unbalance a powerful opponent. The MRI group has developed an intriguing conceptual framework based on the theory of logical types and the theory of groups. Their approach emphasizes the cognitive-meaning dimension, and their interventions are designed to change the frame of reference within which the family has misconstrued its problems, using the paradoxical technique of reframing. Other recent applications of the communicational school approach include Palazzoli and her associates in Milan, Papp's brief therapy for couples, and Rabkin's strategic therapy.

The structural school has a broader frame of reference than the communicational approaches in regard to several aspects of its operational theory: the theory of the family, the approach to the family assessment (which takes into account the influence of the therapist), and the goals of, and techniques used to bring about, family change. The structural school draws on specific techniques to accomplish the three processes of joining the family, assessing the family in order to form an interactional diagnosis, and restructuring the family. Specific applications of structural family therapy have included Minuchin's work with disorganized multiproblem families and with psychosomatic families (particularly those with an anorectic member).

The behavioral school from its early format of conjoint therapy developed rapidly into both training-oriented and eclectic models. It draws on specific social-learning and operant-conditioning techniques for forming the therapeutic alliance, making the behavioral assessment, and implementing behavioral change.

In general, these three schools can be seen to differ markedly from the historical schools, by virtue of their direct, time-limited, problem-solving orientation, in which the goal is to directly alter current family interaction patterns in order to remediate symptoms or presenting problems. No reference is made to the past, the unconscious, transference, insight, or working through, although resistance is acknowledged by two of the schools. These two schools (communicational and structural) have developed highly sophisticated tactical maneuvers for dealing with the family's resistance.

Although the structure/process schools as a group offer a considerably shorter-term model of therapy than the historical schools, they do differ among themselves in the breadth of their goals. Structural therapy has probably the broadest goals, which have been stated as the transformation of the family structure. Communicational approaches are in the middle of this continuum, being problem-focused but also dealing with some alteration of the family system. The behavioral school (specifically, the conjoint format) tends to have the most limited goals, which involve the reduction of the offending behavior, with attention to only the most immediately impinging aspects of the family system.

*RESOURCES: CLINICAL EXAMPLES
OF THE STRUCTURE/PROCESS
APPROACHES*

I. *Communication Systems Theory and its Derivatives*
   A. Jackson
       1. Jackson is one of the participants in the Hillcrest Family Series
           (described in Chapter 4).
       2. Haley and Hoffman (1967) have published an initial interview of
           Jackson with a family with a hospitalized psychotic daughter. The
           presentation interweaves transcripts of the family interview with an
           interview with the therapist, in which the family tape was played
           and the therapist was questioned as to why he did what he did.
   B. Haley
       No tapes are available, to my knowledge, showing Haley's work as a
       therapist. The case studies that are available feature Haley as the super-
       visor or commentator while another therapist demonstrates his approach.
       1. The Philadelphia Child Guidance Clinic (Two Children's Center,
           34th Street and Civic Center Boulevard, Philadelphia, PA 19104—
           brochure available) has available for rental two tapes illustrating
           Haley's problem-solving therapy. *A modern Little Hans* is a 60-
           minute tape with excerpts of the entire treatment by Mariano
           Barragan of a family whose son had a fear of dogs. This tape is
           transcribed and appears in Haley's book *Problem-solving therapy*
           (1976b), and has been reviewed by Greenberg (1980). *Leaving
           home* is a 60-minute tape with excerpts of the treatment by Samuel
           Scott of a family with an adult son unable to leave home, who is
           a deaf-mute, and who has been diagnosed paranoid schizophrenic
           and mentally retarded. This case has been written up as Chapter 10
           of Haley's book *Leaving home* (1980).
       2. The Family Therapy Institute of Washington, D.C. (4602 North
           Park Avenue, Chevy Chase, MD 20815—brochure available) has
           three tapes available for rental. These tapes are unusual in that they
           consist of actual family interviews duplicated by actors in order to
           deal with the issue of confidentiality. However, this results in some
           loss of believability. *Heroin my baby* is a 50-minute tape of excerpts
           of the treatment by Sam Kirschner of a 25-year-old heroin and am-
           phetamine addict and his family. This case was written up in
           Chapters 6 and 9 of Haley's *Leaving home* (1980), and the tape was
           reviewed by La Perriere (1982). *A jealous husband* is the first inter-
           view in a marital treatment, and *Do it on Sunday* illustrates a para-
           doxical approach to a child's symptom.
       3. The South Beach Psychiatric Center (777 Seaview Avenue, Staten
           Island, NY 10305) has one tape available for lecture or purchase,
           Ideas which handicap a therapist, a lecture by Haley on some of his
           ideas.
       4. Haley's book *Leaving home* (1980) has other case material, includ-
           ing interviews by Gary Lande with a family with a hospitalized
           psychotic daughter (Chapters 5 and 8), and by David Heard with
           the family of a hospitalized son (Chapter 7).

C. Mental Research Institute group.

   1. Papp's book (1977a) contains full-length case studies of work by John Weakland with a family of divorced parents and a 15-year-old son with behavior problems (Chapter 2), and by Richard Fisch with a family with a 12-year-old son with behavior problems.

   2. See also the Resources section at the end of Part I of this book for tapes of MRI group members and others that deal with communication theory and pathology of communication.

D. Miscellaneous

   1. The clinical work of Palazzoli and associates (1978) is described in several vignettes in their book *Paradox and counterparadox*.

   2. The brief therapy of Papp is illustrated in two places. The Ackerman Family Institute (149 East 78th Street, New York, NY 10021) has available for rental a 70-minute tape of excerpts of the brief treatment of a 23-year-old anorexic patient and her family—*The daughter who said no*. And a full-length case study of the treatment of family with a 12-year-old son with behavior problems appears in Papp (1977a).

II. *Structural Family Therapy*

A. The Philadelphia Child Guidance Clinic (see above for address) has 10 rental tapes illustrating the structural approach. *I think it's me* is an analysis of an initial interview by Minuchin with a family in which father has experienced several hospitalizations for paranoid and compulsive behavior. This tape is transcribed with commentary in Chapter 9 of Minuchin's book *Families and family therapy* (1974). *A family with a little fire* consists of excerpts of the treatment by Braulio Montalvo of a single-parent family in which the elder daughter has set fires. This tape is also transcribed with commentary in Minuchin (1974) (Chapter 11). *Taming monsters* is a consultation interview with Minuchin, with minimal commentary, with a family with two small daughters, one of whom is described as totally uncontrollable. *The case of the dumb delinquent* is a consultation interview by Minuchin with a single-parent family with a 13-year-old predelinquent boy. *Just a house, not a home* provides excerpts of the treatment by Minuchin of a reconstituted family with two adolescent sons, one each from the prior families. *A family with Minuchin and Whitaker* is a four-tape set in which both therapists interview the family with a young suicidal son and comment on their work. *Between you and me* and *The middleman* both deal with family therapy for anorexia nervosa, the first tape illustrating Minuchin's work, and the second Ronald Liebman's. Finally, *Constructing a workable reality* and *I'd rather forget it* deal with the family treatment of childhood asthma, the first featuring Liebman and the second, Gordon Hotas and Nila Betof.

B. Additional case studies dealing with anorexia can be found in Minuchin (1974) (Chapter 12), and, especially, in Minuchin et al. (1978) (Chapters 8–11).

C. The Boston Family Institute (251 Harvard Street, Brookline MA 02146) has four Minuchin tapes for rental or purchase. *The weekend fights: a growing couple* is a consultation interview with a couple not in therapy, illustrating processes of dealing with conflict and normal adult development. *Anorexia is a Greek word* is a two-tape set, a consultation interview with a family with an anorexic daughter, followed by a discussion with Minuchin about the interview. *Salvador Minuchin* is an interview with Minuchin about his personal history and life work.

D. The South Beach Psychiatric Center (see above for address) has available for rental or purchase three sets of tapes in which Minuchin conducts interviews and discusses his work: *A family interview with an 18 year old schizophrenic, his parents and 3 siblings; Interview with a teenage anorexic patient and her family; Interview with a divorced mother, her son (age 10) and daughter (age 7).*

E. Two full-length case studies using the structural approach appear in Papp (1977a). Aponte treats a lower-socioeconomic-status black family with 12 children (3 still at home) in Chapter 6; and in Chapter 11, Walters presents a crisis case with Minuchin as a consultant.

F. Finally, there is a case study of the marital therapy of a couple whose child was originally presented as the problem (Heard, 1978).

III. *Conjoint Behavioral Family Therapy*

Not much is available on the conjoint form of behavioral family therapy, insofar as the approach evolved fairly quickly into either eclectic or skills-training formats. Liberman (1970), however, briefly describes four cases in his article.

6

The Experiential Model: Gestalt, Experiential, and Client-Centered Schools of Family Therapy

The experiential model, like the structure/process model, focuses on the present rather than on the past, and it is concerned with the immediate experience of family members. Unlike the structure/process schools, and more like the historical model (particularly the psychodynamic school), however, the emphasis is on the individual family member first and foremost. But the experiential schools differ from psychodynamic family therapy in the theoretical orientation toward individual experience. Whereas, in its explanation of causes, strict psychodynamic theory is reductionistic, or mechanistic, and models a closed system, the experiential schools are holistic, organismic, and they model open systems (Ritterman, 1977; Levant, 1980a). Also, whereas psychodynamic theory specifies a particular sequence of development along with a set of issues everyone must deal with, and is thus nomothetic (involving universal laws), the experiential schools are idiographic in their approach: No universal stages or universal conflicts are assumed; instead, each individual is considered unique. The fundamental phenomenological method that characterizes these schools requires that each individual's existential issues be understood from the inner frame of reference of that individual.

The experiential schools are systems-oriented. But, given the emphasis on the individual, systems are conceptualized somewhat differently than in the other systems-oriented schools of family therapy (such as the multigenerational and the structural). The concept of system is used somewhat differently in each of the experiential schools and will be explained in more detail when the specific schools are discussed. Here it will suffice to say that the concept of system used in at least two of the schools derives more directly from the organismic Gestalt psychology of Wertheimer, Kohler, and Goldstein and the field theory of Lewin than it does from the general systems theory of von Bertalanffy.

Unique to this model is its emphasis on experience and affect. Emotional experience is emphasized over awareness, which in turn is emphasized over behavior. These schools are also concerned more with enhancing the quality of life of the individuals in the family than with alleviating symptoms or changing the family's pattern of interaction.

The process of therapy in these schools involves creating a heightened affective experience for family members, in order that ·their own restorative and self-actualizing processes will get started. As Napier and Whitaker describe it:

> Therapy, for us, is related to a growth process that takes place naturally in lives and in families. We assume that the will and the need to expand and integrate experience are universal; and that the family that enters psychotherapy is simply one in which the natural process has become blocked. Therapy is a catalytic "agent" which we hope will help the family unlock their own resources. (Napier & Whitaker, 1978, p. 62)

Resistance is acknowledged by two of the schools (Gestalt and experiential) but not by the client-centered school. The therapist's role in these schools is, for the most part, facilitative, although two of the schools do utilize some directive techniques. All the schools emphasize the person of the therapist as the primary curative factor and require a degree of transparency and openness of the therapist that is not seen in the other models. Indeed, these schools require that as an essential part of the therapy, the therapist must at times engage in personal growth while meeting with a family.

In this chapter, the three major experiential schools will be presented: Gestalt family therapy, experiential family therapy, and client-centered family therapy. Before turning to a discussion of the schools, it should be pointed out that existential and phenomenological theories and experiential techniques have had influence in the two other therapeutic models discussed in Chapters 4 and 5. In the historical model, Boszormenyi-Nagy's intergenerational family therapy is a blend of psychoanalysis, systems concepts, and existentialism. Thomas Fogarty, a former student of Bowen's, has brought an existential perspective to multigenerational family therapy through his concepts of emptiness and the four dimensions of self (Fogarty, 1976a, 1976b, 1976c). In the structure/process model, Minuchin utilizes the phenomenological method and experiential technique in his joining and accommodation operations. And, at MRI, Jackson's family interactional psychotherapy was moving in a phenomenological direction before his death (Jackson, 1965a; Greenberg, 1977), as had Satir's work moved in a humanistic direction before him. Satir's work will not be discussed here because of space limitations, but it should be noted that her approach involved a blending of communication theory within a humanistic frame of reference, with an emphasis on feelings and self-esteem. The interested reader is directed to Satir (1967, 1972), and Satir, Stachowiak, and Taschman (1975).

Finally, it should be briefly noted that in addition to the three major experiential schools, several other approaches have begun to emerge within this model. First, there is a symbolic-interactionist approach to family therapy, based on the principles of the symbolic-interactional school of family sociology, which emphasizes a phenomenological attitude (Hurvitz, 1975). Second, there is an emerging rational emotive therapy (RET) approach to family therapy (Ellis, 1978a). And third, there is some consideration of the use of transactional analysis (TA) in marriage counseling (O'Connor, 1977).

GESTALT FAMILY THERAPY

Gestalt family therapy is derived from Gestalt therapy. Gestalt therapy, originated by Fritz Perls (Perls, Hefferline, & Goodman, 1951), is a synthesis of several psychological traditions (Bauer, 1979). Perls was trained as a psychoanalyst, and his first major work was a version of the reformulation of psychoanalysis from an instinct basis to an ego orientation (Perls, 1947). Object relations theory was central to his thinking, as was Wilhelm Reich's concept of character armor. This mixture of Freudian and neo-Freudian notions was integrated within the frame of reference of Gestalt psychology, a close relative of modern systems theory. Perls had read the works of the academic Gestalt psychologists Wertheimer and Kohler and had worked with Goldstein, a neuropsychiatrist who applied the holistic, organismic principles of Gestalt psychology to the study of neurological impairment. From these sources Perls developed three concepts central to Gestalt therapy: (1) the integral relationships of figure and ground in the formation of the meaningful organized whole, or gestalt; (2) the importance of boundary phenomena; (3) the emphasis on process instead of content. Finally, Perls was also influenced by existential philosophy, which is evident in his emphasis on the here and now of direct encounter and experience. Later workers added an explicit emphasis on the phenomenological method (Stanley & Cooker, 1976).

Gestalt family therapy is an attempt to adapt the principles of Gestalt therapy to the context of working with families. Because of the kinship of Gestalt psychology and modern systems theory, this adaptation would seem to be such a natural progression that it might lead Gestalt therapy to merge eventually with family therapy. The particular character of Gestalt therapy, however, has produced a rather unusual version of family therapy that emphasizes the individual family member and his or her relationships with other family members, rather than the family system as a whole.

Gestalt therapy applied systems thinking to the individual, and it emphasized the intrapsychic-interpersonal boundary. The work was aimed at clarifying this boundary through the reintegration of split-off and projected aspects of self, and, in this manner, facilitating the individuation of the person. The "hot-seat" method of Perls constituted individual therapy in the context of the group. The person working (on the hot-seat) attempted to become aware of projected aspects of self. The other group members were basically bystanders, although some might have helped the person on the hot seat by participating in role plays. In an artificial group it was not expected that individuals' reactions would be so strong as to interrupt the process, although that could and did happen. But by and large it was relatively easy to keep the focus on the individual.

When Gestalt therapy is applied to the family, the focus is on the system of "individual in context" (Kaplan & Kaplan, 1978), which again emphasizes the intrapsychic-interpersonal boundary. The aim is the individuation of each family member and the development of genuine contact between family members. The development of clear individual boundaries is seen as a prerequisite of good intrafamilial relationships.

The problem of keeping a focus on the individual becomes more difficult in the family context, because strong reactions are so much more likely. Owing to the intricate accommodation of family members to each other, one member's moves may touch off numerous responses in the others. This can be handled in a couple of ways. One can work to keep the focus on the individual. Hatcher (1978) opts for this approach and uses for this end a structured method in which the agenda is established through "minicontracts" that are adhered to fairly strictly. Others, such as the Kaplans (1978), do not attempt to keep the focus on the individual, but instead follow the flow of family process, with the aim, though, of promoting the growth of individual family members.

Only a handful of published accounts of Gestalt family therapy appear in the literature. These include: Kempler's pioneering works (1965, 1968, 1974) and the more recent contributions of Hatcher (1978), Kaplan and Kaplan (1978), Bauer (1979), and Rabin (1980). For personal knowledge of Gestalt family therapy, the author is indebted to Dr. Mel Rabin, a Gestalt family therapist in the Boston area, who has guest-lectured in my course on family therapy at Boston University for the past several years.

The discussion in the following pages will first describe the Gestalt experience cycle, a model that summarizes the Gestalt theory of the function and dysfunction of individuals in context. Then the Gestalt approach to therapy, including considerations of process and techniques, will be presented.

The Gestalt Experience Cycle

The Gestalt experience cycle is shown in Figure 6-1. The cycle depicts the elements of experience as a continuous process, wherein organismic needs lead the individual to contacting the environment. When the contact is made, and the needs are met, the individual withdraws, and a complete gestalt is formed. The person is then free to move on to new experiences (Hatcher, 1978). When a person gets stuck at any place in the cycle, the gestalt remains unfinished, and some of the individu-

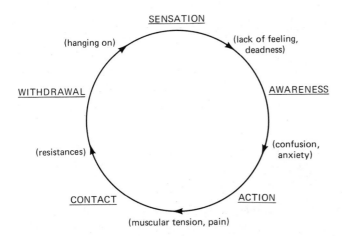

FIGURE 6-1   The Gestalt Experience Cycle. (Adapted from Rabin, 1980.)

al's energy remains bound to that experience. The goal of therapy is to help the individual become aware of the stuck places in order to complete the gestalt.

Sensation.   The cycle begins with sensation, the experiencing of stimuli that may originate in one's organism or in the external world. Sensation and perception are processes that are shaped by our experiences in our families. As a result of these experiences, we have greater or lesser degrees of sensitivity to various kinds of stimuli. For example, children are taught what they can see and hear and what is forbidden. They learn who in their family can be touched and who can't be. They learn whether they are allowed to say that something tastes bad or smells bad. In extreme circumstances, such as some forms of childhood psychosis, the child may not feel free to feel anything. In general, the most serious dysfunctions are those that occur at the level of sensation.

Awareness.   Awareness results from focusing one's attention on a sensation. At any given moment, multiple sensations are emerging into our awareness. Most of these go nowhere; they do not become figural and hence are not acted on. Dysfunctions at the level of awareness can result from family experiences in which mystification (Laing, 1965) is a prominent element. Such individuals may have great difficulty bringing sensations into awareness and will experience confusion and anxiety.

Enhancing awareness is a fundamental aspect of the Gestalt therapy approach. It involves slowing down and being in touch with the small details of one's experience. Hatcher describes the process in the following vignette:

A Gestalt therapist might begin to explore an individual's awareness of an environmental contact in the following manner:
P: I dreamed I was in a car, driving very fast, too fast, on a winding road.
T: Be the road.

P: I am the road. I am demanding and difficult. If you are careful and stay
    in touch with me, I will support you. If you go too fast, you will lose me
    and get hurt.
T: Be the car.
P: I am the car. I am excited by the speed I am moving at, but I am not
    afraid. I am not in control, and Jack is pushing me too far.
T: Be you, the driver.
P: I am trying to get somewhere, and the road is making it hard for me to
    go very fast. I don't like that.

Or other aspects of the contact might be explored, such as what the individual
is hearing, tasting, smelling, or experiencing internally with his body. The
goal, of course is to bring into awareness all aspects of the contact, to complete the gestalt. (Hatcher, 1978, p. 64)

Action. As we become increasingly aware of a sensation—that is, as it becomes figural—we experience an emerging sense of excitement or anticipation. This
facilitates the mobilization of our skeletal-muscular system in order to take action
of some sort. Certain dysfunctions at this level occur in more highly socialized individuals, and result in a "paralysis of will," "inhibition," or an inability to act. Such
individuals block their impulses to action and may experience muscular tension and
pain of various sorts as a result. Other individuals take action that is ineffective or
impotent; for these individuals, the stage of action is not allowed to become sufficiently developed. Finally there are individuals who have an overdeveloped ability to
act, and who short-circuit the awareness phase, taking action that is impulsive and
not well-conceived.

Contact. From the perspective of family therapy, making contact is the
most crucial stage in the cycle. In making contact, one's self moves until one comes
into contact with something else (which can be a person, an object, a memory, anything). That point is the contact boundary.

There are two important characteristics of the contact boundary. The first is
its location. An optimal contact boundary is coterminous with the actual self,
allowing for clear and genuine contact with others. The second important characteristic of the contact boundary is its degree of permeability. An optimal contact
boundary is semipermeable, allowing for selective contact.

Contact may be avoided through the *resistances to contact,* of which there
are five in Gestalt theory. The first three are related to the location of the contact
boundary. In *projection,* the contact boundary is located far in the environment,
where the projecting individual makes contact not with the other, but with the disowned aspects of self. *Introjection* is the complementary situation, in which the
contact boundary is located deep within the self. In this situation, I-Thou contact
is avoided by incorporating aspects of the other into the self, such as when one
acquiesces to attributions made by the other about self. Projection and introjection
function to produce rigidified relationships in a family, in which descriptive terms
are polarized and affectively charged (for example, good-bad; clean-dirty; depen-
dent-independent; drinker-nondrinker). In *retroflection,* the contact boundary is

turned sharply back against the self. One starts to move out to contact the other, but abruptly alters one's course to do to the self what was intended for the other. Retroflection allows for no contact. In its extreme form, it resembles character armor.

The last two resistances to contact concern the permeability of the contact boundary. In *confluence,* the contact boundary is extremely diffuse, and contact is avoided through a failure to differentiate self from other. Confluence is analogous to merger or enmeshment. In *deflection,* the contact boundary is highly rigid, so that when contact is attempted, it bounces off the wall so to speak. Deflection is similar to disengagement.

Rabin (1980) has described how one can begin to observe family process by observing and following the contact boundary as it moves during a family meeting. He has used the image of a tennis ball, tossed from one person to the next, landing short or deep into the receiver's territory, or failing to get over the net, to illustrate this point.

Withdrawal. Withdrawal is the final stage in the cycle, constituting the end of the experience and the completion of the gestalt. After an experience is completed, it goes into background and enriches one's life. An inability to withdraw and let go of experience may result in a hanging-on to unfinished relationships, such as those from one's family of origin.

Process and Techniques of Therapy

The goals of Gestalt family therapy are to help individuals develop clearer self-other boundaries and greater self-awareness in order to break free from stuck patterns and experience life more deeply, particularly in regard to one's family relationships. Different authors have taken different positions in regard to whether the goals are best accomplished by keeping the focus on the individual or by following family process.

Hatcher (1978) recommends blending family and individual therapy, using the former to deal with interpersonal and transactional issues, and the latter to deal with intrapersonal and boundary issues. When an appropriate intrapersonal issue arises, the family member is asked if he or she would like to shift to an individual focus. If the family member opts to work individually, a "minicontract" is established, to which all family members must explicitly agree. Should there not be agreement, this resistance is explored, which helps get at the family's reluctance to permit individuation or separation of its members.

If the family agrees to proceed, the therapist must engage in a fair amount of boundary setting and maintenance as other family members experience strong reactions to the process of the individual of focus. These reactions can be handled either by a simple acknowledgement of the reaction and a return to the individual of focus, or by an agreement to return to the second person's reaction after the first individual's work is completed, depending on the intensity of the reaction.

The individual work is concerned with enhancing self-awareness and promoting differentiation using any or all of the Gestalt techniques, such as the hot seat, the empty chair, the Gestalt experiment, or the person's "becoming" different aspects of his or her projections.

Bauer (1979) uses both individual and family-as-a-whole processes in his approach. For the individual focus, he uses the empty-chair technique with a parent in order to resolve contact-boundary problems between parent and child such as scapegoating, irrational role assignment, and projective identification. The method is based on the notion that, where these problems occur, the parent is projecting split-off, disowned aspects of self onto the child. These projected parts of self are recovered by having the parent enter into a dialogue with the "child" in the empty chair. Bauer describes the process as follows:

> By having the parent give a voice to the child, the parent begins to reown some of the projected part; eventually the focus will shift from the parent and child dialogue to dialogue within the parent himself, or possibly between the parent and his own parent, hence locating the experience historically. The empty chair technique is not a role playing technique to help the parent get along better with the child (although it may be presented that way) but specifically aims at shifting the focus from between parent and child to within the parent himself. (Bauer, 1979, p. 43)

For focusing on the family as a whole, Bauer uses the Gestalt experiment, which is analogous to the directives used in the structure/process schools. The experiments are designed to directly influence the permeability of contact boundaries, particularly those between parents and children, and may be used to correct either confluent, enmeshed boundaries, or rigid, deflecting boundaries. The experiment may involve either straightforward instructions (such as asking confluent parents to not involve their child in their disagreements) or paradoxical directives (such as requiring confluent parents to exaggerate their behavior).

Kaplan and Kaplan (1978) describe a flexible approach which follows the flow of family process, whether its focus is an individual, a subgroup, or the family as a whole. Whatever the specific focus, their work is geared toward the promotion of increased self-awareness and self-responsibility of individuals, in order that they can break out of entrenched positions and make more meaningful relationships with one another. As the Kaplans describe their work:

> In Gestalt therapy, unblocking and exploration come about through expanding awareness of what people do with themselves and with one another. The Gestalt therapist uses the medium of the emergent here-and-now experience to help the family (a) locate current awareness; (b) explore how awareness is blocked; (c) facilitate discovery and expression of hidden (or lost) experiences; (d) experiment with individuation in the family context. (Kaplan & Kaplan, 1978, p. 201)

The choice of where to focus—individual, subsystem, or family group—is made on the basis of the locus of the emergent awareness. Emergent awareness, or "readiness for exploration of awareness" (p. 201), is that which is becoming figural amidst the background of family interaction. Figure in a family context is not what is being talked about (which is *content*); rather, it is what is going on (which is *process*). The content of family communication, although important, is not the most important aspect. The content, or topics of discussion, is organized by the process, that is, by the habitual patterns of interaction. For example, a family may be discussing the misbehavior of their nine-year-old son. Mother criticizes and father mollifies their son. The content is the discussion of the son. The process is the manner in which the parents undercut each other.

Therapists should not point out the process to the family until it is sufficiently figural, so that family members have enough of an experiential sense of the process to be able to become aware of it and integrate it. That is, the therapist should wait until the figure is "phenomenologically loud" (p. 202) before calling the family's attention to it.

In addition to attending to the figural process, the therapist must provide a supportive context in order that family members can risk gaining awareness and making change. The Kaplans describe three functions of the therapist in promoting change: observing, focusing, and facilitating. In observing, the therapist allows the family process to emerge while attending to it very actively. When blocks or resistances are noted, the therapist enters to help focus so that family members may become more aware of their process. Focusing operations can range from simply pointing out the process to using directive techniques (such as exaggerating the process) to heighten awareness. Facilitating is defined as helping family members channel "new awareness and released energy toward constructive reintegration" (p. 205), which may involve the use of Gestalt experiments.

Finally, while working with the family, the therapist also has an ongoing process within, and this is one of the most important therapeutic tools:

> Her/his therapeutic stance is to react with awareness and seek contact and experience with family members to express her/his aroused feelings and needs. In this s/he not only presents a model for taking risks and seeking contacts but by interacting as a person, helps the family achieve awareness of their experience. (Kaplan & Kaplan, 1978, p. 203)

Gestalt Family Therapy: A Unique Approach

Gestalt therapy is an eclectic synthesis of Freudian and neo-Freudian psychoanalytic theory, Gestalt psychology, existentialism, and phenomenology. Gestalt therapy's focus on the individual is carried over into Gestalt family therapy, where the aim is the promotion of individuation as a prerequisite for heightened contact with intimates. In this process, the emphasis is on the necessity for going through the stages (sensation, awareness, action, contact, withdrawal) to complete the Gestalt experience cycle, so that the individual is freed from the consequences of being stuck at any one stage. In family therapy, the contact stage looms large, and it becomes important to deal with the five resistances to contact (introjection, projection, retrojection, confluence, and deflection).

In considering the process and techniques of family therapy, the point of departure is the issue of whether focus is placed on the individual or follows the flow of family process; and, in this, different methods have been suggested by several practitioners (Hatcher's minicontracting, Bauer's use of the empty chair and the Gestalt experiment, and the Kaplans' more general focus on the family process).

In conclusion, I would like to underscore the uniqueness of Gestalt family therapy. It is a method that focuses on the individual in context, yet—because of its eclectic nature—it seems capable of uniting diverse perspectives, from psychoanalytic object relations theory to the structural school. Moreover, because this approach focuses on individual growth, it is possible to conceptualize a broader perspective on treatment in which one could bring into a session (through minicontracting) any of the Gestalt-compatible growth-oriented therapies, such as bioenergetics, Rolfing, transactional analysis, and the like.

EXPERIENTIAL FAMILY THERAPY

The Question of Theory

Experiential family therapy was developed by Carl Whitaker and his associates at Emory University in Atlanta and, from 1965 on, at the University of Wisconsin Medical School. Whitaker's associates include John Warkentin, Thomas Malone, Richard Felder, Gus Napier, and David Keith.

The inclusion of Whitaker as a representative of the experiential model (Levant, 1980a) has been questioned by Keeney and Sprenkle (1980). They comment on Whitaker's use of terms such as "countertransference," "regression," and "primary process" and ask why, then, should he not be grouped among the psychodynamic family therapists. They also raised the question of whether his theory is formally rooted in the writings of any of the existential philosophers. It is true, in fact, that while his writings do contain references to existential philosophers, theologians, and playwrights, his theory is not formally rooted in existentialism.

The reality is that Whitaker's method of therapy is not theory-based. Whatever theory he does have is, indeed, psychodynamic; and he is doing his best to rid himself of that. As he states in his chapter "The hindrance of theory in clinical work": "Theory is the effort to make the unknowable knowable. It's trying to work out a method of forcing the left brain to control the right brain" (Whitaker, 1976a, p. 154). He writes of "the chilling effect [that] theory has on intuition and creativity in general" (p. 155), and he states:

> One of the effects of a therapeutic orientation based on theory is that the therapist becomes an observer. In doing so, he not only avoids his chance to be a person, but he also tends to help the family avoid their courage to be. (Whitaker, 1976a, p. 156)

Pointing out that theory does not work as well for the second-generation therapist (for example, pure psychoanalytic theory didn't work as well for the Freudian as it did for Freud), and referring to the psychotherapy research that finds positive outcomes to be more strongly related to the personal maturity of the therapist than to any theory, he argues that therapy is most appropriately "non theoretical." That term does describe his therapy, which is a highly developed intuitive approach based to a large degree on his person. The nature of his therapy requires a high degree of personal involvement of the therapist with the family, and this provides an intense affective experience for family members—in his words:

> a here-and-now experience with a professional who can share in activating and accelerating the feedback to the family by his own non-rational participation and by his own here-and-now growth process. (Whitaker, 1975, p. 2)

Process of Therapy

Experiential family therapy, as with many therapies, is conceived of in terms of three phases: the beginning ("engagement phase"), the middle ("involvement phase"), and the end ("disentanglement phase"). The process of experiential therapy involves "a pattern of sequential overlapping between the transference relationship and the existential relationship, the existential relating dominating the later stages of psychotherapy" (Whitaker, Felder, & Warkentin, 1965, p. 324). Over the course of therapy, the personal involvement of the therapist with the family grows gradually. This discussion of the process of experiential family therapy will follow the sequential phases, discussing the highlights of each phase: the battles for structure and initiative in the beginning phase; specific techniques used in the middle phase, including extended family consultations and processes for breaking through the "impotence impasse"; and resolving the therapy relationship at the end. At that point, the nature and function of the co-therapy team will be discussed.

The beginning phase. During the beginning phase, two battles must occur—the battle for structure and the battle for initiative.

The *battle for structure* begins at the onset of treatment, during the initial contact with the family, and ends when the therapist succeeds in establishing a two-generational structure to the therapy, with himself in charge.

The battle is often over membership, as is illustrated in the case of the Brice Family, whose course of family therapy is beautifully described in *The family crucible* (Napier & Whitaker, 1978). In this case, the family had agreed during the initial telephone contact to bring to the interview all its members—who included both parents, a teenage daughter (symptom bearer), a young adolescent son, and a six-year-old daughter. At the first interview the son failed to show up. This interview was an intense drama in which the co-therapists had to demonstrate both their firmness and their caringness in a situation where suicide was a potential risk. The parents wanted to focus on the daughter, about whom father was very concerned and mother furious. The co-therapists patiently waited for the son, but when it became clear that he wasn't coming, they attempted to stop the meeting and set up another one. The parents at this point were feeling something along these lines: "We've got a suicidal runaway daughter and you're going to send us away just because our son, who's no trouble at all, is not here!!" Had the co-therapists not paid some attention to this concern, they might have lost the family, and the daughter might have attempted suicide, expressing the family's despair. The resolution required the co-therapists to make a brief assessment of daughter's suicidal potential in order to assure the parents that she would survive until the next meeting, which was set up for the following morning. The resolution was also facilitated by a spontaneous move of Whitaker's at the end of the meeting. After the goodbyes were said, he sat down next to the six-year-old daughter and began to flirt with her, asking if she and he could teach the family to love.

The battle for structure is designed principally to put the therapist in charge of the treatment, as one who has maximum freedom to move in and out of the process, to call the shots and to set the rules. This has the effect of inducing regression in the family and initiating an intense transference relationship. It also communicates to the family that *this* therapy will be serious business and not pseudomutual fooling around. Other aspects of the therapy get defined during this process as well. These include the focus on the family as a whole, the use of the co-therapy team, and Whitaker's admiration of craziness and affection for children.

The *battle for initiative* takes place later in the beginning phase, after the structure is established, the therapeutic relationships formed, and the family's life and problems examined. At this point, the co-therapists work to force the family to take the initiative for their own growth and development, and the responsibility for their own life decisions. Whitaker describes the process as follows:

> Assuming the treatment has been structured, the initial treatment phase includes what I call the battle for initiative. Having set up my own integrity here in my territory, I feel it crucially important to define the integrity of the family. You could call this the "I" position of the family. I demand that their life and their decisions are crucially theirs. For example, mother says in the second interview, "Do you think I ought to get a divorce from this man?" And I answer, "It's fine with me. I'm married and don't expect to divorce my wife and you're free to have the same privilege of either living with him or divorcing him. I'm only concerned with whether you keep coming to therapy. However, if divorce means you aren't coming to the interview, then we better stop now." The battle for initiative includes also the fact that once we're past the initial history, the question of where we go should really be up to the family. I want to participate, but I don't want them to be passive. The ball is in their hands, and although I can coach, I cannot carry the ball of their living and their efforts to make that living more successful. It's not only that I am unwilling to make decision. I try to keep it clear that I am not interested in whether they get a divorce or not. I'm not interested in whether they call the police when the son misbehaves. That's their world and they have to live in it the way they feel right. I don't think that my pattern of living is more valid than theirs, and more important, they can't change their pattern of living unless first they are who they are. Imitating me is not the way to learn how to live. (Whitaker, 1976b, pp. 12–13).

The battle for initiative, when successfully completed, establishes the existential relationship with the family, which has a more adult-to-adult character and a balance between co-therapist team and the family members, with contributions to the process coming from both groups.

The middle phase.   During this phase the family moves into actively defining and working on its life issues as the co-therapists become increasingly personally involved with the family. The outcome of this process varies. Some families leave therapy at this point, having gotten the hang of taking responsibility for their lives, and preferring to go it alone. Others continue to work on their problems in therapy with positive results. Still others get stuck in an impasse. This usually involves a freezing of gears in the shift from the transferential to the existential process of therapy. That is, the family continues with varying degrees of subtlety to demand that the co-therapy team do something to help them change. This kind of impasse most often occurs in less mature families, and it can be traced back to the grandparents and their notions of relationships and living. This impasse is called the *impotence impasse* because "the psychotherapist feels useless despite his best effort and concern" (Keith & Whitaker, 1978, p. 69). Whitaker and his associates have described several ways to resolve this impasse. One is to involve the grandparents and possibly other members of the extended family in treatment, through a grandparent consultation or extended-family reunion. The other ways involve the therapists' using their sense of frustration and helplessness to break through the impasse. This can take the form of absurdity or acting-in.

When a *consultation with the grandparent generation* is set up, the therapists should begin by defining their impotence. The grandparents are thus involved as assistants to the therapists rather than as patients. This kind of meeting can have important effects in helping to establish more of an adult-to-adult existential relationship between the grandparents and parents, which in turn empowers the parents to take more responsibility for their own therapy and life (Whitaker, 1976c).

An *extended-family reunion* may also be useful. This may involve large numbers of people and take place over one or several whole days. The therapists' job is simply to provide the pretext for the meeting. The extended family does the rest, which can

> accomplish a remarkable release of affect, discovery of new realities, detriangulation of some of the family structurings, remobilization of some of the groups that were previously intimate, and cooling off of some of the wars. (Whitaker, 1976c, p. 190)

Absurdity and acting-in are two ways of attempting to directly resolve the impasse, using the therapists' sense of impotence as the reagent.

Psychotherapy of the absurd is a method to disrupt old rigidified patterns of thought and behavior. It is analogous both to paradoxical methods and to the *koans* used by Zen masters to bring about enlightenment. It must be done in a caring, loving way; and, contrary to the usual practice of paradoxical techniques, it is best done without rational thought or plan, but rather intuitively, even unconsciously. It may be a single intervention, which often results in a mood of "creative craziness" facilitative of moving beyond impasse. For example, Whitaker might make an unannounced exit from the therapy room, and return some moments later with the inane explanation "my foot itched" (Whitaker, 1975, p. 6). Or, in another case, Whitaker was seeing a woman who complained about the therapy and threatened to return to her former therapist. During an interview he suddenly grabbed her foot and drew his initials on her canvas shoes with a felt-tipped pen (Haley & Hoffman, 1967, pp. 318-319).

The use of absurdity may also become an ongoing process, taking place over weeks of therapy. In this case, Whitaker builds a precarious tower, taking the patient's initial absurdity and adding layer upon layer of absurdity. At a certain point the patient attempts to break the escalation, which is parried by the therapist's insistence that he is trying to help. Finally there is a break in the patient's integration, and the tower crashes. The patient either develops a deep dependency, as manifested in the statement "we've had a really great week, and I can't understand it"; or rebels and leaves therapy, complaining that the therapist is crazy; or experiences enlightenment, developing a profound understanding of the absurdity of his or her own implicit stance in life.

Whitaker explains this process as follows. The therapist manipulates

> the transference until the therapist's credibility is at the breaking point and the patient must either develop a new *gestalt* that excludes the therapist or regress to keep the transference *gestalt* alive—that is, to keep the therapist magic, keep him the God of their joint reality from which the "therapist-as-a-person" has now withdrawn. (Whitaker, 1975, p. 11)

The third possibility, enlightenment, comes about by transcending the transference relationship and establishing an existential relationship with the therapist.

Keith & Whitaker (1978, pp. 72-73) provide an illustration of the use of psychotherapy of the absurd to resolve the psychosis of a 22-year-old male. The family was at the point of committing their son to a state mental hospital and he was at the point of complying. The therapist made a deal with the family: The son (K) would remain at home and be seen in daily outpatient therapy for at least one week.

The therapist took K's initial absurdity of giving up on life and becoming a chronic mental patient and exaggerated it. He explained that K's problem was that he needed to be productive. He hit upon the idea of K being a statue, and proceeded to arrange him like Rodin's *The thinker*. K complied, but verbally protested that if he did this, he would continue to be dependent on his father. The therapist insisted: "Look, it's art, my friend."

K came to his appointments faithfully and seemed to enjoy them. The content concerned the problems of being a statue, such as the use of isometric exercises to avoid getting out of shape. K stayed at home and actually spent periods of time as a statue. During the week he gradually reintegrated, so that by the week's end he was well-groomed, affable, and driving himself to his appointments. A week later, a series of family interviews was begun, with some significant work on the part of the parents. At two years' follow-up, K was symptom-free, married, and a father.

Acting-in is a procedure that stems from the high degree of personal involve-ment of the therapist. It is a process opposite to acting-out, wherein the patient (usually an adolescent) expresses with "insignificant others" the fundamentals of the family conflict, resulting in a reduction of the patient's affective involvement with the family. In acting-in, the therapist attempts to intensify the therapeutic relationship by bringing in high levels of personal affect. Acting-in usually involves some kind of provocative or challenging act on the part of therapist. It, like absur-dity, is a tricky and risky procedure, and to be handled well, it requires specific training and experience (preferably in a co-therapy teaching context).

Keith & Whitaker (1978, pp. 74–75) give an example of the use of acting-in in a family with two out-of-control adolescent children and a set of intellectual par-ents. The kids started taking the therapist's phone apart and mother objected with, "I feel uncomfortable when you play with the doctor's telephone. Would you please stop." The kids sneered and their play became more destructive. The thera-pist intervened: "Hey you characters, I don't want you doing that to my phone." The kids kept right on, dismantling various components of the phone. The therapist became suddenly angry: "Look, dammit, that's *my* phone, I don't want you play-ing with it, now put it back together and sit down!!" The kids, startled by the anger, complied and went to sit by their mother.

The end phase.   The end phase of therapy involves the disentangling of the co-therapy team and the family. The crucial issues are separation anxiety and any indebtedness that the family might feel. These can be resolved by the co-therapists reversing roles with the family, using them as therapists as they (the co-therapists) talk about their own grieving over the ending of therapy. This process is genuinely possible because the degree of personal involvement of the co-therapists is quite high by this time. As Whitaker expressed it:

> If you didn't grow to love the family you work with, you've not only missed a golden opportunity, you're probably making believe something hasn't hap-pened when indeed it has. A family that is worth treating is worth loving. (Whitaker, 1976b, p. 27)

The therapist's involvement and the co-therapy team.   This is a therapy of in-volvement, which runs the risk of overinvolvement. Whitaker uses his personal pro-cess, particularly the least rational part of it, to a very high degree in his work with families. As he once said, "My therapy is often controlled by my unconscious" (Haley & Hoffman, 1967, p. 353). As a consequence, a co-therapist is quite impor-tant, if not a necessity, to provide a certain degree of security as well as corrective feedback and bail-out when needed. Co-therapy also serves other functions, such as modeling an intimate relationship for the family, and providing opportunities for the therapists' attending to different persons or subunits simultaneously.

Whitaker considers the degree of affective involvement of the co-therapists with the family so critical that he specifically points out that it is inadvisable for co-therapists to engage in extratherapeutic communication: "If therapists joke and complain about the family privately, their involvement with the family is decreased and valuable affect about the family is dissipated" (Napier & Whitaker, 1973, p. 112).

Whitaker keeps his own involvement high by going into therapy intent on serving his own needs for growth:

> I'm trying to expand myself. That's what I'm here for. I'm looking for an experience that will excite me and open me and cause me to grow. (Haley & Hoffman, 1967, p. 277)

To aid their efforts to stay alive to their therapy, Whitaker recommends to therapists the following set of 11 rules:

1. Relegate every significant other to second place.
2. Learn how to love. Flirt with any infant available. Unconditional positive regard probably isn't present after the baby is three years old.
3. Develop a reverence for your own impulses, and be suspicious of your behavior sequences.
4. Enjoy your mate more than your kids, and be childish with your mate.
5. Fracture role structures at will and repeatedly.
6. Learn to retreat and advance from every position that you take.
7. Guard your impotence as one of your most valuable weapons.
8. Build long-term relations so you can be free to hate safely.
9. Face the fact that you must grow until you die. Develop a sense of the benign absurdity of life—yours and those around you—and thus learn to transcend the world of experience. If we can abandon our missionary zeal we have less chance of being eaten by cannibals.
10. Develop your primary process living. Evolve a joint craziness with someone you are safe with. Structure a professional cuddle group so you won't abuse your mate with the garbage left over from the day's work.
11. As Plato said, "practice dying." (Whitaker, 1976a, p. 164)

The Dialectic of Whitaker's Therapy

Although it includes traces of psychodynamic theory and reference to existentialism, Whitaker's therapy is most appropriately viewed as atheoretical and as a highly developed intuitive form of experiential therapy.

He sees therapy as a dialectical process in which the family moves from a transferential mode of relating to an existential, I-Thou form of relationship. The beginning phase includes both the establishment of the transferential relationship with the battle for structure, and the launching of the existential mode with the battle for initiative. In the middle phase, the family members begin to actively engage in their own struggle. Some continue this process in therapy, and some leave and do it on their own. Others get stuck in the transferential-existential dialectic at a place that Whitaker calls "the impotence impasse." Four methods that can be effective in resolving this impasse are grandparent consultations, extended-family reunions, resolution of the impotence impasse through absurdity, and resolution through acting-in. The end phase of therapy involves the successful disentanglement of the highly involved co-therapy team from the family. The therapists' high degree of involvement is offset by the use of the co-therapy team.

CLIENT-CENTERED
FAMILY THERAPY

Client-centered family therapy is a relatively recent entrant into the field. It shares certain characteristics with behavioral family therapy, another "new kid on the block." First, both client-centered and behavioral family therapy developed approaches for working conjointly with the family and then both moved into psychological-educational approaches for training one or more family members in the respective therapeutic techniques for the purpose of either remediation or prevention. The conjoint client-centered family approach was based on the client-centered therapy of Rogers (1951) and was developed by van der Veen and associates at the Institute for Juvenile Research in Chicago (Raskin & van der Veen, 1970) and by Levant (1978a) at Boston University. In this chapter the conjoint approach of client-centered family therapy will be discussed; the psychological-educational approaches will be reserved for discussion in Chapter 9.

Second, both client-centered and behavioral approaches are unique in the family of family therapies for their position on resistance. Resistance is not acknowledged by either school. This position is unique because if one examines the spectrum of family therapy approaches, one finds the concept of resistance to be almost universally accepted. The psychodynamic family therapist describes resistance as the patient's conscious and unconscious countermaneuvers to therapeutic intervention (Framo, 1965b). The family-interactional psychotherapist wrote of family homeostasis, wherein the improvement in one family member would be countered by the behavior of others in the family, or would eventuate in another member becoming disturbed (Jackson & Weakland, 1961). Structure/process therapists have evolved an armory of paradoxical techniques to cope with resistance. And even in the experiential paradigm, the Gestalt family therapist talks of resistance to contact (Rabin, 1980), while the experiential family therapist highlights the impotence impasse (Keith & Whitaker, 1978).

The Family
as a Self-Directed Unit

An alternative view of the family, one which provides the theoretical basis for a client-centered family therapy, is more optimistic about the family's possibility for self-directed change. This alternative conception of the family seems to bridge, and possibly to resolve, a major ideological issue that separates the psychodynamic and family systems camps; that is, whether the focus should be on the individual (oriented to the intrapsychic dynamics) or on the larger social unit (oriented to the multipersonal systems dynamics). This alternative view of the family involves a phenomenological, subjective framing of the concept of the family system.

The individual orientation attempts to explain family dynamics in terms of the intrapsychic dynamics of the individual members of the family. This is not likely to account for much of the variance of family interaction, because family members understand each other's behavior at least in part in terms of the *context* of the family—its relationships, values, and traditions (van der Veen, 1969). On the other hand, the family-systems orientation will not be able to account for much of the variance in individuals' responses to the same objective event, simply because people experience the same events in very different ways.

The phenomenological view surmounts both difficulties. To paraphrase and adapt some of Rogers's propositions (Rogers, 1951), the person exists in, and is the center of, a phenomenal world that includes internal and external realms of experience. The internal realm includes one's experience of one's own intrapsychic dynamics; the external realm includes one's experience of the dynamics of one's family system. One behaves in a goal-directed fashion to maintain and enhance self in response to one's perceived experience in both realms.

This view takes into account both intrapsychic and family systems dynamics. Also, if the person is placed in the center of the phenomenal field, we are in a good position to enlarge intrapsychic explanations of behavior by taking into account the social context of that behavior; and, we can deepen family systems explanations of behavior by considering the subjective basis for idiosyncratic responses to the same objective stimuli. Moreover, this view assumes that individuals are motivated for maintenance *and* enhancement or growth (self-actualization), rather than being motivated to oppose change and growth. Finally, it allows the placing of responsibility for the conceptualization and actualization of family experience with the individual members of the family, who, by virtue of their position at the center of their phenomenal world, are best able to assume this responsibility.

The family concept.   The notion of the "family concept," developed by van der Veen and his group, is a central idea in the phenomenological view of the family. The family concept "denote[s] a person's awareness and conceptualization of his interpersonal family experiences. . . . [It] refer[s] to the person's experience plus the meaning he imparts to this experience" (van der Veen, 1969, p. 20).

> The family concept consists essentially of the feelings, attitudes, and expectations each of us has regarding his or her family life. The family concept encompasses a relatively stable and potent set of psychological attributes. It is assumed to have several characteristics: It influences behavior; it can be referred to and talked about by the individual and it can change as a result of new experience and understanding. (Raskin and van der Veen, 1970, p. 389)

The family concept is analogous to the self-concept, in that it is an organized cognitive-perceptual schema with associated affects, which is based on experience.

The relationship of family concept and self-concept needs to be studied further, since both arise out of family experience. For example, the self-concept develops initially from the evaluation of self by others, particularly parents (Rogers, 1951).

So far, this discussion of the phenomenological conception of the family has focused on how the individual experiences the family. Let us turn now to the family as a whole, continuing in the same theoretical vein. The family as a whole consists of the *"shared consciousness by the parents and the children of their experience together"* (van der Veen, 1969, p. 7). The family concept provides the theoretical foundation for a phenomenological conception of the family as a whole.

> Another way of viewing the importance of the family concept is to consider the role it plays in the members' definition and creation of their lives together as a family. The family is internally created by the members, both children and parents, and is not exclusively or even primarily a "given" of society, even though this may not be clearly apparent to the members themselves. . . . What, after all, would the family be without the ideas that the members themselves have of it? Would it be too extreme to assert that the existence and nature of the family unit depend *foremost* on the members' ideas about it? Our focus on the person's concept of the family seeks to bring the family out of the background of a universal given, into the foreground of an emergent and vital social grouping, a grouping that depends for its shape and substance on the efforts, purposes and ideas of each of its members. (van der Veen, 1969, p. 5)

R. D. Laing develops this argument further. He writes of the "unification by coinherence. . . . We feel ourselves to be one in so far as each of us has inside himself a presence common to all [members of] . . . the family" (Laing, 1969, p. 5).

> Each member incarnates a structure derived from relations between members. This family-in-common shared *group presence* exists *in so far as* each member has it inside himself. . . . Each member of the family may require the other members to keep the same 'family' image inside themselves. Each person's identity then rests on a shared 'family' inside the others who, by that token, are themselves in the same family. *To be in the same family is to feel the same 'family' inside.* (Laing, 1969, p. 13)

It can get considerably more complex, of course:

> The family is united by the reciprocal internalization by each (whose token of membership is precisely this interiorized family) of each other's internalization. The unity of the family is in the interior of each synthesis and each synthesis is bound by reciprocal interiority with each other's internalization of each other's interiorization. (Laing, 1969, p. 5)

To carry this further, the family concept is not simply "a member's view of the rest of the family in relation to himself. It also represents qualities concerning the entire family including oneself. It places more stress on 'we', rather than 'they' versus 'me'" (van der Veen, 1969, p. 4). The family concept, then, is a concept of the multipersonal group, which leaves room for a systems conception. Or, using ideas that Laing developed, "the *family as a* system," "a space-time system," is what is interiorized in the family concept. "Relations and operations between elements and sets of elements are internalized, not elements in isolation" (Laing, 1969, p. 4).

Parenthetically, Laing is an excellent phenomenologist, as has been noted (Curry, 1967a), but he reaches a point where it seems that he loses the internal, subjective frame of reference. This seems to be the point at which he accepts the idea of resistance:

> However, one thing is often clear to an outsider: there is a concerted family *resistance* to discovering what is going on, and there are complicated stratagems to keep everyone in the dark, and in the dark they are in the dark. (Laing, 1969, p. 77)

Client-Centered Family Therapy

The application of client-centered principles to family therapy was a natural development. By 1970, client-centered principles had been applied to several therapeutic modalities, from action-oriented play therapy to interpersonally oriented group therapy, as well as to nontherapy activities such as teaching, administration, training of nonprofessionals, and prevention and enhancement programs (Rogers, 1951; Hart & Tomlinson, 1970). The reason for its wide application, and for its natural fit with family therapy, is that, fundamentally, client-centered theory addresses the processes of enhancing close interpersonal relationships (Rogers, 1961).

A client-centered approach to family therapy requires at base the same attitudes and activities of the therapist that are required in client-centered approaches to other forms of helping. The method begins with a deep trust in the ability of the family members to assume the responsibility for their own change and growth, and a respect for their ability to make the decisions that are best for themselves about all aspects of the therapy, such as who will participate and to what extent, what the significant areas for discussion will be, what meaning will be derived from the experience, and what actions, if any, will be taken. Related to this trust and respect, the therapist experiences a sense of nonpossessive caring and warmth for the family. In this, the therapist attempts to gain an appreciation of the internal frames of reference of the family members and to communicate empathic understanding of family experiences; tries to stay in contact with and follow the moment-to-moment changes in the family's experiential flow; and interacts with the family members on a genuine basis, being transparent about personal feelings and congruent with personal experience.

This is a therapy in which the therapist is not so much expert as coparticipant in, and facilitator of, the process of therapy. The role does not involve history taking, diagnosis, treatment planning, or the use of therapeutic techniques to induce change (whether they be paradoxical maneuvers or interpretations). Rather, it involves facilitating the release and development of self-regenerative and self-enhancing powers within the family members. It also involves a direct encounter on a person-to-person basis with family members. It is a therapy that is based to a very large extent on the person of the therapist.

Development of the approach. Much of the following account of the development of this approach comes from my own involvement with this method since 1972. I did not begin with an explicit intention of developing a method of family therapy. The initial work took place in a therapeutic school for adolescents (Shlien & Levant, 1974). The students were socioeconomically disadvantaged. The majority lived with their families in public housing, subsisting on public welfare. Many came from single-parent families with large numbers of children. The students were many years behind academically, in terms of test scores and prior grade placement. Most of the students were referred for behavioral problems of an aggressive or antisocial nature; however, some were withdrawn, and were referred for problems ranging from school phobia to psychosis.

Our experience with the students and their families took place in a context in which we were a program of last resort. Many other programs had failed with our students, and the next step for many of them would have been some sort of institutional confinement. We offered a broad spectrum of coordinated services: remedial, standard, and advanced instruction in academic and vocational areas (offered initially to students, but later requested by parents for themselves); individual, group, and family therapy, with a client-centered orientation; coordination of services impinging on the families from multiple service agencies, similar to the ecological approach described by Auerswald (1968); and aftercare and placement services. The school was open during the daytime on weekdays during the school year. To cover for the times that the school was not in operation, many additional services were offered: summer programs; neighborhood outreach programs, including home visits and recreational programs in the public housing projects; crisis intervention and emergency services; and temporary shelter and short-term residential placement when students could not live with their families.

During this time we did not focus on family therapy *per se.* It was only one of a range of services that were offered to students and their families. Initially, our stereotypes of the "multiproblem family" were shattered. There were discoveries of strengths and resources in these families that we did not expect to find. More important, many of these families emerged as strongly self-directed, and they used much of what we had to offer to facilitate their own improvement. Normalization and stabilization of previously chaotic family life, followed by planned steps toward upward mobility, were the results that we observed of the families' self-designed programs of change. This took tangible form as (1) reduction of disruptive behavior on the part of the students, concomitant with their reengagement in the process of learning; (2) reduction in family chaos and crisis, attendant upon parents' renewal of hope for improvement in their lives; (3) students coming up to the grade level and returning to public schools; (4) unemployed fathers (and some mothers) seeking and attaining job training and employment; (5) families moving out of public housing and going off of public assistance; (6) students and parents completing their high-school education and entering college (Levant, 1973).

Current practice. For the past eight years, I have been practicing a client-centered form of family therapy in a private psychiatric hospital. The hospital serves adolescents and adults who are generally middle-class and who cover the entire spectrum of diagnostic categories. There are high frequencies of acute psychotic episodes, depressions with suicide potential, and adolescent antisocial behavioral problems. Hospitalizations average just over 30 days. Family therapy is initiated during the hospitalization and continues after discharge.

The membership of the family therapy group is flexibly defined, depending on the family situation and the expressed motivation of family members. Therapy has included three generations of a family, two-generational nuclear families, couples, parents and identified patient, sibling groups, and individual family members. Therapy will often begin with the whole family and then settle on a smaller subgroup. The composition of family meetings may change from time to time, depending on the needs of the family. The situations in which only one member of the family is seen have evolved from seeing the entire family. Such cases usually involve a young adult attempting to separate from the parental family.

This form of therapy seems to be particularly effective in engaging difficult families. The crises that lead to hospitalization usually raise the anxiety or guilt feelings of family members to such an extent that they (the family members) enter into the situation with a great deal of defensiveness, appearing initially to be very closed to any involvement in therapy. Family members seem to particularly welcome an approach that does not force an agenda on them, but that, instead, demonstrates understanding and respect for their situation and allows them some control over the process of therapy, particularly in regard to the timing with which delicate issues are surfaced. I have found that many families that initially seem to be "highly resistant" or even hostile to therapy can be engaged to a significant degree with this approach.

Another interesting finding is that families in client-centered therapy discover and resolve, on their own initiative, dynamic entanglements considered to be of a deeply pathological nature, and thought to require expert-directed resolution by other schools of family therapy. For example, there is the classic set of family dynamics in which chronic conflict between the spouses is not dealt with directly, but rather indirectly through differential, conflicting, and covert policies toward a child, labeled "detouring" by Minuchin (1974).

In a case reported in the literature (Raskin & van der Veen, 1970, p. 399) the parents of an 11-year-old identified patient discovered that their "elongated discussions about Susan are really hedging, away from the basic things that might free us really"—that is, facing the troublesome aspects of their marriage. They worked directly on their relationship and began to own some of their individual contributions to their marital difficulties. As they did this, their daughter "detriangled" herself to the extent of overcoming her difficulties in getting involved in activities outside of the home.

In a family that I saw for seven months in therapy, Sandy, a 29-year-old divorced mother of three, had been experiencing severe migraine headaches and was disabled to the point that she and her children had to live in her parents' home. Contributing to this situation was her long-standing triangulation in her family of origin, in which she felt a great deal of responsibility for her father's happiness, and felt very distant from her mother. As therapy progressed, family members began to speak openly to one another (whereas formerly they would speak critically of another family member only in that person's absence, for fear of causing hurt). A turning point was reached at Christmas, when the parents' conflict was strikingly enacted in their mutually exclusive plans for the holiday celebration. Sandy and her siblings began to point out their parents' need to deal with their relationship. Over the next few months, the parents began to examine and face some of the difficulties in their marriage. As this happened, Sandy felt greater freedom to make a series of decisions that culminated in the establishment of a separate home for herself and her children.

Special Requirements
of a Family Form
of Client-Centered Therapy

Only a little has been written about client-centered family therapy. Aside from the work of the van der Veen group and my own, there is a discussion by Rogers of the effects of individual therapy on the family (1961, pp. 314–328); and a brief note on preventive and therapeutic couples groups and multiple-family therapy is included in Rogers's study of couples (1972, pp. 217–219). This is an underdeveloped area in terms of theoretical and clinical writings. One of the questions that needs to be asked is whether any special modifications of theory or procedures of therapy required in order to take into account the special qualities of the family group. We are just beginning to scratch the surface in this area, but the answer seems to be affirmative, lying with the further conceptual elaboration of two of the basic interpersonal qualities required of the therapist: empathy and genuineness.

With regard to empathy, in family work the focus is not so much on the inner world of each family member (although it is that at times), but rather on the felt meanings as individual family members experience their relationships to other family members. But whereas in individual therapy it is possible to keep the client figural and consider as part of the phenomenal field the persons with whom the client is in relationship, in family therapy, all parties to a relationship (whether dyadic or triadic) must be kept figural (if not simultaneously, then at least within a brief period of time). This requires the balancing of multiple inner frames of reference, in order to be empathic with all family members. With regard to genuineness, similar to what Rogers and his associates (1967) found in their work with schizophrenic patients, this dimension assumes increased importance in family therapy. But, whereas with the nonverbal schizophrenic patients it was necessary to be genuine in order to reach out and build a relationship, with families it is necessary to be genuine in order to be "let in" to the inner family system. Furthermore, the genuine emotional responses of the therapist to family pain or grief, appropriately expressed, can have a powerful impact on unfreezing stuck family relationships. Indeed, the dimension of genuineness has been shown in a recent review to be a key ingredient in family therapy from a wide range of theoretical perspectives (Kaslow, Cooper, & Linsenberg, 1979). These ideas need to be developed further through clinical, theoretical, and research activities.

SUMMARY

The three major experiential schools of family therapy are the Gestalt, the experiential, and the client-centered schools. In general, it can be observed that the distinctive quality of schools in this model is their emphasis on experience in the present, their definition of conflicts in existential rather than psychodynamic terms, and their use of a phenomenological method for understanding the experience and issues of family members (that is, viewing experience through the internal subjective frame of reference of the person).

Gestalt family therapy, based on the eclectic and systemic Gestalt therapy as developed by its principle conceptualizer, Fritz Perls, moves into the interpersonal and familial context while retaining a focus on the individual. The Gestalt experience cycle is taken as the theoretical basis for conceptualizing family experience.

With regard to Whitaker, although his background is in the psychodynamic model, and although he refers to existentialism in his writings, his actual approach is best characterized as atheoretical. Whitaker practices a highly developed intuitive form of therapy, emphasizing the heightening of experience. Therapy for him goes through three phases and involves a dialectical process whereby the family shifts from a transferential to an existential mode of relating.

Client-centered family therapy, like the behavioral school, is relatively new. Both approaches share similar views on the concept of resistance, and both have moved quickly from conjoint family therapy to the development of psychological-educational, skills-training approaches. The client-centered view of the family, based on the notion that persons are motivated for self-enhancement and growth, is optimistic. The family concept is a core construct in the approach; it constitutes a recasting of the notion of the family system into subjective phenomenological terms.

RESOURCES:
CLINICAL EXAMPLES
OF THE EXPERIENTIAL
APPROACHES

   I. *Gestalt Family Therapy*
        1. The Kempler Institute (P.O. Box 1692, Costa Mesa, CA 92626—brochure available) has available for rental or purchase a series of films illustrating the Gestalt-experiential approach to family therapy. Titles

include: *Patient resistance, a myth; A runaway girl from a runaway family; The family is the patient* and *Breaking through; The facts are not enough; Sweet and gentle* and *The court jester gets a transplant; Any topic will do; I know how they feel . . . , I'm sure she is lonely . . . ,* and *I still want her but . . . ; Beyond his many words, sadness and loneliness; A madonna smiles* (two films), *The smile vanishes* (two films), and *Negotiation; A disturbed family* and *The family progresses; The power; Mothers and jobs;* and *One alone.* The first five of these films were reviewed by Gladfelter (1972).

2. Kempler's recent book *Experiential psychotherapy within families* (1981) contains verbatim transcripts with commentary of the brief three-session treatment, with follow-up, of a family with two adolescent sons, the youngest of whom "sets fires, lies, and steals, but is basically a good boy."

3. Netta Kaplan has a videotape of her work (with co-therapist Mark Weinberg). It is of the fifth session in a series of eight with a family with a young adult daughter and an adolescent son who is having difficulty in school. (The tape is available from Media Centre, University of Windsor, Windsor, Ontario, Canada). It has been reviewed by Guerin and Sherman (1982).

II. *Experiential Family Therapy*

1. Whitaker is one of the participants in the Hillcrest Family Series (see Chapter 4).

2. The Philadelphia Child Guidance Clinic (Two Children's Center, 34th Street and Civic Center Boulevard, Philadelphia, PA 19104) has a tape and a four-tape set available for rental. *Affinity* is a consultation interview with a family with an encopretic son; this interview also appears as Chapter 10 of Minuchin (1974). The four-tape set, *A family with Minuchin and Whitaker,* was described in Chapter 5.

3. The Boston Family Institute (251 Harvard Street, Brookline, MA 02146) has two tapes available for rental or purchase. *An isolated father in the family* is a consultation interview with a family with two young daughters and a couple experiencing marital distress; and *Carl Whitaker* is an interview of Whitaker on his personal and professional background.

4. IEA Productions (520 East 77th Street, New York, NY 10021) has three tape sets of Whitaker's work available for purchase only. *The process of family therapy* consists of annotated excerpts of 6 out of 10 sessions of treatment, plus a one-year follow-up interview. The latter shows the family's reactions to the replay of the first part of the tape. This tape has received two recent reviews, one favorable (Berman, 1981) and one unfavorable (Frykman, 1981). *Family therapy consultation, Parts I and II* is a consultation interview and postinterview debriefing session concerning a family in which school-aged daughter and son are both experiencing developmental problems. *Three generational family consultation, Parts I and II* is a similar tape set, this time with a multi-generational focus.

5. South Beach Psychiatric Center (777 Seaview Avenue, S.I., NY 10305) has available for rental or purchase five tapes in which Whitaker conducts interviews and discusses his work: *Co-therapy of chronic schizophrenia; Consultant for a multi-family group; Consultation with a fragmented family at impasse; Consultant for a schizophrenic young man and his family; Consultant with an adolescent boy and his family.*

6. Haley and Hoffman (1967) include in their book an initial interview by

Whitaker with a family in which the teenage son was threatening to assault the father. Their presentation interweaves segments of the family interview with segments from an interview with Whitaker in which the family tape was played and he was queried as to his rationale for his interventions.

7. A full-length case study (Keith and Whitaker) and one-year follow-up (Napier) of a family working out their divorce appears as Chapters 7 and 8 in Papp (1977a).

8. A case study of a "psychoticogenic family" by Keith and Whitaker is presented as Chapter 10 of Andolfi and Zwerling (1980).

9. And, finally, Napier and Whitaker's book *The family crucible* (1978) is a reconstruction of the entire treatment with a family with three children, in which the adolescent daughter was suicidal.

III. *Client-centered Family Therapy*

At this point, little material is available that illustrates client-centered family therapy. Four tapes of Rogers interviewing marital couples are available from American Personnel and Guidance Association (Film Department, 1607 New Hampshire Avenue, N.W., Washington, DC 20009) and several case studies are included in Rogers's book *Becoming partners* (1972); these materials, however, emphasize normal developmental rather than therapeutic processes.

7

Outcome Research,
Training,
and Professional Issues

We are about to conclude our coverage of the field of family therapy, which began with drawing a map of the field and included discussions of the major approaches to therapeutic work with families. We are thus in the position of The Systemic Sheik and Floy Floy in the cartoon depicted in Figure 7-1—aware of our choices and needing to consider what we really want to do (Liddle & Saba, 1981a, 1981b, 1982).

To round out the coverage and, it is hoped, to aid your choices, we will consider several topics in this chapter. First, we will discuss evaluative research on family therapy. As will be seen, this is a field with more unanswered questions than hard facts, and the discussion here may (hopefully) stimulate both an appreciation of the complexities involved in such research and an interest in it. Therapy research in general has been impeded by the distance traditionally maintained between clinicians and researchers, a distance that in recent years has happily decreased. To eventually solve some of the riddles of outcome research, we need clinicians and researchers who understand in depth the "ways of knowing" of their counterparts. We also need more true clinician-researchers, highly skilled professionals comfortable in both realms.

Following this consideration of outcome research, we will take up the topics of training and professional issues. The discussion of training will consider where

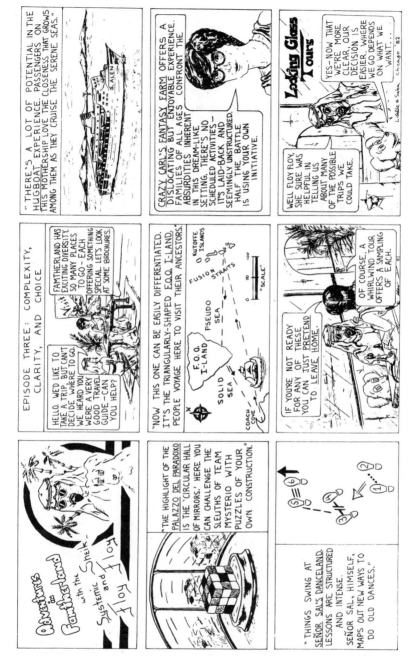

FIGURE 7-1 "Adventures in Famtherland with The Systemic Sheik and Floy Floy: Episode three—Complexity, Clarity, and Choice." Liddle and Saba, 1982, p. 7. Copyright © 1982 by the American Association for Marriage and Family Therapy. Reprinted by permission.)

one can obtain training in family therapy and what one can expect in terms of the components of such training. In addition, research on the effects of training and on the many variations in training patterns will be discussed. Finally, the discussion of professional issues will first cover the regulation of marital and family therapy, with some attention given to the myriad credentialing process extant in the field. After that, the topic of professional associations and ethics will be surveyed.

OUTCOME RESEARCH

In our current era of consumer consciousness and demands for professional accountability, there has been a concomitant emphasis on evaluating help-intended interventions in order to determine their effectiveness. Programs ranging from individual psychotherapy to educational television have increasingly been put under the scrutiny of empirical research to answer the question, Does it work?

The question, of course, cannot be answered in the simplistic manner in which it is phrased. First of all, *it* must be defined. Defining *it* as psychotherapy or family therapy is not sufficient, because there are many types of therapies. Thus the independent variable—the intervention—must be defined specifically: multigenerational, or structural, or experiential family therapy, for example. And since we are talking about therapy, *it* includes both the therapeutic approach (theory and techniques) and the therapist (his or her personal style and interpersonal skills). Then the term *work* must be defined. What are the goals of the therapy, and what outcomes are sought: symptom-abatement, personality change, family restructuring, or some combination of these? And, is the therapy expected to work for everyone, or for only certain specified groups, whether they be diagnostic categories of identified patients, or family types, or members of specific socioeconomic or ethnic groups? Further, is the therapy expected to work under all conditions, or only under certain conditions, such as inpatient or outpatient treatment, treatment in the office or in the home, short-term or long-term treatment, or voluntary or coerced treatment? Thus we get back to G. L. Paul's question (1967, p. 111), quoted in Chapter 3: "*What* treatment, by *whom,* is most effective for *this* individual with *that* specific problem, and under *which* set of circumstances?"

Unfortunately, the state of the art is such that we are only beginning to ask and answer such specific questions. When it is asked, we have been getting useful answers; but most of the research has failed to be sufficiently specific. This discussion will provide an overview of the outcome research, covering both the substantive findings as well as some of the methodological issues. Because family therapy outcome research grew out of psychotherapy outcome research, many current issues of family therapy research issues harken back to the earlier psychotherapy research issues. Thus a tour through psychotherapy research as a starter will benefit our understanding of the issues.

Psychotherapy Outcome Research

Like family therapy, the current interest in psychotherapy outcome research dates back to the 1950s and represents a break with psychoanalytic tradition. The prevailing views at that time regarded therapy as a process of such subtlety that it would defy empirical investigation, and, further, as a process that should not be studied for fear that the delicate therapeutic relationship would be disturbed to the client's detriment. While concern for client's welfare, as well as aspirations to do justice to the complexity of psychotherapy should, and do, guide our research efforts, these caveats are no longer taken as insurmountable barriers.

The Eysenck-Bergin debate. To Hans Eysenck must go the credit for breaking the impasse and stimulating serious interest in psychotherapy research. In 1952 he published the first in a series of review articles in which he purported to demonstrate that approximately two-thirds of all neurotic patients improve within two years, whether treated by psychotherapy or not. The so-called "unbeatable two-thirds law" became a gauntlet thrown down by Eysenck, challenging the psychotherapy field to demonstrate its effectiveness or call it quits. This particular challenge also served for far too long to focus the field on the question, Does it work? thereby impeding the formulation of more specific research questions.

Allen Bergin (1967, 1971) offered the most coherent and comprehensive response to Eysenck's challenge. First, he retabulated the data from the 24 studies initially surveyed by Eysenck (1952), demonstrating that investigators with different biases would arrive at drastically different rates of improvement.

By way of example, consider Fenichel's report (1930) of the results of treatment at the Berlin Psychoanalytic Institute. At the time of the report, a certain percentage of patients had completed treatment, another group had terminated prematurely, and yet another group was still in treatment. Those who had completed treatment were rated as "cured," "very much improved," "improved," or "uncured," using what appear to be very stringent criteria. Eysenck, considering only the first "cured" and "very much improved" categories as improved and regarding the premature terminators as treatment failures, arrived at a 39 percent improvement rate. Bergin showed that a reasonable case could be made for (1) also considering the third category as "improved"; and (2) not considering the premature terminators as treatment failures (excluding them from the analysis). On this basis, he arrived at a 91 percent improvement rate. Bergin's point was not that his rate was more valid than Eysenck's, but rather that the estimation of improvement rates from such uncontrolled studies was itself a subjective process that produced varying results depending on the reviewer's assumptions.

Bergin then went on to show that while Eysenck used stringent assumptions to assess the results of treatment, he used much more lenient criteria to estimate improvement without treatment—the so-called phenomenon of "spontaneous remission." Eysenck's case for a roughly two-thirds rate of spontaneous remission was based initially on two studies, one reporting a 72 percent discharge rate for hospitalized neurotics (Landis, 1937), the other reporting a 72 percent improvement rate over a two-year period for untreated life-insurance disability claimants (Denker, 1947). Bergin and others have pointed out that both studies had major defects and that the figures were misleading.

A wide search of available and emerging studies led to a much lower estimate of the baseline rate for spontaneous recovery—43 percent (Bergin & Lambert, 1978). However, it was also found that spontaneous remission rates vary tremendously, and thus this overall estimate is not a reliable figure for comparison with any and all treatment groups. Instead, future research should draw comparison groups from the population under study, in order to establish a baseline for that specific population.

At this point Bergin, however, had demonstrated the efficacy of psychotherapy—that psychotherapy has at least a modestly positive effect with adult neurotic outpatients, 65 percent of whom recover after two years of treatment, in comparison to 43 percent of untreated controls. Further inquiry indicated that the effects of therapy may be considerably greater. This suggestion rests on three lines of inquiry: (1) the nature of spontaneous recovery; (2) deterioration effects; (3) recent studies on therapeutic efficiency.

Spontaneous recovery, deterioration, and therapeutic efficiency. First, Bergin (1967) pointed out that the term "spontaneous recovery" reflects our lack of understanding of the processes that lead to recovery in the untreated controls. To say that something is spontaneous is simply an admission that we do not know what is going on. In the case of people in distress, there are data that indicate that most do not seek professional help of any kind (relying on self-help procedures or the support of friends or relatives), and that those who do seek help do not turn to mental-health professionals, but seek help instead from clergy and physicians (Gurin, Veroff, & Feld, 1960). Hence, therapy may be but a variant of a broader class of natural therapeutic processes that exist in society.

Second, Bergin (1967) observed in seven well-controlled studies that, although the posttest *mean scores* on the outcome measures differed little between the treatment and control groups, the posttest *variances* differed greatly: relative to the control groups, the spread or range of scores in the treated group significantly increased from pretest to posttest. This led to the conclusion that therapy is "for better or worse," producing both therapeutic change as well as deterioration in a percentage of cases. A schematic illustration of this phenomenon is depicted in Figure 7-2. Although questions have been raised about the phenomenon of deterioration (May, 1971), the evidence for its existence is currently based on more than 40 studies (Lambert, Bergin, & Collins, 1971) and is reasonably well accepted. Rates of deterioration probably average well under 10 percent, but the rates vary according to the type or modality of treatment, and according to therapist and client variables. Although much more research is needed in this area, there is evidence that more severely disturbed clients are more likely to experience negative outcomes.

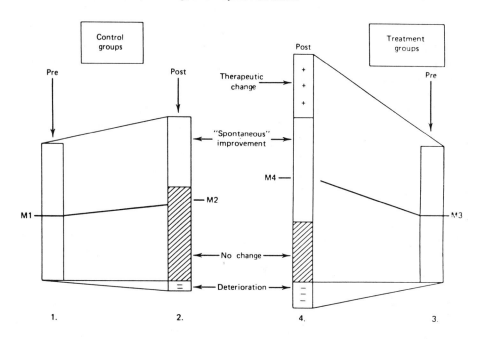

Bar 1   Distribution of test scores for disturbed control groups at beginning of studies.

Bar 2   Distribution of test scores for disturbed control groups at end of study showing increased spread of scores due to "spontaneous" improvement and "spontaneous" deterioration.

Bar 3   Distribution of test scores for disturbed treatment group at beginning of therapy.

Bar 4   Distribution of test scores for disturbed treatment group at end of therapy showing increased spread of scores due to therapeutic change and therapist induced deterioration.

M1,M2,   Median points, pre and post, which show greater change for therapy groups
M3,M4   than control groups.

NOTE: Lengths of bars are approximations.

FIGURE 7-2   The diverse effects of psychotherapy: A schematic illustration. (From Bergin & Lambert, 1978.)

With regard to the effect of therapist variables on deterioration (or on outcome in general), considerable enthusiasm was generated initially when studies seemed to indicate a strong association between the client-centered facilitative conditions (empathy, genuineness, and unconditional positive regard—Rogers, 1957) and outcome. Positive outcomes were associated with high levels of these therapist conditions and negative outcomes were associated with low levels (Truax & Carkhuff, 1967; Truax & Mitchell, 1971). However, critiques of the earlier studies (Lambert, DeJulio, & Stein, 1978), as well as more recent studies that have had nonconfirmatory results (Sloane, Staples, Cristol, Yorkston, & Whipple, 1975; Mitchell, Bozarth, & Krauft, 1977) have led to some qualification of the earlier position. For example, Mitchell and associates (1977, p. 483) conclude: "The recent evidence, although equivocal, does seem to suggest that empathy, warmth, and genuineness are related in some way to client change but that their potency and generalizability are not as great as once thought." (See Parloff, Waskow, & Wolfe, 1978, for a more thorough discussion of therapist variables.)

The third line of inquiry suggesting the potence of psychotherapy concerns the issue of therapeutic efficiency. Recent outcome studies reviewed by Bergin and Lambert (1978) indicate that brief treatment (6 months or less) is effective in providing symptomatic relief. Hence, even if Eysenck's two-thirds spontaneous remission rate were accepted, therapy would be preferable simply on the basis of its efficiency, in that it renders positive results in six months rather than two years.

Thus, there is a reasonably strong case for the efficacy and efficiency of psychotherapy. Bergin and Lambert (1978, p. 170) concluded that "psychoanalytic/ insight therapies, humanistic or client-centered psychotherapy, many behavioral therapy techniques and, to a lesser degree, cognitive therapies, rest on a reasonable empirical base. They do achieve results that are superior to no-treatment and to various placebo treatment procedures." Their conclusion was buttressed by the Smith and Glass (1977) study, in which the results of 375 controlled outcome studies of psychotherapy and counseling were integrated statistically using the procedure known as "meta-analysis." The authors concluded that "on the average, the typical therapy client is better off than 75 percent of untreated individuals" (Smith & Glass, 1977, p. 752).

Specific versus nonspecific effects. Thus it can be said that "psychotherapy works." With regard to more specific guidelines, however, little can be said at this point. First of all, there is an increasingly solid body of research evidence that indicates that the "nonspecific," nontechnical or interpersonal aspects of therapy may be more potent than the more specific technical aspects. The following reviews and studies support this position. First, Luborsky, Singer, and Luborsky's review (1975) of 100 controlled studies of therapy outcome found that most comparisons of different types of psychotherapy revealed few differences among the competing approaches. They concluded with the verdict of the dodo bird in *Alice in Wonderland*: "Everybody has won and all must have prizes" (p. 1003). Second, the Smith and Glass (1977) meta-analysis revealed no differences in effectiveness between the behavioral and nonbehavioral therapies, and few differences among the more specific types of therapy. Third, the recent, exceptionally well-designed Temple study, which compared short-term psychoanalytic psychotherapy, behavioral therapy, and a minimal-treatment wait-list control group, found that on target symptoms at posttest, both treatment groups improved significantly more than the controls, and that there were few significant differences between the two treatment groups (Sloane et al., 1975). And, fourth, the Vanderbilt study found few differences between the results of selected college professors and experienced therapists, both of whom achieved results surpassing those of the control groups (Strupp & Hadley, 1979). While the first three studies indicate the disproportionate influence of nonspecific versus specific factors in the "dead heats" between competing methods, the fourth study directly tests the nonspecific effects of a helping relationship (college professors) against the combined nonspecific and specific effects of a therapeutic relationship (experienced therapists), coming up (again) with a dead heat. As Luborsky and associates (1975, p. 1006) conclude:

> These common ingredients of psychotherapy may be so much more potent than the specific ones that it is wrong to lump them together in the sense of giving them equal weight. It is like making horse and canary pie by the Spanish recipe—horse and canary in equal proportions, one horse and one canary.

So what are these nonspecific effects? At base they are whatever arises from an intense interpersonal relationship between a warm, humane, and caring person of some wisdom and maturity, and a distressed person seeking help. They are the natural healing processes that may account for "spontaneous remission," when a no-treatment control subject seeks out a friend or priest for aid and comfort. They probably involve several client and therapist variables. For the client, there is motivation to change, hope for improvement, expectation of benefit—in short all of the Hawthorne-like or placebo effects that we try to control in our research designs, and that, as Bergin and Lambert (1978, p. 180) point out, may be the "active ingredients we are looking for." For the therapist, the important variables may be some variation of the client-centered facilitative conditions, modified to take into account the different linguistic forms used by the various therapy approaches. It should be noted that the client-centered facilitative conditions have had their most impressive showings with client-centered therapy, and that the measures of these conditions are closely tailored to the linguistic forms used by the client-centered therapist. A broader definition of warmth, empathy, and genuineness, and measures designed to reflect their appearance in the behavior of psychoanalytic, behavioral, and other therapists, might be a fruitful avenue for further study.

In any case, the evidence suggests that nonspecific effects are very potent. Future work should attempt to identify these variables with more precision and perhaps seek to optimize their influence through particular therapist-client matchings. But all this does not mean that there are *no* specific effects. Most of the studies supporting the importance of nonspecific effects are based on somewhat heterogeneous client populations. When certain carefully delineated homogeneous client groupings have been studied, differential effects between methods have been found. This has been true of circumscribed phobias, obesity, compulsions, and certain sexual problems treated by behavioral methods (Luborsky et al., 1975; Frank, 1979) and depression treated by cognitive therapy (Phillips & Bierman, 1981). Further research of this sort is also needed.

Family Therapy Outcome Research

Family therapy outcome research has all the difficulties, pitfalls, and vagaries of psychotherapy outcome research—and then some. The shift to a systemic perspective creates difficulties in defining the target population and in selecting outcome criteria for evaluation. With regard to the first problem, while there is some validity to identifying target populations in terms of psychodiagnostic criteria for assessing psychotherapy outcomes, conceptual and epistemological problems arise when this is done for the assessment of family therapy outcomes. Although it is a frequent practice to use individual nosology in family therapy research, Olson, Russell, and Sprenkle (1980a) have emphasized the importance of shifting to systemic diagnostic categories when assessing systems therapies. Second, the criterion problem becomes very complex in family therapy, because we are not just interested in changes in the identified patient, but also in other individuals, subsystems, and in the family system as a whole. Gurman and Kniskern (1981b) have discussed the criterion problem in depth, establishing a priority sequence for assessing change in families, and discussing the multiple levels of inference at which such assessments can be made.

Despite these increased difficulties, family therapy outcome research has proceeded apace. The first review of family therapy outcome research was published in 1972 (Wells, Dilkes, & Trivelli, 1972). Searching the literature from 1950 to 1970, the reviewers turned up only 18 relevant studies, of which only 13 could be tabulated, and these had a total N of 290. Six years later Gurman and Kniskern (1978a) presented the most comprehensive review of outcome research in marital and family therapy, coming up with 200 studies and a total N approaching 5,000. It should be noted, however, that the latter review is overinclusive from our perspective, in that it includes research on many of the innovative procedures (family crisis therapy, multiple impact therapy, and multiple family therapy) and skills training programs (especially Relationship Enhancement and behavioral skills training programs) that will be the subject of part three of this book. In addition to the Gurman and Kinskern review, recent reviews have also been done by Wells and Dezen (1978), DeWitt (1978), and Olson, Russell, and Sprenkle (1980b).

General findings.   What, then, do the studies show? First, they show rates of improvement comparable to those seen in individual psychotherapy research. For all forms of marital therapy, the average improvement rate is 61 percent (based on 36 studies, $N = 1,528$); and for family therapy (with child, adolescent, adult, and mixed identified patients), the average rate is 73 percent (based on 38 studies, $N = 1,529$) (Gurman & Kniskern, 1978a). The studies also show comparable rates of deterioration: 7.7 percent for marital therapy and 5.4 percent for family therapy. And, as in individual therapy, deterioration is associated with therapists with poor interpersonal skills: those who attack loaded issues early in therapy; who do not intervene in family conflict; who do not structure or guide therapy at the beginning; and who do not support family members (Gurman & Kniskern, 1978b, 1981b).

In marital therapy, both improvement and deterioration rates vary a good deal according to the form of treatment. As discussed in Chapter 3 and in Cookerly (1976), spouses can be seen together in *conjoint* sessions or separately. In the latter case, they can be seen by separate therapists in *collaborative* therapy or by the same therapist individually in *concomitant* (or *concurrent*) therapy. Another alternative is for only one spouse to be seen in *individual* therapy. Finally, the spouses may be seen in *couples group therapy.* According to the Gurman & Kniskern review (1978a), the improvement and deterioration rates are as follows: Conjoint—70 percent and 2.7 percent; collaborative and concomitant—63 percent and 3.3 percent; individual—48 percent and 11.6 percent; and couples group—66 percent and 16.6 percent. This pattern of results clearly contraindicates the use of individual therapy for marital problems, because of both the low improvement rates and high deterioration rates. Couples group therapy is a promising approach, showing particularly favorable results as an adjunct in the treatment of an alcoholic spouse (Gurman & Kniskern, 1981b); however, the exceptionally high deterioration rates are a cause for concern. Gurman & Kniskern (1978a) point out that these rates are artificially inflated by the inclusion of a study that focused on the effects of video-playback in couples groups, finding a high rate of casualities (Alkire & Brunse, 1974). Removing this study, however, only reduces the rate to 12 percent, which is still very high. The basis for this high rate of deterioration deserves further study.

In family therapy, improvement rates vary a little according to the development level of the identified patient: 71 percent for children and adolescents and 65 percent for adults. In general—on the basis of uncontrolled, controlled, and comparative studies—family therapy has been shown to be at least as good if not better than individual therapy for problems involving marital and family conflict, and even for problems presented as individual (Gurman & Kniskern, 1978a, 1981b). This conclusion lumps together various types of family therapy, and although it is a very general statement, it does indicate that family therapy must be taken seriously as a therapeutic modality.

Specific findings. With regard to more specific findings, Olson, Russell, and Sprenkle (1980b) developed a matrix that identifies those family therapy approaches that have received some modest degree of support for their efficacy with a number of specific presenting problems. The usefulness of this grid is limited because it only covers studies published in 1970–79, and because it is overinclusive in ways similar to the Gurman and Kniskern (1978a) review. An extension and modification of Olson and colleagues' grid, developed by using other reviews as sources, is displayed in Table 7-1.

It can be seen that the structure/process approaches have received the most support and research attention, with the historical schools coming in second. So far no evaluations of experiential approaches have been reported. It should be noted that these findings are *very tentative,* in that they are based for the most part on uncontrolled studies or on studies lacking in methodological rigor. (See Gurman & Kniskern, 1978a, for evaluations of the available studies according to their methodological adequacy.)

Outcome also varies as a function of certain general treatment factors, as well as patient/family variables and therapist variables. Gurman and Kniskern (1981b)

TABLE 7-1   Specific Conjoint Family Therapy Approaches Yielding Some Degree of Documented Effectiveness by Presenting Problem

PRESENTING PROBLEM	HISTORICAL		STRUCTURE/PROCESS			
	Psychodynamic	Multigenerational	Communicational and derivatives	Structural (pure and eclectic)	Functional	Triadic
Alcoholism			X			
Drug Abuse			X	X		
Juvenile Offender				X	X	
Adolescent Psychopathology			X			X
Phobias	X					
Psychosomatic Problems			X	X		
Schizophrenia		X	X			

have summarized these in their chapter on "knowns and unknowns" in family-therapy-outcome research. First, with regard to treatment factors, two generalizations can be made: Time-limited and brief treatment (approximately 20 sessions) seems to be about as effective as open-ended treatment; and the involvement of the father in family therapy improves the likelihood of good outcomes in many cases. Second, with regard to therapist variables, there are three conclusions: Therapist experience level has an unreliable relationship to outcome, but differences in the experience levels of co-therapists weaken therapeutic effectiveness; there are no data to support the superiority of co-therapy over single-therapist therapy; and, therapist relationship skills are strongly associated with outcome, both positive and negative (as discussed above).

Finally, with regard to patient-family factors, several conclusions can be drawn. (1) The severity and chronicity of the identified patient's disturbance is negatively related to outcome. (2) Improvement rates vary as a function of the identified patient's diagnosis. Examining the studies which listed specific diagnoses ($N = 1,343$ cases), Gurman and Kniskern (1978a) found the following improvement rates for various diagnostic categories: neurotic and other nonpsychotic—69 percent; psychotic—68 percent; behavior problem—64 percent; anorexia and other psychosomatic—91 percent; drug abuse—90 percent; alcoholism—60 percent. Although calculated for the most part on uncontrolled studies, the improvement rates with psychosomatic and drug-abuse problems are particularly striking. These problems have been treated with eclectic versions of structural family therapy, (structural/behavioral for anorexia and structural/strategic for drug abuse), which must be regarded as the treatment of choice based on current data. (3) The variables of family type (for example, enmeshed or disengaged), family-interaction style, family constellation, and demographic factors have not shown consistent or strong associations with family-therapy outcome.

TRAINING

In this discussion of family therapy training, we will first consider the question of where family therapy is offered. Two groups of training programs will be discussed: those offering training in family therapy as part of a larger training program in one of the mental health professions; and those offering training specifically and/or exclusively in family therapy. Second, we will consider the components of family therapy training, including didactic inputs, experiential processes, and supervised practical experience. Finally, we will discuss the question of research on training, including outcome issues as well as considerations regarding variations in the methods of training.

Where Is Family Therapy Training Offered

Training in family therapy is offered in a growing and varied matrix of programs. Bloch and Weiss (1981) conducted a national survey of training programs in family therapy. They found great diversity and also discovered that the establishment of family therapy training programs grew exponentially between the years 1942 and 1980. They have compiled an *International Master List of Training Programs in Family Therapy* that lists programs within geographic regions, coding them according to six variables: type of program, clinic affiliation, entrance requirements, degree granted, institutional auspices, and accreditation status (Weiss & Bloch, 1981).

Family therapy training occurs in a large number of programs, which form into two primary groups. In the first group, training in family therapy is offered as part of the overall training program of one of the mental health or human-service professions. In the second, training in family therapy becomes focal, in programs that are specifically designed to train family therapists.

Family therapy training in the mental health professions.   With regard to the first group of programs, family-therapy training is offered in the training programs of a wide range of established and emergent professions: psychiatry and other medical specialities (pediatrics, family practice), professional psychology (clinical, counseling, and school), social work, psychiatric nursing, pastoral counseling, law, special education, rehabilitation counseling, mental health and school counseling, applied human development, and human services. These graduate-level programs are degree-granting, and they offer a variety of degrees at both the masters level (Ed.M., M.A., M.S., M.S.W., M.S.N., M.Div.) and the doctoral level (Ph.D., Psy.D., Ed.D., M.D., D.S.W., D.Sc., D.Min.). The programs usually provide, as part of the graduate program, supervised practical experience in the delivery of their respective professional services (clerkship, practicum, internship). Some professions also require postgraduate supervised experience (internship, residency, fellowship) for admission to various levels of professional status. The supervised experiences take place in a wide range of facilities, including hospitals, clinics, schools, churches, counseling centers, family-service associations, and other community agencies.

The importance ascribed to family therapy varies a great deal within this range of programs, and exposure to family therapy in both academic course work and practicum training ranges from virtually nonexistent to highly intensive. In recent years, several articles have appeared in the literature, describing family therapy training within a specific profession. With regard to psychiatry residencies, Martin (1979) presented an overview of training in marital therapy at university-based training centers and a detailed discussion of the program at the University of Michigan; and Sugarman (1981) reported the results of a national survey of 80 general psychiatry residencies. In psychology, Stanton (1975) described the academic and internship opportunities available to psychologists; Cooper, Rampage, and Soucy (1981) reported the results of a survey of 102 doctoral programs in clinical psychology; and Liddle, Vance, and Pastushak (1979) reported the results of a survey of 108 American Psychological Association-approved doctoral programs in clinical and counseling psychology and of 125 doctoral programs in counseling/counselor education. In nursing, Shapiro (1975) described a training program at the University of Rochester. And, in social work, Erickson (1973) discussed the teaching of family therapy.

Training in family therapy as a profession in its own right.   The second group of programs offering training in family therapy differs from the first in that their focus is squarely on family therapy. In contrast also to the first group of programs, which rely on the credentialing processes of their respective professions, the family therapy programs rely on the credentialing processes for family therapists developed by the American Association of Marriage and Family Therapy (AAMFT, see below). This group consists of two types of programs: graduate programs offering degrees in marital and family therapy, and family therapy institutes.

The graduate programs in marital and family therapy have evolved within schools of home economics, social sciences, and education, and they are most frequently housed in departments of family and child development or family studies. Training is offered at both masters and doctoral levels, though the masters-degree programs are more common. In a special issue of the *Journal of Marital and Family Therapy* devoted to education and training issues (Nichols, 1979a), Everett (1979) described the masters-degree programs, and Nichols (1979b) described the doctoral programs. A discussion of the unique Hahnemann Master of Family Therapy Program (which requires a masters degree in a mental health profession for admission) is provided by Garfield (1979). Additional discussions of the core curriculum can be found in Nichols (1979c) and Winkle, Piercy, and Hovestadt (1981). A listing of AAMFT-accredited programs can also be found in Nichols (1979a, p. 129).

The family therapy institutes date back to the beginning of marital counseling in the 1940s and the emergence of family therapy in the 1950s. The most complete listing of the institutes can be found in Weiss and Bloch (1981), and a listing of AAMFT-accredited institutes can be found in Nichols (1979a, p. 128). Most of the institutes are free-standing, established independent of a university or teaching hospital, though some are partially embedded within, or affiliated with, a larger institution. Most, also, are established to offer postgraduate training to people who have earned, or are in the process of completing, their professional degrees, though some offer training to individuals without professional degrees. The institutes offer certificates of completion, but do not offer graduate degrees. Bloch and Weiss (1981) found that the programs of the family therapy institutes that they surveyed varied considerably in their length (1–3 years) and intensity (2–40 hours per week), despite the fact that they all viewed themselves as training journeyman-level practitioners. Although some of this variation may be the result of differing points of departure and varying objectives, the extent of the variation highlights the need for uniform standards for a minimal acceptable level of training for family therapists.

Several discussions of particular family therapy institutes have been published. In the special issue of the *Journal of Marital and Family Therapy* referred to above (Nichols, 1979a), Berman and Dixon-Murphy (1979) discussed two of the oldest marital counseling institutes, the Marriage Council of Philadelphia and the Blanton-Peale Graduate Institute. The Marriage Council of Philadelphia is also the subject of a special issue of the *American Journal of Family Therapy* (Berman, 1982). The Ackerman Institute is described by La Perriere (1979); the Boston Family Institute is discussed by Duhl and Duhl (1979), and Constantine (1976) described its precursor (the Center for Training in Family Therapy at Boston State Hospital); and the Family Systems Program at the Institute for Juvenile Research is discussed by Falicov, Constantine, and Breunlin (1981).

Variations in both types of training programs.   Overall, both groups of programs that offer training in family therapy vary along several additional general dimensions. First, there is the level at which training is offered, which includes non-professional, masters-degree, doctoral-degree, and postgraduate programs. Second, there is the level of exposure to family therapy, which can vary from minimal "enrichment" programs (Bloch & Weiss, 1981) to intensive training. Although it is more likely that the explicitly family therapy programs would offer more intensive training in family therapy, this issue cuts across the primary categorization of training programs into two groups; some mental health professional training programs offer highly intensive training in family therapy, and some family therapy institutes offer only a range of enrichment-type courses. Third, there is the issue of professional ideology: Is family therapy seen as a fundamentally new paradigm for mental health or as an additional treatment modality in the practitioner's armamentarium? Although this issue was much more polarized in the 1960s, it still exists; and while many training centers take middle-of-the-road, integrative positions, others continue to espouse more extreme views. Fourth, and related to the third issue, when family therapy is taught intensively, is it taught exclusively? That is, are traditional courses and skills such as personality theory, human development, psychopathology, and individual and group psychotherapy seen as necessary background, or as a hindrance to the development of a systems perspective? This issue also has implications for the selection of trainees. While some of the family therapy institutes teach family therapy exclusively and seek trainees "unburdened" by backgrounds in traditional methods (for example, Haley, 1976b), others only accept trainees with expertise in psychotherapy, or require concomitant preparation in individual methods, or both (Nichols, 1979c).

The final issue has to do with the degree to which the program emphasizes the development of a set of skills or the personal growth of its trainees. Liddle and Halpin (1978), in a comparative review of the training and supervision literature, found that programs providing training in the historical and experiential models tend to emphasize the personal growth and affective lives of their trainees, whereas structure/process programs emphasize the development of a set of cognitive and behavioral skills for intervening in family systems. For example, Cleghorn and Levin (1973) developed checklists of basic and advanced objectives for trainees, framed in terms of three sets of skills: "perceptual" or observational (recognizing family interaction patterns); "conceptual" (formulating family's problems in systems terms); and "executive" (establishing the treatment relationship and implementing change). Tomm and Wright (1979) recently extended this model, embedding it within a set of four therapist functions ("engagement," "problem identification," "change facilitation," and "termination") and the attendant competencies. Related to this is the relative ease of training students in the more straightforward operationalized structure/process approaches of Haley or Minuchin when compared to some of the historical and experiential approaches that rely heavily on the use of self (for example, Whitaker's experiential therapy).

Thus, training in family therapy is offered both in mental health professional training programs and in family therapy training programs, at educational levels ranging from the nonprofessional to the postgraduate, and with exposure ranging from enrichment to intensive training. Programs vary both in terms of their ideological stance on family therapy and in whether they require or include training in traditional psychotherapeutic methods along with family therapy training. Finally, programs vary in terms of their focus on affective (personal growth) or cognitive-behavioral (skills) objectives. We will now turn from this general discussion to a consideration of the specific components of family therapy training.

The Components
of Family Therapy Training

Training methods fall into three general categories: didactic, experiential, and supervisory (Kniskern & Gurman, 1979). There is considerable variation among training programs in terms of their emphasis on one or the other of these learning processes, and in terms of other, more specific, issues (Liddle & Halpin, 1978).

Didactic methods. One of these more specific issues concerns the approach to didactic course work: Should trainees be systematically exposed to the range of approaches that exist in the field or intensively instructed in one approach? Until recently, no integrative textbooks were available, so that it was often difficult, if not impossible, to provide introductory courses with a coherent view of the field.

In the absence of such introductory texts, attempts to teach such courses ran the risk of confusing and disorienting the students. The alternative, adopted by many of the leading family therapy institutes, is to offer training in a single approach. This latter course makes it difficult for students to compare and integrate formulations and perspectives that arise from approaches outside of their frame of reference, handicapping their ability to work with colleagues. Perhaps the optimal approach—given the increasing availability of integrative texts—is to offer comparative overviews early in training, and then to offer advanced work in one or more specific approaches.

Didactic courses, at either the introductory or advanced levels, include readings, lectures, group discussions, and demonstrations of techniques (both live and on tape and film). Readings should include theory and practice. The current text has emphasized an introduction to theory, supplying references for more advanced theoretical readings and suggestions for practical examples or case studies exemplifying a particular approach. Resources suggested for specific approaches have also included films and videotapes available from various sources. Beyond this, several other bibliographies are available: Framo and Green (1980); Glick, Weber, Rubenstein, and Patten (1981); and Brown (1981). Finally, serious research-oriented readers should be aware of the *Inventory of Marriage and Family Literature,* published annually by Sage publications and edited by D. H. Olson at the Family Social Science Department of the University of Minnesota.

Experiential methods.   Experiential processes usually begin early in training and often continue on into the more advanced stages. Initial experiences occurring in introductory courses include role-plays in simulated families (Weingarten, 1979) or behavioral rehearsal of interviewing techniques. In addition, a technique unique to family therapy training is usually initiated early in training, wherein students work on their own families of origin. This technique has most often been used in the historical approaches, particularly Bowen's multigenerational school (Carter & Orfanidis, 1976). It varies from the construction of one's own genogram, to role-playing one's own family, and to extended efforts to increase one's differentiation of self through planned home visits in which one is supported by "coaching" seminars.

A final experiential process is participating in therapy—individual, group, marital, or family. Such an experience is much more likely to be recommended or required of trainees in traditional mental health professional training programs and psychodynamically oriented family therapy training programs (Liddle & Halpin, 1978; Kniskern & Gurman, 1979). It should also be noted that the AAMFT guidelines for accreditation (American Association of Marriage and Family Therapy, 1979) recommend that opportunities for personal therapy should be available to, but not required of, trainees.

Supervision.   Supervision of one's work with families is generally considered to be one of the most potent learning experiences on the road to becoming a family therapist. Supervisory methods vary considerably. Traditionally, supervisors relied on the method of reviewing written process notes in individual supervision, though this approach is used less frequently nowadays. Because of economic advantages and the benefits of peer-group influence, group supervision seminars are much more common today (Tucker, Hart & Liddle, 1976; Dell, Sheely, Pulliam, Goolishian, 1977; Steir & Goldenberg, 1975; O'Hare, Heinrich, Kirschner, Oberstone, & Ritz, 1975). Such group supervision seminars often use videotapes of family interviews as the data base (Kramer & Reitz, 1980).

Within the context of group supervision, methods vary according to the theoretical orientation of the supervisors. In group supervision seminars in which the theoretical orientation is historical or experiential, co-therapy is often utilized. Teams may be formed of supervisor-trainee, trainee-trainee, or supervisor-supervisor (Tucker et al., 1976). In using co-therapy in training, however, care must be taken to match co-therapists on their level of experience (Steir & Goldenberg, 1975), given the research findings indicating negative relationships between experience-level differences of co-therapists and therapy outcome (Gurman & Kniskern, 1978a).

In group supervision seminars with an orientation toward structure/process theories, live supervision is often used (Haley, 1976b). In this approach, the supervisor (and the trainees) observe an ongoing therapy session through a one-way mirror, or by using a video monitor (Cornwell & Pearson, 1981). The supervisor and trainees can then meet and discuss the interview after it is completed. More commonly, the supervisor prearranges to provide instant feedback to the trainee-therapist during the course of the interview. This may be done through one of several ways: (1) the use of a "bug-in-the-ear" wireless transmitter; (2) the use of a CB radio or walkie-talkie system; (3) the use of the telephone; or (4) the supervisor's entering the therapy room to consult with the trainee-therapist (Birchler, 1975). Variations of live supervision include Papp's (1977b) adaptation of the brief/paradoxical approaches of the Mental Research Institute and Palazzoli's Milan team approach. In the Milan approach, a team of four therapists work together, one conducting the interview and three observing. The observers may call the therapist out of the room after 30 minutes for a conference lasting up to 10 minutes, in order to help the therapist formulate directives to give to the family. Additionally, Coppersmith (1980a) has described expanded uses of the telephone, wherein the observing team not only sends in strategic signals to the therapist but also speak directly to family members; and family members can also call one another. Live supervision techniques are quite controversial, and they have been criticized on several grounds —particularly, their possible promotion of the therapist's dependence on the supervisor and the potential disruption of the therapeutic process (Liddle & Halpin, 1978).

Research on Family Therapy Training

Kniskern and Gurman (1979), in their recent discussion of the state of our knowledge regarding training, made several interesting points. The first is that research on the process and outcome of family-therapy training is nonexistent. Thus no direct empirical support is available for any training procedure or program at this point in time. Second, findings from family therapy outcome research on the importance of therapists' interpersonal skills have clear implications for the selection of trainees, implications that happily turn out to be congruent with actual selection practices in the field. Many training centers accord more weight to the trainee's personal attributes and relationship skills (as reflected in personal interviews and occasionally in tapes of therapeutic interviews) than to traditional academic criteria (which, in the case of postgraduate trainees, have been tested many times in the past). Third, if anything has been learned from the voluminous research on psychotherapy and family therapy research outcomes, it is that we have been asking too broad a question (Does therapy work?). Hence, it would behoove us to not repeat the same mistake with family therapy training research, and to avoid asking, Does family therapy training work? Instead, our attention should be directed to examining some of the more specific issues along which actual training practices vary. To this end, Kniskern and Gurman (1979) listed a number of "important and researchable questions regarding family therapy training." Some of these questions are paraphrased below, along with several additional questions.

1. Questions regarding *selection*.
   - What is the relationship between prior training in individual psychotherapy and family therapy training? Does it improve or impede family therapy training? Do the effects of prior training vary with the family therapy model (historical, structure/process, experiential)?
   - What is the relationship between a therapist's interpersonal skills and success in training?
   - Can success in training be predicted on the basis of a personal interview?
   - Does a sample of therapeutic work improve selection?
2. Questions regarding *didactic methods*.
   - Is it better to present a comprehensive overview of the field or to focus on one method?
   - Should didactic courses be scheduled before, during, or after the family therapy practicum?
   - Does the viewing of videotapes of master family therapists help or hinder the trainee's development?
3. Questions regarding *experiential methods*.
   - What are the effects of role-play exercises on trainees' anxieties about their competence, and on the development of clinical skills?
   - What effects does working on one's own family have on trainees? Are effects primarily cognitive? Affective? Behavioral?
   - What are the positive and negative effects of personal therapy on trainees when it is a required experience? At what point in training would personal therapy be most beneficial?
4. Questions regarding *supervision*.
   - What are the advantages of group supervision?
   - What are the advantages of using videotape?
   - What are the effects (positive and negative) of co-therapy as a training procedure?
   - What are the effects (positive and negative) of live supervision with immediate feedback?

PROFESSIONAL ISSUES

At last we come to a discussion of professional issues in family therapy. Two topics will be taken up at this point. First, we will discuss the issue of the regulation of marital and family therapy, considering such procedures of accreditation, certification, and licensure. Second, we will describe the professional associations that exist in family therapy and will consider the topic of professional ethics.

The Regulation of Marital and Family Therapy

The regulation of the mental health professions has become an increasingly absorbing professional and political issue over the past 10 to 15 years. The basic issues involved are twofold: (1) the protection of the public, insuring that people will be served by qualified practitioners; (2) the protection of the "turf" of particular professions vis-à-vis other professions. A comprehensive study of the regulation of psychotherapists, recently completed by Hogan (1979a, 1979b, 1979c, 1979d), challenges current trends toward restrictive licensure and professional fragmentation. In addition to this major resource, the reader is also referred to Fretz and Mills (1980) for additional information regarding the licensure and certification of psychologists and counselors.

Credentialing processes: General considerations. The regulation of the mental health professions occurs through a myriad of credentialing processes, so that definitions of certain terms are in order at this point. We will consider the following credentialing processes: accreditation, approval, and designation; licensure and certification; diplomate boards, register listing, and provider status.

Accreditation refers to the process whereby the training facilities of professional programs in academic institutions and field-based practicums become certified as having met certain standards or qualifications. For academic institutions, two types of accreditation are available: the accreditation of the institution itself, by the regional Association of Schools and Colleges; and the accreditation of the professional training program by the appropriate professional organization. The latter process also applies to the accreditation of field-based training facilities. The mental health professions (psychiatry, psychology, social work, nursing, and the various counseling professions) have, or are in the process of establishing, procedures for the accreditation of academic-based professional training programs and field-based training facilities. Once a program is accredited, it is listed as *approved* (as in "APA-approved"). Short of accreditation, some professions are experimenting with the process of *designation,* whereby degree-granting programs that meet definitional standards of what constitutes a degree in that field are so designated. This process is currently being developed in psychology in order to help state psychology-licensing boards determine who is qualified (on the basis of academic credentials) to take the licensing examination.

Licensing and *certification* both refer to the credentialing of individuals. Licensure refers to laws that regulate both the use of a title (such as "psychologist" or "physician") and the scope and content of practice of a particular profession. Licensure violations usually carry significant legal penalities. Certification can be of two types: Statutory certification is mandated by law, but is less comprehensive than licensure, regulating only the use of a professional title; nonstatutory certification is a process whereby an agency or professional association grants recognition to an individual for having met certain professional qualifications. In general, all three processes are designed to insure that professionals have met certain minimal standards of education, training, and supervised experience. As Koocher (1979) has pointed out, licensure and certification are "secondary credentials," based in part on the candidates' possession of "primary credentials" such as a graduate degree or internship certificate. And although secondary credentialing usually samples the candidate's professional functioning through some sort of examination, the sample is brief and cross-sectional, in contrast to the long-term and longitudinal sampling that occurs in primary credentialing. Hence, although licensure and certification have the advantage of setting minimal standards in professions characterized by great diversity in training practices, they have the disadvantage of not getting very close to the data, which may handicap their ability to adequately assess actual competence.

Diplomate boards offer a secondary credential that attempts to assess competence more adequately, through assessing work samples and through live observation of candidates' work. In this case, the level of competence sought is excellence rather than minimal adequacy. Diplomate boards have been established in psychology to certify advanced competence in one of the professional specialities (clinical, counseling, school, and industrial/organization) and in certain special proficiencies (psychological hypnosis, forensic psychology, and family psychology).

Register listing, as in the National Register of Health Service Providers in Psychology, is a "tertiary credential," relying totally on the candidate's possession of primary and secondary credentials. As such, Koocher (1979) has concluded that it is at the "bottom of the heap" with regard to considerations of its validity as an assessment of competence.

Finally, *provider status* refers to the process of being designated as a reimbursable mental health service provider by an insurance company (such as Blue Shield) or other third party payor. The process of attaining provider status for professional groups involves a complex series of state legislation, including: (1) "freedom-of-choice" legislation, which enables consumers to obtain health services from any qualified practitioner rather than being limited to physicians; (2) mandated mental health coverage, requiring health insurance companies to provide mental health coverage; (3) licensure of the specific professional group; (4) and, finally, the passage of a "vendorship" bill, which recognizes the professional group as qualified health service providers. Currently in Massachusetts, for example, psychiatrists, psychologists, and licensed independent clinical social workers have provider status.

   Credentialing processes in the family therapy field.   Having completed a brief tour through credentialing processes in general, we shall now turn to an examination of family therapy. Here we find, as we did in our discussion of training, a two-track system. In the first track, mental health professionals earn graduate degrees and obtain training and supervised experience in programs accredited or designated by their respective professional associations. Upon the completion of their training, they seek whatever licensure, certification, or register listing is available to their profession, and qualify—or hope to qualify—for provider status. Five or so years down the road, some may seek diplomate status. In the second track, marital and family therapists earn graduate degrees and obtain professional training in programs accredited by AAMFT. On the completion of their training, they may apply for nonstatutory certification as a clinical member of AAMFT, and for statutory certification or licensure in those states where it is available.

   The second track clearly has fewer credentialing options, and those that exist are limited in their availability at this time. Currently, only eight graduate programs and six training centers are accredited by AAMFT; five states have licensing laws, and three have certification laws. This situation may change, as the effects have yet to be seen of the U.S. Office of Education's recognition in 1978 of the Committee on Accreditation of AAMFT as the official body for accrediting educational and training programs in marital and family therapy. (The reader is directed to Smith & Nichols, 1979, for further discussion of AAMFT accreditation, and to Sporakowski & Staniszewski, 1980, for a complete discussion of licensure and certification in marital and family therapy).

   The existence of two tracks has generated some polarized opinions regarding the credentialing of marriage and family therapy. On the one hand, the established mental health professions have argued that marital and family therapy is but a sub-branch of psychotherapy, and that as such, it is not an independent profession. Representatives of several of these professions have spoken in opposition to the granting of accreditation authority to AAMFT. On the other hand, marital and family therapists have argued that there is nothing in the credentialing procedures of the established professions that adequately assesses and certifies education and training in family therapy; hence, it is argued, mental health professionals who wish to specialize in family therapy should seek appropriate additional education and training, and obtain certification and licensure as marital and family therapists. This issue was recently tested in California, where it was held that, although licensed psychologists could practice marital and family therapy, they could not advertise marital and family therapy as a service, unless they were also licensed as marriage and family therapists (Hansen & L'Abate, 1982). It is difficult to forsee how these issues will be resolved, especially since they are part of a much larger pattern of interprofessional competition and conflict.

Professional Associations
and Ethics

The mental health professions have professional associations, such as the American Psychiatric Association, the American Psychological Association, the National Association of Social Workers, and the American Personnel and Guidance Association. To be a member of one's professional association usually requires meeting certain requirements in terms of education, training, and current professional functioning. As mentioned earlier, the associations are involved in credentialing process of various sorts, including accreditation and designation of programs and, in some cases, nonstatutory certification of individuals. In addition, the associations are usually active in promoting statutory certification and licensure. The associations are also involved in setting standards for professional behavior, particularly ethical behavior, and all the associations have codes of ethics. Continued membership in the association requires a commitment to abide by the code of ethics. Ethical violations are dealt with by ethics committees, who generally take an educative-remediative rather than a punitive stance.

Marital and family therapists can turn, in addition, to several professional associations. First and foremost is the American Association of Marriage and Family Therapy (AAMFT). Founded in 1942 as the American Association of Marriage Counselors, and representing for many years the specific discipline of marriage counseling, this organization has recently come to the fore as the recognized association for marriage and family therapy. AAMFT has authority to accredit graduate programs and training centers and has been active in pursuing state certification and licensure for marriage and family therapists. In addition, it offers credentials of its own for those who meet certain qualifications as clinical member, fellow, and approved supervisor. The AAMFT has recently published a draft version of its ethical code (AAMFT, 1982), which includes eight principles: responsibility to clients, competence, integrity, confidentiality, professional responsibility, professional development, research responsibility, and social responsibility.

Second, there is the American Family Therapy Association (AFTA). Founded in 1978, AFTA has been viewed by some as a rival organization to AAMFT, representing the interests of (systemic) family therapists as distinct from (psychodynamic) marriage counselors. A joint liaison committee was established between the two organizations, which met from spring 1981 to spring 1982. Through the process, much was clarified regarding the respective roles of the two organizations, with AAMFT retaining the burden of credentialing (Williamson, 1982).

Third, for psychologists who are also marriage and family therapists, there is the Academy of Psychologists in Marital, Family, and Sex Therapy. Founded in 1958, the organization exists in recognition of the fact that training in professional psychology does not always provide adequate preparation in marital and family therapy. The organization sets standards and conducts continuing education programs in this area. Recently, the Academy sponsored the formation of the American Board of Family Psychology (ABFamP). ABFamP is a diplomate board designed to assess and recognize qualified psychologists with advanced competence in those specialized areas of psychotherapy primarily involving marital and family therapy.

Finally, two additional organizations should be mentioned, as they are indirectly involved in, or connected with, family therapy: (1) The National Council on Family Relations is concerned with the family along the spectrum from basic research and theory to political action, and it has sections on family therapy and on education and enrichment. NCFR sponsors several of the primary journals in the field of family studies (*Journal of Marriage and the Family, Journal of Family Issues, Family Relations*). (2) The American Association of Sex Educators, Counselors, and Therapists (AASECT) was founded in 1974, and it provides nonstatutory certification for sex-educators and counselors.

A full treatment of professional ethics is beyond the scope of this volume, and is covered elsewhere (see Hobbs, 1965; Koocher, 1976; Mailloux, 1977; American Psychological Association, 1981). It should be pointed out, however, that certain specific ethical issues may arise when doing family therapy, such as: Whose interest is the therapist ethically bound to serve in situations of conflicting interests? When requiring all family members to participate in family therapy, do individuals have the right to *not* be treated? Is the expression of intense hostility and the escalation of family conflicts ethically advisable? (These tactics run the risk of family dissolution, which may be in the interests of some but not other family members.) And what about the use of paradoxical techniques, such as telling family members to continue or exaggerate their dysfunctional behavior? Are directive techniques an unethical form of manipulation? (Haley, 1976b, maintains that all therapies are manipulative, and that his therapy is simply explicit about it; he argues that a more cogent ethical issue is whether the treatment is effective in solving the family's problems.) What about the sharing of intimate details or secrets? Therapists who advocate such openness may find it hard to maintain their positions when the consequences for all participants are thoroughly examined. And, finally, how do therapists' implicit values influence choice of treatment goals? For extended discussions of these and other ethical concerns specific to family therapy, the reader is advised to consult Hines and Hare-Mustin (1978) and Hansen and L'Abate (1982).

SUMMARY

In this chapter, the topics of outcome research, training, and professional issues were treated. The foundation for outcome research in family therapy lies in prior developments in psychotherapy outcome research. The major findings of family therapy outcome research indicate that family therapy is a potent intervention, that certain forms can have dramatically positive results (such as eclectic versions of structural family therapy with psychosomatic and drug-abuse problems), and that in other instances, dramatic degrees of deterioration can result (for example, the use of videotape playback in couples-group therapy). Additional, more fine-grained research is clearly needed.

In family therapy training, two tracks of preparation are available for entering the field: (1) programs for training in an established (or emerging) mental health profession; and (2) programs designed to offer training singularly in family therapy. In family therapy training, a fair amount of variation exists in the way didactic, experiential, and supervisory components of the training are provided. Research on family therapy training has been rare, and a number of potential research issues have emerged.

Myriad credentialing processes are awash in the mental health field today. In the specific regulating processes in the marital-family field, again, two tracks can be noted—one providing a set of credentialing procedures for the established mental health professions, and another, for marital and family therapists. Some conflicts have been engendered by these separate tracks. Several professional associations currently operate to set credentialing and ethical standards for the profession; and within the context of family therapy, a number of specific ethical issues arise.

8

Beyond Conjoint Family Therapy: Special Forms and Techniques of Working Therapeutically with Families

In this chapter we will consider a set of family-oriented therapeutic approaches that amplify or extend beyond the parameters of the conjoint model discussed in Part II of this book. The approaches to be considered here vary in the degree of their development, ranging from full-fledged therapeutic modalities that are widely applied, to special techniques used for more limited purposes; and, some are more potential than actual, constituting areas for future development.

These approaches fall into five groups. First, there are crisis-oriented approaches that apply crisis theory and crisis-intervention techniques to the family. Two crisis approaches will be considered: family crisis therapy and multiple impact therapy. Second, there are the megagroup approaches, which extend the intervention beyond the family to groups of families and ultimately to the community. Two megagroup approaches will be discussed: multiple family therapy (and couples groups) and social network intervention. Third, there is a set of nonverbal techniques or adjuncts to treatment which are applicable to a range of therapeutic approaches: family sculpture and choreography, and the use of videotape and other aids (family photos, home movies, and floor plans) in treatment. Fourth, there are specialized approaches for working with aspects of the marital relationship: sex therapy and divorce therapy. And finally, there is the area of special techniques for working with children in family therapy. The last area is the one referred to as more potential than actual, and the discussion here will focus on the need to develop some integration between the disparate disciplines of child therapy and family therapy.

CRISIS-ORIENTED APPROACHES

The two approaches to be discussed here (family crisis therapy and multiple impact therapy) are based on the theory and practice of crisis intervention (Caplan, 1964; Lindemann, 1965). Emotional crisis arises when "a person faces an obstacle to important life goals that is, for a time, insurmountable through the utilization of customary methods of problem-solving" (Caplan, 1964). A self-limiting period of disorganization ensues, accompanied by intense anxiety and distress. The person or system in crisis utilizes available coping mechanisms, particularly those that have worked in past difficult situations. The crisis typically lasts four to six weeks, and it is a period of both increased vulnerability as well as an opportunity for growth. The outcome could go either way, depending on the availability of timely and appropriate help. Thus, the theory proposes that a relatively small intervention, applied for a brief period, can shift the balance to the side of mental health.

Family Crisis Therapy

Family crisis therapy (FCT) was developed at the Family Treatment Unit at Colorado Psychiatric Hospital from 1964 to 1971. The original aim was to evaluate the efficacy of crisis intervention applied to the family unit as an alternative to psychiatric hospitalization. It was expected that FCT would reduce chronicity and rehospitalization rates. Subsequently, the approach has been applied in other settings: a rural community mental health center, a general hospital emergency room, and in private practice (Langsley & Kaplan, 1968; Pittman, 1973).

FCT focuses on defining and resolving the crisis. The request for psychiatric hospitalization is seen as a part of the crisis process. Crisis is viewed as a time of impending change, characterized by a disruption of normal patterns of behavior, increased tension, suspension of long-term objectives, and revival of past conflicts. The crisis is resolved by making specific changes in order to accommodate to or remove the stress that precipitated it.

Stresses come in all forms, and the stress value of a particular event can only be assessed in terms of its meaning to, and impact on, a particular family. The Colorado team, in an effort to classify the types of stress that families experience, came up with four dimensions: overt versus covert, temporary versus permanent, unique versus habitual, and situational versus structural. The crisis-resolution process will be more manageable according to the degree to which the crisis-inducing stress is overt, temporary, unique, and situational.

Another variable that can affect outcome is the family's response to the crisis. Some families respond with dysfunctional efforts to resolve the crisis, which exacerbate the original stress. Three kinds of faulty resolutions have been described by Pittman (1973): (1) ignoring the stress; (2) overreacting to the stress; (3) placing full responsibility for the stress on one individual, making that person the family scapegoat or the family healer. (Parenthetically, note the similarity of this formulation of problems with that of Watzlawick et al., 1974.)

Treatment is aimed at clarifying the crisis in order to facilitate its resolution. Treatment requires an average of five office visits and one home visit (scheduled for the first 24–36 hours of the crisis) over a three-week period. Seven overlapping steps are involved in treatment (Langsley & Kaplan, 1968):

1. *Providing immediate aid.* The family is seen at once, at any hour of the day or night, and is given promise of immediate availability around the clock from that moment on.
2. *Defining the crisis as a family problem.* Absent members are called in and efforts to define the problem as the craziness of one member are blocked.
3. *Focusing on the current crisis.* The team attempts to define the current crisis, avoiding extensive discussion of past crises, conflicts, or problems.
4. *General prescription.* This step involves the use of nonspecific treatment factors to reduce the level of tension and distress and to provide reassurance and hope. Psychotropic medications are used as needed to reduce tension and provide symptom relief.
5. *Specific prescription.* As the nature of the crisis becomes clearer, specific activities are recommended to resolve the crisis. These may take the form of tasks that are assigned to family members.
6. *Negotiating role conflicts.* The structural aspects of the family that had hindered their attempts to cope with the original stress, or that are manifested as resistance to treatment, are clarified and negotiated in this step. A long-term referral for family therapy may be made for this purpose.
7. *Terminating with an open door.* The availability of the treatment unit for subsequent crises is stressed.

A controlled evaluation of FCT was conducted, in which 300 patients were randomly assigned to FCT or psychiatric hospitalization. The hospitalized patients stayed an average of 26 days and received the usual hospital regimen: individual and group psychotherapy, milieu therapy, and chemotherapy. Results were assessed at 6-month, 18-month, and 3-year follow-up. FCT patients were significantly less likely to require hospitalization at 6-month follow-up, although the differences in hospitalization rates tended to even out over time. FCT patients performed as well as hospitalized patients on measures of functioning, symptoms, and family relationships. The average number of days lost before resuming performance of patient's usual role was 25 days for FCT and 72.5 days for hospitalized patients, and the cost of care for hospitalized patients was 6½ times that of FCT patients. Thus, there is support for the proposition that FCT is an effective and cost-effective alternative to psychiatric hospitalization (Langsley, Pittman, Machotka, & Flomenhaft, 1968; Langsley, Pittman, & Swank, 1969).

Multiple Impact Therapy

Multiple impact therapy (MIT) was developed by Robert MacGregor and colleagues at the University of Texas Medical Branch at Galveston (MacGregor, Ritchie, Serrano, & Schuster, 1964; MacGregor, 1971). Like FCT, the program is a brief crisis-oriented intervention; but whereas the focus of the FCT project was hospitalized young adults, MIT focuses on adolescents with behavior problems. Serving as an alternative treatment for families not engagable through the usual child guidance clinic procedures, the program involves the efforts of a team of professionals (two psychologists, one psychiatrist, and one social worker) working with the family (parents, identified patient, selected siblings and involved relatives, and representatives of the care-giving community agency) over a two-day-plus period. This program combines elements of an extended intake procedure with the intensive quality of a marathon experience, and it is designed both to pinpoint the family's problems and to move rapidly toward their resolution.

The procedure is both structured and flexible. The first day begins with a team conference, in which available information is reviewed, clinical hypotheses are generated, and tentative assignments are made for the first set of individual interviews. This is followed by the initial team–family conference, which is a frank and open discussion of the family's problems. When the family members have difficulty communicating, the team members might debate the issues in front of them, different members of the team taking the sides of various family members.

At this point, family members feel considerable pressure to have their point of view understood and accepted, and they welcome the individual interviews that follow the team–family conference as an opportunity to ventilate. The interview for the identified patient is typically shorter than that for the parents. At the conclusion of the interview, the teenager is sent off to take psychological tests, and his or her interviewer joins one of the ongoing interviews with a parent in what is termed an "overlapping session." In the overlapping session, the parents' interviewer summarizes the content of the interview to the overlapping therapist, thus giving the parent an opportunity to see how well he or she has been understood, and to comment on any aspects of the summary. The overlapping therapist then might comment on how the evolving interpretation fits in with what was learned from the teenager.

At noon, the family goes to lunch, encouraged to discuss their impressions of the morning sessions, since the team will do likewise. The team also maps out strategy for the afternoon session. The afternoon session starts out with individual interviews with the parents, with the interviewers switching assignments, so that each interviewer has an opportunity to see both sides of the marital relationship. During the parents' interviews, the teenager will complete the psychological testing. Other siblings, when present, may also be tested. During the afternoon, frequent use is made of overlapping sessions, often with two team members and two family members. A chain of overlapping sessions may be employed, where one member of the team goes from office to office to confer with each member of the family on a family pattern that has been uncovered.

The first day ends with a final team–family conference, which is an attempt to capitalize on the movement that individuals have been making during the course of the day in order to break through family resistance to change. Members of the family who attempt to go back to old patterns often find they do not receive reciprocal responses; and, the prospect of spending an evening together in which the old defenses and barriers to communication are partially disabled provides momentum for more open communication. During this session, the team models open expression of feeling and conflict resolution behaviors in order to both encourage and teach the family to do the same.

The second day follows the basic pattern of the first day, but with more flexibility and variability. The movement begun on the first day usually accelerates on the second, with family members dealing with more emotionally charged issues, such as the marital relationship. The final team–family conference is concerned with how the family can continue to grow and deal with the "back home problems." At this time, arrangements are made for the follow-up visit, to be held six months later. On occasion, two days are not sufficient, and the process is continued for an additional half day. With about one-fourth of the cases, a booster session of one day's length is arranged after about two months.

An uncontrolled evaluation of MIT with 62 families indicated results somewhat better than traditional psychotherapy (79 percent rated improved by therapists). Further, MIT is able to engage families who would not ordinarily avail themselves of psychotherapeutic help. In terms of cost efficiency, although the method is brief, it does involve the efforts of a team, and it consumes between 36 and 50 hours of professional time per family.

MEGAGROUP APPROACHES

The next set of innovative approaches is characterized by an emphasis on treatment in large groups: multiple family therapy (and couples groups), and social network intervention. These approaches have been strongly influenced by the principles and practices of group therapy, but the phenomenon of large-group therapy is distinctly different from that of small therapeutic groups. Large groups would seem to be unwieldy, yet the clinical impression of those who lead them is that they are surprisingly effective in producing significant change for sets of patients in a relatively short-term treatment interval. This apparant paradox has not provoked much study. Only Curry (1967b) attempted to formulate a theory of megagroup therapy. He based his work on situational analysis and behavioral systems theory, and attempted to explain the paradoxical utility of large groups in terms of the process of forming subgroups of various kinds.

But perhaps the paradox is only apparent. Perhaps there is something intrinsically beneficial in participating in large groups. We are living in an era of increasing fragmentation of society, evident at both micro and macro levels. Witness the breakup of the extended family early in the twentieth century and the breakup of the nuclear family impending in recent years, and also the increasing international tension as small and emerging nations struggle to attain their goals. States of loneliness, alienation, isolation, and anxiety are all too common. The opportunity to "reconnect," when it presents itself, can be quite enriching. Recently a newspaper article discussed the large crowds that gather for the Boston Marathon in terms of the deeply human need for large-group rituals. Perhaps an element in the success of large-group therapeutic approaches, then, is their ability to help restore a "psychological sense of community" (Sarason, 1974).

Multiple Family Therapy
(and Couples Groups)

The principal architect of multiple family therapy (MFT) is H. P. Laquer. Although Bowen (1971) developed a form of MFT (discussed above, in Chapter 4), and others have contributed to the approach (N. L. Paul, Bloom, & B. B. Paul, 1981; Dreikurs, Corsini, Lowe, & Sonstegard, 1959; Sauber, 1971), Laquer's work in this area is indisputably seminal (see Strelnick, 1977, for a review of the literature on MFT, and Mackler, 1980, for Laquer's bibliography).

Laquer began his work on MFT in 1950, while he was in charge of a 100-bed ward in a New York state hospital in which schizophrenic patients were treated with insulin coma therapy. Noticing the deterioration in patients' functioning after their first home visit, he decided to study the families more closely. He then observed that informational meetings with the families made the patients suspicious that the therapists were conspiring with their families. An attempt to correct for this by meeting subsequently with the patients made the families suspicious. Thus was born the idea of bringing together groups of patients and their families for ward meetings. The therapeutic efficiency of this method was quickly observed, and, serendipitously, a new therapeutic modality came into being. The approach has grown (along with the field of family therapy as a whole) from an initial focus on schizophrenia to the application to families of the most diversely diagnosed identified patients (Laquer, 1976, 1980; Strelnick, 1977).

MFT groups consist of the families of four to five identified patients, including parents, spouses, siblings and children, and the therapist, co-therapist, and trainee-observers. All told, such a group of 25–35 people meet from 60 to 90 minutes, usually in the evening, and preferably in a room with access to video equipment. Groups are formed randomly, with no attempt to impose any selection criteria, and are open-ended. A family leaving the group for whatever reason is replaced by a newly referred family. In general, MFT groups are freely structured (Bowen's highly structured approach being the exception), with open-group discussion facilitated by the therapists' clarifications and interpretations. Laquer (1976) recommended the use of role-playing exercises and psychodrama and sculpture techniques.

MFT is a hybrid of group and family therapy. It is unique among the therapies in that it allows "society" (in the form of several family units other than the identified parents) to enter into the therapeutic relationship (Laquer, 1976).

Laquer used the language of general systems theory to discuss his work, viewing MFT as a system composed of a number of subsystems (families), each in turn composed of smaller units (dyads, individuals). The therapist functions as the central processing unit in this feedback-governed system (Laquer, 1969). He conceived of the process of MFT as occurring through three phases: (1) initial interest, in which hope is generated for improvement; (2) resistance, when the family realizes that change will be required of all, and not just of the identified patient, and (3) working through, wherein significant change begins to occur.

Certain "mechanisms of change" are operative during this process (Laquer, 1972). "Delineation of the field of interaction" is the process whereby the family comes to understand that the problem is not resident in the identified patient but rather in the interactional patterns in which that patient is embedded. The presence of other families is often helpful in "breaking the intrafamilial codes" by which disturbed families close off discussion of touchy areas and defend against outside intervention. Sensitive patients often pick up "signals" from the therapist, which they then "amplify or modulate," allowing the message to be heard by others. In the open-ended MFT groups, families are at various stages of growth and problem resolution. Consequently, healthier aspects of certain families serve as "models" for other families, and healthier families sometimes function informally as "co-therapists." Also, because of the presence of families who are struggling with similar issues, MFT members "learn by analogy"—that is, they observe how other families handle analogous problem situations. Related to this is "learning through identification," where fathers learn from fathers, patients from patients, and so forth. When this concept is applied to the family as a whole, Laquer uses the term "identification constellation." Moreover, group members "learn through trial and error"—that is, through trying out behaviors in the group and receiving feedback on their utility. The last mechanism described by Laquer is based on information theory, in which it is postulated that events that have a low probability of occurrence have the highest information value. Translated into MFT, any new, more appropriate, or functional behavior that occurs becomes the "focus of excitation" for the whole group, which serves to reinforce the change and replenish hope in other group members.

During a period of nearly 30 years Laquer (1980) and his associates treated about 1,500 families in New York and another 250 in Vermont. Informal uncontrolled evaluation indicated that MFT is effective in reducing frequency and duration of hospitalization, and in promoting improved communication and resolution of pathological interactional patterns. The outcome research on MFT is still undeveloped, but the few studies available have been reviewed by Strelnick (1977). In general, there is modest support for the proposition that MFT "works," but controlled studies are needed for confirmation.

Couples groups are a variation of MFT, in which the focus is squarely in the marital relationship. Couples group therapy is useful both when the marriage is the presenting problem, and when—in child-focused families—the therapy has evolved to the point that serious difficulties in the parents' relationship have been identified. Although many of the processes described in MFT also occur in couples groups, the latter are unique in the opportunities that they provide for observing other peoples' marriages in depth. In and of itself, this allows couples to see that their difficulties are not unique and that all couples must work out a complementarity and a set of accommodations in the universal areas of sex, money, parenting, and handling the families of origin. In addition, the couples are excellent sources of support and honest confrontation of one another, picking up some of the functions that used to be served by the extended family. As mentioned in Chapter 4, Framo (1973) has done extensive work with couples group therapy; see also Alger (1976b) for a more complete discussion of this approach. Neiberg (1976) treated the subject from the perspective of group therapy, and Papp (1976a) described a brief format of couples group therapy, which utilizes choreography and task assignment to facilitate "accelerated change." The evaluative research on couples groups was discussed above, in Chapter 7.

Social Network Intervention

Social network intervention, or network therapy, is a radical form of treatment that was developed originally as the treatment of last resort in situations where other methods of therapy had failed. The approach involves the assembly and mobilization of the entire social network of a troubled family and identified patient. A minimum of 40 people are called together, including extended family, neighbors, friends, co-workers or colleagues, adolescent peer groups, professional and paraprofessional caregivers, and community leaders. Initially, this group may share only a common concern for the plight of the family and patient.

The social network is brought together at the patient's home, and it will typically meet six times, for an entire evening each time, at one-week to four-week intervals. The network-intervention team consists of a leader or conductor and one to two "intervenors." Optimally, the team should be diverse in age, personality style, and other traits, in order to be able to blend in with and relate well to all sections of the network.

The approach, as described by its pioneers (Speck & Attneave, 1973; Ruevini, 1979), attempts to mobilize, empower, or otherwise facilitate the group's efforts to find and implement effective solutions for the patient's and family's problems. Clinical problems are redefined as problems in living, and they become recognized as utterly common, shared in varying degrees by others in the network. In this context, human rather than professional resources are viewed as the solution, whether it be sitting around the clock with anxious parents while they let their son make some of his own mistakes and find his independence, inviting an embattled, defensive couple to a card party or over to dinner, or finding job after job for an unwilling and inept depressed person, helping him to succeed in spite of himself (Speck & Attneave, 1971).

But it is not only the identified patient and family who receive help. Others in need bring forth their problems, permitted to do so by the acceptant atmosphere created in the network. Those with energy and resources to share come forth as "activists," providing aid and comfort to those in need. A sharing community is thus created, revitalizing the attenuated social bonds. In fact, many networks continue to meet or stay in contact (for example, through newsletters) long after the intervention is over.

Network therapy depends on creating what its originators term the "network effect," a group "high" or euphoric sense of belonging in which old barriers are dissolved and new bonds readily form—a process such as was alluded to in the introduction to this section, one that is probably the common denominator in tribal healing ceremonies, religious revival meetings, city-wide Fourth of July or New Years Eve celebrations, Rotary Club picnics, Columbus Day parades, "big-game" celebrations, large outdoor concerts, and, yes, the Boston Marathon.

To achieve this state in such a sustained way as to enable substantial solutions to serious human problems, the network must go through a dialectical process consisting of six stages. The first stage, called *retribalization,* depends heavily on nonverbal encounter-group techniques, such as "war whoops and yells," vigorously jumping up and down, and holding hands and swaying. The purpose of these exercises is to induct the network into a preliminary state of "tribal" connectedness marked by enthusiasm and freedom from conventional restraint. The second stage (*polarization*) consists of bringing out into the open the various antinomies of living or polarities that exist in the network (such as young versus old, men versus women, family versus friends, and conservatives versus liberals). This is done through a series of discussions, in which one subgroup of 6 to 10 persons takes the inner circle and is allowed free discussion. Those in the outer circle must be quiet until it is their turn. Often the initial subgroups will naturally form along generational lines, with the younger generation sitting on the floor in the middle of the room and the parent generation sitting on the comfortable furniture along the periphery. If the inner and outer subgroups are naturally polarized (as in this instance), it is often necessary to place one or two chairs in the center of the room in order to allow members of the outer circle to come forward and speak. Attempts by network members to resolve the differences that emerge are avoided at this stage, which is designed to survey the range of problems and select one or more as the object of the network's focus. The first session typically ends at this point, with the network team excusing themselves during a free-floating visiting and refreshment period, which often continues late into the night.

Subsequent sessions usually begin with the nonverbal exercises followed by a recap of where things stand. The third stage, *mobilization,* begins when a group of network activists come forward with a preliminary solution. Often such a solution is inadequate to the task and fails to achieve the desired results, bringing the network into the fourth stage of *depression.* It is here that the group makes the decision to gather its forces for a concerted effort to solve the problem, which often requires a serious attempt to resolve the relevant polarities within which the problem is embedded. In so doing, the dialectical synthesis is achieved, and the *breakthrough* stage results. The intervention ends with the group in the stage of *exhaustion/elation.*

Network therapy is a radical intervention in several ways: in calling together such a group in the first place; in its de-professional attitude of eschewing confidentiality and relabeling problems as human rather than clinical; and in its attempt to revitalize social networks and whole communities. But most significantly, it is radical in the sense of being a distinctly new departure, the full potential of which is only beginning to be apprehended. As Speck and Attneave wrote:

> It is part of the fascination of network study and intervention that there are unmapped vistas and old mountains to be climbed before new ones are glimpsed. The sequences and patterning sketched here may after some years seem like the early maps of the new world that showed California as an island and connected the Great Lakes to the western seas. (Speck & Attneave, 1971, p. 317)

The full treatment of the emerging developments within social-network intervention and the delineation of this field are beyond the scope of this section. A recent journal issue, however, was devoted to this very task, and interested readers are urged to consult Pattison (1981; see also Speck & Speck, 1979).

NONVERBAL TECHNIQUES

Most approaches to family therapy utilize a range of verbal and nonverbal techniques, from interpretation to changing seats, and these have been discussed in Part II. In addition, several other nonverbal techniques can be used to "make the invisible visible." These techniques will be discussed here because they are applicable to a range of therapeutic approaches and can be used as adjuncts to treatment by a variety of therapists. The techniques to be discussed are (1) family sculpture and choreography, (2) the use of videotape, and (3) other aids (family photos, home movies, and floor plans) in family therapy.

Family Sculpture and Choreography

Family sculpture was developed originally at the Boston Family Institute by Kantor, with contributions from the Duhls (Duhl, Kantor, & Duhl, 1973), and it is conceptually related to both psychodrama (Moreno, 1946) and general systems theory. Satir (1972) and Papp (1976b) have also contributed to the development of this approach.

Sculpture is based on the use of space as a metaphor for human relationships. "Closeness" and "distance" are, of course, spatial metaphors. The concepts of "boundaries," "personal space," and "interpersonal space" bring in the systems idea. Fundamentally, sculpture involves the arrangement of the bodies of the family members in terms of their positioning and posture, in order to depict family relationships. What results is a *tableau vivant* (Simon, 1972) or freeze-frame that graphically portrays the hidden and poignant aspects of family life—those private perceptions or invisible structures that come to light only very slowly through verbal techniques.

Sculpture can be used as a diagnostic aid or as a therapeutic intervention. In the latter case it is particularly valuable for breaking through stuck patterns maintained by verbal communication, and also for involving adolescents and older children, who often find it easier to participate in an actional mode than a verbal one. Sculpture has also been used as a training procedure and as an educational or preventive mental-health intervention (Papp, Silverstein, & Carter, 1973).

There are several types of sculpture. Duhl and colleagues (1973) described three types, according to the number of people participating as sculptors. In individual sculpture, one person portrays his or her relationship with family members, who, here, are played by family nonmembers. This is a sculpture of the family as seen from the perspective of one person. "Boundary" or "dyadic" sculpture involves two people who, in turn, portray their own personal space and boundaries. In the process, the conditions for entering an individual's personal space are explicated. This type of sculpture helps clarify the rules governing each part of the two-part system. Family or group sculpture involves three or more family members and helps to define the larger and more complex system. In this sculpture, each person portrays his or her relationship with other family members and understanding of the family rules. In all three types of sculpture, participants can not only portray family relationships as they are, but also as they ideally would like them to be. The former tends to emphasize each person's unique perspective on the family; the latter can bring out hopes and failed expectations. Additional types of sculpture have been described by Constantine (1978).

Sculpture is, in some respects, a misnomer, unless one has in mind kinetic sculpture. Not a static process, family sculpture involves much change and motion in the dimensions of both space and time. Papp (1976b) has coined the term "family choreography" to capture this quality, which she accentuates in her approach. Papp's emphasis is more on creating new patterns and changing the family system than on understanding the system as it is. She uses choreography as a technique of active intervention to realign family relationships through exploring alternative transactional patterns in terms of physical movement and positioning in space.

Use of Videotape
in Family Therapy

Videotape technology has been strongly associated with the family therapy movement. There are several reasons for this. First, there is historical contiguity: Videotape technology became available at a time when communication and general systems theories were turning clinicians' attention toward the interactional field within which the symptomatic person was embedded. Videotape, because it provided a means for directly studying this field or interactional matrix, was quickly adopted. Second, there is the extraordinary openness (some critics would say exhibitionism) that has characterized the family therapy movement. In contrast to the psychoanalytic attitude of mystery (which for many years regarded the therapeutic process as too delicate to even be studied), family therapy has a tradition of bringing the family's dynamics and the therapeutic process out into the light of day. Even before the introduction of videotape, movies were made of family interviews, such as the famous Hillcrest Family Series, which consists of series of consultation interviews with the Hillcrest family by several family therapy pioneers (Don Jackson, Nathan Ackerman, Murray Bowen, and Carl Whitaker). Videotape soon replaced the use of film because of its technical advantages, such as immediate availability without processing, and its ability to focus on particular aspects of family interaction through various special effects.

Videotape is used for teaching, supervision, research, and therapy. The focus in this section will be on its use in therapy. (Some of the other applications have been covered in Chapter 7.) The coverage here will be of necessity brief. For additional information the reader is referred to Alger (1973, 1976a), N.L. Paul (1976), and Berger (1978).

A wide selection of video equipment is available. In my own work I use a three-quarter-inch cassette videotape deck (VTR), a TV monitor, and a camera with tripod. The camera is equipped with a zoom lens for close-up shots and a wide-angle lens for observing group interactions. An omnidirectional microphone placed in the center of the group is usually sufficient, but individual lavaliere microphones may also be used. A second unit and a special-effects generator are also available, which allows the mixing of inputs from two cameras and achieves certain interesting effects, such as split-screen images (which can focus on two interactants, or on two parts of the group); corner inserts (of one individual in close-up while the rest of the screen shows the whole group in wide angle); and superimposition of images.

Alger (1973) recommended letting different members of the family operate the camera, which helps them develop an observational capacity and also is particularly revealing in terms of which aspects of the family are focused on or excluded by each member. More commonly, the camera is operated by a co-therapist or technician. Tapes may be made available for later viewing by family members, or they may be stopped for "instant replay" during the session itself. The particular sequence can then be played back several times, each time revealing additional information; or it may be played in slow motion, still-framing, or fast motion. The slow-motion technique is particularly valuable for revealing a particular movement by one family member that initiates a sequence of interaction, or for capturing a shift in facial expression, whereas still-framing allows the isolation of particularly poignant nuances in interaction of facial expression. Such images have a far greater impact than verbal insights ("I'll never forget that look on my face when . . . ").

Video replay is very useful for highlighting descrepancies between verbal and nonverbal communication, and for cutting through verbal denials of nonverbal behavior through self-confrontation. Alger (1973, p. 69) described a case in which the son's defense to his father's reproach was " 'What do you mean disrespectful, I was *just* sitting here listening to you.' True, he was listening, but even he nodded his head in understanding when he recognized his sneer in replay." Moreover, the synchronized movements of family members are often dramatically revealing of the family system. A family in which father formed a coalition with his 11-year-old daughter against his wife was caught on tape in a particularly revealing split-second interaction. The interaction was preceded by husband and wife reaching an impasse in their angry hurling of charges and countercharges. The family was seated in a semicircle, with father in the middle and mother and daughter seated on either side of him. At the point of impasse father abruptly moved his chair a quarter turn away from his wife, and crossed his legs so as to form a barrier against her; almost simultaneously wife shifted her position in her seat, and crossed her legs as a barricade, and daughter shifted her chair a quarter turn toward her father, crossing her legs so as to form a boundary around her and her father.

Gurman and Kniskern (1978a) have reviewed the few available studies regarding the effects of videotape feedback. Several studies have shown beneficial effects, but Alkire and Brunse (1974) found powerful negative results from the use of video playback in a couples group, both on individuals and on relationships. Gurman and Kniskern concluded that videotape feedback can have profound effects, both for better or worse; and that it may be a useful adjunct to family therapy, "but its independent use to effect change is questionable" (p. 180). Additional research into the conditions under which video playback promotes deterioration is urgently needed.

Family Photos, Home Movies, and Floor Plans

Several authors have described the use of family photographs (Anderson & Malloy, 1976; Kaslow & Friedman, 1977), family home movies (Kaslow & Friedman, 1977), and family floor plans (Coppersmith, 1980b) as aids in family therapy. In general, these adjuncts are used for memory-evoking purposes, to call forth into the present vivid images of the past.

Anderson and Malloy (1976) used family photos in a task-assignment procedure that can be structured in several ways. Each individual may be asked to bring in two to three photos chosen as representing important aspects of the family relationships. Alternatively, to study families of origin and multigenerational themes, the family is asked to bring in one to three photos from each generation or photos of the extended family. The process of collecting and selecting the photos for the session is usually emotionally charged, calling forth memories of the way things were at various epochs or of deceased or forgotten relatives. In the session this material becomes available for therapeutic work.

Kaslow and Friedman (1977) combine family photos and home movies in a procedure called Family Photo Reconnaisance. In contrast to Anderson and Malloy, they do not limit the numbers of photos, nor do they set up the task as a homework assignment. Reconnaisance may be conducted in the office or during a home visit, and it may continue over several therapy sessions. Kaslow and Friedman listed the following advantages of using photos and movies: (1) They provide much factual historical information; (2) they help members retrieve memories and modify memory distortions; (3) they elicit emotionally meaningful material and evoke affect; (4) they help family members break through stereotyped perception and see each other in new ways; (5) they help the therapist to identify crucial times in the family's life cycle; (6) they elicit information regarding parental expectations of their children; and (7) they help understand the family's role network.

Finally, Coppersmith (1980) described the use of the Family Floor Plan as an aid in assessment and therapy. In this procedure, individuals are asked to draw floor plans of the homes in which they lived at various times of their lives, while being prompted to recall specific details such as smells, sounds, colors, moods, people, and typical events. One variation involves having parents draw the floor plans of their families of origin while their children watch. A second approach has each family member drawing the floor plan of the family's current dwelling. Finally, children may be asked to draw the current floor plan while parents observe. Coppersmith has found this technique useful in providing the therapist with information not readily available through purely verbal means and in providing the family with an experience that promotes both interpersonal involvement and differentiation.

SPECIALIZED APPROACHES
FOR CERTAIN ASPECTS OF MARRIAGE

As discussed in Part II, all the family therapy approaches can be and are utilized for marital therapy (that is, when the presenting complaint is a problem in the marriage), and practitioners of many of the approaches agree that the marital relationship is at the core of the family problem, even when the presenting complaint is a symptomatic individual. Supplementary to these general approaches to marital therapy are two specialized approaches aimed at particular aspects of marriage: sex therapy and divorce therapy. These specialized approaches will be discussed in this section.

Sex Therapy

Sex therapy as a professional field is of relatively recent origin, coming into its own around 1970. Since then, two professional journals have been founded (*Journal of Sex and Marital Therapy* and *Journal of Sex Education and Therapy*), and the American Association of Sex Educators and Counselors has established standards for certifying qualified sex therapists.

The reasons for this rapid recent development lie in a combination of the liberalization of attitudes regarding sexuality and a tremendous explosion of knowledge about the human sexual response and its dysfunctions. Work by early pioneers such as Havelock Ellis (1936) and Alfred Kinsey and associates (Kinsey, Pomeroy & Martin, 1948; Kinsey, Pomeroy, Martin, & Gebbard, 1953) was overshadowed by the monumental studies of Masters and Johnson (1966), who studied in great detail the physiological and behavioral events during masturbation and sexual intercourse. Masters and Johnson's initial research (1966) established the four phases of the human sexual response cycle (excitement, plateau, orgasm, and resolution) and discredited a number of established beliefs, such as Freud's doctrine (1938) of the superiority of the vaginal orgasm and the general cultural evaluation of the benefits of penis size.

It was Masters and Johnson's (1970) clinical work, however, that revolutionized the field. Breaking with psychodynamic tradition, which regarded sexual dysfunction as a manifestation of psychopathology and requiring extensive treatment (Freud, 1953), they focused only on the immediate causes of sexual dysfunction in short-term problem-focused treatment. The treatment program requires that both partners spend two weeks at the Reproductive Biology Research Foundation in St. Louis. The couple is treated conjointly by a co-therapist team, consisting of one male and one female (in order to avoid misunderstandings due to sexual bias), preferably one trained in the biological sciences and the other in the behavioral sciences.

The treatment program begins with an extensive two-day evaluation, taking an in-depth sexual history (including experiences, attitudes, and feelings) and doing a physical history and medical examination. On the third day, the first round-table meeting is held, in which the co-therapists present their findings regarding the etiology of the couple's sexual problem and the plan for treatment that is to follow. Masters and Johnson conceptualize sexual inadequacy as arising from lack of information regarding sexual matters, difficulties in communication, performance anxiety, taking a spectator role rather than abandoning oneself to the mutual sexual experience, or combinations of these elements. Treatment is thus geared toward three areas: (1) educational counseling to provide accurate information about sexuality and eliminate myths and erroneous views; (2) facilitation of open communication; (3) a graded series of sensual-sexual tasks, termed "sensate focus." The couple is instructed to begin the tasks with an emphasis on discovery and communication about sensual pleasures; performance (erection, orgasm) is to be disregarded. The stages of the sensual-sexual encounter are generally as follows: (1) nonerotic physical contact; (2) nonbreast, nongenital touching and exploration, while the partner communicates pleasure or nonpleasure; (3) breast and genital touching in the same manner; (4) self-masturbation to orgasm; (5) mutual masturbation to orgasm; (6) intercourse. The tasks include specific procedures for altering the couple's sexual dysfunction. Regular round-table meetings are held to deal with feelings that arise in the course of implementing the tasks.

Masters and Johnson (1970) have achieved impressive results with their approach, reporting an overall success rate of 81.1 percent after treatment, which decreased only slightly at five-year follow-up (80 percent). The best results have been obtained with premature ejaculation in men (97.8 percent) and primary orgasmic dysfunction in women (never having achieved an orgasm—83.4 percent).

The clinical work of Masters and Johnson was actually preceded by that of several behaviorists: Semans (1956) developed a treatment for premature ejaculation; and Wolpe (1958) applied *in vivo* systematic desensitization to the treatment of sexual dysfunctions. In fact, the sensate focus technique is based on systematic desensitization; Masters and Johnson's original contributions are the use of the conjoint format and the focus on communication and sexual education. Most recently, an explicitly behavioral wing of sex therapy has emerged (LoPiccolo & LoPiccolo, 1978). This group has developed such innovations as self-monitoring, masturbation training, orgasmic reconditioning, social-skill training, and motivation contracts. Reviews of recent outcome studies indicate the behavioral approach to be about as effective as Masters and Johnson's approach for premature ejaculation and primary orgasmic dysfunction, but that the behavioral treatment of secondary orgasmic dysfunction is not as successful (Kinder & Blakeney, 1977); and that both approaches are effective with highly selected populations but may not be very effective with unselected outpatient populations who have varying degrees and types of psychopathology (Wright, Perreault, & Mathieu, 1977). These results indicate that careful screening is needed when using a strict sex-therapy approach outside of the context of an ongoing therapeutic relationship.

Kaplan (1974) provides a model for a more general approach, providing sex therapy within a broader therapeutic context that systematically takes into account individual and relationship factors. She utilizes the assignment of sensate-focus exercises and prescriptive erotic techniques for specific sexual dysfunctions in the context of a conjoint therapeutic relationship of a mixed psychodynamic-behavioral orientation. She reports results similar to the other two groups, but is in a better position to provide longer-term treatment for more serious individual psychopathology and marital discord, when indicated.

Divorce Therapy

Divorce has become a strikingly frequent phenomenon in our society during the last decade. Divorce rates had been increasing very gradually overall (with fluctuations here and there) during the twentieth century, going from 1/1,000 (one divorce per 1,000 population) in 1910 to 2/1,000 in 1940 to 3/1,000 by 1970. But during the 1970s the rates skyrocketed, hitting 5.3/1,000 in 1979. During that year, 1.17 million divorces involved an estimated 1.2 million children. And this is in relationship to a marriage rate of 10.7/1,000, indicating that one out of every two marriages ends in divorce (U.S. Bureau of the Census, 1979, 1980).

Correspondingly, social scientists and mental health professionals have given increased attention to various aspects of divorce. Studies of the effects on children (Wallerstein & Kelley, 1974, 1975, 1976; Lamb, 1977) have indicated that divorce is a highly stressful experience, the favorable resolution of which depends on a careful assessment of, and attention to, the needs of both parents as well as the needs of the children. Other researchers have focused on the stages of the divorce experience, and on the interventions indicated at the various stages (Salts, 1979). Judicial reforms have humanized the divorce process through the enactment of "no-fault" divorce laws in many states; and changes in the long-prevailing practice of automatically awarding custody to mothers (based on the "tender years" doctrine) have led to more frequent awards of joint custody and father custody (Family Advocate, 1978). Remarriage after divorce has led to a new family form—the "reconstituted" or "blended" stepfamily (Duberman, 1975), for whom specialized counseling procedures have been developed (Visher & Visher, 1979).

Divorce therapy, as a professional field, is voluminous in some respects and underdeveloped in others. On the one hand, most existing therapeutic approaches have been applied in individual, couples, family, and group formats to the spouses and children at all stages of the divorce process. Yet, as Gurman and Kniskern (1981a, p. 682) point out, "the existence of such a 'broad spectrum' of treatment approaches about divorce problems reflects the undeniable fact that there have been developed essentially no intervention strategies or treatment techniques that are specific to the emotional, behavioral and interpersonal difficulties caused by separation and divorce." Furthermore, the research in the outcome of divorce therapy is very sparse, and efficacy has yet to be established (Gurman and Kniskern, 1978a; Kaslow, 1981). Kaslow (1981) provides a review of the literature on divorce and divorce therapy, to which the interested reader is directed. The coverage here will be, of necessity, brief.

During the *predivorce period,* Whitaker and Miller (1969, p. 57) caution against the use of individual therapy, in that "intervention on one side or another in a marriage when divorce is being considered may serve to destroy the probability of reconciliation." Several clinicians recommend couples-group therapy at this stage because of the support and confrontation that such a group can offer (Kaslow, 1981).

During the *divorce period,* Kaslow (1981) recommends that the therapists be attuned to the potentially corrosive adversarial aspects of the process, and that they maintain a list of attorneys who are concerned about their clients' psychological well-being and not just "getting the best deal" no matter how much "hard ball" they have to play. In addition, an alternative to traditional divorce procedures has recently come into being: the Family Mediation Program (Coogler, 1978). In this highly structured program, couples sign a legal document that binds them to work out a mutual settlement on issues of custody, support, alimony, and division of property. If they are unable to do so, they are required to enter into binding arbitration. Couples are "walked through" the process, using a set of "Marital Mediation Rules," which are well-worked-out methods of conflict resolution.

Kressel and Deutsch (1977) surveyed 21 experienced divorce therapists regarding their criteria for a constructive divorce, impediments to its achievement, and strategies and tactics of divorce therapy. A constructive divorce had the following hallmarks: a successful completion of the process of psychological separation; and the protection of the welfare of the dependent children. They found three types of therapeutic strategies: "Reflexive interventions by which the therapist orients himself to the marital partners and attempts to gain the trust and confidence of the partners; contextual interventions by which he tries to promote a climate conducive to decision-making; and substantive interventions intended to produce resolution on terms the therapist has come to believe are inevitable or necessary" (p. 413).

In many cases, therapy continues in the *postdivorce* period; it is often initiated at this time. Recent innovations include attention to the father (Dreyfus, 1979; Leader, 1973)—traditionally, the neglected person in the family unit—and the use of family therapy after divorce (Leader, 1973; Goldman & Coane, 1977). Support groups, such as Parents Without Partners, are also often helpful at this stage.

SPECIAL TECHNIQUES
FOR CHILDREN:
TOWARD THE INTEGRATION
OF CHILD
AND FAMILY THERAPY

The clinical specializations of child therapy and family therapy have developed along parallel paths, with scant collaboration and cross-fertilization. Child therapists tend to describe their work in child therapy journals such as the *Journal of the American Academy of Child Psychiatry*, the *International Journal of Child Psychotherapy*, the *Psychoanalytic Study of the Child*, and the *Journal of Child Psychology and Psychiatry*. Family therapists tend to discuss their work in family therapy journals such as the *American Journal of Family Therapy*, the *Journal of Marital and Family Therapy*, the *International Journal of Family Therapy*, and *Family Process*. At the level of practice, there are those who have been trained in child therapy programs who practice child therapy, and who may or may not see the members of the child's family, but who are usually not knowledgeable about the expanding array of family therapy approaches and techniques. And there are family therapists who see the whole family, or the mother-father-child triad, yet who demonstrate a remarkable lack of knowledge regarding the techniques of child therapy.

This unspoken, stubborn refusal of each speciality field to even take interest in the other has been referred to as the "undeclared war between child and family therapy" (McDermott & Char, 1974). The primary victims of this war are, of course, the children, whose symptoms initiate the treatment process.

What is needed is an integration of the theory and techniques of child therapy with those of family therapy. The child needs to be seen within the context of the family: yet the child (as well as each parent) exists not only as a member of the family system, but also as an individual at a certain stage of development in his or her life cycle. The family therapist must have knowledge not only of the family system, but also of the particular stage of development of the individual family members, including the children. The family therapist also needs to understand the child's nonverbal language and use of play to express fantasies, feelings, and conflicts, and to be able to communicate with the child through the use of play.

Such an integrated approach has only rarely been suggested in the literature.

Levant and Haffey's recent review (1981) of current forms of treatment for the symptomatic child found four general approaches (individual child psychotherapy, conjoint parent-child psychotherapy and counseling, parent therapy and counseling, and conjoint family therapy), and scant attention directed towards the integration of child and family therapy. McDermott and Char's perspective (1974) on the polarization of child and family therapy techniques is that family therapists have tended to replace or compete with individual child therapists, rather than to integrate child therapy skills into their approach. Suggesting that techniques need to be conceived that will effectively involve children in family therapy, they posed the problem of "how to understand, relate, and integrate the multiple levels of communication and interaction that occur so naturally in every family into a therapeutic process" (McDermott & Char, 1974, p. 435). Finally, Malone (1979) explored the polarization of child and family therapy, which he viewed as a reflection of the longstanding controversy between intrapsychic and interpersonal theories of motivation. The polarization is exacerbated by theorists with extreme positions, while the overlap of the theories and therapeutic approaches has been ignored. He pointed out that the growing overlap is evidenced by the use of family interviews to aid in the diagnosis of children, the incorporation of developmental concepts into theories of family interaction and therapy, and the inclusion of children in family therapy by therapists who are able to understand and utilize the children's play.

A few reports of attempts to move in the direction of a more thoroughgoing integration of child and family therapy have begun to appear in the literature. These either attempt the integration within the context of conjoint family therapy or provide concurrent child and family therapy.

In the conjoint approaches, Dare and Lindsey (1979) reported the development of a conjoint family therapy approach to the child-focused family, combining techniques of family therapy with techniques of play therapy. Toys are used not "as a distraction to keep children quiet, but are deliberately being used as a vehicle for understanding them" (p. 260). In addition, Tasem and colleagues (Augenbraun & Tasem, 1966; Tasem, Augenbraun, & Brown, 1965) have described a method in which the families of preschool children are seen in a playroom setting. The therapist responds to both the child and the parents, interpreting the child's behavior to the parents, exploring the parent-child interaction, and reflecting the affective meaning of the child's behavior.

Dowling and Jones (1978) described both the problems and benefits inherent in such conjoint therapy that integrates child therapy skills with family therapy sessions. While it is difficult for the therapist to cope with the abundance of nonverbal communication offered by the children, understanding the children's communication is invaluable for understanding the family. The therapist utilizes child therapy techniques in order to better understand the child, the family dynamics, and the parent-child relationship, and to allow the child to benefit directly from their involvement in the family sessions. Moreover, Dare and Lindsey (1979) point out that when therapists are able to accept and understand the children's communication, this acceptance encourages and allows the adults to share their more immature and childlike feelings.

In the concurrent model of integrated play therapy and family therapy, the therapist sees the child individually, at which time the child's language of play predominates. The therapist also sees the family as a unit (or at times, the parents alone), and the verbal communication of adults predominates. With the sole exception of the paper by Haffey (1980), this technique as a treatment of choice has not been reported in the literature. Taichert (1973) described a limited use of this technique; however, his treatment of choice appears to be family therapy. Individual play therapy is used with the child concurrent with family therapy to help the child deal with issues of control and mastery. The content of the individual sessions is shared with the parents so they will better understand their child. Charney (1966) has also discussed concurrent individual and family therapy, concluding that such a concurrent approach would be useful when neither individual nor family therapy seemed sufficient. Although Charney described concurrent individual and family treatment with a preadolescent boy, it is not reported whether play techniques were used. Finally, Smith and Loeb (1965) discussed the use of sequential individual, family, and group therapy for the families of atypical or severely disturbed young children.

SUMMARY

Thus we conclude our kaleidoscopic survey of special forms and techniques of working therapeutically with families. These approaches include not only the well-established theory and practice of crisis intervention (family crisis therapy and multiple impact therapy), but also the megagroup approaches in need of a meta-theory (multiple family therapy and social network intervention). Nonverbal adjunctive techniques (sculpture and choreography, and the use of videotape, family photos, home movies, and floor plans) are also useful in a range of therapeutic approaches. Two specialized approaches are available for working with certain aspects of the marriage (sex therapy and divorce therapy). Finally, the integration of child and family therapy is potentially of great value, but it remains to be more fully developed.

No general conclusion for such a diverse set of techniques is really possible, except to point out that these represent the edges around the field of family therapy, and as such, they should be mentioned in any literate discussion of the field. Some of these edges were growth areas in the past and have not seen much current development (such as the crisis approaches), whereas others are of more recent origin (sex therapy and divorce therapy). Some have histories that stretch back to· the beginnings of family therapy and futures that appear limitless (such as mega-group approaches, particularly social-network intervention). And still others have yet to develop fully (the integration of child and family therapy).

RESOURCES: CLINICAL EXAMPLES
OF SPECIAL FORMS
AND TECHNIQUES OF FAMILY WORK

I. *Crisis-Oriented Approaches*
   A. Family Crisis Therapy
      1. Haley and Hoffman (1967) present an initial interview with a middle-aged psychotic woman, her sister and her young adult son by Pittman and associates. As mentioned before, the format interweaves the interview with extensive commentary on the interview, derived from a postinterview debriefing session.
      2. Several case studies are included in Langsley & Kaplan's book *The treatment of families in crisis* (1968).
   B. Multiple Impact Therapy
      1. The Boston Family Institute (251 Harvard Street, Brookline, MA 02146) has two tapes available for rental or purchase: *Single parent struggles* includes segments of interviews with the family unit, the parents, and the children; *Robert and Mary MacGregor* is an interview with the MacGregors on the evolution of their approach and their work together as a co-therapy team.
      2. Israela Meyerstein (2910 Highland Street, Allentown, PA 18104) has a four-part tape set available for rental, *Promise her anything but send her a postcard,* illustrating the MIT approach with a family with multiple problems. This tape set was recently reviewed by Schultz (1981).
II. *Megagroup Approaches*
   A. Multiple Family Therapy (and Couples Groups).
      1. IEA Productions (520 East 77th Street, New York, NY 10021) has two tapes available for purchase only, illustrating Alger's work with couples groups: *Videotape in couples group therapy* and *Multiple couple therapy.*
      2. See also the Boston Family Institute's tape of Framo's work with a couples group, described in Chapter 4, and the South Beach Psychiatric Center's tape of Whitaker's consultation with a multiple-family group, described in Chapter 5.
   B. Social Network Intervention
      1. The Boston Family Institute (see above) has available for rental or purchase two interviews with social network and ecological therapists, *Carolyn Attneave* and *Edgar Auerswald,* in which they describe their lives and work.
      2. A demonstration of network therapy with Attneave as conductor is available from Groome Child Guidance Center (Hayes Hall, Sibley Hospital, 5225 Loughboro Road NW, Washington, DC 20016).
      3. Case studies of network interventions are included in Speck and Attneave (1973) and Rueveni (1979).
III. *Nonverbal Techniques*
   A. Sculpture and Choreography
      1. The Ackerman Institute (149 East 78th Street, New York, NY 10021) has available for rental the tape *Making the invisible visible,* in which Papp demonstrates her use of sculpture as a therapeutic technique. This tape was reviewed by Greenberg (1979a).

2. The Boston Family Institute (see above) has several tapes available for rental or purchase on Satir's work. *Sisters and parents* is an interview that includes a demonstration of sculpture; *The light and the dark* is a follow-up interview of the same family following the suicide of one of the daughters; and *Virginia Satir* is a interview with Satir about her background and development as a therapist.

B. Video Replay
1. The South Beach Psychiatric Center (777 Seaview Ave., S.I., N.Y. 10305) has available for rental or purchase *Basic equipment for effective use in psychiatry,* a videotape illustrating the use of video equipment.
2. IEA Productions (see above) has available for purchase three tapes illustrating Alger's use of video playback: *Videotape in couples group therapy* (mentioned above), *Family circle,* and *Time-mirror.* The last tape was reviewed by Salin (1980).

IV. *Specialized Approaches for Certain Aspects of Marriage*
A. Sex Therapy
1. South Beach Psychiatric Center (777 Seaview Avenue, S.I., NY 10305) has available for purchase or rental the tape *Psycho-sexual therapy,* illustrating the work of Helen Singer Kaplan.
2. See also the South Beach Psychiatric Center's tape by Sager, *Marital or sex therapy,* discussed in Chapter 4.

B. Divorce Therapy
1. The American Personnel and Guidance Association has available a two-part film set, *Divorce* (available from APGA Film Dept., 1607 New Hampshire Avenue NW, Washington, DC 20009).
2. See also the case study and follow-up on divorce by Whitaker and associates in Papp (1977a), described in Chapter 5, and the Bowen tape *Divorcing family systems,* available from the Georgetown University Family Center and described in Chapter 4.

9

Psychological-Educational and Skills-Training Family Programs for Treatment, Prevention, and Development

This chapter will address the task of taking stock of an expanding array of programs designed for families and using psychological-educational and skills-training approaches. These are generally brief or time-limited, systematic or structured, experiential and didactic training programs, designed to remediate individual and family problems, to enhance aspects of family life, or both. These programs have arisen in the last 15 years from several sources, and amount to what some are calling a "new professional field" (R. M. Smith, Shoffner, & Scott, 1979; L'Abate, 1981).

OVERVIEW

Many of these programs have emerged as a growing trend within the field of family therapy (Olson, 1976; Olson & Sprenkle, 1976). Two of the most recent entrants into the field of family therapy—client-centered and behavioral approaches—quickly moved from a focus on conjoint family therapy to the development of skills-training programs. These programs, deriving from a therapeutic approach, have been influenced by certain tenets of the community mental-health movement, particularly the emphasis on prevention and the use of nonprofessional helpers (Iscoe, Bloom & Spielberger, 1977; Kessler & Albee, 1975; L. F. Guerney, 1969; Carkhuff, 1969a, 1969b). Moreover, these particular programs, developed primarily by psychologists, were responsive to Miller's call (1969) to "give psychology away" to the public. They represent a shift from a medical model to an educational model as the basis for psychological practice (B. G. Guerney, Stollak, & L. Guerney, 1971).

Other skill-training programs for families have developed within several related fields: parent education, marriage enrichment, family-life education, childbirth education, premarital counseling, and divorce counseling (Tavormina, 1974; Gurman & Kniskern, 1977; Fisher & Kerckhoff, 1981; Bagarozzi & Rauen, 1981; Kaslow, 1981; L'Abate, 1981). Thus, the array of skills-training programs to be discussed in this chapter represent an emergent confluence of trends that began in a number of separate fields. Together, they form the basis for a field in which the promotion of well-being is given status at least equal to that of the remediation of dysfunction, and in which educational approaches are seen as serious alternatives to approaches based on the medical model.

Classification
of Skills-Training Programs

The skills-training programs can be classified in a nested schema with four dimensions. The first dimension concerns the *objective* of the program, along a continuum from the remediation of dysfunction to the enhancement of functioning. Nested within the first dimension of program objective is the second dimension, which concerns the *focus* of the intervention, or the particular problem, relationship, role, or developmental transition to which it is applied. The third dimension concerns the *field* within which the program originated, such as psychotherapy and family therapy, parent education, or marriage enrichment. Nested within the third dimension of field of origin is the fourth dimension, which concerns the theoretical *orientation* that has informed the development of the skills-training program.

Objective and focus. Within the broad framework of the shift from the medical to the educational model discussed above, there are three distinct approaches, varying according to their emphasis on remediation or prevention and development. The first and historically earliest position involves the training of family members as therapeutic helpers who then treat another family member. This approach could be termed *training for treatment.* It has evolved from a larger class of programs concerned with the training of "significant others," or "symbionts" (B. G. Guerney, 1969). The training of symbionts is itself a component of the broader field of paraprofessional training. The rationale for the training of symbionts is that, by virtue of their close ties with clients, symbionts are in a good position to affect clients' functioning or development in positive and significant ways, if provided with the necessary training. The training of symbionts dates back to the early 1900s, when Freud (1959) trained the father to carry out the treatment of Little Hans. The current programs have retained this focus on training a parent to help a disturbed child.

The second approach focuses on training family members in certain skills (such as communication, problem solving, or conflict negotiation) in which deficiencies are thought to exist, as a means of helping the family resolve its problems. This approach, termed *training as treatment* by Carkhuff (1971a), takes an additional step in the shift toward the educational model: Human problems are conceptualized as deficits in psychological or interpersonal skills that can be learned, rather than as impairments that require a corrective experience administered by a helper. The training-as-treatment concept originated with the training of psychiatric inpatients in communicational and social skills (Pierce & Drasgow, 1969; Vitalo, 1971). The application of this approach to the family has usually focused on a dyadic relationship—either the marital partners or a parent-adolescent dyad—and has involved conjoint skill training for both members of the pair. Recently, this approach has been applied to the family as a whole.

The third approach uses psychological-educational methods to enhance the quality of family life as a means of either preventing the emergence of problems or of stimulating the development of family members. When thought of as a preventive measure, the aim is primary prevention—reduction of the incidence of mental health problems by strengthening the coping capacity of individuals who do not have clinical problems (Caplan & Grunebaum, 1967). When viewed as a developmental intervention, it reflects John Dewey's position that "true education *is* development." This approach will be termed *training for enhancement*. It has been applied to marriage, parenthood, and the family as a whole, at various stages of the life cycle. For marriage, there are programs designed for premarital ("pre"), newlywed ("neo"), married ("meso"), and divorcing couples ("post"). For parenthood, there are programs designed to prepare adolescents for parenthood ("pre"), to support young marrieds through pregnancy and childbirth ("neo"), and to help parents improve their parental functioning ("meso"). For the family as a whole, programs have tended to concentrate on the stage when children have reached adolescence, although one program has modules for all stages of the family life cycle.

Field of origin and theoretical orientation. The psychological-educational and skills-training approaches can also be grouped according to the field of origin and theoretical framework from which they have been developed. The two groups of approaches that originated in the therapy field—client-centered and behavioral skills-training programs—are the broadest and most comprehensive. They include programs developed for all three objectives and most of the foci described above. The parent-education and marriage-enrichment fields have each produced a number of single-objective, single-focus programs from several theoretical orientations, as well as eclectic and atheoretical programs. Psychodynamic, Adlerian, Kohlbergian, systemic, transactional-analytic, rational-emotive, reality-therapeutic, eclectic, and atheoretical programs have been developed for parent education. For marriage enrichment, communication-systems, Gestalt, transactional-analytic, Rankian, eclectic, and atheoretical programs have been developed.

Family life education is a separate field that developed within the home economics profession and that has been concerned with the offering of college-level

TABLE 9-1 Skill Training Programs for Families Classified According to Their Objectives, Foci, Fields of Origin, and Theoretical Orientation

OBJECTIVE AND FOCUS		FIELD OF ORIGIN AND THEORETICAL ORIENTATION	
		Family therapy	
		Client-Centered	Behavioral
TRAINING FOR TREATMENT		Filial Therapy and extensions; Human Resource Development; Microcounseling	behavioral parent training
TRAINING AS TREATMENT	Marital	Conjugal Relationship Therapy; Human Resource Development	behavioral marital therapy
	Parent-Adolescent	Parent Adolescent Relationship Therapy	
	Family	Relationship Enhancement; Dialoguing	
TRAINING FOR ENHANCEMENT	Marital (pre, neo, meso, post)	PRIMES; Conjugal Relationship Enhancement; Children of Divorce; communication skills for divorced persons	PREP; Mutual Problem Solving Program; group behavioral marital training
	Parental (pre, neo, meso)	Filial Parent Education; Parent Adolescent Relationship Development; Communication and Parenting Skills; Human Resource Development; Personal Development Program; Parent Effectiveness Training	group behavioral parent training
	Family		

TABLE 9-1 (Continued)

OBJECTIVE AND FOCUS		FIELD OF ORIGIN AND THEORETICAL ORIENTATION	
		Parent education, family life education, childbirth education	Marriage enrichment, premarital counseling, divorce counseling
		Psychodynamic, Adlerian, Kohlbergian, Systemic, TA, RET, Reality Therapy, Eclectic, Atheoretical	Communication Systems, Gestalt, TA, Rankian, Eclectic, Atheoretical
TRAINING FOR TREATMENT			
TRAINING AS TREATMENT	Marital		
	Parent-Adolescent		
	Family		
TRAINING FOR ENHANCEMENT	Marital (pre, neo, meso, post)		premarital programs (various); religious programs (Marriage Encounter, Quaker, Methodist); ACME; theoretical programs (Gestalt, TA, Marital Rebirth); skills-training programs (CCP and others); children-of-divorce programs; Family Mediation; divorce adjustment groups
	Parental (pre, neo, meso)	Exploring Childhood and other preparental Programs; childbirth-education classes (various); parent discusssion groups (psychodynamic); didactic/discussion groups (Adlerian, humanistic, systemic, TA, RET, Reality Guidance, and eclectic); skills-training programs (STEP and others)	
	Family	Moral Development Program; Structured Family Enrichment; Understanding Us	

(and, more recently, high-school-level) courses that are designed to have a more personal impact on students' lives than the traditional fare of "cooking, sewing and money-management." These courses were intended to "improve the courtship and marriage of the students" (Broderick & Schrader, 1981, pp. 10–11) and prepare them for parenthood (Kerckhoff, Ulmschneider, & Adams, 1976). The field of family life education will not be covered separately in this chapter because of space limitations, but some of the preparenthood and premarital programs will be grouped with the parent-education and marriage-enrichment programs, respectively.

It should be pointed out that this nested classification of theories within fields does not yield mutually exclusive categories. The client-centered and behavioral approaches have produced several programs that are commonly grouped under the rubrics of parent education or marriage enrichment. However, it seems more parsimonious to include these particular programs under the umbrella of their theoretical orientation; it is also truer to their conceptual lineage.

The skills-training programs, classified according to their objectives, foci, fields of origin, and theoretical orientation, are displayed in Table 9-1. The next four sections of this chapter will provide overviews of the various programs, grouped according to the columns on Table 9-1: client-centered, behavioral, parenting, and marriage programs. The last section will discuss directions for the future.

CLIENT-CENTERED PROGRAMS

The client-centered skills-training programs for families began in the early 1960s. These programs are based on the concepts that the client-centered facilitative conditions of empathy, genuineness, and regard (Rogers, 1957) are at the core of good interpersonal relationships in general (Rogers, 1961), and that people can be trained to improve their interpersonal functioning (Carkhuff, 1971b). During the 1960s, encouraged by the emerging psychotherapy research findings indicating the importance that these facilitative conditions have for psychotherapy outcome (Bergin, 1967), and mobilized by an acute awareness of the shortages of mental-health personnel (Albee, 1967), a growing number of client-centered therapists began to train professional and lay helpers to enhance their interpersonal functioning in terms of the facilitative conditions (Truax & Carkhuff, 1967; B. G. Guerney, 1969). The facilitative conditions became known as skills, and systematic skills-training programs emerged (Carkhuff, 1969a, 1969b). A concern with having an impact beyond the individual and on the smaller and larger social systems led to their application to the family.

Several groups have developed family skills-training programs from a client-centered orientation. These include (1) the Relationship Enhancement (RE) programs based at Pennsylvania State University, under the leadership of Bernard Guerney, Jr. (1977); (2) two efforts related to RE—Dialoguing (van der Veen, 1977) and the Communication and Parenting Skills (CAPS) program (D'Augelli & Weener, 1978); (3) the Human Resource Development (HRD) programs of Robert

Carkhuff and associates (1971b); (4) Ivey's related Microcounseling (1971); (5) the Personal Development Program (PDP) of Levant, Slattery, and Slobodian (1981); and (6) the Parent Effectiveness Training (PET) of Thomas Gordon (1970).

Relationship Enhancement and Related Programs

Relationship Enhancement (RE) constitutes the best-developed and best-evaluated set of client-centered skills-training programs for the family. Although aspects of social learning theory and other theoretical perspectives have influenced the development of the RE programs (B. G. Guerney & Vogelsong, 1980), they are at their core client-centered. This is evident not only in the content but also in the method of training, which is explicitly trainee-centered (van der Veen, 1977). The RE programs provide training in four sets of skills, or behavioral modes: (1) *the expressor mode,* wherein the individual learns skills of self-awareness and genuine self-expression; (2) the *empathic responder mode,* which includes listening and reflective responding skills; (3) *mode switching,* which involves learning how to change modes in order to facilitate communication; (4) the *facilitator mode,* in which participants learn to help others develop the first three sets of skills. Recently two new sets of skills have been developed: (5) *problem-solving and conflict-resolution* skills, which are based on the use of the first three skills in a six-step method; (6) *maintenance and generalization* skills, which involve the use of home practice, relying on the use of the facilitator mode (Vogelsong, B. G. Guerney, & L. F. Guerney, in press). The programs are didactic and experiential, and they include homework.

RE programs have been developed for all three objectives and for most of the foci described in the previous section (see Table 9-1). The first development was in the training for treatment area, with the Filial Therapy program, which began in 1962 (L. F. Guerney, 1976). Filial Therapy involves training the parent (most often the mother) in the application of client-centered play therapy as a method of treating mild to severe emotional disturbance in preadolescent children. In Filial Therapy, parents are trained in groups of six to eight parents, meeting weekly for two hours for 12 to 18 months.

In the training-as-treatment area, marital and parent-adolescent programs are available now, and whole-family programs are being developed. The marital (Conjugal Relationship Enhancement, or CRE–Rappaport, 1976) and parent-adolescent (Parent Adolescent Relationship Development, or PARD–Grando & Ginsberg, 1976) programs involve training both members of the dyadic relationship, usually in a brief group program of 10 to 15 weeks (20 to 30 hours), although longer programs with varying formats have been tried. Family relationship programs are being developed for psychiatric inpatients and their families (Vogelsong et al., in press), and for clinically symptomatic families in general (Dialoguing–van der Veen, 1977).

In the training-for-enhancement area, both the CRE and the PARD programs, originally intended as therapeutic programs, are also used as preventive programs. In addition, there are five other programs: (1) A version of CRE has been developed for premarital couples (The Program for Relationship Improvement by Maximizing Empathy and Self-Disclosure, or PRIMES—Ginsberg & Vogelsong, 1977). (2) Filial Parent Education, a didactic version of Filial Therapy has been developed as a parent-education course (L. Guerney, 1976). (3) An RE-related program (Communication and Parenting Skills, or CAPS—D'Augelli & Weener, 1978) has been developed for parents. (4) A divorce program for children (Children of Divorce, or COD—L. Guerney & Jordan, 1979) is in the process of development. (5) A communication skills training program for divorced persons has also been recently developed (Avery & Thiessen, 1982).

The evaluative research literature has been reviewed by Levant (1978b, 1983). The RE programs have demonstrated their efficacy in teaching communication skills, improving parental attitudes and the functioning of disturbed children, improving relationships, and facilitating the adjustment of stressed adults. The changes in communication skills, parental attitudes, child adjustment, and relationships have been shown to be maintained at follow-up intervals ranging from 10 weeks to three years. Compared with other treatments, RE has been found to be superior to Gestalt Relationship Awareness Facilitation, lecture/discussion programs, and discussion-group approaches, and to be equivalent to a behavioral approach. Only the Filial Parent Education program has received no empirical support; and the COD, family RE, and Dialoguing programs have yet to be systematically evaluated. To fill in various gaps in the empirical literature, future research should include assessments of individual and relationship changes with more objective measures; tests with clinical populations (particularly for PARD) and with a broader socioeconomic spectrum; and additional follow-ups and comparisons with alternative treatments.

Human Resource Development Program and Microcounseling

Robert Carkhuff is one of the pioneers of the skills-training and psychoeducational approaches, and he has been seen as the original prime mover in this area (Kagan, 1972). His Human Resource Development (HRD) program involves training in the "responsive" dimensions of empathy, respect, and genuineness; the "initiative" dimensions of self-disclosure, confrontation, and immediacy; and the general dimension of concreteness. Training occurs in a two-stage process in which discrimination training is followed by communication training. The trainers must function at high levels on the facilitative conditions, and they must provide a student-centered climate for the trainees (Carkhuff, 1969a). Microcounseling (Ivey, 1971) is conceptually related to, and a refinement of, Carkhuff's approach, focusing on specific skills and using videotaped feedback. Both programs are didactic and experiential, and both include homework exercises.

The HRD program has been applied to all three training objectives, but with limited foci. In training for treatment, it has been applied to training parents in interpersonal skills, in a brief group program, in order to help disturbed children

(Carkhuff & Bierman, 1970). A version of Microcounseling has been similarly applied (Durrett & Kelly, 1974). In training as treatment, it has been applied to the marital relationship (Pierce, 1973) in a brief group program. Finally, in training for enhancement, it has been applied to training parents as trainers of their children (Bendix, 1977).

Unfortunately, there is not much empirical support for the efficacy of the HRD and Microcounseling family programs. Only a few studies have been done, and these are of limited scope and complicated by methodological problems. The literature in this area is consistent with the larger HRD literature, which has been criticized on methodological grounds (Resnikoff, 1972; Gormally & Hill, 1974; Lambert & De Julio, 1977).

Personal Developmental Program

The Personal Developmental Program (PDP), developed by Levant and associates, is a client-centered skills-training program. It includes a set of modules that focuses on specific skills and that can be used in varying combinations: Attending; Listening and Responding to Content; Listening and Responding to Feelings; Speaking for Oneself—Self-Awareness; Speaking for Oneself—Genuineness; Acceptance; Structuring; Rules, Limits and Consequences; Conflict Resolution; Skill Integration. The program is a brief didactic and experiential group program that includes homework exercises. It has been applied as a training-for-treatment program with foster mothers of lower socioeconomic status (Levant et al., 1981) and as training-for-enhancement programs, both with working-class parents (Haffey & Levant, 1982; Kanigsberg & Levant, 1982) and with fathers of school-age children who wanted to increase their parental role (Levant & Doyle, 1983). The evaluative research has provided modest support for this program, which is still very much in the beginning stages of development.

Parent Effectiveness Training

Parent Effectiveness Training, or PET (Gordon, 1970, 1976), is used widely throughout the country. A training-for-enhancement program, it consists of eight three-hour group sessions, which are didactic and experiential and include homework. PET emphasizes "active listening," which involves acceptance and empathy; owning or "I-messages," in which the parent communicates feelings directly, without blaming the child; and a specific program of conflict-resolution called the "no-lose method," which involves a search for mutually acceptable solutions to problems.

The evaluative research literature, which has been reviewed twice in recent years, is somewhat controversial. Rinn and Markle (1977) reviewed 14 studies dating up to 1975, which included 5 single-group-outcome studies (all unpublished papers or masters' theses) and 9 comparative-group studies (1 unpublished study, 7 doctoral dissertations, and 1 published study). They found these studies to be plagued with methodological flaws and concluded that "the effectiveness of PET as a prevention or intervention strategy was not supported" (p. 95). More recently, Levant (1983) reviewed the studies available through 1981, focusing only on doctoral dissertations (17) or published studies (6). After reviewing the methodological features of the group of studies, he categorized them according to their adequacy. Examining the findings of the adequate group of studies, he concluded that there is some support for the efficacy of PET. PET appears to result in positive changes in parent attitudes (self-report) and behavior (child-rated), and improvement in children's self-concept (self-report) and behavior (teacher-rated).

BEHAVIORAL PROGRAMS

Behavioral training programs for families began in the mid-1960s. As in the client-centered training programs, the initial focus was on training a parent to participate in the treatment of a child. The impetus for this development came from a combination of sources: dissatisfaction with the results of traditional child therapy; the growth in the application of the principles of the experimental analysis of behavior; the shortages of mental-health personnel; and the potential expansion of the personnel pool through the use of paraprofessionals, particularly symbionts (Cone & Sloop, 1974). The major reason for training parents in behavioral (particularly operant) techniques, however, was that the principles of behavior therapy logically required it: Although certain child behaviors may be brought under control in the treatment session, there is little reason to expect that they will *generalize* to the home if the contingencies of reinforcement in the home remain unchanged (O'Dell, 1974).

Behavioral skills-training programs for families cluster into two general categories: behavioral parent training (BPT) and behavioral marital therapy (BMT). Although all three behavioral theories—classical or respondent, operant and social-learning, and self-control or cognitive—have been used, the major approach is operant/social-learning theory. Operant/social-learning theory is a loosely systematized collection of ideas that includes the principles of operant learning (such as reinforcement and extinction) and social-psychological influencing processes such as modeling. Classical conditioning procedures have been used in BPT to treat enuretic children (Berkowitz & Graziano, 1970); in BMT, classical conditioning procedures include systematic desensitization to reduce one spouse's dysfunctional emotional responses to the other's behavior (Epstein & Williams, 1981), and also, assertiveness training (Alberti & Emmons, 1974). Self-control strategies have started to emerge in BPT (Brown, Gamboa, Birkimer, & Brown, 1976) and BMT (O'Leary & Turkewitz, 1978; Jacobson, 1980), but these have not yet been applied widely.

Another general characteristic of the behavioral training programs is their preponderant use in an individual-family format. BPT does utilize some group training procedures, but in the more sophisticated studies, the group approach is integrated with individual consultations (O'Dell, 1974; Johnson & Katz, 1973). When used alone, the group-training format is most often used for preventive goals (Cone & Sloop, 1974). In BMT, group training procedures have been developed for teaching communication skills to couples in a preventive program (Witkin & Rose, 1978). Jacobson and Margolin (1979) have suggested group training in problem-solving skills for treatment programs, but they have cautioned that this approach is "still very much in the experimental stage."

The focus on individual families is based on the principle of specificity. Simply teaching family members the general principles of behavior therapy is not considered sufficient to enable them to alter dysfunctional patterns. What is required is a very specific application of these principles, based on a detailed idiographic analysis of the contingencies of reinforcement operative in the family, and resulting in the construction of a carefully designed treatment plan. These are tasks that are not easily accomplished in a group-training format.

Related to this is the preponderant emphasis on treatment rather than enhancement. Behavioral parent training fits the training-for-treatment paradigm, and behavioral marital therapy fits the training-as-treatment model. Behavioral training for enhancement, though not nearly so well developed as are the treatment-oriented programs, is represented by some of the group-training programs in BPT (for example, Hall, 1976; Brockway & Williams, 1976; Dubanoski & Tanabe, 1980) and BMT. For group BMT, both marital programs (Harrell & B. G. Guerney, 1976; Witkin & Rose, 1978) and premarital programs (Markman & Floyd, 1980; Ridley, Avery, Harrell, Leslie, & Dent, 1981) have recently emerged.

Thus the behavioral training programs are predominantly based on operant principles and social-learning theory and are mainly geared toward remediation. Most often, families are trained individually. Group training is sometimes used in conjunction with individual consultation. When used alone, it is usually reserved for prevention programs.

Behavioral Parent Training

Behavioral parent training is characterized by considerable diversity in its conceptualization, implementation, and evaluation. In the face of this diversity, Mash, Handy and Hamerlynck (1976) considered the question of whether BPT represents a unitary approach. They answered the question in the affirmative, pointing to the general adherence to experimentally established behavioral principles and commitment to empirical research.

Parent involvement. One of the key dimensions along which behavioral programs have varied is the nature and extent of parental involvement. Berkowitz and Graziano (1972) reviewed 32 experimental case studies ($N = 1$), and sorted them into five groups based on the nature and extent of parents' involvement and degree of training, the complexity of the child's problem, and the methodological sophistication of the studies. The authors observed a shift from a focus on relatively uncomplicated presenting problems (such as mild conduct problems) using minimal parental involvement and no systematic evaluation, to a concern with serious clinical problems (such as psychosis) and complex multiple-problem behaviors (or syndromes) in which parents—trained to fairly high degree of proficiency—carried out extensive home programs, and in which evaluation was careful and rigorous. Even in the better developed programs, however, parents were not included in many aspects of the treatment, particularly observation, treatment planning, and evaluation, and their training was not sufficient to enable them to formulate and carry out programs independently.

In general, then, the parents' role in this training-for-treatment approach (BPT) stops just short of being equal co-therapists. Whether the parents' role will develop further is uncertain. However, emergent trends in BPT are shifting the focus from the parent as change agent to modifying the parent-child interactional system (Berkowitz & Graziano, 1972). Recent innovations along this theme have included training children as modifiers of their parents' behavior (Benassi & Larson, 1976) and dyadic training of parents and adolescents in problem-solving and communication skills (Robin, Kent, O'Leary, Foster, & Prinz, 1977). This latter approach begins to extend BPT into the training-as-treatment area.

Nature of training programs. A related issue is the nature of the training program. O'Dell (1974) reviewed 70 studies with a focus on variations in the technology of BPT. *Training approaches* include individual consultations, educational groups, and "controlled learning environments" in which parental behavior is shaped in order to alter parents' responses to their children. *Training content* emphasizes either behavioral knowledge or behavioral skills. Knowledge-oriented programs teach operant-learning principles with an emphasis on how negative behavior is produced and maintained in the child's social environment through reinforcement contingencies. Skills-oriented programs teach parents to define, count, and chart behaviors, and to apply consequences to either accelerate (reinforce) or decelerate (extinguish) their frequency (see Chapter 5). *Training techniques* include simple advice and direction; didactic instruction using programed texts, such as Patterson & Gullion's *Living with children* (1976) and Becker's *Parents are teachers* (1971) (see Bernal & North, 1978, for a review of 26 commercially available parent training texts and manuals); and skill-building practices, such as observation with feedback, use of videotape, modeling, and behavioral rehearsal. Finally, under the heading of *implementation and maintenance,* O'Dell discussed the use of various contingencies (such as social rewards, monetary reimbursement, and written contracts) to increase parent attendance and participation, and techniques (such as telephone contacts after treatment and periodic retraining) to promote generalization of treatment effects.

Types of child problems. Several reviewers have discussed the type of child problems treated by BPT. Johnson and Katz (1973) listed antisocial and immature behavior, speech dysfunction, school phobia, encopresis and enuresis, seizures, self-injurious behavior, and oppositional behavior. Cone and Sloop (1974) provided detailed lists of the specific child behaviors treated in the 49 studies that they reviewed. Berkowitz and Graziano (1972) noted that most of the work has focused on the reduction of surplus maladaptive behavior. Finally, O'Dell (1974, p. 421) noted that the types of child problems treated by BPT have ranged from specific problem behaviors in children who have been labeled as brain-damaged, retarded, autistic, psychotic, and school-phobic, on the one hand, to complex behavioral syndromes, on the other hand, and he concluded that "There does not appear to be any type of overt child behaviors that parents cannot be trained to modify."

Evaluation. In general, the evaluative research indicates that parents can be used to modify their children's maladaptive behavior. Also, the sophistication of the evaluation research has increased over time. Johnson & Katz (1973) reviewed 49 studies, summarizing their methodological characteristics in tables. For each study they provided information on the number of subjects treated; the adequacy of the description of the parent-training operations; whether reliability data for dependent measures were provided; whether behavioral control was demonstrated using reversal techniques in the experimental designs; the length of follow-up (if any); and cost-efficiency data (estimate of therapist time), where available. Although noting the general empirical support for BPT, they pointed out that additional research is needed not only to identify the critical components of parent training but also to determine the most efficient means to maintain positive behavior after the end of the intervention. For the latter, they recommended routine follow-up and the systematic programing of generalization-of-treatment effects.

O'Dell provided a detailed methodological critique of the 70 studies that he reviewed according to general criteria for research in applied behavioral analysis (Baer, Wolfe, & Risley, 1968). He concluded more cautiously than Johnson and Katz, noting that the usefulness of BPT is "more promise than fact" (O'Dell, 1974, p. 430). The major problem is the lack of information regarding changes in parents' behavior as a result of BPT. Evaluation has focused exclusively on changes in children's behavior. Without demonstrations that parents acquired behavioral skills and utilized them in the home, one cannot unequivocally attribute the results of treatment to the training of the parents. Another (related) neglected area has been the generalization and maintenance of changes in parents' behavior.

Finally, Forehand & Atkeson (1977) reviewed the research on generalization-of-treatment effects, focusing on the procedures used to implement and assess temporal, setting, behavioral, and sibling generalization (see Chapter 5). They found few clear-cut findings, noting that the more rigorous the method of assessment, the more negative were the results. However, suggestive evidence was found for temporal generalization and for setting generalization from clinic to home, whereas the evidence was much less compelling for setting generalization from home to school and for behavioral generalization. Sibling generalization has been examined only infrequently, but the few studies available suggest positive changes in untreated siblings. Finally, very little is known about which training procedures promote generalization.

Behavioral Marital Therapy

Behavioral marital therapy got started a few years after BPT, in the late 1960s (Lazarus, 1968; Stuart, 1969a). Since then there have been a number of reports on the use of BMT. Although approaches vary a good deal, the central thrust is based on a combination of social-learning theory and theories of social-psychological exchange (Thibaut & Kelley, 1959; Homans, 1961). Troubled marriages are viewed as a function of a low rate of exchange of positive reinforcers, which leads either to withdrawal (Stuart, 1969a) or to the use of aversive control strategies (Weiss, Hops, & Patterson, 1973). And, whereas nondisturbed couples exchange reinforcers on an equitable basis over time (reciprocity), distressed couples have an inequitable exchange (coercion), wherein one spouse's behavior is controlled by positive reinforcement and the other's by negative reinforcement (Patterson & Reid, 1970—see Chapter 5).

The central objective of BMT is to help couples learn more positive means of effecting changes in each other's behavior. Ultimately, this involves a reorganization of their contingencies of reinforcement, so that positive interaction is increased and aversive interaction is decreased. Before the contingencies can be renegotiated, however, the couples must receive training in communication skills. The generally accepted rationale for this is that distressed couples are usually deficient in this area and would not be able to negotiate a meaningful contract without such skill training. Jacobson (1978), however, has argued that skill training is the essential process, and that contingency contracting may be unnecessary. He argues that the conditions under which the agreement is negotiated (conditions that are determined in large part by the couple's communication skills) are the primary determinants of whether the agreement is upheld, irrespective of the specific content of the agreement. There are some data to support his position (Jacobson & Margolin, 1979).

In any case, BMT as currently practiced involves a two-stage process of skills training followed by contingency contracting. Several modular packages have been developed, the most researched of which is the 10-session Oregon package (Weiss et al., 1973). A less technical package has been developed by Azrin, Naster, and Jones (1973).

Skills training focuses on communication, and it aims at the retraining of the couple's interactional repertoire in four areas: (1) helping the couples learn to communicate more specifically (pinpointing and discrimination training) and effectively; (2) teaching problem-solving, conflict-resolution, and negotiation skills; (3) increasing the expression of appropriate feelings; and (4) increasing positive interaction. Skill training generally takes place in the clinic and utilizes the skill-building practices of therapist feedback, modeling, and behavioral rehearsal. Empathy training, borrowed from the client-centered school, is often included (O'Leary & Turkewitz, 1978; Epstein & Williams, 1981).

Contingency contracting takes place in the home, and it involves the use of written agreements between the spouses for specific changes in behavior. The focus is on selecting positive behaviors for acceleration, rather than on decelerating negative behaviors, because the latter process requires the use of aversive stimulation. Contracts may be buttressed by the use of token economies (Stuart, 1969a, 1969b). Contracts are of two types: *Quid-pro-quo* contracts are "cross-linked," taking the form "If you do X, I'll do Y." These are used in the program devised by Azrin and colleagues (1973). This type of contract has the disadvantage of requiring one spouse to "go first"; it also sanctions the abandonment of contractual responsibilities if one member fails to fulfill his or her responsibilities. The Oregon package (Weiss et al., 1973) uses an alternative format—the "good-faith" contract, in which, "if X, then W+; if Y, then H+." That is, each spouse is reinforced independently for performing targeted behaviors. The latter form of contract is more cumbersome, and Jacobson and Martin (1976) recommend that it be used only when it is necessary. The available research suggests that the good-faith contract may be necessary with more disturbed couples, or in the earlier stages of therapy (O'Leary & Turkewitz, 1978).

BMT is a brief treatment, used in a conjoint individual-couple format, primarily for mild to moderately distressed couples, although its application to severely distressed couples is being investigated (Jacobson & Weiss, 1978). As mentioned above, couples groups have been used for preventive marital programs (Harrell & Guerney, 1976; Witkin & Rose, 1978) and premarital programs (Markman & Floyd, 1980; Ridley et al., 1981), but not yet for treatment programs.

The evaluative research on BMT has been reviewed several times (Greer & D'Zurilla, 1975; Jacobson & Martin, 1976; Jacobson & Margolin, 1979), and the base of empirical support is increasing. Although there is some controversy about its precise empirical status (Gurman & Kniskern, 1978c; Jacobson & Weiss, 1978; Gurman, Knudson, & Kniskern, 1978), BMT has demonstrated that it is an effective treatment for many couples. There is at this point a substantial body of studies, including uncontrolled studies, controlled clinical studies, and controlled group-design analogue studies. The studies have used a combination of self-report measures of satisfaction and behavioral-observation measures of communication skills. The most impressive are Jacobson's studies (reviewed in Jacobson & Margolin, 1979), which replicated the work of the Oregon group (Weiss et al., 1973). Future research should aim at further replication and should include follow-up studies.

A key issue for the future of BMT concerns the effective elements within the complex treatment packages. Jacobson and Margolin (1979, p. 359) noted that the available research indicates that "communication training seems to be an often necessary and at times sufficient treatment for many couples," whereas "there is some empirical basis for doubting the general effectiveness of contingency contracting." This prompted Jacobson to observe that "it may be that the most effective element of the behavioral approach is the one which is least unique to a behavioral approach."

PARENTING PROGRAMS

Parent education fits the training-for-enhancement paradigm. This selection will review the programs focused on parenting, at the preparental, neoparental, and meso-parental stages. Also to be discussed are several programs that are derived from parent education but that focus on the family as a whole.

Preparental Programs

The preparental programs are education-for-parenthood courses for teenagers and young adults developed by family-life educators. The *Exploring Childhood* curriculum, developed by the Education Development Center (1977) in Cambridge, Massachusetts, is one of the better-known programs. Designed for high-school students, the program is eclectic and integrates didactic instruction in child development (written by some of the leading experts in developmental psychology) with practical experiences in child care. An extensive evaluation found gains in knowledge, attitudes, and behavior in child care (Education Development Center, 1976). However, de Lissovoy (1978) pointed out that such short-term gains do not insure long-term preparation for parenthood. Making the case that adolescents are not ready developmentally to prepare themselves for parenthood, he argued that *Exploring Childhood* is a "white elephant in the classroom," one that might be better utilized for an audience of prospective parents.

Neoparental programs

Neoparental programs consist of various forms of childbirth education classes offered in many local communities through prenatal clinics, maternity hospitals, the Red Cross, and the Childbirth Education Association. The courses are usually led by nurses, and the content typically includes information on the health needs of pregnant women, labor and delivery, and the care of the newborn infant. These classes are designed to help prepare women for the birth process. Whether or not they go beyond this to help prospective parents cope with the developmental transition to parenthood varies a great deal, depending on the skills and awareness of the instructor. Prepared childbirth classes, especially the Lamaze method (Bing, 1969), provide more systematic attention to these psychological needs of parents-to-be.

A recent trend is the inclusion of expectant fathers in childbirth-education classes (Barnhill, Rubenstein, & Rocklin, 1979; Gearing, 1978; Resnick, Resnick, Packer, & Wilson, 1978). One of these programs has been extended to provide education for fathers of infants from birth to the preschool stage (Resnick et al., 1978). The available research literature indicates that developing a coherent father role is important for men's postpartum adjustment (Fein, 1976), and that lack of knowledge about parenting is predictive of high postpartum adjustment difficulty (Wente & Crockenberg, 1976). Whether expectant father education is effective in facilitating postpartum adjustment, however, has yet to be shown.

Mesoparental Programs

Mesoparental programs are the programs that are most commonly thought of as parent education—or parent education proper. Parent education has been defined as "purposive learning activity of parents who are attempting to change their method of interaction with their children for the purpose of encouraging positive behavior in their children" (Croake & Glover, 1977, p. 151). The first recorded parent-education group in the United States was formed in 1815. Several such groups, or "maternal associations," were soon developed for the purpose of encouraging mothers to discuss their child-rearing concerns and promote the moral and religious development of their children. In 1888 the organization now known as the Child Study Association of America was founded and began to sponsor ongoing parent-education groups (Croake & Glover, 1977).

By the middle of the twentieth century, the parent-education groups sponsored by the Child Study Association were based on Freudian psychology (especially the work of Anna Freud) and on child-development research such as that conducted at the Gesell Institute (Cable, 1975). It was assumed that parental motives, thoughts, and feelings were more important than overt behavior (Brim, 1965). These assumptions were reflected in the structure and format of the programs. The programs utilized a discussion-group format in which the parents developed the agenda based on their interests and problems, and in which the group leaders attempted to provide support and advice (Auerbach, 1968). While these discussion groups varied in terms of the size of the group, the homogeneity of its members, and the length and number of meetings, they shared the following goals for parents: to be more loving and accepting of their children; to understand child development and the causes of the child's behavior; to understand the effect of parent behavior on children; to develop problem-solving skills; and to feel relaxed, secure, and natural (Brim, 1965).

Tavormina (1974) reviewed the discussion-group approach to parent education, as well as the associated evaluative research. The initial evaluations ranged from parent testimonials and clinical impressions to evaluations of changes in parental attitudes. Although Hereford's four-year study (1963) reported changes in parent attitudes as a result of discussion-group parent education, his results were not replicated in subsequent research. Moreover, other studies found that changes in parent attitudes were not consistently associated with changes in children's behavior. Furthermore, Chilman's review (1973) of parent-education programs indicated that most discussion-group programs failed to attract and hold many parents, especially those of lower socioeconomic status. In a later review article, Tavormina (1980) criticized the discussion-group approach to parent education for its lack of specificity and pointed to the more recently developed didactic/discussion and skills-training programs as the direction for the future.

Didactic/discussion groups differ from discussion groups in that more time is spent in a structured presentation of didactic material. Child-rearing principles are taught from a variety of theoretical perspectives. The original didactic/discussion groups were either Adlerian Parent Study groups (Dreikurs & Soltz, 1974) or Ginottian humanistic groups (Ginott, 1957). Recently a spate of new didactic/discussion programs have appeared, described in several new texts and handbooks on parent education (Lamb & Lamb, 1978; Arnold, 1978a; Fine, 1980; Abidin, 1980). These new programs include theoretically pure and eclectic programs. The theoretically pure programs include models developed from systems theory (Arnold, 1978b; Benson, Berger, & Mease, 1975), transactional analysis (Sirridge, 1980; James & James, 1978; Lamb & Lamb, 1978), rational-emotive therapy or RET (Ellis, 1978b; Lamb & Lamb, 1978), and reality therapy (McGuiness & Glasser, 1978; Lamb & Lamb, 1978). Numerous eclectic programs have been developed. Representative examples include Developing the Productive Child (Gilmore & Gilmore, 1978); Becoming Us (Carnes & Laube, 1975); the Solution Oriented Approach to Problems, or SOAP program (Lamb & Lamb, 1978); and Parenting Skills (Abidin, 1976). These didactic/discussion programs are for the most part fairly new and many have not yet developed a set of teaching materials or techniques. With three exceptions, they have not yet been evaluated. The exceptions are the programs by Benson and colleagues (1975), Gilmore and Gilmore (1978), and Abidin (1976), all of which have received some empirical support.

Regarding the skills-training programs, the more-established programs include client-centered programs (Parent Effectiveness Training—Gordon, 1970; and Parent Adolescent Relationship Development—B. G. Guerney, 1977); a behavioral program (group behavioral parent training); and an Adlerian program (Systematic Training for Effective Parenting—Dinkmeyer & McKay, 1976). The client-centered and behavioral programs have been described above, and the Adlerian programs will be described below, in a general discussion of Adlerian parent education.

Adlerian parent education.   There are two basic models of Adlerian parent education: Parent Study Groups and Systematic Training for Effective Parenting. (The Adlerian Parent Teacher Education Center is a related program, but it will not be covered because its focus is on counseling parents and children and on training teachers as Adlerian counselors—see Lowe & Morse, 1977). For parent study groups, the format is a didactic/discussion group. Groups have been run for mothers only, fathers only, both parents, and whole families (Lamb & Lamb, 1978; Christensen & Thomas, 1980). Groups consist of 8–12 members; they meet weekly for two hours over 8–12 weeks. The content is based on the Dreikurs and Soltz text *Children: The challenge* (1964), for which there is a leader's manual (Soltz, 1973). The objective is to teach Adlerian-Dreikursian principles of democratic child-rearing, which, in brief, include the following: (1) understanding the four goals of children's misbehavior (attention, power, revenge, or inadequacy), and learning to use one's impulsive responses to children's misdeeds to identify the child's goal; (2) understanding that the misbehaving child is a discouraged child, and learning to use encouragement in a broad form, which communicates respect and love to the child; (3) replacing the authoritarian discipline techniques of reward and punishment with the democratic techniques of natural and logical consequences; and (4) learning to hold family councils. The evaluative research on Adlerian parent study groups has been recently reviewed and was found to generally support the effectiveness of these groups in improving parents' knowledge of course content, and changing parents' attitudes, perceptions of their children's behavior, and self-reported childrearing practices (McDonough, 1976; Croake & Glover, 1977; Christensen & Thomas, 1980).

Systematic Training for Effective Parenting, or STEP (Dinkmeyer & McKay, 1976) is a skills-training version of Adlerian parent education, and it also incorporates training in communicational skills. It is designed for up to 12 participants, who meet weekly for two hours over nine weeks. Research so far has been very limited (Dinkmeyer & Dinkmeyer, Jr., 1979) but is clearly needed, given the widespread use of this program.

Family Programs

This category has three entries: Kohlbergian family education, Structured Family Enrichment, and the Understanding Us program. Although these programs are designed for whole families, they are included under parent education because of their derivation from parent-education programs.

Kohlbergian family education.   A rather unusual program was recently developed, utilizing components of other programs, but integrating them within an intervention framework aimed at altering the justice structure of the family according to Kohlbergian principles (Stanley, 1980).

The 10-session, 25-hour program includes elements of Parent Effectiveness Training and Adlerian Parent Education, and it consists of four phases. In phase I, the PET skills of empathic listening and "I-messages" are taught. In phase II, the Adlerian family council is introduced in order to discuss family rules and promote more justice and democracy in the family. In phase III, PET's "no-lose" method of conflict resolution is taught. In part IV, those conflicts that could not be resolved with the "no-lose" method—namely, those having to do with basic differences in values—became grist for the mill; since this phase is focused on the value and moral dimensions and uses values clarification and the discussion of moral dilemmas. An evaluation of the program administered to families (both parents and their adolescent children), compared to parents-only and no-contact groups, indicated that while parents in both treatment groups improved their equalitarian attitudes and effectiveness in collective decision making, the family group showed greater improvement, and their adolescent children showed gains in moral reasoning—gains that were maintained at one-year follow-up (Stanley, 1978).

Structured Family Enrichment.   The Structured Family Enrichment program, developed by L'Abate (1977) and colleagues at Georgia State University, is based on the educational methods of programed instruction. The theoretical base lies in general information-processing systems, communication theory, and transactional psychology. The model consists of written programs with detailed instructions that a specially trained individual then reads to the participants. Each program consists of three to six lessons, each containing five to six exercises in which the whole family participates. In all, there are 26 different programs with 139 structured lessons. These programs and accompanying lessons are developed around specific topics of relevance to family living (such as democratic living, financial management, values clarification, assertiveness, helpfulness, and negotiation). The selection of a particular program for each family varies according to those areas of most concern to the particular family participating. This feature allows a great deal of flexibility, as well as the ability to tailor the intervention to specific family needs. Programs also vary in complexity and can be matched to the family's educational level. In focus, some are cognitive (or didactic), some are affective (or experiential), and others are problem solving (combining didactic and experiential). Most of the above program elements are included in L'Abate's first manual (1975a).

A second manual (L'Abate, 1975b) contains several enrichment programs written from a developmental perspective and focusing on various issues confronting families over the life cycle. Programs have been also developed which address specific family forms or situations (such as single parents, adoptive families, families with drug problems, families with a physically handicapped member, and families of alcoholics). Preliminary research on this model provides some support for its efficacy (L'Abate, 1977).

Understanding Us.   The most recently developed family-education program is the Understanding Us (UU) program. UU is the first in a planned series of "Whole Family Programs" and was developed by Carnes (1981a, 1981b), one of the originators of the Becoming Us parent-education program (Carnes & Laube, 1975). Sponsored by Interpersonal Communication Programs, Inc. (the first effort of which was the well-known Couples Communication Program), the UU program is based on the "circumplex model" of family systems, recently developed by Olson, Sprenkle, & Russell (1979). In their circumplex model, they propose that the dimensions of "cohesion" and "adaptability" are central to family functioning and identify 16 family types according to their placement in a circumplex formed by these two orthogonal dimensions. The UU program adds the individual concepts of identity development and personal responsibility in an integrated set of systems principles (Carnes, 1981a).

The program is offered to groups of 10 to 12 families (primarily parents and adolescent children) who meet with a certified UU instructor for four weekly sessions, two hours in length. The topics of the four sessions are adapting, caring, growing, and changing. The program is didactic and experiential, and family members are given a book with homework assignments (*Understanding us*—Carnes, 1981b). Given the newness of the program, it has yet to be evaluated, although such research is planned.

MARRIAGE PROGRAMS

Marriage programs are training for enhancement programs. This section will review three groups of programs: premarital and neomarital programs; mesomarital programs (marriage enrichment); and postmarital or divorce programs.

Premarital and Neomarital Programs

The field of premarital counseling dates back to 1932 (Bagarozzi & Rauen, 1981; Mudd, Freeman, & Rose, 1941). It derives from two main sources: (1) high-school and college programs in family-life education (Figley, 1977); (2) instructional counseling offered by clergy and family physicians (Schumm & Denton, 1979). Recently, the marital-enrichment movement has contributed to development of new premarital programs.

Programs have been developed from a client-centered perspective (PRIMES— Schlien, 1971; Ginsberg & Vogelsong, 1977) and from a behavioral perspective (Premarital Relationship Enhancement Program, or PREP—Markman & Floyd, 1980; Mutual Problem Solving Program—Ridley et al., 1981). In addition, the Couples Communication Program (discussed below) was initially designed to facilitate the developmental transition to marriage (Miller, 1971). Finally, numerous atheoretical programs are offered from religious (Boike, 1977) and nonreligious (Hinkle & Moore, 1971) perspectives. Five atheoretical programs were recently evaluated by Olson and Norem (1977).

Bagarozzi and Rauen (1981) reviewed the evaluative research literature, limiting their review to the 13 studies in which "standardized procedures and intervention technique were . . . followed systematically," and in which "some type of outcome measure was employed" (p. 14). These 13 studies suffered from several methodological flaws: Only 7 used a control or comparison group; only 2 of these 7 used standardized assessment procedures, and only 2 studies attempted follow-ups. While there is modest support for the notion that premarital enrichment programs improve communication and problem-solving skills, there is no evidence that these programs either reduce the incidence of divorce or promote more successful marriages. Believing that existing programs have little likelihood of accomplishing these long-term goals, Bagarozzi and Rauen (1981) recommended more ambitious programs that help couples preview their upcoming developmental tasks, teach a wide range of behavioral skills, and provide an opportunity to reevaluate the decision to marry.

Schumm and Denton (1979) dealt with a related problem, namely the question raised by Emily Mudd over 40 years ago: "How far can one help to prepare another person for an experience which he has not had" (Mudd, et al., 1941, p. 114). Reviewing the literature on "postwedding" or neomarital counseling, they conclude that the most "teachable moment" probably occurs after the marriage, and that the most important product of premarital counseling may be the establishment of a positive relationship as a basis for neomarital sessions. Future work in this area thus might investigate the relative efficacy of premarital versus neomarital versus combined premarital and neomarital enrichment programs, investigating some of the better-developed programs, and utilizing reliable evaluative procedures, including follow-ups.

Mesomarital Programs.

Mesomarital programs are marital-enrichment programs. Marital enrichment is a recent phenomenon that emerged in the 1960s as part of the humanistic wave of that period. It has been characterized as "a response to the transition from institutional to companionship marriage in our contemporary world" (Mace & Mace, 1975, p. 131). The marital-enrichment movement has roots in humanistic psychology, the human-potential movement, and affective education, and it relies heavily on group-process techniques developed in the encounter-group movement (R. M. Smith et al., 1981; Hof & Miller, 1980). The movement has grown tremendously. On the basis of a survey conducted in 1973-74, Otto (1975) estimated that 180,000 couples had participated in a marital-enrichment program. In 1976 he reported a revised estimate of 420,000 couples (Otto, 1976).

The marital-enrichment movement was started by several religious and secular groups. Herbert and Roberta Otto first led marriage groups on the West Coast in 1961 (Otto, 1969); and David and Vera Mace began leading weekend retreats for the Quakers the following year on the East Coast (Quaker Marriage Enrichment Retreats—Mace & Mace, 1973). Leon and Antoinette Smith began their work in 1964, developing the Marriage Communication Labs sponsored by the United Methodist Church (L. Smith & A. Smith, 1976). In 1967 the Catholic Marriage Encounter program (begun in Spain in 1958) reached the United States (Bosco, 1973). Acknowledging its strong ties to the Catholic Church and having differing needs, several Protestant and Jewish groups developed their own versions of Marriage Encounter (Genovese, 1975). In 1968 Sherod Miller and colleagues began work on the Minnesota Couples Communication Program (now known as the Couples Communication Program—Miller, Nunnally, & Wackman, 1976). In 1973, the Maces (1975) founded the Association of Couples for Marriage Enrichment (ACME) in an effort to coordinate the burgeoning movement. In addition, marital-enrichment programs were developed during the late 1960s and early 1970s by client-centered and behavioral workers.

At present a large number of programs are available (Hof & Miller, 1980, report a knowledge of 50 programs). Many of these programs are described in two edited texts (Otto, 1976; Miller, 1975). Unfortunately, many programs are not well developed conceptually, consisting of a "hodge-podge" or "smorgasbord" of various concepts and techniques (Hof & Miller, 1980). The emphasis in this brief overview will be on the better-developed programs.

As a group, the marital-enrichment programs are concerned with enhancing normal marriages (that is, those with no clinical problems), and they focus on enhancing communication, negotiation, and conflict-resolution skills, deepening emotional and sexual satisfaction, and fostering and supporting existing marital strengths (Gurman & Kniskern, 1977). Marital enrichment programs are of four types:

First, there are the programs sponsored by religious organizations. These include Marriage Encounter (Catholic, Jewish, and Protestant forms—Genovese, 1975), the Quaker Marital Enrichment Program (Mace & Mace, 1973), the Methodist Marriage Communication Labs (L. Smith & A. Smith, 1976), and others (see Otto, 1976; Ulrici, L'Abate, & Wagner, 1981). The religious programs generally take the form of intensive weekend retreats or marathons for groups of couples. But whereas Marriage Encounter involves a private encounter between husband and wife, with group interaction occurring only at religious or social levels, the Methodist and Quaker programs consist almost entirely of group interaction and are modeled after the encounter-group movement. Marriage Encounter, the largest marriage-enrichment program, has recently been criticized on theoretical and clinical grounds, and concerns have been raised about potential harmful effects (Doherty, McCabe, & Ryder, 1978; De Young, 1979).

Second, there are the nonprofessional programs offered by the Association of Couples for Marriage Enrichment (ACME). ACME offers weekend retreats similar to the Methodist and Quaker programs, as well as growth groups that meet weekly for 6–8 weeks; both the retreats and the growth groups are led by nonprofessionals selected, trained, and certified by ACME (Hopkins, Hopkins, Mace, & Mace, 1978). In addition to group interaction, ACME also incorporates elements of some of the systematic skills programs, such as the Couples Communication Program.

Third, several theoretically based group programs have recently emerged. These include Gestalt Marriage Enrichment (Zinker & Leon, 1976); Transactional Analysis Program (Capers & Capers, 1976); and the Rankian Marital Rebirth Program (Schmitt & Schmitt, 1976). These new programs are still in the early stages of their development.

Fourth, there are the systematic skills-training programs, of which the major ones are the client-centered Conjugal Relationship Enhancement (Collins, 1977) and group behavioral marital training programs (Harrell & Guerney, 1976; Witkin & Rose, 1978) discussed above, and the Couples Communication Program (Miller et al., 1976), which will be discussed below. In addition, there are several other less well known skills-training programs: the Pairing Enrichment Program (Travis & Travis, 1975); MARDILAB—the Marital Diagnostic Laboratory (Stein, 1975); the Structured Marital Enrichment Program (L'Abate, 1977); and Fair Fight Training (Bach & Bernard, 1971).

The evaluative research literature on the marital enrichment programs has been reviewed by Gurman and Kniskern (1977) and by Hof and Miller (1980). Although the results of controlled studies are generally positive (67 percent of the controlled studies reviewed by Gurman & Kniskern found program effects to exceed those of control groups) there are a number of methodological flaws: lack of attention to placebo control groups; overreliance on subject self-report or trainer assessments; and relative lack of follow-ups. Thus, although there is modest support for the proposition that marital-enrichment programs enhance short-term communication skills and satisfaction with the relationship, the empirical basis for this conclusion needs to be strengthened through improved studies. In addition, Gurman & Kniskern (1977) recommend attention to several related issues: (1) the durability of enrichment-induced change; (2) the generalizability of enrichment-induced change to other family relationships; (3) the range of potential participants (most research has focused on educated couples from university communities or couples closely affiliated with a religious organization); (4) the timing of enrichment programs to fit with developmental needs; and (5) investigations of the relative efficacy of various program forms, including separating out the most potent program components.

The Couples Communication Program.   The Couples Communication Program (CCP) has been identified as one of the most promising marital-enrichment programs (Otto, 1975; Olson, 1976; Olson & Sprenkle, 1976). The program, as originally developed, is a brief (4-session, 12-hour) systematic training program based somewhat on the family sociological frameworks of family development (Hill & Rodgers, 1964) and symbolic interaction (Foote & Cottrell, 1955), but primarily on communication-systems theory (Watzlawick et al., 1967). There is a text, *Talking together* (Miller, Wackman, & Nunnally, 1983) and an instructor's manual (Nunnally, Miller & Wackman, 1983). The program is designed to equip normal couples to meet the challenge of their developmental tasks, at all stages of the life cycle (premarriage, during marriage, or in anticipation of remarriage), through teaching two sets of skills: (1) speaking skills to help partners express themselves more completely and clearly; (2) listening skills to help partners understand each other more fully and accurately. Wampler and Sprenkle (1980) reviewed the past research on the Couples Communication Program and reported the results of a follow-up study. Correcting for several of the methodological flaws of earlier studies, they found that while the program had a positive effect on communication skills (assessed behaviorally) and on relationship quality (self-reported) at posttest, only the positive changes in relationship quality persisted at 4-months' to 6-months' follow-up. They recommended an expanded program, perhaps using booster sessions, to improve the staying power of the communication skills.

Postmarital Programs

Divorce is a very difficult human experience, stressful and often traumatic for all members of the family. The field of divorce therapy was discussed in Chapter 8. The discussion here will touch briefly on the structured or skill-training approaches that have been developed.

These fall into three categories. First, there are programs for the children. Open-ended discussion groups or "rap sessions" are offered to children of divorce by Parents Without Partners (Parks, 1977) and Children Helped in Litigated Divorce (Anderson, 1977). Young (1980) reported the use of court-mandated workshops (two hours in length) for adolescent children of divorcing parents, with participants reporting positive attitudes toward the program. Structured Children's Divorce Groups for elementary school children have been described by Wilkinson and Bleck (1977) and Sonnenshein-Schneider and Baird (1980). Finally, there are two skills-training programs: L. Guerney and Jordan's client-centered Children of Divorce Program (1979) was offered to children 9–13 years of age and met for one hour for six weekly meetings; and Kessler and Bostwick's assertion-training program (1977) was offered to children 10–17 years of age and consisted of a one-day (six-hour) workshop.

Second, there is the Family Mediation Program (Coogler, 1978), discussed in Chapter 8. At present, the approach utilizes very little skills training, but given the limitations of the approach found in a recent evaluation (Kressel, Deutsch, Jaffe, Tuchman, & Watson, 1977), some skills training might well become a useful component of this promising approach.

Finally, there are divorce-adjustment groups that utilize an educational approach. Three such programs are known to the author: a seven-week cognitive-behavioral treatment seminar (Granvold & Welch, 1977); an open-ended eclectic didactic/discussion group (Kessler, 1976); and a client-centered training workshop in communication skills that has been offered both as a 5-week, 15-hour course (Thiessen, Avery, & Joanning, 1980) and as a 2-day, 13-hour weekend workshop (Avery & Thiessen, 1982).

CONCLUSIONS

Six issues are important to discuss by way of closing: (1) the overselling of family-oriented skills-training programs; (2) staffing and training issues; (3) the combination of theoretically distinct program elements; (4) sex-role stereotyping in programs; (5) the family-systems perspective; and (6) future developments for enhancement programs.

Overselling of programs. As is the case with any new intervention or method of helping people, there is the risk that the enthusiasm for skills training will outdistance its demonstrated efficacy. Definite limits exist for what any intervention can accomplish, and we would do well to insure that any claims of efficacy are founded on a solid empirical base. There is some indication that enrichment programs are being oversold (L'Abate, 1981; R. M. Smith et al., 1979), and several programs have recently been taken to task on this account (Doherty, McCabe, & Ryder, 1978; Doherty & Ryder, 1980).

Staffing and training. As the field of marriage and family enrichment becomes a new professional area, questions arise about who provides these services and what their training should be. L'Abate (1981) pointed out the reluctance of many highly trained mental-health practitioners to involve themselves in these kinds of activities, seeing them as "second-class" in relationship to psychotherapy; and, R. M. Smith and colleagues (1979) noted that many current practitioners of the family skills programs have little or no training. While Durlak's review (1979) finds evidence for the efficacy of paraprofessional helpers in service activities, there is an important role for professionals, both in the selection and training of paraprofessionals, and in the design, evaluation, and refinement of programs. These issues are beginning to surface and will be much discussed in coming years.

Combination of theoretically distinct program elements. Tavormina (1980) has been one of the chief proponents of what is called the "combination format," wherein elements of two markedly different programs (for example, communication-skills training and behavioral child management) are brought together in a single program. There is a temptation in this field to do this, and at times this is done somewhat thoughtlessly, creating "hodge-podges" or "smorgasbords" of enrichment activities. Many investigators do not recommend this approach, seeing value in maintaining the theoretical integrity and conceptual consistency of intervention programs. It should also be observed, however, that the better-developed programs are incorporating aspects of other models, but that they are doing so by extending their own theoretical orientation. For example, behavioral marital therapy has incorporated communication-skills training but has conceptualized it in behavioral terms, regarding it as a means of enhancing stimulus control; so, too, Relationship Enhancement has begun to "program" generalization and maintenance effects, but does so using client-centered methods.

Sex-role stereotyping. The issue of sex-role stereotyping has recently come into focus in regard to parent education programs (De Frain, 1977; Resnick, 1981). Parent education has usually meant "mother education," and until very recently, little systematic attention was given to involving fathers in these programs. In the current "era of paternal rediscovery" (Lamb, 1979, p. 938), this is starting to change; and, as mentioned above, attention is now being given to fathers in childbirth education and other programs (Filial Therapy—Stollak, 1981; Parent Adolescent Relationship Development—Grando & Ginsberg, 1976; Personal Development Program—Levant & Doyle, 1983). Two recent studies evaluated the differential effects of including or excluding fathers in behavioral parent training, and these studies found no difference in mother-child interaction (Martin, 1977) and children's classroom behavior (Firestone, Kelley, & Fike, 1980) attributable to father involvement. These findings should not be interpreted as indicating that father involvement is unimportant, given the very distal relationship between the criterion measures and probable father effects, and given the fact that these studies are limited to one approach to working with a particular population (problem children).

Parent education has also not served mothers well, as Resnick (1981) has pointed out, ignoring their needs as persons and perpetuating the "motherhood mystique." Furthermore, preparental programs do not adequately address the decision to have a child, often treating motherhood as a mandate rather than a choice.

Finally, the programs give little emphasis to the later stages of parenting and to helping full-time mothers disengage from the maternal role. These issues should be attended to in future program development and refinement.

The family-systems perspective.   There is a limited but growing awareness in this field of the family-systems perspective. Most of the programs focus on one subsystem of the family (usually a dyad) and do not take into account the potential consequences of such an intervention on other subsystems or the family as a whole. For instance, we have mentioned the fact that most parent education is mother education. How does training one parent affect the other parent, the parental subsystem, and the parents-child triad? What are the effects on the other children of a training-for-treatment program geared to one child? What are the effects of a parent-education program on the marital relationship? (or of marriage enrichment on parenting?) Research addressing these issues is just starting to appear (Levant & Doyle, 1983; Patterson & Fleischman, 1979), and it seems that parent education does have beneficial effects on marital adjustment (Scovern, Bukstel, Kilmann, Laval, Busemeyer, & Smith, 1980), at least with troubled marriages (Forehand, Griest, Wells, & McMahon, 1982). This matter of system effects deserves attention in future studies.

Future developments for enhancement programs.   The last issue concerns the future development of the training-for-enhancement area. While it is easy to understand why theories of therapy can serve as the foundation for the two treatment areas (training for treatment and training as treatment), it is less clear that such theories can be a viable intellectual basis for enhancement. Doherty and Ryder (1980) criticized PET for training parents to be therapists, but the issue is really much broader than that. The problem resides in the lack of differentiation of the objectives of enhancement programs. Most enhancement programs are designed to "improve" parenting or "enrich" marriages. Programs should become more sharply focused, as either prevention programs or development programs. In the case of prevention, populations at risk could be identified, their vulnerabilities and strengths assessed, and appropriate interventions designed (using therapy and other relevant theories). Good examples of this approach can be found in the new divorce programs. With regard to development, a good deal of rethinking is necessary. Parenting programs, for example, should be based to a greater degree on child-development research (Griffore, 1980) and on the research regarding the adult development of parents (Newberger, 1980); and different kinds of programs should be offered to parents at different stages of their own and their children's life cycles. Regarding marriage programs, little is known about the development of the marriage over the life cycle (Levant, 1982). The premarital and neomarital stages are key points for intervention, however, and future work in this area is urged, taking into account the suggestions of Bagarrozi and Rauen (1981) for improved programs and evaluations and of Schumm and Denton (1979) regarding the timing of the intervention.

References

ABELES, G. Researching the unresearchable: Experimentation on the double bind. In C. E. Sluzki & D. C. Ransom (Eds.), *Double Bind: The foundation of the communicational approach to the family.* New York: Grune & Stratton, 1976.

ABIDIN, R. D. *Parenting skills.* New York: Human Sciences Press, 1976.

ABIDIN, R. D. (Ed.). *Parent education and intervention handbook.* Springfield, IL: Charles C. Thomas, 1980.

ACKERMAN, N. W. *Treating the troubled family.* New York: Basic Books, 1966.

ACKERMAN, N. W. Prejudice and scapegoating in the family. In G. H. Zuk and I. Boszormenyi-Nagy (Eds.), *Family therapy and disturbed families.* Palo Alto, CA: Science and Behavior Books, 1967.

ALBEE, G. W. The relationship of conceptual models to manpower needs. In E. L. Cowen, E. A. Gardner, & M. Zak (Eds.), *Emergent approaches to mental health problems.* New York: Meredith Publishers, 1967.

ALBERTI, R. E., & EMMONS, M. L. *Your perfect right: A guide to assertive behavior.* San Luis Opispo, CA: Impact, 1974.

ALEXANDER, I. E. Family therapy. *Marriage and family living,* 1963, *25,* 146–154.

ALGER, I. Audio-visual techniques in family therapy. In D. Bloch (Ed.), *Techniques of family psychotherapy: A primer.* New York: Grune & Stratton, 1973.

ALGER, I. Integrating immediate videoplayback in family therapy. In P. J. Guerin (Ed.), *Family therapy: Theory and practice.* New York: Gardner Press, 1976 (a).

ALGER, I. A. Multiple couple therapy. In P. J. Guerin, Jr. (Ed.), *Family therapy: Theory and practice.* New York: Gardner Press, 1976 (b).

ALKIRE, A. A., & BRUNSE, A. J. Impact and possible casualty from videotape feedback in marital therapy. *Journal of Consulting and Clinical Psychology,* 1974, *42,* 203–210.

AMERICAN ASSOCIATION OF MARRIAGE AND FAMILY THERAPY. *Manual on accreditation.* Upland, CA: AAMFT, 1979.

AMERICAN ASSOCIATION OF MARRIAGE AND FAMILY THERAPY. Draft version of "AAMFT code of ethical principles" is available for review. *Family Therapy News,* 1982, *13*(3), 10.

AMERICAN PSYCHOLOGICAL ASSOCIATION. *Ethical Principles of Psychologists* (1981 rev.), Washington, DC: A.P.A., 1981.

ANDERSON, C. M., & MALLOY, E. S. Family photographs: In treatment and training. *Family Process,* 1976, *15*(2), 259.

ANDERSON, H. Children of divorce. *Journal of Clinical Child Psychology,* 1977, *6*(2), 41–44.

ANDOLFI, M. Prescribing the families' own dysfunctional rules as a therapeutic strategy. *Journal of Mental and Family Therapy,* 1980, *6,* 29–36.

ANDOLFI, M., & ZWERLING, I. (Eds.). *Dimensions of family therapy.* New York: Guilford, 1980.

ANGYAL, A. *Foundations for a science of personality.* New York: Commonwealth Fund, 1941.

ANONYMOUS. Toward the differentiation of self in one's own family. In J. L. Framo (Ed.), *Family interaction: A dialogue between family researchers and family therapists.* New York: Springer, 1972.

ARNOLD, L. E. (Ed.). *Helping parents help their children.* New York: Brunner/ Mazel, 1978 (a).

ARNOLD, L. E. Helping parents beat the system. In L. E. Arnold (Ed.), *Helping parents help their children.* New York: Brunner/Mazel, 1978 (b).

AUERBACH, A. B. *Parents learn through discussion: Principles and practices of parent group education.* New York: John Wiley, 1968.

AUERSWALD, E. Interdisciplinary versus ecological approach. *Family Process,* 1968, *7,* 202–215.

AUGENBRAUN, B., & TASEM, M. Differential techniques in family interviewing with both parents and preschool child. *Journal of the American Academy of Child Psychiatry,* 1966, *5,* 721–730.

AVERY, A. W., & THIESSEN, J. D. Communication skills training for divorces. *Journal of Counseling Psychology,* 1982, *29,* 203–205.

AZRIN, N. H., NASTER, B. J., & JONES, R. Reciprocity counseling: A rapid learning-based procedure for marital counseling. *Behavior Research and Therapy,* 1973, *11,* 365–382.

BACH, G., & BERNARD, Y. *Aggression laboratory: The fair fight training manual.* Los Angeles: Kendall Hunt Publishing Company, 1971.

BAER, D. M., WOLFE, M. M., & RISLEY, T. R. Some current dimensions of applied behavior analysis. *Journal of Applied Behavior Analysis,* 1968, *1,* 91–97.

BAGAROZZI, D. A., & RAUEN, P. Premarital counseling: Appraisal and status. *American Journal of Family Therapy,* 1981, *9*(3), 13–30.

BAKAN, D. *The duality of human existence.* Chicago: Rand McNally, 1966.

BANDURA, A. *Principles of behavior modification.* New York: Holt, Rinehart and Winston, 1969.

BARNHILL, L., RUBENSTEIN, G., & ROCKLIN, N. From generation to generation: Fathers-to-be in transition. *The Family Coordinator,* 1979, *28,* 229–235.

BARTON, C., & ALEXANDER, J. F.   Functional family therapy: In A. S. Gurman & D. P. Kniskern (Eds.), *Handbook of family therapy.* New York: Brunner/ Mazel, 1981.

BATESON, G.   *Steps to an ecology of mind.* New York: Chandler, 1972 (a).

BATESON, G.   Double bind—1969. In G. Bateson, *Steps to an ecology of mind.* New York: Chandler, 1972 (b).

BATESON, G., JACKSON, D. D., HALEY, J., & WEAKLAND, J. H.   Toward a theory of schizophrenia. *Behavioral Science,* 1956, *1,* 251–261.

BATESON, G., JACKSON, D. D., HALEY, J., & WEAKLAND, J. H.   A note on the double bind—1962. *Family Process,* 1963, *2*(1), 154–161.

BAUER, R.   Gestalt approach to family therapy. *American Journal of Family Therapy,* 1979, *7*(3), 41–45.

BECKER, W. C.   *Parents are teachers.* Champaign, IL: Research Press, 1971.

BEELS, C. C.   Family and social management of schizophrenia. In P. J. Guerin, Jr. (Ed.), *Family therapy: Theory and practice.* New York: Gardner Press, 1976.

BEELS, C. C., & FERBER, A.   Family therapy: A view. *Family Process,* 1969, 280–332.

BELL, N. W., & VOGEL, E. F.   Toward a framework for the functional analysis of family behavior. In N. W. Bell & E. F. Vogel (Eds.), *A modern introduction to the family* (Rev. ed.). New York: The Free Press, 1968.

BEM, S. L.   The measurement of psychological androgeny. *Journal of Consulting and Clinical Psychology,* 1974, *42,* 155–162.

BEM, S. L., MARTYNA, W., & WATSON, C.   Sex typing and androgeny: Further explorations of the expressive domain. *Journal of Personality and Social Psychology,* 1976, *34,* 1016–1023.

BENASSI, V. A., & LARSON, K. M.   Modification of parent interaction with the child as the behavior-change agent. In E. J. Mash, L. A. Hamerlynck, & L. C. Handy (Eds.), *Behavior modification and families.* New York: Brunner/Mazel, 1976.

BENDIX, L. A.   The differential effectiveness on parents and their children of training parents to be helpers or life skill trainers for their children (Doctoral dissertation, Boston University, 1977). *Dissertation Abstracts International,* 1977, *38,* 1869–1870 B. (University Microfilms No. 77-21, 688).

BENSON, L., BERGER, M., & MEASE, W.   Family communication systems. *Small Group Behavior,* 1975, *6*(1), 91–105.

BERENSON, D.   An interview with Murray Bowen. *The Family,* 1976, *3,* 50–62.

BERGER, M. M. (Ed.).   *Videotape techniques in psychiatric training and treatment* (Rev. ed.). New York: Brunner/Mazel, 1978.

BERGIN, A. E.   Some implications of psychotherapy research for therapeutic practice. *International Journal of Psychiatry,* 1967, *3,* 136–150.

BERGIN, A. E.   The evaluation of therapeutic outcomes. In A. E. Bergin & S. L. Garfield (Eds.), *Handbook of psychotherapy and behavior change,* New York: John Wiley, 1971.

BERGIN, A. E., & LAMBERT, M. J.   The evaluation of therapeutic outcomes. In S. L. Garfield & A. E. Bergin (Eds.), *Handbook of psychotherapy and behavior change: An empirical analysis* (2nd ed.). New York: John Wiley, 1978.

BERKOWITZ, B. P., & GRAZIANO, A. M.   Training parents as behavior therapists: A review. *Behavioral Research and Therapy,* 1972, *10,* 297–317.

BERMAN, E. M. (Ed.).   Special issue on Marriage Council of Philadelphia. *American Journal of Family Therapy,* 1982, *10*(1), 1–104.

BERMAN, E. M., & DIXON-MURPHY, T. F.   Training in marital and family therapy at free-standing institutes. *Journal of Marital and Family Therapy,* 1979, *5,* 29–41.

BERMAN, L.   Review of "The process of family therapy." *American Journal of Family Therapy,* 1981, *9*(2), 102–103.

BERNAL, M. E., & NORTH, J. A.   A survey of parent training manuals. *Journal of Applied Behavior Analysis,* 1978, *11,* 533–544.

BING, E.   *Six practical lessons for easier childbirth.* New York: Bantam Books, 1969.

BIRCHLER, G. R.   Live supervision and instant feedback in marriage and family therapy. *Journal of Marriage and Family Counseling,* 1975, *1,* 331–342.

BIRCHLER, G. R., & SPINKS, S. H.   Behavioral-systems marital and family therapy: Integration and clinical application. *The American Journal of Family Therapy,* 1980, *8*(2), 6–28.

BLOCH, D. A.   The clinical home visit. In D. A. Bloch (Ed.), *Techniques of family psychotherapy: A primer.* New York: Grune & Stratton, 1973 (a).

BLOCH, D. A.   The family of the psychiatric patient. In S. Arieti (Ed.), *American handbook of psychiatry* (Vol. 1). New York: Basic Books, 1973 (b).

BLOCH, D. A., & WEISS, H. M.   Training facilities in marital and family therapy. *Family Process,* 1981, *20,* 133–146.

BODIN, A. M.   Conjoint family assessment: An evolving field. In P. McReynolds (Ed.), *Advances in Psychological Assessment* (Vol. 1). Palo Alto, CA: Science and Behavior Books, 1968.

BODIN, A. M.   Family interaction: A social-clinical study of synthetic, normal, and problem family triads. In W. D. Winter & A. J. Ferreira (Eds.), *Research in family interaction.* Palo Alto, CA: Science and Behavior Books, 1969.

BODIN, A. M.   The interactional view: Family therapy approaches of the Mental Research Institute. In A. S. Gurman & D. P. Knistern (Eds.), *Handbook of family therapy.* New York: Brunner/Mazel, 1981.

BOIKE, D.   *The impact of a premarital program on communication process, communication facilitativeness, and personality trait variables of engaged couples.* Unpublished doctoral dissertation, Florida State University, 1977.

BOSCO, A.   *Marriage encounter: The rediscovery of love.* St. Meinard, IN: Abbey Press, 1973.

BOSZORMENYI-NAGY, I.   A theory of relationships: Experience and transaction. In I. Boszormenyi-Nagy & J. L. Framo (Eds.), *Intensive family therapy: Theoretical and practical aspects.* Hagerstown, MD: Harper & Row, 1965.

BOSZORMENYI-NAGY, I. & KRASNER, B. R.   Trust-based therapy: A contextual approach. *American Journal of Psychiatry,* 1980, *137*(7), 767–775.

BOSZORMENYI-NAGY, I., & SPARK, G. M.   *Invisible loyalties.* Hagerstown, MD: Harper & Row, 1973.

BOSZORMENYI-NAGY, I., & ULRICH, D. M.   Contextual family therapy. In A. S. Gurman & D. P. Kniskern (Eds.), *Handbook of family therapy.* New York: Brunner/Mazel, 1981.

BOWEN, M.   A family concept of schizophrenia. In D. D. Jackson (Ed.), *The etiology of schizophrenia.* New York: Basic Books, 1960.

BOWEN, M.   Family psychotherapy. *American Journal of Orthopsychiatry,* 1961, *31,* 40–60.

BOWEN, M.   The use of family theory in clinical practice. *Comprehensive Psychiatry,* 1966, *7,* 345–374.

BOWEN, M.   Principles and techniques of multiple family therapy. In J. O. Bradt & C. J. Moynihan (Eds.), *Systems therapy selected papers: Theory, technique, research.* Washington, DC: Groome Child Guidance Center, 1971.

BOWEN, M.   Toward the differentiation of self in one's family of origin. In F. Andres and J. Loria (Eds.), *Georgetown family symposia* (Vol. 1, 1971–72), Washington, DC: Georgetown University Medical Center, 1974.

BOWEN, M.   Family therapy after twenty years. In S. Arieti (Ed.), *American handbook of psychiatry* (2nd Ed., Vol. 5). New York: Basic Books, 1975.

BOWEN, M.   Theory in the practice of psychotherapy. In P. J. Guerin (Ed.), *Family therapy: Theory and practice*. New York: Gardner Press, 1976.

BOWEN, M.   *Family therapy in clinical practice*. New York: Jason Aronson, 1978.

BRIM, O. G., JR.   *Education for childrearing*. New York: The Free Press, 1965.

BROCKWAY, B. S., & WILLIAMS, W. W.   Training in child management: A prevention-oriented model. In E. J. Mash, L. C. Handy, & L. A. Hamerlynck (Eds.), *Behavior modification approaches to parenting*. New York: Brunner/Mazel, 1976.

BRODERICK, C. B.   Beyond the five conceptual frameworks: A decade of development in family theory. *Journal of Marriage and the Family*, 1971, *33*, 139–159.

BRODERICK, C. B., & SCHRADER, S. S.   The history of professional marriage and family therapy. In A. S. Gurman & D. P. Kniskern (Eds.), *Handbook of family therapy*. New York: Brunner/Mazel, 1981.

BRODEY, W. M.   Some family operations and schizophrenia: A study of five hospitalized families each with a schizophrenic mother. *Archives of General Psychiatry*, 1959, *1*, 379–402.

BRONFENBRENNER, V.   Toward an experimental ecology of human development. *American Psychologist*, 1977, *32*, 513–531.

BROWN, J. H., GAMBOA, A. M., JR., BIRKIMER, J., & BROWN, R.   Some possible effects of parent self-control training on parent child interactions. In E. J. Mash, L. C. Handy, & L. A. Hamerlynck (Eds.), *Behavior modification approaches to parenting*. New York: Brunner/Mazel, 1976.

BROWN, K.   *Family counseling: An annotated bibliography*. Cambridge, MA: Oelgeschlager, Gunn, & Hain, 1981.

BUBER, M.   *I and thou*. New York: Charles Scribner's Sons, 1958.

BUCKLEY, W.   *Sociology and modern systems theory*. Englewood Cliffs, NJ: Prentice-Hall, 1967.

BURGESS, E. W.   The family as a unity of interacting personalities. *Family*, 1926, *7*, 3–9.

CABLE, M.   *The little darlings: A history of child rearing in America*. New York: Charles Scribner, 1975.

CAPERS, H., & CAPERS, B.   Transactional analysis tools for use in marriage enrichment programs. In H. A. Otto (Ed.), *Marriage and family enrichment: New perspectives and programs*. Nashville: Abington, 1976.

CAPLAN, G.   *Principles of preventive psychiatry*. New York: Basic Books, 1964.

CAPLAN, G., & GRUNEBAUM, H.   Perspectives on primary prevention: A review. *Archives of General Psychiatry*, 1967, *17*, 331–346.

CARKHUFF, R. R.   *Helping and human relations. Vol. I: Selection and training*. New York: Holt, Rinehart and Winston, 1969 (a).

CARKHUFF, R. R.   *Helping and human relations. Vol II: Practice and research*. New York: Holt, Rinehart and Winston, 1969 (b).

CARKHUFF, R. R.   Training as a preferred mode of treatment. *Journal of Counseling Psychology*, 1971, *18*, 123–131 (a).

CARKHUFF, R. R.   *The development of human resources: Education, psychology, and social change*. New York: Holt, Rinehart and Winston, 1971 (b).

CARKHUFF, R. R., & BIERMAN, R.   Training as a preferred mode of treatment of parents of emotionally disturbed children. *Journal of Counseling Psychology*, 1970, *17*, 157–161.

CARNES, P. J.   *Family development instructors manual*. Minneapolis MN: Interpersonal Communication Programs, 1981 (a).

CARNES, P. J. *Family development I: Understanding us.* Minneapolis MN: Interpersonal Communication Programs, 1981 (b).

CARNES, P. J., & LAUBE, H. Becoming us: An experiment on family learning and teaching. *Small Group Behavior,* 1975, *6*(1), 106–119.

CARTER, E. A., & MCGOLDRICK, M. (Eds.). *The family life cycle: A framework for family therapy.* New York: Gardner Press, 1980.

CARTER, E., & ORFANIDIS, M. M. Family therapy with one person and the family therapist's own family. In P. J. Guerin, Jr. (Ed.), *Family therapy: Theory and practice.* New York: Gardner Press, 1976.

CHARNEY, I. W. Integrated individual and family psychotherapy. *Family process,* 1966, *5,* 179–198.

CHASIN, R., & GRUNEBAUM, H. A brief synopsis of current concepts and practices in family therapy. In J. K. Pearce and L. J. Friedman (Eds.), *Family therapy: Combining psychodynamic and systems approaches.* New York: Grune & Stratton, 1980.

CHILMAN, C. S. Programs for disadvantaged parents. In B. M. Caldwell & H. N. Ricciuti (Eds.), *Review of child development research* (Vol. 3). Chicago: University of Chicago Press, 1973.

CHRISTENSEN, H. T. (Ed.). *Handbook of marriage and the family.* Chicago: Rand McNally, 1964 (a).

CHRISTENSEN, H. T. Development of the family field of study. In H. T. Christensen (Ed.), *Handbook of marriage and the family.* Chicago: Rand McNally, 1964 (b).

CHRISTENSEN, O. C., & THOMAS, C. R. Dreikurs and the search for equality. In M. J. Fine (Ed.), *Handbook on parent education.* New York: Academic Press, 1980.

CLEGHORN, J. M., & LEVIN, S. Training family therapists by setting learning objectives. *American Journal of Orthopsychiatry,* 1973, *13,* 439–446.

CLEVELAND, E. J., & LONGAKER, W. D. Neurotic patterns in the family. In A. Leighton (Ed.), *Explorations in social psychiatry,* New York: Basic Books, 1957.

COLLINS, J. D. Experimental evaluation of a six-month conjugal therapy and relationship enhancement program. In B. G. Guerney, Jr. (Ed.), *Relationship enhancement.* San Francisco: Jossey-Bass, 1977.

CONE, J. D., & SLOOP, W. E. Parents as agents of change. In A. Jacobs & W. W. Spradling (Eds.), *The group as agent of change: Treatment, prevention, personal growth in the family, the school, the mental hospital, and the community.* New York: Behavioral Publications, 1974.

CONSTANTINE, L. L. Designed experience: A multiple, goal-directed training program in family therapy. *Family Process,* 1976, *15,* 373–385.

CONSTANTINE, L. L. Family sculpture and relationship mapping techniques. *Journal of Marriage and Family Counseling,* 1978, *4*(2), 13–24.

COOGLER, O. J. *Structured mediation in divorce settlement.* Lexington, MA: Lexington Books, 1978.

COOKERLY, J. R. Evaluating different approaches to marriage counseling. In D. H. L. Olson (Ed.), *Treating relationships.* Lake Mills, IA: Graphic Publishing Company, 1976.

COOPER, A., RAMPAGE, C., & SOUCY, G. Family therapy training in clinical psychology programs. *Family Process,* 1981, *20,* 155–166.

COPPERSMITH, E. Expanding uses of the telephone in family therapy. *Family Process,* 1980, *19,* 411–417 (a).

COPPERSMITH, E. The family floor plan: A tool of training, assessment, and intervention in family therapy. *Journal of Marital and Family Therapy*, 1980, *6*(2), 141–145 (b).

CORNWELL, M., & PEARSON, R.   Cotherapy teams and one-way screen in family therapy practice and training. *Family Process*, 1981, *20*, 199–229.

CROAKE, J. W., & GLOVER, K. E.   A history and evaluation of parent education. *The Family Coordinator*, 1977, *26*(2), 151–158.

CROMWELL, R. E., OLSON, D. H. L., & FOURNIER, D. G.   Diagnosis and evaluation in marital and family counseling. In D. H. L. Olson (Ed.), *Treating relationships*. Lake Mills, IA: Graphic Publishing Company, 1976.

CURRY, A. E.   Toward the phenomenological study of the family. *Existential Psychiatry*, 1967, *6*, 35–44 (a).

CURRY, A. E.   Large therapeutic groups: A critique and appraisal of selected literature. *International Journal of Group Psychotherapy*, 1967, *17*, 536–547 (b).

DARE, C., & LINDSEY, C.   Children in family therapy. *Journal of Family Therapy*, 1979, *1*, 253–269.

D'AUGELLI, J. F., & WEENER, J. M.   Training parents as mental health agents. *Community Mental Health Journal*, 1978, *14*(1), 14–25.

DE FRAIN, J.   Sexism in parenting manuals. *Family Coordinator*, 1977, *26*(3), 245–251.

DE LISSOVOY, V.   Parent education: White elephant in the classroom? *Youth and Society*, 1978, *9*(3), 315–338.

DELL, P. F., SHEELY, M. D., PULLIAM, G. P., & GOOLISHIAN, H. A.   Family therapy process in a family therapy seminar. *Journal of Marriage and Family Counseling*, 1977, *3*, 43–48.

DENKER, P. G.   Results of treatment of psychoneuroses by the general practitioner. *New York State Journal of Medicine*, 1946, *46*, 2164–2166.

DEWITT, K. N.   The effectiveness of family therapy: A review of outcome research. *Archives of General Psychiatry*, 1978, *35*, 549–561.

DE YOUNG, A. J.   Marriage encounter: A critical examination. *Journal of Marital and Family Therapy*, 1979, *5*(2), 27–30.

DICKS, H. V.   *Marital tensions*. New York: Basic Books, 1967.

DINKMEYER, D., & DINKMEYER, D., JR.   A comprehensive and systematic approach to parent education. *American Journal of Family Therapy*, 1979, *7*(2), 46–50.

DINKMEYER, D., & MCKAY, G. D.   *Systematic training for effective parenting*. Circle Pines, MN: American Guidance Service, 1976.

DOANE, J. A.   Family interaction and communication training in disturbed and normal families: A review of research. *Family Process*, 1978, *17*, 357–376 (a).

DOANE, J. A.   Questions of strategy: Rejoinder to Jacob and Grounds. *Family Process*, 1978, *17*, 389–399 (b).

DOHERTY, W. J., MCCABE, P., & RYDER, R. G.   Marriage encounter: A critical appraisal. *Journal of Marriage and Family Counseling*, 1978, *4*(4), 99–107.

DOHERTY, W. J., & RYDER, R. G.   Parent effectiveness training (PET): Criticisms and caveats. *Journal of Marital and Family Therapy*, 1980, *6*, 409–419.

DOWLING, E., & JONES, H. V. R.   Small children seen and heard in family therapy. *Journal of Child Psychotherapy*, 1978, *4*, 87–96.

DREIKURS, R., & SOLTZ, V.   *Children: The challenge*. New York: Meredith Press, 1964.

DREIKURS, R., CORSINI, R., LOWE, R. & SONSTEGARD, M.   Adlerian family counseling—*A manual for counseling centers*. Eugene, OR: University of Oregon Press, 1959.

DREYFUS, E. A. Counseling the divorced father. *Journal of Marital and Family Therapy,* 1979, *5,* 77–86.

DUBANOSKI, R. A., & TANABE, G. Parent education: A classroom program on social learning principles. *Family Relations,* 1980, *29*(1), 15–20.

DUBERMAN, L. *The reconstituted family: A study of remarried couples and their children.* Chicago: Nelson-Hall Publishers, 1975.

DUHL, J. B., & DUHL, F. J. Integrative family therapy. In A. S. Gurman & D. P. Kniskern (Eds.), *Handbook of family therapy.* New York: Brunner/Mazel, 1981.

DUHL, F. J., & DUHL, B. S. "Structured spontaneity": The thoughtful art of integrative family therapy at BFI. *Journal of Marital and Family Therapy,* 1979, *5,* 59–75.

DUHL, F. J., KANTOR, D., & DUHL, B. S. Learning, space, and action in family therapy: A primer of sculpture. In D. A. Bloch (Ed.), *Techniques of family psychotherapy: A primer.* New York: Grune & Stratton, 1973.

DURLAK, J. H. Comparative effectiveness of paraprofessional and professional helpers. *Psychological Bulletin,* 1979, *66,* 80–92.

DURRETT, D. D., & KELLEY, P. A. Can you really talk with your child? A parental training program in communication skills toward the improvement of parent-child interaction. *Group Psychotherapy and Psychodrama,* 1974, *27,* 98–109.

EDUCATION DEVELOPMENT CENTER. *Exploring childhood: National field test. Summary of evaluation findings, year two.* Cambridge, MA: Author, 1976.

EDUCATION DEVELOPMENT CENTER. *Exploring childhood: Program overview and catalogue of materials.* Cambridge, MA: Author, 1977.

ELBERT, S., ROSMAN, B., MINUCHIN, S., & GUERNEY, B. A method for the clinical study of family interaction. *American Journal of Orthopsychiatry,* 1964, *34,* 885–899.

ELLIS, A. Family therapy: A phenomenological and active directive approach. *Journal of Marriage and Family Counseling,* 1978, *4*(2), 43–50 (a).

ELLIS, A. Rational-emotive guidance. In L. E. Arnold (Ed.), *Helping parents help their children.* New York: Brunner/Mazel, 1978 (b).

ELLIS, H. *Studies in the psychology of sex.* New York: Random House, 1936.

EPSTEIN, N., & WILLIAMS, A. M. Behavioral approaches to the treatment of marital discord. In G. P. Sholevar (Ed.), *The handbook of marriage and marital therapy.* New York: S. P. Medical and Scientific Books, 1981.

EPSTEIN, N. B., & BISHOP, D. S. Problem-centered systems therapy of the family. In A. S. Gurman & D. P. Kniskern (Eds.), *Handbook of Family Therapy.* New York: Brunner/Mazel, 1981.

EPSTEIN, N. B., BISHOP, D. S., & LEVIN, S. The McMaster model of family functioning. *Journal of Marriage and Family Counseling,* 1978, *4,* 29–31.

ERICKSON, G. Teaching family therapy. *Journal of Education for Social Work,* 1973, *9,* 9–15.

EVERETT, C. A. The masters degree in marriage and family therapy. *Journal of Marital and Family Therapy,* 1979, *5,* 7–13.

EYSENCK, H. J. The effects of psychotherapy: An evaluation. *Journal of Consulting Psychology,* 1952, *16,* 319–324.

FALICOV, C. J., CONSTANTINE, J. A., & BREUNLIN, D. C. Teaching family therapy: A program based on training objectives. *Journal of Marital and Family Therapy,* 1981, *7,* 497–505.

FAMILY ADVOCATE. *Joint custody: What does it mean? How does it work?* Chicago: American Bar Association Section of Family Law, Summer 1978.

FEIN, R. A. Men's entrance to parenthood. *The Family Coordinator,* 1976, *25,* 341–348.

FENICHEL, D. *Ten years of the Berlin Psychoanalytic Institute,* 1920–1930.

FERREIRA, A. The double bind and delinquent behavior. *Archives of General Psychiatry,* 1960, *3,* 359–367.

FIGLEY, C. R. Family life education: Teacher selection, education, and training issues—a selected bibliography. *Family Coordinator,* 1977, *26,* 160–165.

FINE, M. J. (Ed.). *Handbook on parent education.* New York: Academic Press, 1980.

FIRESTONE, E., & MOSCHETTA, P. Behavioral contracting in family therapy. *Journal of Family Counseling,* 1975, *3*(2), 27–31.

FIRESTONE, P., KELLEY, M. J., & FIKE, S. Are fathers necessary in parent training groups? *Journal of Clinical Child Psychology,* 1980, *9,* 44–47.

FISHER, B. L., & KERCKHOFF, F. K. Family life education: Generating cohesion out of chaos. *Family Relations,* 1981, *30*(4), 505–510.

FISHER, L. Dimensions of family assessment: A critical review. *Journal of Marriage and Family Counseling,* 1976, *2,* 367–382.

FLECK, S., LIDZ, T., & CORNELISON, A. R. Comparison of parent-child relationships of male and female schizophrenic patients. *Archives of General Psychiatry,* 1963, *8,* 1–7.

FOGARTY, T. F. On emptiness and closeness: Part I. *The Family,* 1976, *3*(1), 3–10 (a).

FOGARTY, T. F. On emptiness and closeness: Part II. *The Family,* 1976, *3*(2), 37–49 (b).

FOGARTY, T. F. System concepts and the dimensions of self. In P. J. Guerin, Jr. (Ed.), *Family therapy: Theory and practice.* New York: Gardner Press, 1976 (c).

FOGARTY, T. F. Marital crisis. In P. J. Guerin, Jr. (Ed.), *Family therapy: Theory and practice.* New York: Gardner Press, 1976 (d).

FOLEY, V. D. *An introduction to family therapy.* New York: Grune & Stratton, 1974.

FOOTE, N. H., & COTTRELL, L. S., JR. *Identity and interpersonal competence: A new direction in family research.* Chicago: University of Chicago Press, 1955.

FOREHAND, R., & ATKESON, B. M. Generality of treatment effects with parents as therapists: A review of assessment and implementation procedures. *Behavior Therapy,* 1977, *8,* 575–593.

FOREHAND, R., GREIST, D. C., WELLS, K., & MCMAHON, R. J. Side effects of parent counseling on marital satisfaction. *Journal of Counseling Psychology,* 1982, *29,* 104–107.

FRAMO, J. L. Systematic research on family dynamics. In I. Boszormenyi-Nagy & J. L. Framo (Eds.), *Intensive family therapy: Theoretical and practical aspects.* Hagerstown, MD: Harper & Row, 1965 (a).

FRAMO, J. L. Rationale and techniques of intensive family therapy. In I. Boszormenyi-Nagy & J. L. Framo (Eds.), *Intensive family therapy: Theoretical and practical aspects.* Hagerstown, MD: Harper & Row, 1965 (b).

FRAMO, J. L. Symptoms from a family transactional viewpoint. In N. W. Ackerman (Ed.), *Family therapy in transition.* Boston: Little, Brown, 1970.

FRAMO, J. L. Marriage therapy in a couples group. In D. A. Bloch (Ed.), *Techniques of family psychotherapy: A primer.* New York: Grune & Stratton, 1973.

FRAMO, J. L. Personal reflections of a family therapist. *Journal of Marriage and Family Counseling,* 1975, *1,* 15–28.

FRAMO, J. L.   Family of origin as a therapeutic resource for adults in marital and family therapy: You can and should go home again. *Family Process*, 1976, *15*(2), 193–210.

FRAMO, J. L.   *Explorations in marital and family therapy*. New York: Springer, 1982.

FRAMO, J. L., & GREEN, R. T.   *Bibliography of books related to family and marital systems theory and therapy*. Upland, CA: American Association for Marriage and Family Therapy, 1980.

FRANK, G. H.   The role of the family in the development of psychopathology. *Psychological Bulletin*, 1965, *64*, 191–205.

FRANK, J. D.   The present status of outcome studies. *Journal of Consulting and Clinical Psychology*, 1979, *47*, 310–316.

FRANKLIN, P., & PROSKY, P.   A standard initial interview. In D. A. Bloch (Ed.), *Techniques of family psychotherapy: A primer*. New York: Grune & Stratton, 1973.

FRETZ, B. R., & MILLS, D. H.   *Licensing and certification of psychologists and counselors*. San Francisco, CA: Jossey-Bass, 1980.

FREUD, S.   The transformation of puberty. *The basic writings* (A. A. Brill, Ed. and trans). New York: The Modern Library, 1938.

FREUD, S.   *Three essays on the theory of sexuality. Standard edition of the complete psychological work of Sigmund Freud* (J. Strachey, Ed.) (Vol. 7). London: Hogarth Press, 1953.

FREUD, S.   Analysis of a phobia in a five-year-old boy. In *Collected papers*. New York: Basic Books, 1959.

FRIEDMAN, A. S.   Implications of the time setting for family treatment. In A. S. Friedman, I. Boszormenyi-Nagy, J. E. Jungreis, G. Lincoln, H. E. Mitchell, J. C. Sonne, R. V. Speck, & G. Spivack. *Psychotherapy of the whole family*. New York: Springer, 1965.

FRIEDMAN, A. S., BOSZORMENYI-NAGY, I., JUNGREIS, J. E., LINCOLN, G., MITCHELL, H. E., SONNE, J. C., SPECK, R. V., & SPIVACK, G.   *Psychotherapy for the whole family*. New York: Springer, 1965.

FRIEDMAN, A. S., SONNE, J. C., BARR, J. P., BOSZORMENYI-NAGY, I., COHEN, G., SPECK, R. V., JUNGREIS, J. E., LINCOLN, G., SPARK, G., & WEINER, O. R.   *Therapy with families of sexually acting-out girls*. New York: Springer, 1971.

FROMM-REICHMAN, F.   Notes on the treatment of schizophrenia by psychoanalytic psychotherapy. *Psychiatry*, 1948, *11*, 267–277.

FRYKMAN, J. H.   Review of "The process of family therapy." *Family Process*, 1981, *20*(1), 128–129.

GARFIELD, R.   An integrative training model for family therapists: The Hahneman master of family therapy program. *Journal of Marital and Family Therapy*, 1979, *5*, 15–22.

GARMEZY, N.   Children at risk: The search for the antecedents of schizophrenia. Part I: Conceptual models and research methods. *Schizophrenia Bulletin*, 1974, *8*, 14–90 (a).

GARMEZY, N.   Children at risk: The search for the antecedents of schizophrenia. Part II: Ongoing research programs, issues, and interventions. *Schizophrenia Bulletin*, 1974, *9*, 55–125 (b).

GEARING, J.   Facilitating the birth process and father-child bonding. *The Counseling Psychologist*, 1978, *7*(4), 53–56.

GENOVESE, R. J.   Marriage encounter. *Small Group Behavior*, 1975, *6*, 45–46.

GILMORE, J. V., & GILMORE, E. C.   *A more productive child: Guidelines for parents*. Boston: The Gilmore Institute, 1978.

GINOTT, H. G. Parent education groups in a child guidance clinic. *Mental Hygiene,* 1957, *41,* 82-86.

GINSBERG, B., & VOGELSONG, E. L. Premarital relationship improvement by maximizing empathy and self-disclosure: The PRIMES program. In B. G. Guerney, Jr. (Ed.), *Relationship enhancement.* San Francisco: Jossey-Bass, 1977.

GLADFELTER, J. Films on group and family psychotherapy. In C. J. Sager & H. S. Kaplan (Eds.), *Progress in group and family therapy.* New York: Brunner/Mazel, 1972.

GLICK, I. D., WEBER, D. H., RUBINSTEIN, D., & PATTEN, J. T. *Family therapy and research: An annotated bibliography* (2nd ed.). New York: Grune & Stratton, 1981.

GOLDMAN, J., & COANE, J. Family therapy after the divorce: Developing a strategy. *Family Process,* 1977, *16,* 357-362.

GOLDSTEIN, M. J., & RODNICK, E. H. The family's contribution to the etiology of schizophrenia: Current status. *Schizophrenia Bulletin,* 1975, *14,* 48-63.

GORDON, T. *P.E.T.: Parent effectiveness training.* New York: Peter H. Wyden, 1970.

GORDON, T. *P.E.T. in action.* New York: Peter H. Wyden, 1976.

GORMALLY, J., & HILL, C. E. Guidelines for research on Carkhuff's training model. *Journal of Counseling Psychology,* 1974, *21*(6), 539-547.

GRANDO, R., & GINSBERG, B. G. Communication in the father-son relationship: The parent adolescent relationship development program. *The Family Coordinator,* 1976, *4*(24), 465-473.

GRANVOLD, D. K., & WELCH, G. J. Intervention for postdivorce adjustment problems. The treatment seminar. *Journal of Divorce,* 1977, *1,* 81-91.

GRAY, W., & RIZZO, N. D. History and development of general systems theory. In W. Gray, F. J. Duhl, & N. D. Rizzo (Eds.). *General systems theory and psychiatry.* Boston: Little, Brown, 1969.

GREENBERG, G. S. The family interactional perspective: A study and examination of the work of Don D. Jackson. *Family Process,* 1977, *16,* 385-412.

GREENBERG, G. S. Review of "Making the invisible visible." *Family Process,* 1979, *18*(3), 367-369 (a).

GREENBERG, G. S. Review of "The initial interview." *Family Process,* 1979, *18*(4), 503-509 (b).

GREENBERG, G. S. Review of "A modern little Hans." *Family Process,* 1980, *19*(2), 207-209.

GREER, S. E., & D'ZURILLA, T. J. Behavioral approaches to marital discord and conflict. *Journal of Marriage and Family Counseling,* 1975, *1*(4), 299-316.

GRIFFORE, R. J. Toward the use of child development research in informed parenting. *Journal of Clinical Child Psychology,* 1980, *9,* 48-51.

GAP (Group for the Advancement of Psychiatry). *Treatment of families in conflict: The clinical study of family process.* New York: Jason Aronson, 1970.

GUERIN, P. J., JR. Family therapy: The first twenty-five years. In P. J. Guerin, Jr. (Ed.), *Family therapy: Theory and practice.* New York: Gardner Press, 1976.

GUERIN, P. J., JR., & PENDAGAST, E. G. Evaluation of family system and genogram. In P. J. Guerin, Jr. (Ed.), *Family therapy: Theory and practice.* New York: Gardner Press, 1976.

GUERIN, P.J., & SHERMAN, C. O. Review of "Gestalt-system family therapy." *American Journal of Family Therapy,* 1982, *10*(2), 86-87.

GUERNEY, B. G., JR. (Ed.). *Psychotherapeutic agents: New roles for nonprofessionals, parents, and teachers.* New York: Holt, Rinehart and Winston, 1969.

GUERNEY, B. G., JR. (Ed.). *Relationship enhancement.* San Francisco: Jossey-Bass, 1977.

GUERNEY, B. G., JR., STOLLAK, G., & GUERNEY, L.   The practicing psychologist as educator—An alternative to the medical practitioner model. *Professional Psychology,* 1971, *2*(3), 276–282.

GUERNEY, B. G., JR., & VOGELSONG, E. L.   Relationship enhancement therapy. In R. Herink (Ed.), *The psychotherapy handbook.* New York: The New American Library, 1980.

GUERNEY, L. F.   Filial therapy programs. In D. H. Olson (Ed.), *Treating relationships.* Lake Mills, IA: Graphic Publishing Company, 1976.

GUERNEY, L., & JORDAN, L.   Children of divorce—a community support group. *Journal of Divorce,* 1979, *2*(3), 283–294.

GUNTRIP, H. J. S.   *Psychoanalytic theory, therapy, and the self.* New York: Basic Books, 1971.

GURIN, G., VEROFF, J., & FELD, S.   *Americans view their mental health.* New York: Basic Books, 1960.

GURMAN, A. S.   Behavior marriage therapy in the 1980's: The challenge of integration. *The American Journal of Family Therapy,* 1980, *8*(2), 86–96.

GURMAN, A. S., & KNISKERN, D. P.   Enriching research on marital enrichment programs. *Journal of Marriage and Family Counseling,* 1977, *3*(2), 3–11.

GURMAN, A. S., & KNISKERN, D. P.   Research on marital and family therapy: Progress, perspective and prospect. In S. L. Garfield & A. E. Bergin (Eds.), *Handbook of psychotherapy and behavior change: An empirical analysis.* (2nd ed.). New York: John Wiley, 1978 (a).

GURMAN, A. S., & KNISKERN, D. P.   Deterioration in marital and family therapy: Empirical, clinical, and conceptual issues. *Family Process,* 1978, *17,* 3–20 (b).

GURMAN, A. S., & KNISKERN, D. P.   Behavior marriage therapy: II. Empirical perspective. *Family Process,* 1978, *17,* 139–148 (c).

GURMAN, A. S., & KNISKERN, D. P. (Eds.).   *Handbook of family therapy.* New York: Brunner/Mazel, 1981 (a).

GURMAN, A. S., & KNISKERN, D. P.   Family therapy outcome research: Knowns and unknowns. In A. S. Gurman & D. P. Kniskern (Eds.), *Handbook of family therapy.* New York: Brunner/Mazel, 1981 (b).

GURMAN, A. S., KNUDSON, R. M., & KNISKERN, D. P.   Behavior marriage therapy: IV. Take two aspirin and call us in the morning. *Family Process,* 1978, *17,* 165–180.

HAFFEY, N. A.   Integrated child and family therapy. In R. F. Levant (Chair), *Toward the integration of child and family therapy: A symposium on conceptual models and techniques.* Symposium presented at Annual Meeting, American Psychological Association, Montreal, P.Q., Canada, 1980. ERIC/CAPS, *Resources in Education,* September, 1980, *15*(9), ED 199577.

HAFFEY, N., & LEVANT, R. F.   *The differential effectiveness of two models of skill training for working class mothers.* Manuscript submitted for publication, 1982.

HALEY, J.   Whither family therapy? *Family Process,* 1962, *1,* 69–100.

HALEY, J.   *Strategies of psychotherapy.* New York: Grune & Stratton, 1963.

HALEY, J.   Family therapy: A radical change. In J. Haley (Ed.), *Changing families: A family therapy reader.* New York: Grune & Stratton, 1971 (a).

HALEY, J.   A review of the family therapy field. In J. Haley (Ed.), *Changing families: A family therapy reader.* New York: Grune & Stratton, 1971 (b).

HALEY, J.   Critical overview of present status of family interaction research. In J. Framo (Ed.), *Family interaction—A dialogue between family researchers and family therapists.* New York: Springer, 1972.

HALEY, J. *Uncommon therapy: The psychiatric techniques of Milton H. Erickson, M.D.: A workbook of an innovative psychiatrist's work in short-term therapy.* New York: Norton, 1973.

HALEY, J. Development of a theory: A history of a research project. In C. E. Sluzki and D. C. Ransom (Eds.), *Double bind: The foundation of the communicational approach to the family.* New York: Grune & Stratton, 1976 (a).

HALEY, J. *Problem solving therapy.* San Francisco: Jossey-Bass, 1976 (b).

HALEY, J. *Leaving home: The therapy of disturbed young people.* New York: McGraw-Hill, 1980.

HALEY, J., & HOFFMAN, L. *Techniques of family therapy.* New York: Basic Books, 1967.

HALL, R. V. *Parent training: A preventive mental health program (Responsive Parent Training Program).* National Institute of Mental Health Grant, University of Kansas, 1976.

HANSEN, J. C., & L'ABATE, L. (Eds.). *Values, ethics, legalities and the family therapist.* Rockville, MD: Aspen Systems Corporation, 1982.

HARRELL, J., & GUERNEY, B. G., JR. Training married couples in conflict negotiation skills. In D. H. Olson (Ed.), *Treating relationships.* Lake Mills, IA: Graphic Publishing Company, 1976.

HART, J. T., & TOMLINSON, T. M. *New directions in client-centered therapy.* Boston: Houghton Mifflin, 1970.

HATCHER, C. Intrapersonal and interpersonal models: Blending Gestalt and family therapies. *Journal of Marriage and Family Counseling,* 1978, *4*(1), 63–68.

HEARD, D. B. Keith: A case study of structural family therapy. *Family Process,* 1978, *17*(3), 338–356.

HENRY, J. *Pathways to madness.* New York: Vintage Books, 1973.

HEREFORD, C. F. *Changing parental attitudes through group discussion.* Austin: University of Texas Press, 1963.

HILL, R. Contemporary developments in family theory. *Journal of Marriage and the Family,* 1966, *28,* 10–25.

HILL, R. Modern systems theory and the family: A confrontation. In M. B. Sussman (Ed.), *Sourcebook in marriage and the family* (2nd ed.). Boston: Houghton Mifflin, 1974.

HILL, R., & HANSEN, D. A. The identification of conceptual frameworks utilized in family study. *Marriage and Family Living,* 1960, *22,* 299–311.

HILL, R., KATZ, A. M., & SIMPSON, R. L. An inventory of research in marriage and family behavior: A statement of objectives and progress. *Marriage and Family Living,* 1957, *19,* 89–92.

HILL, R., & RODGERS, R. H. The developmental approach. In H. T. Christensen (Ed.), *Handbook of marriage and the family.* Chicago: Rand McNally, 1964.

HINES, R. M., & HARE-MUSTIN, R. T. Ethical concerns in family therapy. *Professional Psychology,* 1978, *9,* 165–170.

HINKLE, J. E., & MOORE, M. A student couples program. *Family Coordinator,* 1971, *20,* 153–158.

HOBBS, N. Ethics in clinical psychology. In B. Wolman (Ed.), *Handbook of clinical psychology.* New York: McGraw Hill, 1965.

HOF, L., & MILLER, W. R. Marriage enrichment. *Marriage and Family Review,* 1980, *3,* 1–27.

HOFFMAN, L. Deviation-amplifying processes in natural groups. In J. Haley (Ed.), *Changing families: A family therapy reader.* New York: Grune & Stratton, 1971.

HOGAN, D. B. *The regulation of psychotherapists. Vol I: A study in the philosophy and practice of professional regulation.* Cambridge, MA: Ballinger, 1979 (a).

HOGAN, D. B. *The regulation of psychotherapists. Vol. II: A handbook of state licensure laws.* Cambridge, MA: Ballinger, 1979 (b).

HOGAN, D. B. *The regulation of psychotherapists. Vol. III: A review of malpractice suits in the United States.* Cambridge, MA: Ballinger, 1979 (c).

HOGAN, D. B. *The regulation of psychotherapists. Vol. IV: A resource bibliography.* Cambridge, MA: Ballinger, 1979 (d).

HOMANS, C. G. *Social behavior: Its elementary forms.* New York: Harcourt Brace, 1961.

HOPKINS, L., HOPKINS, P., MACE, D., & MACE, V. *Toward better marriages.* Winston-Salem: ACME, 1978.

HOWELLS, J. G. (Ed.). *Therapy and practice of family psychiatry.* New York: Brunner/Mazel, 1971.

HURVITZ, N. The Miller family: Illustrating the symbolic interactionist approach to family therapy. *The Counseling Psychologist,* 1975, *5,* 57–109.

ISCOE, I., BLOOM, B., & SPIELBERGER, C. D. (Eds.). *Community psychology in transition: Proceedings of the national conference on training in community psychology.* Washington, DC: Hemisphere Publishing Corporation, 1977.

IVEY, A. E. *Microcounseling: Innovations in interviewing training.* Springfield, IL: Charles C. Thomas, 1971.

JACKSON, D. D. The question of family homeostasis. *Psychiatric Quarterly Supplement,* 1957, *31* (Part I), 79–90.

JACKSON, D. D. The study of the family. *Family Process,* 1965, *4,* 1–20 (a).

JACKSON, D. D. Family rules: Marital quid pro quo. *Archives of General Psychiatry,* 1965, *12,* 589–594 (b).

JACKSON, D. D., & WEAKLAND, J. H. Conjoint family therapy: Some considerations on theory, technique, and results. *Psychiatry,* 1961, *24,* 30–45.

JACOB, T. Family interaction in disturbed and normal families: A methodological and substantive review. *Psychological Bulletin,* 1975, *82*(1), 33–65.

JACOB, T., & GROUNDS, L. Confusions and conclusions: A response to Doane. *Family Process,* 1978, *17,* 377–387.

JACOBSON, N. S. Training couples to solve their marital problems: A behavioral approach to relationship discord. *International Journal of Family Counseling,* 1977, *5*(1), 22–31 (a).

JACOBSON, N. S. Training couples to solve their marital problems: A behavioral approach to relationship discord (Part II). *International Journal of Family Counseling,* 1977, *5*(2), 20–28 (b).

JACOBSON, N. S. A stimulus control model of change in behavioral couples' therapy: Implications for contingency contracting. *Journal of Marriage and Family Counseling,* 1978, *4*(3), 29–36.

JACOBSON, N. S. Behavioral marital therapy: Current trends in research, assessment and practice. *American Journal of Family Therapy,* 1980, *8*(2), 3–5.

JACOBSON, N. S., & MARGOLIN, G. *Marital therapy: Strategies based on social learning and behavioral exchange principles.* New York: Brunner/Mazel, 1979.

JACOBSON, N. S., & MARTIN, B. Behavioral marriage therapy: Current status. *Psychological Bulletin,* 1976, *83*(4), 540–556.

JACOBSON, N. S., & WEISS, R. L. Behavior marriage therapy: III. The contents of Gurman et al. may be hazardous to our health. *Family Process,* 1978, *17,* 149–163.

JAMES, M., & JAMES, J. Games parents play. In L. E. Arnold (Ed.), *Helping parents help their children.* New York: Brunner/Mazel, 1978.

JOHNSON, A. M., & SZUREK, S. A. Etiology of anti-social behavior in delinquents and psychopaths. *Journal of the American Medical Association,* 1954, *154,* 814–817.

JOHNSON, C. A., & KATZ, R. C.   Using parents as change agents for their children: A review. *Journal of Child Psychology and Psychiatry,* 1973, *14,* 181–200.

KAFKA, J. S.   Ambiguity for individuation: A critique and reformation of double-bind theory. *Archives of General Psychiatry,* 1971, *25,* 232–239.

KAGAN, N.   Observation and suggestions. *The Counseling Psychologist,* 1972, *3*(3), 42–45.

KANFER, F. H., & KAROLY, P.   Self-control: A behavioristic excursion into the lion's den. *Behavior Therapy,* 1972, *3,* 398–416.

KANIGSBERG, J., & LEVANT, R. F.   *Changes in parental attitudes, children's self-concept and behavior following parental participation in skills training programs.* Manuscript submitted for publication, 1982.

KANTOR, D., & LEHR, W.   *Inside the family: Toward a theory of family process.* San Francisco: Jossey-Bass, 1975.

KAPLAN, H. S.   *The new sex therapy: Active treatment of sexual dysfunction.* New York: Brunner/Mazel, 1974.

KAPLAN, M. L., & KAPLAN, N. R.   Individual and family growth: A Gestalt approach. *Family Process,* 1978, *17,* 195–206.

KARPEL, M.   Individuation: From fusion to dialogue. *Family Process,* 1976, *15,* 65–82.

KASLOW, F. W.   Divorce and divorce therapy. In A. S. Gurman & D. P. Kniskern (Eds.), *Handbook of family therapy.* New York: Brunner/Mazel, 1981.

KASLOW, F., COOPER, B., & LINSENBERG, B.   Family therapist authenticity as a key factor in outcome. *International Journal of Family Therapy,* 1979, *1*(2), 184–199.

KASLOW, F. W., & FRIEDMAN, J.   Utilization of family photos and movies in family therapy. *Journal of Marriage and Family Counseling,* 1977, *3*(1), 19–25.

KEENEY, B. P., & SPRENKLE, D. H.   *Reactions to Levant's classification of family therapy classifications.* Unpublished manuscript, 1980. (Available from Sprenkle, Department of Child and Family Studies, Purdue University, W. Lafayette, IN 47907).

KEITH, D. V., & WHITAKER, C. A.   Struggling with the impotence impasse: Absurdity and acting in. *Journal of Marriage and Family Counseling,* 1978, *4*(1), 69–77.

KEMPLER, W.   Experiential family therapy. *The International Journal of Group Psychotherapy,* 1965, *15,* 57–71.

KEMPLER, W.   Experiential psychotherapy with families. *Family Process,* 1968, *7*(1), 88–99.

KEMPLER, W.   *Principles of Gestalt family therapy.* Salt Lake City: Deseret Press, 1974.

KEMPLER, W.   *Experiential psychotherapy within families.* New York: Brunner/Mazel, 1981.

KENDON, A.   How people interact. In A. Ferber, M. Mendelsohn, & A. Napier (Eds.), *The book of family therapy.* Boston: Houghton Mifflin, 1973.

KERCKHOFF, F. G., ULMSCHNEIDER, A., & ADAMS, C.   College and university programs in parent education. *Family Coordinator,* 1976, *25*(2), 131–133.

KESSLER, M., & ALBEE, G. W.   Primary prevention. *Annual Review of Psychology,* 1975, *26,* 557–572.

KESSLER, S.   Divorce adjustment groups. *Personnel and Guidance Journal,* 1976, *54*(5), 251–255.

KESSLER, S., & BOSTWICK, S.   Beyond divorce: Coping skills for children. *Journal of Clinical Child Psychology,* 1977, *6,* 38–41.

KINDER, B. N., & BLAKENEY, P.   Treatment of sexual dysfunction: A review of outcome studies. *Journal of Clinical Psychology,* 1977, *33*(2), 523–530.

KINSEY, A. C., POMEROY, W. E., & MARTIN, L. E.   *Sexual behavior in the human male.* Philadelphia: W. B. Saunders Company, 1948.

KINSEY, A. C., POMEROY, W. E., MARTIN, C. E., & GEBBARD, P. H.   *Sexual behavior in the human female.* Philadelphia: W. B. Saunders Company, 1953.

KLEIN, J. F., CALVERT, G. P., GARLAND, T. N., & PALOMA, M. M.   Pilgrim's progress I: Recent developments in family theory. *Journal of Marriage and the Family,* 1969, *31,* 677–687.

KLEIN, M.   Notes on some schizoid mechanisms. *International Journal of Psychoanalysis,* 1946, *27,* 99–110.

KNISKERN, D. P., & GURMAN, A. S.   Research on training in marriage and family therapy: Status, issues, and directions. *Journal of Marital and Family Therapy,* 1979, *5,* 83–96.

KOOCHER, G. (Ed.).   *Children's rights and the mental health professions.* New York: John Wiley, 1976.

KOOCHER. G. P.   Credentialing in psychology: Close encounters with competence. *American Psychologist,* 1979, *34,* 696–702.

KRAMER, J. R., & REITZ, M.   Using video playback to train family therapists. *Family Process,* 1980, *19,* 145–150.

KRESSEL, K., & DEUTSCH, M.   Divorce therapy: An in-depth survey of therapists' views. *Family Process,* 1977, *16,* 413–443.

KRESSEL, K., DEUTSCH, M., JAFFEE, N., TUCHMAN, B., & WATSON, C.   Mediated negotiations in divorce and labor disputes. *Conciliation Courts Review,* 1977, *15,* 9–12.

KUHN, T. T.   *The structure of scientific revolutions* (2nd ed.). Chicago: University of Chicago Press, 1970.

L'ABATE, L.   *Enrichment: Structured interventions with couples, families, and groups.* Washington, DC: University Press of America, 1977.

L'ABATE, L.   Skill training programs for couples and families. In A. S. Gurman & D. P. Kniskern (Eds.), *Handbook of family therapy.* New York: Brunner/Mazel, 1981.

L'ABATE, L., & COLLABORATORS.   *A Manual: Family enrichment program.* Atlanta, GA: Social Research Laboratories, 1975 (a).

L'ABATE, L., & COLLABORATORS.   *Manual: Enrichment programs for the family life cycle.* Atlanta, GA: Social Research Laboratories, 1975 (b).

L'ABATE, L., & FREY, J., III.   The E-R-A model: The role of feelings in family therapy reconsidered: Implications for a classification of theories in family therapy. *Journal of Marital and Family Therapy,* 1981, 7(2), 143–150.

LAING, R. D.   *The self and others: Further studies in sanity and madness.* London: Tavistock Press, 1961.

LAING, R. D.   Mystification, confusion, and conflict. In I. Boszormenyi-Nagy & J. L. Framo (Eds.), *Intensive family therapy: Theoretical and practical asaspects.* Hagerstown, MD: Harper & Row, 1965.

LAING, R. D.   *The politics of the family and other essays.* New York: Pantheon Books, 1969, 1971.

LAING, R. D. & ESTERSON, A.   *Sanity, madness, and the family.* London: Penguin Books, 1970.

LAMB, J., & LAMB, W. A.   *Parent education and elementary counseling.* New York: Human Sciences Press, 1978.

LAMB, M. E.   The effects of divorce on children's personality development. *Journal of Divorce,* 1977, *1*(2), 163–174.

LAMB, M. E.   Paternal influences and the father's role: A personal perspective. *American Psychologist,* 1979, *34,* 938–943.

LAMBERT, M. J., BERGIN, A. E., & COLLINS, J. L.   Therapist-induced deterioration in psychotherapy. In A. S. Gurman & A. M. Razin (Eds.), *Effective psychotherapy: A handbook of research.* New York: Pergamon Press, 1977.

LAMBERT, M. J., & DE JULIO, S. S.   Outcome research in Carkhuff's Human Resource Development training programs: Where is the donut? *The Counseling Psychologist,* 1977, *6*(4), 79–86.

LAMBERT, M. J., DE JULIO, S. S., & STEIN, D. M.   Therapist interpersonal skills: Process, outcome, methodological considerations and recommendations for further research. *Psychological Bulletin,* 1978, *85,* 467–489.

LANDIS, C.   A statistical evaluation of psychotherapeutic methods. In L. E. Hinsie (Ed.), *Concepts and problems of psychotherapy.* New York: Columbia University Press, 1937.

LANGSLEY, D. G., & KAPLAN, D. M.   *The treatment of families in crisis.* New York: Grune & Stratton, 1968.

LANGSLEY, D. G., PITTMAN, F. S., III, MACHOTKA, P., & FLOMENHAFT, K.   Family crisis therapy: Results and implications. *Family Process,* 1968, *7,* 145–148.

LANGSLEY, D. G., PITTMAN, F. S., III, & SWANK, G. E.   Family crisis in schizophrenics and other mental patients. *Journal of Nervous and Mental Disease,* 1969, *149,* 270–276.

LA PERRIERE, K.   Family therapy training at the Ackerman Institute: Thoughts of form and substance. *Journal of Mental and Family Therapy,* 1979, *5,* 53–58.

LA PERRIERE, K.   Review of "Heroin my baby." *American Journal of Family Therapy,* 1982, *10*(1), 90–91.

LAQUER, H. P.   General systems theory and multiple family therapy. In W. Gray, F. J. Duhl, & N. D. Rizzo (Eds.), *General systems theory and psychiatry.* Boston: Little, Brown, 1969.

LAQUER, H. P.   Mechanisms of change in multiple family therapy. In C. J. Sager & H. S. Kaplan (Eds.), *Progress in group and family therapy.* New York: Brunner/Mazel, 1972.

LAQUER, H. P.   Multiple family therapy. In P. J. Guerin, Jr. (Ed.), *Family therapy: Theory and practice.* New York: Gardner Press, 1976.

LAQUER, H. P.   The theory and practice of multiple family therapy. In L. R. Wolberg & M. L. Aronson (Eds.), *Group and family therapy: 1980.* New York: Brunner/Mazel, 1980.

LAZARUS, A. A.   Behavior therapy and group marriage counseling. *Journal of the American Society of Psychosomatic Medicine and Dentistry,* 1968, *15,* 49–56.

LEADER, A. L.   Family therapy for divorced fathers and others out of home. *Social Casework,* 1973, *54,* 13–19.

LEBOW, M. D.   Behavior modification for the family. In G. D. Erickson & T. P. Hogan (Eds.), *Family therapy: An introduction to theory and technique.* Monterey, CA: Brooks/Cole, 1972.

LECKER, S.   Family therapies. In B. Wolman (Ed.), *The therapist's Handbook.* New York: Van Nostrand, 1976.

LERNER, P. M.   Rorschach measures of family interaction: A review. In P. M. Lerner (Ed.), *Handbook of Rorschach scales.* New York: International Universities Press, 1975.

LEVANT, R. F.   The planning, development, and administration of a therapeutic school for adolescents (The Robert W. White School) (Doctoral dissertation, Harvard University, 1973). *Dissertation Abstracts International,* 1974, *35,* 5684-B. (University Microfilms No. 74-11, 324).

LEVANT, R. F. Family therapy: A client-centered perspective. *Journal of Marriage and Family Counseling,* 1978, *4*(2), 35–42 (a).

LEVANT, R. F. Client-centered approaches to working with the family: An overview of new developments in therapeutic, educational, and preventive methods. *International Journal of Family Counseling,* 1978, *6*(1), 31–44 (b).

LEVANT, R. F. A classification of the field of family therapy: A review of prior attempts and a new paradigmatic model. *American Journal of Family Therapy,* 1980, *8*(1), 3–16 (a).

LEVANT, R. F. Sociological and clinical models of the family: An attempt to identify paradigms. *American Journal of Family Therapy,* 1980, *8*(4), 5–20. (b)

LEVANT, R. F. Developmental processes in marriage. *Medical Aspects of Human Sexuality,* 1982, *16*(8), 77–94.

LEVANT, R. F. Toward a counseling psychology of the family: Psychological-educational and skills-training programs for treatment, prevention, and development. *The Counseling Psychologist,* 1983, *11,* in press.

LEVANT, R. F. Client-centered skill training programs for the family: A review of the literature. *The Counseling Psychologist,* 1983, in press.

LEVANT, R. F., & DOYLE, G. A systematic evaluation of a parent education program for fathers of school-aged children. *Family Relations,* 1983, *32,* 29–37.

LEVANT, R. F., & HAFFEY, N. A. Toward an integration of child and family therapy. *International Journal of Family Therapy,* 1981, *3*(2), 130–143.

LEVANT, R. F., SLATTERY, S. C., & SLOBODIAN, P. E. A systematic skills approach to the selection and training of foster parents as mental health paraprofessionals, II: Training. *Journal of Community Psychology,* 1981, *9,* 231–238.

LEVY, D. *Maternal overprotection.* New York: Columbia University Press, 1943.

LIBERMAN, R. Behavioral approaches to family and couple therapy. *American Journal of Orthopsychiatry,* 1970, *40*(1), 106–118.

LICKORISH, J. R. The psychometric assessment of the family. In J. G. Howells (Ed.), *Theory and practice of family psychiatry.* New York: Brunner/Mazel, 1971.

LIDDLE, H. A., & HALPIN, R. J. Family therapy training and supervision: A comparative review. *Journal of Marriage and Family Counseling,* 1978, *4,* 77–98.

LIDDLE, H. A., & SABA, G. W. Systemic chic I: Family therapy's new wave. *Journal of Systemic and Strategic Therapies,* 1981, *1*(2), 36–39 (a).

LIDDLE, H. A., & SABA, G. W. Systemic chic II: Can family therapy maintain its Floy Floy? *Journal of Systemic and Strategic Therapies,* 1981, *1*(2), 40–43 (b).

LIDDLE, H. A., & SABA, G. W. Adventures in famtherland with the Systemic Sheik and Floy Floy: Episode three—complexity, clarity, and choice. *Family Therapy News,* 1982, *13*(3), 7.

LIDDLE, H. A., VANCE, S., & PASTUSHAK, R. J. Family therapy training opportunities in psychology and counselor education. *Professional Psychology,* 1979, *10,* 760–765.

LIDZ, T. *The family and human adaptation.* New York: International Universities Press, 1963.

LIDZ, T. *The origins and treatment of schizophrenic disorders.* New York: Basic Books, 1973.

LIDZ, T., CORNELISON, A. R., & FLECK, S. The limitations of extrafamilial socialization. In T. Lidz, S. Fleck, & A. R. Cornelison (Eds.), *Schizophrenia and the family.* New York: International Universities Press, 1965.

LIDZ, T., CORNELISON, A. R., FLECK, S., & TERRY, D. The intrafamilial environment of schizophrenic patients: II. Marital schism and marital skew. *American Journal of Psychiatry, 1957, 114,* 241-248 (a).

LIDZ, T., CORNELISON, A. R., FLECK, S., & TERRY, D. The intrafamilial environment of the schizophrenic patient: I. The father. *Psychiatry, 1957, 20,* 329-342 (b).

LIDZ, T., CORNELISON, A. R., TERRY, D., & FLECK, S. Intra-familial environment of the schizophrenic patient: IV. The transmission of irrationality. *A. M. A. Archives of Neurology and Psychiatry, 1958, 79,* 305-316.

LIDZ, T., CORNELISON, A. R., SINGER, M. T., SCHAFER, S., & FLECK, S. The mothers of schizophrenic patients. In T. Lidz, S. Fleck, & A. R. Cornelison (Eds.), *Schizophrenia and the family.* New York: International Universities Press, 1965.

LIDZ, T., & FLECK, S. Family studies and a theory of schizophrenia. In *The American family in crisis.* Des Plaines, IL: Forest Hospital Publications, 1965.

LIDZ, T., FLECK, S., ALANEN, Y. O., & CORNELISON, A. R. Schizophrenic patients and their siblings. *Psychiatry, 1963, 26,* 1-18.

LIDZ, T., FLECK, S., & CORNELISON, A. R. (Eds.), *Schizophrenia and the family.* New York: International Universities Press, 1965.

LIDZ, R. W., & LIDZ, T. The family environment of schizophrenic patients. *American Journal of Psychiatry, 1949, 106,* 332-345.

LIEBMAN, R., MINUCHIN, S., & BAKER, L. An integrated treatment program for anorexia nervosa. *American Journal of Psychiatry, 1974, 131,* 432-436.

LINDEMANN, E. Symptomatology and management of acute grief. In H. Parad (Ed.), *Crisis intervention: Selected readings.* New York: Family Service Association of America, 1965.

LOPICCOLO, J., & LOPICCOLO, L. *Handbook of sex therapy.* New York: Plenum, 1978.

LOVELAND, N. T. The relation Rorschach: A technique for studying interaction. *Journal of Nervous and Mental Diseases, 1967, 145,* 93-105.

LOWE, R. N., & MORSE, C. Parent child education centers. In C. Hatcher & B. J. Brooks (Eds.), *Innovations in counseling psychology: Developing new roles, settings, techniques.* San Francisco, CA: Jossey-Bass, 1977.

LUBORSKY, L., SINGER, B., & LUBORSKY, L. Comparative studies of psychotherapies. *Archives of General Psychiatry, 1973, 29,* 719-729.

MACE, D., & MACE, V. *Marriage enrichment retreats: Story of a Quaker project.* Philadelphia: Friends General Conference, 1973.

MACE, D. R., & MACE, V. C. Marriage enrichment—wave of the future? *The Family Coordinator, 1975, 24,* 131-135.

MACGREGOR, R. Multiple impact psychotherapy with families. In J. G. Howells (Ed.), *Theory and practice of family psychiatry.* New York: Brunner/Mazel, 1971.

MACGREGOR, R., RITCHIE, A. N., SERRANO, A. C., & SCHUSTER, F. P. *Multiple impact theory with families.* New York: McGraw-Hill, 1964.

MACKLER, L. H. P. Laquer, M. D. 1909-1977: Bibliography. In L. R. Wolberg & M. L. Aronson (Eds.), *Group and family therapy: 1980.* New York: Brunner/Mazel, 1980.

MAILLOUX, N. Ethical issues in the psychologist-client relationship. *International Journal of Psychology, 1977, 16,* 115-119.

MALONE, C. A. Child psychiatry and family therapy. *Journal of the American Academy of Child Psychiatry,* 1979, *18,* 4–21.

MARKMAN, H. J., & FLOYD, F. Possibilities for the prevention of marital discord: A behavioral perspective. *American Journal of Family Therapy,* 1980, *8*(2), 29–48.

MARTIN, B. Brief family intervention: Effectiveness and the importance of including the father. *Journal of Consulting and Clinical Psychology,* 1977, *45,* 1002–1010.

MARTIN, P. A. Training of psychiatric residents in family therapy. *Journal of Marital and Family Therapy,* 1979, *5,* 43–52.

MASH, E. J., HANDY, L. C., & HAMERLYNCK, L. A. (Eds.). *Behavioral modification approaches to parenting.* New York: Brunner/Mazel, 1976.

MASTERS, W. H., & JOHNSON, V. E. *Human sexual response.* Boston: Little, Brown, 1966.

MASTERS, W. H., JOHNSON, V. E. *Human sexual inadequacy.* Boston: Little, Brown, 1970.

MAY, P. R. For better or worse? Psychotherapy and variance change: A critical review of the literature. *The Journal of Nervous and Mental Disease,* 1971, *152,* 184–192.

MCDERMOTT, J. F., & CHAR, W. F. The undeclared war between child and family therapy. *Journal of the American Academy of Child Psychiatry,* 1974, *13,* 422–426.

MCDONOUGH, J. J. Approaches to Adlerian family education research. *Journal of Individual Psychology,* 1976, *32*(2), 224–231.

MCGUINESS, T., & GLASSER, W. Reality guidance. In L. E. Arnold (Ed.), *Helping parents help their children.* New York: Brunner/Mazel, 1978.

MEALIEA, W. J., JR. Conjoint-behavior therapy: The modification of family constellations. In E. J. Mash, L. C. Handy, & L. A. Hamerlynck (Eds.), *Behavior modification approaches to parenting.* New York: Brunner/Mazel, 1976.

MEISSNER, W. W. Thinking about the family: Psychiatric aspects. *Family Process,* 1964, *3*(1), 1–40.

MEISSNER, W. W. Family dynamics and psychosomatic processes. *Family Process,* 1966, *5,* 142–161.

MENDELSOHN, H. Review of "Down on Jack Night." *American Journal of Family Therapy,* 1981, *9*(3), 103–104.

MENN, A. Z. Review of "Family systems therapy with schizophrenia." *Family Process,* 1981, *20*(4), 473.

MILLER, G. A. Psychology as a means of promoting human welfare. *American Psychologist,* 1969, *24,* 1063–1071.

MILLER, S. The effects of communication training in small groups upon self-disclosure and openness in engaged couples' systems of interaction: A field experiment (Doctoral dissertation, University of Minnesota, 1971). *Dissertation Abstracts International,* 1971, *32,* 2819-A-2820-A. (University Microfilms no. 71-28, 263).

MILLER, S. (Ed.). *Marriages and families: Enrichment through communication.* Beverly Hills, CA: Sage, 1975.

MILLER, S., NUNNALLY, E. W., & WACKMAN, D. B. A communication training program for couples. *Social Casework,* 1976, *57,* 9–18.

MILLER, S., WACKMAN, D. B., & NUNNALLY, E. W. *Talking together.* Minneapolis: Interpersonal Communication Programs, 1983.

MINUCHIN, S. Conflict-resolution family therapy. *Psychiatry,* 1965, *28,* 278–286.

MINUCHIN, S. *Families and family therapy.* Cambridge: Harvard University Press, 1974.

MINUCHIN, S., & MONTALVO, B.   Techniques for working with disorganized low socioeconomic families. *American Journal of Orthopsychiatry*, 1967, *37*, 880–887.

MINUCHIN, S., MONTALVO, B., GUERNEY, B. G., JR., ROSMAN, B. L., & SCHUMER, F.   *Families of the slums: An exploration of their structure and treatment.* New York: Basic Books, 1967.

MINUCHIN, S., ROSMAN, B. L., & BAKER, L.   *Psychosomatic families: Anorexia nervosa in context.* Cambridge, MA: Harvard University Press, 1978.

MISHLER, E. G., & WAXLER, N. E.   *Interaction in families: An experimental study of family processes and schizophrenia.* New York: John Wiley, 1968.

MITCHELL, K. M., BOZARTH, J. D., & KRAUFT, C. C.   A reappraisal of the therapeutic effectiveness of accurate empathy, nonpossessive warmth, and genuineness. In A. S. Gurman & A. M. Razin (Eds.), *Effective psychotherapy: A handbook of research.* New York: Pergamon Press, 1977.

MORENO, J. L.   *Psychodrama.* Beacon, NY: Beacon House, 1946.

MORRIS, G. C., & WYNNE, L. C.   Schizophrenic offspring and parental styles of communication: A predictive study using excerpts of family therapy recordings. *Psychiatry,* 1965, *28,* 19–44.

MUDD, W., FREEMAN, C., & ROSE, E.   Premarital counseling in the Philadelphia Marriage Council. *Mental Hygiene,* 1941, *25,* 98–119.

NAPIER, A. Y., & WHITAKER, C.   Problems of the beginning family therapist. In D. A. Bloch (Ed.), *Techniques of family psychotherapy: A primer.* New York: Grune & Stratton, 1973.

NAPIER, A. Y., & WHITAKER, C. A.   *The family crucible.* New York: Harper & Row, 1978.

NEIBERG, N. A.   The group psychotherapy of married couples. In H. Grunebaum & J. Christ (Eds.), *Contemporary marriage: Structure, dynamics, and therapy.* Boston: Little, Brown, 1976.

NEWBERGER, C. M.   The cognitive structure of parenthood: Designing a descriptive measure. *New Directions for Child Development,* 1980, *7,* 45–67.

NEWTON, J. R.   Therapeutic paradoxes, paradoxical intentions and negative practice. *American Journal of Psychotherapy,* 1968, *22,* 68–81.

NICHOLS, W. C. (Ed.).   Special issue: Education and training in marital and family therapy. *Journal of Marital and Family Therapy,* 1979, *5,* 1–106 (a).

NICHOLS, W. C.   Doctoral programs in marital and family therapy. *Journal of Marital and Family Therapy,* 1979, *5,* 23–28 (b).

NICHOLS, W. C.   Education of marriage and family therapists: Some trends and implications. *Journal of Marital and Family Therapy,* 1979, *5,* 19–28 (c).

NUNNALLY, E. W., MILLER, S., & WACKMAN, D. B.   *Couple communication instructor manual.* Minneapolis: Interpersonal Communication Programs, 1983.

NYE, F. I., & BERARDO, F. M. (Eds.).   *Emerging conceptual frameworks in family analysis.* New York: Macmillan, 1966.

O'CONNOR, W. J.   Some observations on the use of TA in marriage counseling. *Journal of Marriage and Family Counseling,* 1977, *3*(1), 27–34.

O'DELL, S.   Training parents in behavior modification: A review. *Psychological Bulletin,* 1974, *81*(7), 418–433.

O'HARE, C., HEINRICH, A. G., KIRSCHNER, N. N., OBERSTONE, A. V., & RITZ, M. G.   Group training in family therapy—the students' perspective. *Journal of Marriage and Family Counseling,* 1975, *1,* 157–162.

O'LEARY, K. D., & TURKEWITZ, H.   Marital therapy from a behavioral perspective. In T. J. Paolino & B. S. McCrady (Eds.), *Marriage and marital therapy:*

Psychoanalytic, behavioral and systems theory perspectives. New York: Brunner/Mazel, 1978.

OLSON, D. H. Empirically unbinding the double bind: Review of research and conceptual reformulations. *Family Process,* 1972, *11,* 69–94.

OLSON, D. H. Treating relationships: Trends and overview. In D. H. Olson (Ed.), *Treating relationships.* Lake Mills, IA: Graphic Publishing Company, 1976.

OLSON, D. H., & NOREM, R. *Evaluation of five pre-marital programs.* Unpublished manuscript, 1977. (Available from author at Family Social Science, University of Minnesota, 218 North Hall, St. Paul, MN. 55108.)

OLSON, D. H., RUSSELL, C., & SPRENKLE, D. H. Circumplex model of marital and family systems II: Empirical studies and clinical intervention. In J. P. Vincent (Ed.), *Advances in family intervention, assessment and theory (Vol. 1).* Greenwich, CT: JAI Press, 1980 (a).

OLSON, D. H., RUSSELL, C., & SPRENKLE, D. H. Marriage and family therapy: A decade review. *Journal of Marriage and the Family,* 1980, *42,* 973–993 (b).

OLSON, D. H., & SPRENKLE, D. H. Emerging trends in treating relationships. *Journal of Marriage and Family Counseling,* 1976, *2*(4), 317–329.

OLSON, D. H., SPRENKLE, D. H., & RUSSELL, C. Circumplex model of marital and family systems: I. Cohesion and adaptability dimensions, family types, and clinical applications. *Family Process,* 1979, *18,* 3–28.

OTTO, H. A. *More joy in your marriage.* New York: Hawthorne, 1969.

OTTO, H. A. Marriage and family enrichment programs in North America—report and analysis. *The Family Coordinator,* 1975, *24,* 137–142.

OTTO, H. A. (Ed.). *Marriage and family enrichment: New perspectives and programs.* Nashville: Abington, 1976.

PALAZZOLI, M. S. *Self-starvation: From individual to family therapy in the treatment of anorexia nervosa.* New York: Jason Aronson, 1978.

PALAZZOLI, M. S., CECCHIN, G., PRATA, G., & BOSCOLO, L. *Paradox and counterparadox: A new model in the therapy of the family in schizophrenic transaction.* New York: Jason Aronson, 1978.

PAPP, P. Brief therapy with couple groups. In P. J. Guerin, Jr. (Ed.), *Family therapy: Theory and practice.* New York: Gardner Press, 1976 (a).

PAPP, P. Family choreography. In P. J. Guerin, Jr. (Ed.), *Family therapy: Theory and practice.* New York: Gardner Press, 1976 (b).

PAPP, P. (Ed.). *Family therapy: Full length case studies.* New York: Gardner Press, 1977 (a).

PAPP, P. The family who had all the answers. In P. Papp (Ed.), *Family therapy: Full length case studies.* New York: Gardner Press, 1977 (b).

PAPP, P., SILVERSTEIN, O., & CARTER, E. Family sculpting in preventive work with "well-families." *Family Process,* 1973, *12,* 197–212.

PARKS, A. Children and youth of divorce in Parents Without Partners, Inc. *Journal of Clinical Child Psychology,* 1977, *6*(2), 44–48.

PARLOFF, M. S., WASKOW, I. E., & WOLFE, B. E. Research on therapist variables in relation to process and outcome. In S. L. Garfield & A. E. Bergin (Eds.), *Handbook of psychotherapy and behavior change: An empirical analysis.* (2nd ed.). New York: John Wiley, 1978.

PARSONS, T. Family structure and the socialization of the child. In T. Parsons & R. F. Bales (Eds.), *Family, socialization and interaction process.* New York: The Free Press, 1955.

PARSONS, T., & BALES, R. F. *Family, socialization and interaction process.* New York: The Free Press, 1955.

PATTERSON, G. R., & FLEISCHMAN, M. J. Maintenance of treatment effects.

Some considerations concerning family systems and follow-up data. *Behavioral Therapy,* 1979, *10,* 168–185.

PATTERSON, G. R., & GULLION, M. E. *Living with children: New methods for parents and teachers* (Rev. ed.). Champaign, IL: Research Press, 1976.

PATTERSON, G. R., RAY, R. S., & SHAW, D. A. Direct intervention in families of deviant children. *Oregon Research Institute Research Bulletin,* 1968, *8,* No. 9.

PATTERSON, G. R., & RIED, J. B. Reciprocity and coercion: Two facets of social systems. In C. Neulinger & J. L. Michael (Eds.), *Behavior modification in clinical psychology.* New York: Appleton-Century-Crofts, 1970.

PATTERSON, G. R., WEISS, R. L., & HOPS, H. Training of marital skills. In H. Leitenberg (Ed.), *Handbook of behavior modification and behavior therapy.* New York: Prentice-Hall, 1976.

PATTISON, E. M. (Ed.). Clinical applications of social network therapy. *International Journal of Family Therapy,* 1981, *3*(4), 241–320.

PAUL, G. L. Strategy of outcome research in psychotherapy. *Journal of Consulting Psychology,* 1967, *31,* 109–118.

PAUL, N. L. The role of mourning and empathy in conjoint marital therapy. In G. H. Zuk & I. Boszormenyi-Nagy (Eds.), *Family therapy and disturbed families.* Palo Alto, CA: Science & Behavior Books, 1967.

PAUL, N. L. Cross-confrontation. In P. J. Guerin (Ed.), *Family therapy: Theory and Practice.* New York: Gardner Press, 1976.

PAUL, N. L., BLOOM, J. D., & PAUL, B. B. Outpatient multiple family group therapy—why not? In L. R. Wolberg & M. L. Aronson (Eds.), *Group and family therapy: 1981.* New York: Brunner/Mazel, 1981.

PENDAGAST, E. G., & SHERMAN, C. O. A guide to the genogram family systems training. *The Family,* 1977, *5*(1), 3–14.

PERLMAN, L. M., & BENDER, S. S. Operant reinforcement in structural family therapy in treating anorexia nervosa. *Journal of Family Counseling,* 1975, *3*(2), 38–46.

PERLS, F. S. *Ego, hunger and aggression.* London: Allen & Unwin, 1947.

PERLS, F., HEFFERLINE, R. F., & GOODMAN, P. *Gestalt therapy: Excitement and growth in the human personality.* New York: Delta Books, 1951.

PERRUCCI, C. C., & TARG, D. B. (Eds.). *Marriage and the family: A critical analysis and proposals for change.* New York: David McKay, 1974.

PERTSHUK, M. J. Behavior therapy: Extended follow-up. In R. A. Vigersky (Ed.), *Anorexia nervosa.* New York: Raven Press, 1977.

PHILLIPS, J. S., & BIERMAN, K. L. Clinical psychology: Individual methods. *Annual Review of Psychology,* 1981, *32,* 405–438.

PIAGET, J. *The origins of intelligence in children* (Margaret Cook, Trans.). New York: Norton, 1963.

PIERCE, R. M. Training in interpersonal communication skills with the partners of deteriorated marriages. *The Family Coordinator,* 1973, *21,* 223–227.

PIERCE, R., & DRASGOW, J. Teaching facilitative interpersonal functioning to psychiatric patients. *Journal of Counseling Psychology,* 1969, *16,* 295–298.

PIERCY, F. P., LAIRD, R. A., & MOHAMMED, Z. A family therapist rating scale. *Journal of Marital and Family Therapy,* 1983, *9*(1), 49–59.

PITTMAN, F. S., III. Managing psychiatric emergencies: Defining the family crisis. In D. A. Bloch (Ed.), *Techniques of family psychotherapy: A primer.* New York: Grune & Stratton, 1973.

PITTS, J. R. The structure-functional approach. In H. T. Christensen (Ed.), *Handbook of marriage and the family.* Chicago: Rand McNally, 1964.

POWERS, W. T.   Feedback: Beyond behaviorism. *Science,* 1973, *179,* 351–356.
RABIN, M.   Gestalt therapy and therapy of intimate systems. In R. F. Levant (Chair), *The field of family therapy: A Paradigmatic classification and presentation of three major approaches.* Symposium presented at Annual meeting of the American Personnel and Guidance Association, Atlanta, 1980.
RABKIN, R.   *Strategic psychotherapy: Brief and symptomatic treatment.* New York: Basic Books, 1977.
RAKOFF, V., SIGAL, J. J., & EPSTEIN, N. B.   Working-through in conjoint family therapy. *American Journal of Psychotherapy,* 1967, *21,* 782–790.
RAPPAPORT, A. F.   Conjugal relationship enhancement program. In D. H. Olson (Ed.), *Treating relationships.* Lake Mills, IA: Graphic Publishing Co., 1976.
RASKIN, N. J., & VAN DER VEEN, F.   Client-centered family therapy: Some clinical and research perspectives. In J. T. Hart & T. M. Tomlinson (Eds.), *New directions in client-centered therapy.* Boston: Houghton Mifflin, 1970.
REISS, D.   Varieties of consensual experience: I. A theory for relating family interaction to individual thinking. *Family Process,* 1971, *10,* 1–28 (a).
REISS, D.   Varieties of consensual experience: II. Dimensions of a family's experience of its environment. *Family Process,* 1971, *10,* 28–35 (b).
REISS, D.´   Varieties of consensual experience: III. Contrast between families of normals, delinquents, and schizophrenics. *Journal of Nervous and Mental Disease,* 1971, *152,* 73–95 (c).
REISS, D., & SHERIFF, W. H., JR.   A computer-automated procedure for testing some experiences of family membership. *Behavioral Science,* 1970, *15,* 431–443.
RESNICK, J. L.   Parent education and the female parent. *The Counseling Psychologist,* 1981, *9*(4), 55–62.
RESNICK, J. L., RESNICK, M. B., PACKER, A. B., & WILSON, J.   Fathering classes: A psychoeducational model. *The Counseling Psychologist,* 1978, *7*(4), 56–60.
RESNIKOFF, A.   A critique of the Human Resource Development model from the viewpoint of rigor. *The Counseling Psychologist,* 1972, *3*(3), 46–55.
RIDLEY, C. A., AVERY, A. W., HARRELL, J. E., LESLIE, L. A., & DENT, J.   Conflict management: A premarital training program in mutual problem solving. *American Journal of Family Therapy,* 1981, *9*(4), 23–32.
RINN, R. C., & MARKLE, A.   Parent effectiveness training: A review. *Psychological Reports,* 1977, *41,* 95–109.
RISKIN, J., & FAUNCE, E. E.   An evaluative review of family interaction research. *Family Process,* 1972, *11*(4), 365–455.
RITTERMAN, M. K.   Paradigmatic classification of family therapy theories. *Family Process,* 1977, *16,* 29–48.
ROBIN, A. L., KENT, R., O'LEARY, D., FOSTER, S., & PRINZ, R.   An approach to teaching parents and adolescents problem-solving communication skills: A preliminary report. *Behavior Therapy,* 1977, *8,* 639–643.
RODGERS, R. H.   Toward a theory of family development. *Journal of Marriage and the Family,* 1964, *26,* 262–270.
ROGERS, C. R.   *Client-centered therapy.* Boston: Houghton Mifflin, 1951.
ROGERS, C.   The necessary and sufficient conditions of therapeutic personality change. *Journal of Consulting Psychology,* 1957, *21,* 95–103.
ROGERS, C. R.   *On becoming a person: A therapist's view of psychotherapy.* Boston: Houghton Mifflin, 1961.
ROGERS, C. R. (Ed.),   *The therapeutic relationship and its impact: A study of*

psychotherapy with schizophrenics. Madison: University of Wisconsin Press, 1967.

ROGERS, C. R.   *Becoming partners.* New York: Dell, 1972.

ROSENBERG, J. B.   Two is better than one: Use of behavioral techniques within a structural family model. *Journal of Marriage and Family Counseling,* 1978, *4*(1), 31–37.

RUESCH, J., & BATESON, G.   *Communication: The social matrix of psychiatry.* New York: Norton, 1951.

RUEVENI, V.   *Networking families in crisis.* New York: Human Sciences Press, 1979.

RYCKOFF, I., DAY, J., & WYNNE, L. C.   Maintenance of stereotyped roles in the families of schizophrenics. *Archives of General Psychiatry,* 1959, *1,* 93–98.

SAGER, C. J.   *Marriage contracts and couple therapy: Hidden forces in intimate relationships.* New York: Brunner/Mazel, 1976.

SALIN, L.   Review of "Time-mirror." *Family Process,* 1980, *19*(4), 427–428.

SALTS, C. J.   Divorce process: Integration of theory. *Journal of Divorce,* 1979, *2,* 233–240.

SARASON, S. B.   *The psychological sense of community: Prospects for a community psychology.* San Francisco: Jossey-Bass, 1974.

SATIR, V.   *Notes on the structured interview.* Unpublished manuscript, Mental Research Institute, Palo Alto, CA, 1966.

SATIR, V.   *Conjoint family therapy: A guide to theory and technique.* Palo Alto, CA: Science and Behavior Books, 1967.

SATIR, V.   *Peoplemaking.* Palo Alto, CA: Science and Behavior Books, 1972.

SATIR, V., STACHOWIAK, J., & TASCHMAN, H. A.   *Helping families to change.* New York: Jason Aronson, 1975.

SAUBER, S. R.   Multiple-family group counseling. *Personnel and Guidance Journal,* 1971, *49,* 459–465.

SCHATZMAN, M.   Paranoia or persecution: The case of Schreber. *Family Process,* 1971, *10,* 177–212.

SCHEFLEN, A. E., & SCHEFLEN, N.   *Body language and the social order.* Englewood Cliffs, NJ: Prentice-Hall, 1972.

SCHLIEN, S.   *Training dating couples in empathic and open communications: An experimental evaluation of a potential preventive mental health program.* Unpublished doctoral dissertation, Pennsylvania State University, 1971.

SCHMITT, A., & SCHMITT, D.   Marriage renewal retreats. In H. A. Otto (Ed.), *Marriage and family enrichment: New perspectives and programs.* Nashville: Abington, 1976.

SCHULTZ, S. J.   Review of "Promise her anything but send her a postcard." *Family Process,* 1981, *20*(1), 127–128.

SCHUMM, W. R., & DENTON, W.   Trends in premarital counseling. *Journal of Marital and Family Therapy,* 1979, *5*(4), 23–32.

SCOVERN, A. W., BUKSTEL, L. H., KILMANN, P. R., LAVAL, R. A., BUSEMEYER, J., & SMITH, V.   Effects of parent counseling on the family system. *Journal of Counseling Psychology,* 1980, *27,* 268–275.

SEARLES, H. F.   The effort to drive the other person crazy—an element in the aetiology and psychotherapy of schizophrenia. *British Journal of Medical Psychology,* 1959, *32,* 1–18.

SEARLES, H. F.   The contributions of family treatment to the psychotherapy of schizophrenia. In I. Boszormenyi-Nagy & J. L. Framo (Eds.), *Intensive family therapy: Theoretical and practical aspects.* Hagerstown, MD: Harper & Row, 1965.

SEMANS, J. H.   Premature ejaculation: A new approach. *Southern Medical Journal*, 1956, *49*, 353–358.

SHAPIRO, R. J.   Some implications of training psychiatric nurses in family therapy. *Journal of Marriage and Family Counseling*, 1975, *1*, 323–330.

SHLIEN, J. M., & LEVANT, R. F.   The Robert W. White School. *Harvard Graduate School of Education Association Bulletin*, 1974, *19*, 12–18.

SIMON, R. M.   Sculpting the family. *Family Process*, 1972, *11*, 49–57.

SINGER, M. T.   Family transactions and schizophrenia: I. Recent research findings. In J. Romano (Ed.), *The origins of schizophrenia: Proceedings of the first Rochester conference on schizophrenia, March 30–31, 1967.* New York: Excerpta Medica Foundation, 1967.

SINGER, M. T.   The consensus Rorschach and family transaction. *Journal of Protective Techniques*, 1968, *32*, 348–351.

SINGER, M. T., & WYNNE, L. C.   Thought disorder and family relations of schizophrenics: III. Methodology using projective techniques. *Archives of General Psychiatry*, 1965, *12*, 187–200 (a).

SINGER, M. T., & WYNNE, L. C.   Thought disorder and family relations of schizophrenics: IV. Results and implications. *Archives of General Psychiatry*, 1965, *12*, 201–212 (b).

SINGER, M. T., & WYNNE, L. C.   Principles for scoring communication defects and deviances in parents of schizophrenics: Rorschach and TAT scoring manuals. *Psychiatry*, 1966, *29*, 260–288.

SINGER, M. T., WYNNE, L. C., LEVI, L. D., & SOJIT, C.   Proverbs interpretation reconsidered: A transactional approach to schizophrenics and their families. Presented at *Symposium on Language and Thought in Schizophrenia*, 1968, Newport Beach, CA, November 23, 1968.

SIRJAMAKI, J.   The institutional approach. In H. T. Christensen (Ed.), *Handbook of marriage and the family.* Chicago: Rand McNally, 1964.

SIRRIDGE, S. T.   Transactional analysis: Promoting OK'ness. In M. J. Fine (Ed.), *Handbook on parent education.* New York: Academic Press, 1980.

SKYNNER, A. C. R.   *Systems of family and marital psychotherapy.* New York: Brunner/Mazel, 1976.

SKYNNER, A. C. R.   An open-systems, group-analytic approach to family therapy. In A. S. Gurman & D. P. Kniskern (Eds.), *Handbook of family therapy.* New York: Brunner/Mazel, 1981.

SLOANE, R. B., STAPLES, F. R., CRISTOL, A. H., YORKSTON, N. J., & WHIPPLE, K.   *Short-term analytically oriented psychotherapy vs. behavior therapy.* Cambridge, MA: Harvard University Press, 1975.

SLUZKI, C. E., BEAVIN, J., TARNOPOLSKY, A., & VERON, E.   Transactional disqualification: Research on the double bind. *Archives of General Psychiatry*, 1967, *3*(10), 494–504.

SLUZKI, C. E., & RANSOM, D. C. (Eds.).   *Double bind: The foundation of the communicational approach to the family.* New York: Grune & Stratton, 1976.

SLUZKI, C. E., & VERON, E.   The double bind as universal pathogenic situation. *Family Process*, 1971, *10*(4), 397–410.

SMITH, I. W., & LOEB, D.   The stable extended family as a model in treatment of atypical children. *Social Work*, 1965, *10*, 75–81.

SMITH, L., & SMITH, A.   Developing a nationwide marriage communication labs program. In H. A. Otto (Ed.), *Marriage and family enrichment: New perspectives and programs.* Nashville: Abington, 1976.

SMITH, M. L., & GLASS, G. V.   Meta-analysis of psychotherapy outcome studies. *American Psychologist*, 1977, *32*, 752–760.

SMITH, R. M., SHOFFNER, S. M., & SCOTT, J. P.   Marriage and family enrichment: A new professional area. *The Family Coordinator*, 1979, *28*, 87–93.

SMITH, V. G., & NICHOLS, W. C. Accreditation in marital and family therapy. *Journal of Marital and Family Therapy*, 1979, *5*, 95–100.

SOLOMON, M. A. A developmental, conceptual premise for family therapy. *Family Process*, 1973, *12*, 179–188.

SOLTZ, V. *Study group leader's manual for children: The challenge.* Chicago: Alfred Adler Institute, 1973.

SONNENSHEIN-SCHNEIDER, M., & BAIRD, K. L. Group counseling children of divorce in the elementary schools: Understanding process and technique. *Personnel and Guidance Journal*, 1980, *59*(2), 88–91.

SOPER, P., & L'ABATE, L. Paradox as a therapeutic technique. A review. *International Journal of Family Counseling*, 1977, *5*, 10–21.

SPECK, R. V., & ATTNEAVE, C. L. Social network intervention. In J. Haley (Ed.), *Changing families: A family therapy reader.* New York: Grune & Stratton, 1971.

SPECK, R. V., & ATTNEAVE, C. L. *Family networks.* New York: Vintage Books, 1973.

SPECK, R. V., & SPECK, S. L. On networks: Network therapy, network intervention, and networking. *International Journal of Family Therapy*, 1979, *1*(4), 333–337.

SPEIGEL, J. P., & BELL, N. W. The family of the psychiatric patient. In S. Arieti (Ed.), *American handbook of psychiatry* (Vol. 1). New York: Basic Books, 1959.

SPORAKOWSKI, M. J., & STANISZEWSKI, W. P. The regulation of marriage and family therapy: An update. *Journal of Marital and Family Therapy*, 1980, *6*, 335–348.

STANLEY, C. S., & COOKER, P. G. Gestalt therapy and the core conditions of communication: A synergistic approach. In E. W. Smith (Ed.), *The growing edge of Gestalt therapy.* New York: Brunner/Mazel, 1976.

STANLEY, S. F. Family education to enhance the moral atmosphere of the family and the moral development of adolescents. *Journal of Counseling Psychology*, 1978, *25*, 110–118.

STANLEY, S. F. The family and moral education. In R. L. Mosher (Ed.), *Adolescents' development and education: A Janus Knot.* Berkeley: McCutchan, 1980.

STANTON, M. D. Family therapy training: Academic and internship opportunities for psychologists. *Family Process*, 1975, *14*, 433–439.

STANTON, M. D. An integrated structural/strategic approach to family therapy. *Journal of Marital and Family Therapy*, 1981, *7*(4), 427–439.

STEIDL, J. H., & WEXLER, J. P. What's a clinician to do with so many approaches to family therapy? *The Family*, 1977, *4*, 51–66.

STEIN, E. V. MARDILAB: An experiment in marriage enrichment. *Family Coordinator*, 1975, *24*, 167–170.

STIER, S., & GOLDENBERG, I. Training issues in family therapy. *Journal of Marriage and Family Counseling*, 1975, *1*, 63–66.

STIERLIN, H., RÜCKER-EMBDEN, I., WETZEL, N. & WIRSCHING, M. *The first interview with the family.* New York: Brunner/Mazel, 1980.

STOLLAK, G. G. Variations and extensions of filial therapy. *Family Process*, 1981, *20*, 305–309.

STRAUS, M. A., & BROWN, B. W. *Family measurement techniques: Abstracts of published instruments, 1935–1974* (Rev. ed.). Minneapolis: University of Minnesota Press, 1978.

STRAUS, M. A. & TALLMAN, I. SIMFAM: A technique for observational measurement and experimental study of families. In J. Aldous (Eds.), *Family problem solving.* Hinsdale, IL: Dryden Press, 1971.

STREAN, H. S.   A family therapist looks at "Little Hans." *Family Process,* 1967, *6,* 227–234.

STRELNICK, A. H.   Multiple family group therapy: A review of the literature. *Family Process,* 1977, *16,* 307–325.

STRODTBECK, F. L.   The family as a three-person group. *American Sociological Review,* 1954, *19,* 23–29.

STRUPP, H. H., & HADLEY, S. W.   Specific v. nonspecific factors in psychotherapy: A controlled study of outcome. *Archives of General Psychiatry,* 1979, *36,* 1125–1136.

STRYKER, S.   The interactional and situational approaches. In H. T. Christensen (Ed.), *Handbook of marriage and the family.* Chicago: Rand McNally, 1964.

STUART, R. B.   Operant-interpersonal treatment for marital discord. *Journal of Consulting and Clinical Psychology,* 1969, *33,* 675–682 (a).

STUART, R. B.   Token reinforcement in marital treatment. In R. D. Rubin & C. M. Franks (Eds.), *Advances in behavior therapy.* New York: Academic Press, 1969, (b).

SUGARMAN, S.   Family therapy training in selected general psychiatry residency programs. *Family Process,* 1981, *20,* 147–154.

TAICHERT, L. C.   *Childhood learning, behavior and the family.* New York: Behavioral Publishers, 1973.

TASEM, M., AUGENBRAUN, B., & BROWN, S. L.   Family group interviewing with the preschool child and both parents. *Journal of the American Academy of Child Psychiatry,* 1965, *4,* 330–340.

TAVORMINA, J. B.   Basic models of parent counseling: A critical review. *Psychological Bulletin,* 1974, *81,* 827–835.

TAVORMINA, J. B.   Evaluation and comparative studies of parent education. In R. R. Abidin (Ed.), *Parent education and intervention handbook.* Springfield, IL: Charles C. Thomas, 1980.

THIABUT, J. W., & KELLEY, H. S.   *The social psychology of groups.* New York: Wiley, 1959.

THIESSEN, J. D., AVERY, A. W., & JOANNING, H.   Facilitating post-divorce adjustment among women: A communication skills training approach. *Journal of Divorce,* 1980, *4*(2), 35–44.

THOMAS, E. J., CARTER, R. D., GAMBRILL, E. D., & BUTTERFIELD, W. H.   A signal system for the assessment and modification of behavior (SAM). *Behavior Therapy,* 1970, *1,* 252–259.

THOMAS, W. I., & THOMAS, D. S.   *The child in America.* New York: Knopf, 1928.

TOMAN, W.   *Family constellation: Its effects on personality and social behavior* (3rd ed.). New York: Springer, 1976.

TOMM, K. M., & WRIGHT, L. M.   Training in family therapy: Perceptual, conceptual, and executive skills. *Family Process,* 1979, *18,* 227–250.

TRAVIS, R. P., & TRAVIS, P. Y.   The pairing enrichment program: Actualizing the marriage. *Family Coordinator,* 1975, *24,* 161–165.

TRUAX, C. B., & CARKHUFF, R. R.   *Toward effective counseling and psychotherapy: Training and practice.* Chicago: Aldine, 1967.

TRUAX, C. B., & MITCHELL, K. M.   Research on certain therapist interpersonal skills in relation to process and outcome. In A. E. Bergin & S. L. Garfield (Eds.), *Handbook of psychotherapy and behavior change: An empirical analysis.* New York: John Wiley, 1971.

TSOI-HOSHMAND, L.   Marital therapy: An integrative behavioral-learning model. *Journal of Marriage and Family Counseling,* 1976, *2*(2), 179–191.

TUCKER, B. Z., HART, G., & LIDDLE, H. A.   Supervision in family therapy: A developmental perspective. *Journal of Marriage and Family Counseling,* 1976, *2,* 269–276.

ULRICI, D., L'ABATE, L., & WAGNER, V. The E-R-A Model: A heuristic framework for classification of skill training programs for couples and families. *Family Relations,* 1981, *30,* 307–315.

U.S. BUREAU OF THE CENSUS. Divorce, child custody, and child support. *Current Population Reports,* Series P-23, No. 84. Washington, DC: U.S. Government Printing Office, 1979.

U.S. BUREAU OF THE CENSUS. Marital status and living arrangements: March 1979. *Current Population Reports,* Series P-20, No. 349. Washington, DC: U.S. Government Printing Office, 1980.

VAN DER VEEN, F. Family psychotherapy and a person's concept of his family: Some clinical and research formulations. *Institute for Juvenile Research Reports,* 1969, *6*(16).

VAN DER VEEN, F. *Three client-centered alternatives: A therapy collective, therapeutic community and skill training for relationships.* Paper presented symposium honoring Carl Rogers at 75 at the Annual Meeting of the American Psychological Association, 1977.

VISHER, J. B., & VISHER, J. S. *Stepfamilies: A guide to working with stepparents and stepchildren.* New York: Brunner/Mazel, 1979.

VITALO, R. Teaching improved interpersonal functioning as a preferred mode of treatment. *Journal of Consulting and Clinical Psychology,* 1971, *35,* 166–171.

VOGEL, E. F., & BELL, N. W. The emotionally disturbed child as the family scapegoat. In N. W. Bell & E. F. Vogel (Eds.), *A modern introduction to the family.* New York: Free Press, 1968.

VOGELSONG, E. L., GUERNEY, B. G., JR., & GUERNEY, L. F. Relationship enhancement with inpatients and their families. In R. Luber & C. Anderson (Eds.), *Communication training approaches to family intervention with psychiatric patients.* New York: Human Sciences Press, in press.

VON BERTALANFFY, L. *General systems theory: Foundation, development, applications.* New York: Braziller, 1968.

VON BERTALANFFY, L. General systems theory and psychiatry—an overview. In W. Gray, F. J. Duhl, & N. P. Rizzo (Eds.), *General systems theory and psychiatry.* Boston: Little, Brown, 1969.

VYGOTSKY, L. S. *Thought and language.* New York and Cambridge, MA: John Wiley & MIT Press, 1962.

WALLERSTEIN, J. S., & KELLEY, J. B. The effects of parental divorce: The adolescent experience. In E. J. Anthony & C. Koupernik (Eds.), *The child in his family—children at a psychiatric risk* (Vol. 3). New York: John Wiley, 1974.

WALLERSTEIN, J. S., & KELLEY, J. B. The effects of parental divorce: Experiences of the preschool child. *Journal of the American Academy of Child Psychiatry,* 1975, *14*(4), 600–616.

WALLERSTEIN, J. S., & KELLEY, J. B. The effects of parental divorce: Experiences of the child in later latency. *American Journal of Orthopsychiatry,* 1976, *46*(2), 256–269.

WAMPLER, K. S., & SPRENKLE, D. H. The Minnesota Couple Communication Program: A follow-up study. *Journal of Marriage and the Family,* 1980, *42*(3), 577–584.

WATZLAWICK, P. A review of the double bind theory. *Family Process,* 1963, *2,* 132–153.

WATZLAWICK, P. A structured family interview. *Family Process,* 1973, *12,* 127–144.

WATZLAWICK, P., BEAVIN, J. H., & JACKSON, D. D. *Pragmatics of human communication: A study of interactional patterns, pathologies, and paradoxes.* New York: Norton, 1967.

WATZLAWICK, P., WEAKLAND, J., & FISCH, R. *Change: Principles of problem formation and problem resolution.* New York: Norton, 1974.

WEAKLAND, J. H. The "double bind" hypothesis of schizophrenia and three-party interaction. In D. D. Jackson (Ed.), *The etiology of schizophrenia.* New York: Basic Books, 1960.

WEAKLAND, J. G., FISCH, R., WATZLAWICK, P., & BODIN, A. M. Brief therapy: Focused problem resolution. *Family Process,* 1974, *13,* 141–168.

WEEKS, G. R., & L'ABATE, L. A bibliography of paradoxical methods: The psychotherapy of family systems. *Family Process,* 1978, *17,* 95–98.

WEEKS, G. R., & L'ABATE, L. A compilation of paradoxical methods. *American Journal of Family Therapy,* 1979, 7(4), 61–76.

WEINGARTEN, K. Family awareness for nonclinicians: Participation in a simulated family as a teaching technique. *Family Process,* 1979, *18,* 143–150.

WEISS, H. M., & BLOCH, D. A. *International master list of training programs in marital and family therapy.* Unpublished manuscript, 1981. (available from *Family Process,* 149 East 78th Street, New York, NY. 10021).

WEISS, R. L., HOPS, H., & PATTERSON, G. R. A framework for conceptualizing marital conflict, a technology for altering it, some data for evaluating it. In L. A. Hamerlynck, L. C. Handy, & E. J. Mash (Eds.), *Behavioral change: Methodology, concepts, and practice.* Champaign, IL: Research Press, 1973.

WEISS, R. L., & MARGOLIN, G. Marital conflict and accord. In A. R. Ciminero, K. S. Calhoun, & H. E. Adams (Eds.), *Handbook for behavioral assessment.* New York: John Wiley, 1977.

WELLS, R. A., & DEZEN, A. E. The results of family therapy revisited: The nonbehavioral methods. *Family Process,* 1978, *17,* 251–274.

WELLS, R. A., DILKES, T. C., & TRIVELLI, N. The results of family therapy: A critical review of the literature. *Family Process,* 1972, *11,* 189–207.

WENTE, A. S., & CROCKENBERG, S. B. Transition to fatherhood: Lamaze preparation, adjustment difficulty, and the husband-wife relationship. *The Family Coordinator,* 1976, *25,* 351–357.

WERNER, H. The concept of development from a comparative and organismic point of view. In D. B. Harris (Ed.), *The concept of development: An issue in study of human behavior.* Minneapolis: University of Minnesota Press, 1957.

WHITAKER, C. A. Psychotherapy of the absurd: With a special emphasis on psychotherapy of aggression. *Family Process,* 1975, *14,* 1–16.

WHITAKER, C. The hindrance of theory in clinical work. In P. J. Guerin, Jr. (Ed.), *Family therapy: Theory and practice.* New York: Gardner Press, 1976 (a).

WHITAKER, C. A. *Process techniques of family therapy.* Unpublished manuscript, 1976 (Available from Boston Society for Family Therapy and Research, 94 Lewis Road, Belmont, MA. 02178) (b).

WHITAKER, C. A. A family is a four dimensional relationship. In P. J. Guerin, Jr. (Ed.), *Family therapy: Theory and practice.* New York: Gardner Press, 1976 (c).

WHITAKER, C. A., FELDER, R. E., & WARKENTIN, J. Countertransference in the family treatment of schizophrenia. In I. Boszormenyi-Nagy & J. L. Framo (Eds.), *Intensive family therapy: Theoretical and practical aspects.* Hagerstown, MD: Harper & Row, 1965.

WHITAKER, C. A., & MILLER, M. H. A re-evaluation of 'psychiatric help' when divorce impends. *American Journal of Psychiatry,* 1969, *126,* 57–64.

WHITEHEAD, A. N., & RUSSELL, B. *Principia mathematica.* Cambridge, Eng.: Cambridge University Press, 1910.

WILD, C., SINGER, M. T., ROSMAN, B., RICCI, J., & LIDZ, T. Measuring disordered styles of thinking. *Archives of General Psychiatry,* 1965, *13,* 471–476.

WILKINSON, G. S., & BLECK, R. T. Children's divorce groups. *Elementary School Guidance and Counseling,* 1977, *11,* 205–213.

WILLIAMSON, D. S. AAMFT and AFTA: Epilogue. *Family Therapy News,* 1982, *13*(3), 2.

WILTZ, N. A. Behavioral therapy techniques in treatment of emotionally disturbed children and their families. *Child Welfare,* 1972, *52*(8), 483–490.

WINKLE, C. W., PIERCY, F. P., & HOVESTADT, A. J. A curriculum for graduate level marriage and family therapy education. *Journal of Marital and Family Therapy,* 1981, *7,* 201–210.

WITKIN, S. L., & ROSE, S. D. Group training in communication skills for couples: A preliminary report. *International Journal of Family Counseling,* 1978, *6*(2), 45–56.

WOLPE, J. *Psychotherapy by reciprocal inhibition.* Palo Alto, CA: Stanford University Press, 1958.

WRIGHT, J., PERREAULT, R., & MATHIEU, M. The treatment of sexual dysfunction. *Archives of General Psychiatry,* 1977, *34,* 881–890.

WYNNE, L. C. The study of intrafamilial alignments and splits in exploratory family therapy. In N. W. Ackerman, F. L. Beatman, & S. N. Sherman (Eds.), *Exploring the base for family therapy: Papers from the M. Robert Gomberg Memorial Conference.* New York: Family Service Association of America, 1961.

WYNNE, L. C. Some indications and contraindications for exploratory family therapy. In I. Boszormenyi-Nagy & J. L. Framo (Eds.), *Intensive family therapy: Theoretical and practical aspects.* Hagerstown, MD: Harper & Row, 1965.

WYNNE, L. C. Family transactions and schizophrenia: II. Conceptual considerations for a research strategy. In J. Romano (Ed.), *The origins of schizophrenia: Proceedings of the first Rochester conference on schizophrenia, March 29–31, 1967.* New York: Excerpta Medica Foundation, 1967.

WYNNE, L. C. Consensus Rorschachs and related procedures for studying interpersonal patterns. *Journal of Projective Techniques,* 1968, *32,* 352–356.

WYNNE, L. C. Communication disorders and the quest for relatedness in families of schizophrenics. *The American Journal of Psychoanalysis,* 1970, *30*(2), 100–111.

WYNNE, L. C. Some guidelines for exploratory conjoint family therapy. In J. Haley (Ed.), *Changing families: A family therapy reader.* New York: Grune & Stratton, 1971.

WYNNE, L. C. Family and group treatment of schizophrenia: An interim view. In R. Cancro, N. Fox, & L. Shapiro (Eds.), *Strategic intervention in schizophrenia.* New York: Behavioral Publishers, 1974.

WYNNE, L. C. On the anguish, and creative passions, of not escaping double binds. In C. E. Sluzki & D. C. Ransom (Eds.), *Double bind: The foundation of the communicational approach to the family.* New York: Grune & Stratton, 1976.

WYNNE, L. C., RYCKOFF, I. M., DAY, J., & HIRSCH, S. I. Pseudo-mutuality in the family relations of schizophrenics. *Psychiatry,* 1958, *21,* 205–220.

WYNNE, L. C., & SINGER, M. T. Thought disorder and family relations of schizophrenics: I. A research strategy. *Archives of General Psychiatry*, 1963, *9*, 191-198 (a).

WYNNE, L. C., & SINGER, M. T.   Thought disorder and family relations of schizophrenics: II. A classification of forms of thinking. *Archives of General Psychiatry*, 1963, *9*, 199-206 (b).

YOUNG, D. M.   A court-mandated workshop for adolescent children of divorcing parents: A program evaluation. *Adolescence,* 1980, *15,* 763-774.

ZEIG, J. K. (Ed.).   *A teaching seminar with Milton H. Erickson.* New York: Brunner/Mazel, 1980.

ZINKER, J. C., & LEON, J. P.   The Gestalt perspective: A marriage enrichment program. In H. A. Otto (Ed.), *Marriage and family enrichment: New perspectives and programs.* Nashville: Abington, 1976.

ZINNER, J., & SHAPIRO, R.   Projective identification as a mode of perception and behavior in families of adolescents. *International Journal of Psychoanalysis,* 1972, *53,* 523-530.

ZUK, G. H.   Family therapy: 1964-1970. *Psychotherapy: Therapy, Research and Practice,* 1971, *8,* 90-97 (a).

ZUK, G. H.   *Family therapy: A triadic-based approach.* New York: Behavioral Publications, 1971 (b).

ZUK, G. H.   Family therapy: Clinical hodgepodge or clinical science? *Journal of Marriage and Family Counseling,* 1976, *2*(4), 299-303.

ZUK, G. H., & RUBINSTEIN, D.   A review of concepts in the study and treatment of families of schizophrenics. In I. Boszormenyi-Nagy & J. L. Framo (Eds.), *Intensive family therapy: Theoretical and practical aspects.* Hagerstown, MD: Harper & Row, 1965.

AUTHOR INDEX